ONLY TWO FOR EVEREST

Dedicated to Ed Cotter, gentle man of the mountains

My life has been a great series of journeys. It has always been my way to take on any adventure in the offing. I've always said, 'Let's be travellers in our short time here, not tourists. Let's just go and do it.' But as I look back, I'm amazed so many spur-of-the-moment decisions actually worked out.

To me, the mountains always meant a taste of freedom and adventure. When I was young, being in the back country with seasoned mountaineers was a lasting adventure in itself. Those early years in the Canterbury mountain valleys, and the association with so many returned servicemen, led us into a new world enhanced by true companionship.

From those early years sprang lifelong friendships. We grew in confidence, and we passed that on when we became adults. As the years went by I continued to enjoy the freedom of the back country. The love of the mountains stayed with us and united us.

May the mountain clubs, and all those who follow our paths into the hills, continue to prosper. – *Ed Cotter*

ONLY TWO FOR EVEREST

How a first ascent by Riddiford and Cotter shaped climbing history

Lyn McKinnon

OTAGO
UNIVERSITY PRESS

Published by Otago University Press
Level 1, 398 Cumberland Street
Dunedin, New Zealand
university.press@otago.ac.nz
www.otago.ac.nz/press

First published 2016
Revised reprint 2017
Copyright © Lyn McKinnon
The moral rights of the author have been asserted.
Royalties from the sale of this book will be directed towards the NZAC DOW Hall Publications Fund.

The publisher gratefully acknowledges financial assistance from Creative New Zealand and the New Zealand Alpine Club.

ISBN 978-1-927322-40-6
A catalogue record for this book is available from the National Library of New Zealand.

This book is copyright. Except for the purpose of fair review, no part may be stored or transmitted in any form or by any means, electronic or mechanical, including recording or storage in any information retrieval system, without permission in writing from the publishers. No reproduction may be made, whether by photocopying or by any other means, unless a licence has been obtained from the publisher.

Editors: Imogen Coxhead, Rachel Scott
Design/layout: Christine Buess

Back cover: Mukut Parbat (Crown Mountain) was the jewel in the crown of the successful 1951 First New Zealand Himalayan Expedition. *Watercolour by Jacqui Cotter*

Front cover: From left: George Lowe, Earle Riddiford, Ed Hillary, Ed Cotter (seated). (Cotter Archives)
Ed Cotter explains how he came to take the chair: When we were in Badrinath the local doctor wanted to take our photo and brought out a chair for the leader of the expedition. We didn't really have a leader, but his assumption that we did started a discussion about whether we ought to or not. Ed Hillary thought we should appoint a leader to make major decisions while we were climbing – and clearly he thought it should be himself. But Earle Riddiford had organised everything, so if we needed a leader, why wasn't it him? There was a long discussion about how we could make all those major decisions between us. I got a bit sick of it, and I knew I certainly wasn't going to be appointed leader, so while they carried on arguing I saw the chair there and for a bit of a laugh I went and sat in it. Then along came the doctor and took the photo.

Dedication page: Ed Cotter on a trip to the Copland, 2005. Guy Cotter

Printed in China by Asia Pacific Offset

Contents

FOREWORD by Philip Temple 7
PREFACE 9

PART 1 LEADING THE WAY: THE FIRST NEW ZEALAND HIMALAYAN EXPEDITION: May–August 1951

1: Magnificent Obsession: A dream team for the Himalaya 15
2: Master Planner: Riddiford moves mountains 27
3: Awesome Elie: A feat unequalled for 30 years 35
4: En Route to Nilkanta: Indian reality and a steep learning curve 47
5: 'We Long Way Come': The conquest of Mukut Parbat 69
6: Monsoon Woes: 'We have not one rupee among us.' 87
7: Into the Crucible: An agonising impasse 97

PART 2 MAN OF PURPOSE: HAROLD EARLE RIDDIFORD: 1921–1989

8: Pioneer Spirit: 'Determination was the secret of his success.' 107
9: The 1951 Everest Reconnaissance: Negotiating the Khumbu death-trap 121
10: Cho Oyu: Shipton's folly 137
11: Fallout: Ripple effects from a frightfully British bungle 149
12: New Directions: The joyous adventure into marriage and fatherhood 157
13: Orongorongo Station: Living another dream 171

PART 3 SPUR OF THE MOMENT: EDMUND M^CCARTHNY COTTER: 1927–

14: Born for Adventure: At home in the hills *185*
15: Reaching for the Sky: To the high Himalaya *197*
16: Southward Bound: Time out in the magnificent Hollyford Valley *207*
17: The 1964 New Zealand Andean Expedition: Alpamayo by accident *223*
18: Trailblazing the Hollyford: Heroic failure *247*
19: Vailima and Beyond: From the mountains to the sea *259*
20: Everest at Last: The son lives the life the father imagined *269*
Conclusion: Putting the record straight *285*

APPENDIX 1: Return to Mukut Parbat by Evangeline Riddiford Graham *297*
APPENDIX 2: What Happened to the Dream Team? *302*
APPENDIX 3: British and New Zealand Expeditions to the Himalaya 1950–55 *308*
APPENDIX 4: Pasang the Indestructible *311*

NOTES *314*
BIBLIOGRAPHY *332*
ACKNOWLEDGEMENTS *337*
INDEX *339*

FOREWORD
Philip Temple

In May 1967 I went to interview Sir Edmund Hillary at his Remuera home as part of research for a book about the exploits of New Zealand climbers in the great mountain ranges of the world.[1] I had met Sir Ed before, but only on formal occasions, and was a tad nervous as I knocked on the door. I was taken aback when it was thrown open and I was greeted by his wife Louise with a wry smile and the words, 'Oh hello! Come to see the great man have you?' Perhaps there had been a minor domestic just before my arrival, but the interview was all downhill from there. Hillary told me he could only spare an hour and there were some things he was not going to talk about because he was writing a book himself.[2] He was guarded, often monosyllabic, and I went away feeling frustrated and a little angry.

What he did not say heightened my interest in what had actually happened during Hillary's first Himalayan expeditions, in 1951 and 1952, and which had led to his ascent of Everest in 1953. What were the achievements of other New Zealand climbers involved that had led to his success, but which had become buried beneath the avalanche of publicity and honours heaped upon him? Although, in subsequent years, Hillary would sometimes acknowledge his mate on Everest, George Lowe, he either ignored the key contributions of his other companions on his first Himalayan expedition in 1951, Earle Riddiford and Ed Cotter, or actively denigrated Riddiford. Why?

There were four members of the First New Zealand Himalayan Expedition in 1951: Ed Cotter, Ed Hillary, George Lowe and Earle Riddiford. In my book I told how Riddiford made the expedition happen through his drive, organisational ability and financial input; and how he and Cotter made the first ascent of their objective, Mukut Parbat, when Hillary and Lowe did not. Their success prompted an invitation for two of the four to join a British reconnaissance expedition to Everest that same year, and led to Hillary and Lowe joining the successful climb two years later.

I did not have room in my book to discuss the acrimony surrounding the decision that Hillary and Riddiford should join the 1951 Everest Reconnaissance, nor the pair's later relationship, nor much of what Ed Cotter – possibly the best climber of the four – went on to do. Now, in a detailed and authoritative account, drawing on the widest possible sources, Lyn McKinnon tells the full story of what happened in 1951. She also gives us, for the first time, the life stories and achievements of its two most successful climbers, which Hillary's 'most iconic climb of all time' has almost obliterated.

Lyn McKinnon tells of the 1951 expedition's enormous contribution to New Zealand and indeed world mountaineering history, and makes a good fist of giving 'more credit where credit is due'. It is a fascinating account, accompanied by many hitherto unpublished photographs. It will be seen as controversial by many – but that is often the case when the record is finally put straight.

Philip Temple
Dunedin, May 2016

---

1 *The World at their Feet*, 1969.
2 His book *Nothing Venture, Nothing Win* was published in 1975.

PREFACE

Autobiography can prove a deeply satisfying genre, as the reader is brought ever closer to the author. In 1951 four men took part in what was known as the First New Zealand Himalayan Expedition. Two members of the party – Edmund Hillary and George Lowe – recorded their achievements in autobiographies and authorised biographies, works that will continue to increase their stature beyond the grave.

But autobiography is very selective: it is, after all, just one person's version of events. Earle Riddiford and Ed Cotter, who accompanied Hillary and Lowe on the 1951 expedition, never wrote their own stories. Their rather different perspectives of that journey deserve to be passed on to those who love New Zealand's mountains and mountaineering history.

Fate took a hand in this project through the destruction wrought by the Canterbury earthquake on 22 February 2011. In a few minutes, Ed Cotter's stone and timber villa on the hill above Sumner Beach was torn apart. A concerted effort by friends and family saw a few of his effects saved before the building was 'red-zoned'. Just as I was invited to write his memoirs, Cotter's marvellous diaries of his 1951 Himalayan expedition were shaken onto my desk. I found them fascinating because they transported me back to the golden days of mountaineering, when so many unexplored ranges offered an irresistible palette of glistening untouched summits. But I was also intrigued, as others have been, by a compelling tale of human nature and how it defines and divides us. One simple event that has simmered away for more than six decades had far-reaching consequences, as the rope linking four climbers stretched taut and snapped over several days of bitter dissension.

The crowning achievement of the First New Zealand Himalayan Expedition was Riddiford and Cotter's ascent, with Pasang Dawa Lama, of Mukut Parbat, a previously unclimbed 23,760ft peak near Kamet in the Himalaya. But through a combination of extraordinary circumstances it was the two other members of the party – Hillary and Lowe – who became New Zealand's glory boys of the 1953 Everest expedition.

At first this book was intended to be Cotter's story, but very soon I became convinced that Riddiford's special brand of vision and determination was a major influence on the course of New Zealand mountaineering, and that his contribution deserved much wider acknowledgement. Serendipitously launched into an absorbing project, I was very aware that with such a lapse of time, face-to-face interviews with the men's surviving climbing contemporaries, friends and family members would have to be my priority. Those whom I was personally able to visit are acknowledged in the bibliography. My approaches to the Riddiford family were warmly rewarded, as they generously made available all of Earle's personal records of his Himalayan experiences. This account will, I hope, reflect how much we owe to him.

Lyn McKinnon

Left: For their first foray together into the mountains, the members of the First New Zealand Himalayan Expedition chose a ground-breaking assault on Elie de Beaumont via the unclimbed Maximilian Ridge. That highly successful ascent was to be the only target summit they shared as a team. This aerial view taken during a winter flight in 2015 shows the formidable nature of the ridge, which still remains unclimbed in winter. Colin Monteath/Hedgehog House

PART 1: LEADING THE WAY
The First New Zealand Himalayan Expedition: May–August 1951

The Sherpas
Pasang Dawa Lama, 40, Darjeeling
Nima, Pasang's brother
Thundu, cook
Yila Tenzing, 31
Ed Cotter's 1951 diary

The Sahibs
Harold Earle Riddiford, 29, lawyer, Christchurch
Edmund McCarthny Cotter, 24, office manager, Christchurch
Wallace George Lowe, 27, schoolteacher, Hastings
Edmund Percival Hillary, 31, beekeeper, Auckland
All from Riddiford collection

The Dream Team: from left, Bill Beaven, Jim McFarlane, Norman Hardie, Earle Riddiford.
Riddiford collection

1. MAGNIFICENT OBSESSION

A Dream Team for the Himalaya

When young people dream, occasionally the dream will flare into heroic exploits.

Half a world away from the high horizons of the Himalaya, in a student flat in postwar Christchurch, New Zealand, a daring plan took shape. The instigator was Earle Riddiford, a University of Canterbury law student not long returned from overseas service with New Zealand army intelligence.

He had been climbing since 1941 when he tackled Mt Sefton[1] from the west, but after his return to Christchurch in 1944 the mountains became his overriding passion. In 1946 Riddiford met Bill Beaven, an engineering student, and the two became regular climbing partners. In the third term of the 1947 university year Riddiford moved into the flat of Norman Hardie – another engineering student and, like Riddiford, a member of the Canterbury–Westland committee of the New Zealand Alpine Club (NZAC). Beaven and a third engineering student, Jim McFarlane, became regular visitors to that flat, as did many other prominent local mountaineers. By 1948, Hardie, Beaven, Riddiford and McFarlane had settled firmly into a strong, cohesive climbing partnership, a happy combination of complementary, dedicated amateurs with an impressive list of achievements. This was the dream team that Riddiford hoped would undertake the First New Zealand Himalayan Expedition.[2]

Hardie and McFarlane had been the first to team up. Hardie grew up on a small farm on the outskirts of Timaru, and after completing his university entrance exams he took up deer culling. On a solo shooting expedition in the Arthur's Pass area he met McFarlane in a mountaineering club shelter. The two students were taking the same course at university, and soon became close friends and hunting companions. Through the university tramping club Hardie was soon introduced to mountaineering – with a walk up the Waimakariri Valley to climb Mt Isobel in marginal visibility and then Mt Rolleston in wintry conditions without crampons. Though it wasn't an altogether happy experience,[3] it sparked his interest and, with McFarlane, he switched focus from tramping to mountaineering.

At the end of 1946 at the head of the Landsborough River[4] they encountered Riddiford and Beaven, who had just followed a new route into the Douglas Glacier via Christopher Col, making the first ascent of Mt Brunner and then Mt Townsend (see Chapter 8). Over the next year the 'dream team' consolidated its experience. In February 1947 McFarlane, Beaven and Hardie made the first ascent of Mt Elliot, summited Mt Strachan, and the next day climbed Fettes Peak. Crossing Mueller Pass, they made their way out down the Mahitahi Valley, shooting a few deer on the way.[5] That year Riddiford climbed 14 peaks, mostly first ascents, and after every Alpine Club committee meeting he pressed Hardie to let him join the flat. Halfway through the year he squeezed into the two rooms shared by Hardie and Bill Packard, a geography student and former captain of the Canterbury University Tramping Club. Riddiford brought with him not only his taste for classical music and an extensive collection of Benny Goodman big band records, but also his low-slung Riley car – an unusual luxury for a student – and much wit and challenging conversation.

Most of that conversation revolved around mountains, though there was occasional mention of plans to farm cattle on the West Coast. Riddiford, who was working for a law firm while studying, was held in high regard for the adventures he planned and the detailed and interesting articles he contributed to the *New Zealand Alpine Journal (NZAJ)*. He and Hardie avidly read and studied every book about mountaineering they could track down in Christchurch libraries. (Hardie remembers the only non-mountain book he ever saw Riddiford read: it was the hilarious *Uncommon Law*,[6] from which Riddiford often quoted.) All that reading and talk was certain to broaden their mountaineering horizons.

Occasionally Riddiford mentioned the Himalaya as an ultimate objective. Personally well resourced, he seemed most likely to realise the Himalayan dream. Beaven and McFarlane were also enthused by the idea, but Hardie was a down-to-earth, debt-burdened student who felt such ambitions were probably beyond his reach. Nevertheless, one weekend Hardie accompanied Riddiford to Dunedin to talk to Noel Odell, professor of geology at Otago University and the last man to see Mallory and Irvine on Everest in 1924. Odell was supportive of their Himalayan aspirations but surprisingly casual. He considered there was no special magic about British expeditions or famed mountaineers such as Eric Shipton and Frank Smythe,[7] and suggested that keen young New Zealanders could get just as far with their own experience and gear. He advised planning for at least two Himalayan expeditions, however, because of difficulties with strange food, foreign languages, acclimatisation and the challenges in adapting to the scale of the bigger peaks.

As the four members of Riddiford's dream team strengthened their skills, there was plenty of competition among climbers who wanted to join them, but by staying together as much as possible they developed an enviable esprit de corps. Resourceful and intelligent, always cheerful and optimistic, the four shared an easy camaraderie unaffected by challenges such as heavy loads and bad weather. Riddiford, who was lightly built but had great mental toughness, took on the role of initiator and meticulous organiser of trips; Beaven was very sound on technique, and Hardie and McFarlane were especially powerful as a climbing pair.[8] They all thrived on expedition-style climbing; in what is now nostalgically seen as a golden era of New Zealand mountaineering, their trips were mainly exploratory. Many questions of topography remained to be solved, and they had to look out for unknown difficulties on both ascents and descents. Successful exploration further fuelled Riddiford's imagination.

The Southern Alps may not compare in height to the Himalaya, but they certainly do in terms of the difficulties that confront the mountaineer.[9] In that respect, the challenges undertaken by Riddiford's group were equipping them very well for wider horizons. Two expeditions in particular gave notice that these four climbers were destined to make their mark overseas. One was the ascent of Mt Sefton from the south, which took place in the 1947–48 Christmas holidays. Riddiford initially planned a new route up an elusive ice shelf to the east, but such were the difficulties that they abandoned the plan in favour of an alternative approach from the Landsborough. There were numerous delays after a terrific nor'west storm on 26 December brought new snow to Sefton that reduced the chances of a south ridge climb, but eventually, from a base at Harpers Rock, they were able to mount their attack.

From 31 December they enjoyed five faultlessly fine days. From a vantage point on the Douglas névé they saw a snow route that reached the south ridge about halfway up. On New Year's Day they cramponed up the mixed snow and ice face on two ropes – McFarlane with Hardie, and Beaven with Riddiford. They achieved the icy high peak of Sefton at 10.15am and, after moving on to the southern summit, descended via the west ridge. That afternoon, after a thrilling traverse, the party added the northern Sharks Tooth and Mt Thomson to their bag before making it back to Harpers Rock at 6.30pm. On the following three fine days they climbed several other Landsborough peaks, including Mt Burns, Vampire, a first ascent of Mt Foster, a first ascent of Mt Hopkins from the north, and Mt Spence. Riddiford's *NZAJ* account reflects his exhilaration as they examined views from all angles, in perfect visibility, into a fascinating area of mountain country.[10]

Crossing Zora Creek, a tributary of the Landsborough River, during their Mt Sefton trip. Using crossed ice axes, Bill Beaven takes the current, McFarlane the middle, and Riddiford the easier end. Riddiford collection

On 6 January they began the long tramp down the Landsborough Valley to Makarora, to be picked up on 10 January by Packard (in itself a mission of great courage, as Packard had never driven a car before.) During their trip out to Haast Pass the four men were amazed by the splendid isolation and topography of the Landsborough Valley, so greatly admired by Riddiford that he would long harbour an ambition to own Landsborough Station, a freehold cattle run with grazing rights over extensive valley flats. Today, the station is part of Te Wāhipounamu, the South West New Zealand World Heritage Site. Riddiford's commitment to a legal career was clearly shaky (it was 1951 before he was finally awarded his Bachelor of Laws), and it came as no surprise to Hardie to learn from Beaven early in 1948 that their friend had left university and was working on the Sullivans' cattle property in South Westland.

In February 1948 the dramatic rescue of Ruth Adams[11] on La Perouse, a 10,098ft peak on the Main Divide above the Hooker Glacier, brought many experienced amateur and professional climbers together. Adams and another client, North Island amateur Edmund Hillary, were attempting an ascent with

A brief respite for the overworked Riley: from left, Beaven, McFarlane and Riddiford, just before the Makarora Bridge. Riddiford collection

guides Mick Sullivan and Harry Ayres when a rope broke and Adams fell, breaking a wrist and hurting her back. In 'an incredible display of stamina and endurance'[12] Ayres ran down the glacier in his crampons to the Hermitage to report the accident to guide Mick Bowie, who then controlled the rescue operation. A call was put through to Christchurch for a group of strong climbers to assist. One of them was Bill Beaven, who woke Hardie (then an engineer at Lake Pukaki) at 4am the following morning to ask him to join the party. Towards nightfall, working their way up the face of Mt Jellicoe, Hardie and Beaven were roped together in the darkness. The next morning they were at the accident site, where Hardie first met Hillary. To reduce the risks in getting the patient safely off the mountain, Bowie chose to descend to the West Coast side and out via the Cook River. This was the most arduous rescue in New Zealand's climbing history.[13] Adams was carried on a stretcher virtually over the summit and through deep gorges to the West Coast road. Riddiford, released from his work at Fox Glacier, was among the first to meet the rescue party from the West Coast side. It was his first meeting with Hillary also.

For Hardie, Beaven and Riddiford, the La Perouse experience was a significant event in their climbing careers because they gained so much confidence from it. They had always climbed without the professional guides generally regarded as the top climbers, whereas Ed Hillary, though fit and hard working, had regularly engaged Ayres. Now, after seeing guides in action on La Perouse, Riddiford realised that the skills of his own team were easily comparable. In some ways, since as eager amateurs they had read widely about mountaineering and attended many instruction courses, they were even ahead of the professionals. Now they knew for certain they were competent to attempt much bigger mountains in the future, and the Himalaya – though still a long way off and well beyond their budget – no longer seemed so improbable.[14]

The ascent of Sefton from the south in 1947–48 had defined the special talents of Riddiford's team: at the end of 1948 a second expedition, the ascent of Mt Tasman from the Balfour Glacier, signalled just how proficient the party had become. When mountaineering writer Philip Temple singled out 1948 as the year that more than any other marked the ascendancy of amateur achievement, he used these two ground-breaking trips as examples.[15] On the Balfour trip, their plan was to traverse the three parallel West Coast glaciers – Fox, Balfour and La Perouse[16] – with attempts on Tasman, La Perouse and possibly Dampier. Three weeks were set aside. After they packed in food and supplies from the West Coast in torrential rain, a week of fine weather followed. From their first high camp at Katie's Col they reconnoitred a route into the Balfour. 'It was something of a thrill to know that this broken ice field below us had never been trodden on before. In fact it

The Riley bulging at the seams, Jim McFarlane and Bill Beaven stretch their legs on the Mt Cook road. Aoraki/Cook centre left, La Perouse far left. Riddiford collection

seemed amazing that such a state of affairs could exist right in the heart of the Alps,' Riddiford wrote in the *NZAJ*.[17]

On Christmas Day they were soon in the Balfour Valley. After scrambling up an ice wall, cramponing up the steeper slopes and a spell of step cutting, they moved into the sun on the Main Divide, about four hours from camp, and proceeded up a new route to the summit of Silberhorn (10,800ft) then on to Tasman. 'Like others before us, we were rather appalled by the look of the knife-edge ridge leading up to Tasman … but it turned out to be thoroughly enjoyable work,' Riddiford wrote. They were on the top (11,473ft) at midday, absorbing the magnificent view. From Katie's Col over the next few days they climbed more neighbouring peaks before packing for the Balfour Valley. From there they crossed the Balfour Range and the La Perouse Glacier, and on 29 December reached the

McFarlane, Beaven and Riddiford take in the magnificent view from above the Balfour Glacier. Aoraki/Cook left, La Perouse right. Riddiford collection

summit of La Perouse. The next day they collected supplies from their Cook River dump, then spent several days in a snow cave in the Upper La Perouse waiting for a chance to attempt Dampier. This they did on 4 January, but at 10,000ft the weather packed up and they retreated, finally making it out from Gulch Creek to the Haast highway just in time to avoid a river in high flood. 'It was a disappointment that the trip could not be completed by traversing to the Hermitage, but we could wait no longer.'[18]

The following year, McFarlane and Hardie teamed up for the 77th ascent of Aoraki/Mt Cook on New Year's Day 1950.[19] The summer of 1949–50 was distinguished by poor climbing conditions. Because his usual companions had 'other fish to fry',[20] Riddiford took another party into the Callery and Tatare region with the object of tackling Elie de Beaumont via the unclimbed Maximilian Ridge, following the route taken via the Burton and Spencer glaciers by D.A. Carty in 1937. But they struck wet, deep, slushy snow and heavy nor'west rain, and on a second attempt were frustrated by whiteout blizzard conditions and continual rain. Last-minute hopes of an attempt on the ridge were finally dashed when the weather broke again, forcing a retreat to Franz Josef. Riddiford made a promise to himself to return.

In the meantime Bill Packard had been awarded a Rhodes Scholarship to Oxford University and, after a chance meeting with H.W. (Bill) Tilman at an Oxford Mountaineering Club meeting, was invited to join the 1950 British West Nepal Expedition, which came close to the summit of Annapurna IV. Tilman had climbed frequently with Eric Shipton and in 1936 had led the first ascent of Nanda Devi, accompanied by Noel Odell. When Tilman heard that Packard knew L.V. (Dan) Bryant, a New Zealander whose brilliant ice-climbing had so impressed the British on Shipton's small, low-cost 1935 Everest Reconnaissance, he instantly made Packard the expedition geographer. Packard acquitted himself extremely well on Annapurna IV, but his climbing career was suddenly curtailed when, on reaching the Nepalese lowland at the end of the expedition, he was struck down by polio.

Also in 1950, two years after the three flatmates had dispersed to pursue their careers, Riddiford was back in Christchurch to complete his law degree while working part time for Christchurch solicitors Bell and Taylor. He boarded with Bill Beaven's mother, and was busy planning a Himalayan expedition for mid-1951. Packard's thrilling inclusion in Tilman's party fired his imagination – could another party of skilled, experienced New Zealanders tackle a major objective like 28,208ft Kangchenjunga,[21] or even Everest itself? Riddiford was also inspired by Tilman's descriptions of British reconnaissance trips in the 1930s. 'It occurred to me that the British ideal of not trying very hard was being taken to its absolute limit, and I came to the conclusion that if we couldn't do better than that, there was something wrong with us.'[22] As the magnificent obsession took hold, Riddiford's courage never faltered. He placed enormous confidence in his dream team: McFarlane, always cheerful and able to endure hardship with a great sense of humour; Beaven, highly skilled and reliable; and Hardie, without a doubt the fittest and most determined climber he knew.[23]

2. MASTER PLANNER

Riddiford moves mountains

Riddiford's private 1951 expedition to the Garhwal Himalaya was one of the smallest to set foot on the roof of the world, with few of the resources enjoyed by larger expeditions financed by governments and sponsor organisations. Tackling the logistics of such a trip was a huge challenge and a terrific leap of faith for the New Zealand party: from familiar climbing conditions and equipment into the complete unknown.

Riddiford was just the man to lead them. His planning abilities had been honed on exploratory expeditions in the Southern Alps. He had also read assiduously, and his painstaking research was followed by an unrelenting flow of correspondence as he negotiated permits. His friend Archie Scott,[1] a Christchurch sharebroker and NZAC member, approached the then minister of education, R.M. Algie, on Riddiford's behalf, for advice on the best method of gaining permission to enter Tibet. By mid-April 1950 Algie had arranged a meeting in Christchurch between Riddiford and the minister of external affairs, F.W. Doidge, whose private secretary, R.H. Wade, was to prove most helpful. A memorandum Riddiford prepared for that meeting emphasised that although an attempt on Everest might seem ambitious, it was a choice well suited to his party: 'We fully realise the difficulties involved … but we feel that as New Zealanders we can give a good account of ourselves in the Himalaya and do as well and we hope better than the British expeditions.'[2]

By mid-May, however, Doidge was warning that the highly unstable political situation in Tibet would make it difficult to get permission from the Tibetan government. He asked Riddiford to provide as much information as possible about expedition plans and the climbers' experience, in order to approach the government of India to request assistance in communicating with the Tibetan authorities. Riddiford sent him an exhaustive list of the climbs undertaken by his team of four, outlining their thorough mountaineering training, the expert advice they had taken on the timing of the expedition, and the planned approach to Everest.[3]

By this time Hardie was working in State Hydro Design with the Ministry of Works in Wellington, which made it easy for him to consult extensively with Doidge's secretary, Wade. He explained that Riddiford was the leader who would make all the big decisions. Hardie's feedback to Riddiford was encouraging: 'Wade is to handle the whole affair … he is bloody good and co-operative and approachable and satisfied that the Minister thought we were the best party New Zealand could send.'[4] But with Everest in mind the team was now aiming for a complement of eight. Hardie broached the subject with George Lowe, a primary-school teacher in Hawke's Bay who was climbing strongly in the Southern Alps during his holidays. In May Hardie wrote to Riddiford saying he had met Lowe at a Federated Mountain Clubs of New Zealand (FMC) meeting and invited him along to their 'little do'.[5] Hardie was sure Lowe's inclusion was an excellent move and he reported that Lowe was keen because he and Ed Hillary were themselves considering a Himalayan expedition in 1952.

When Lowe put up a strong case for Hillary's inclusion, Hardie concurred. He had worked with Hillary at Pukaki and described him as the easiest of blokes to get along with, possessed of plenty of general ruggedness. There was some uncertainty because Hillary had climbed mainly with guides and never with Lowe, although they had met up in the mountains. But Lowe assured Hardie that Hillary would be a tower of strength, and said the party would have no regrets if he were included. In Lowe's letters to Riddiford he explained that Hillary had climbed with guides simply because his early climbing contacts were not enthusiastic high climbers. 'I'm sure Ed is as good as you will get in ability and temperament.'[6]

Lowe also backed Riddiford's plans for a training expedition – a 'Christmas rehearsal', suggesting that if numbers were short, his climbing companions Geoff Milne and Ed Cotter would join in. Another high-profile mountaineer on Riddiford's wishlist was Harry Ayres, who would lend the party impressive skill, maturity and experience. Ayres enthusiastically accepted Riddiford's invitation. As plans moved forward, Riddiford authorised Lowe to invite Hillary, who was then in England, stressing that nothing should be said publicly about their objectives. (In 1950 Nepal was opened to foreign expeditions, but only one nation was permitted each season: Riddiford was acutely aware that in the matter of getting permission for any major peak in the Himalaya, New Zealand was likely to be competing with the British.)[7]

In early June the New Zealand government sent a recommendation to the Indian government requesting that they approach the Tibetan authorities on New Zealand's behalf. In August, Hardie reported that as Tibet looked likely to be overrun by China, Wade believed there was 'not a show of a capitalist expedition in that direction'. One of Lowe's suggested alternatives was the Zemu Glacier, which drained Kangchenjunga and was reasonably handy to Darjeeling. Riddiford outlined that option to Doidge, asking for assistance with permission from the state of Sikkim, and Doidge passed his request on to the Indian government.[8] But the months were slipping by in what Hardie termed 'one long story of duck-shoving' through the 'Department of Infernal Affairs'.[9]

Ed Cotter, a young Canterbury Mountaineering Club (CMC) member with a big reputation for rapid ascents on the Canterbury mountains, was the next recruit. Riddiford invited Cotter to give a lantern-slide lecture to the NZAC in August, and after the lecture asked if he would like a trip to the Himalaya. Cotter was delighted to be asked, but there was a stumbling block – he could not afford to pay his way in a privately funded expedition. Riddiford was not to regret his impulsive invitation, however. As he wrote to Hardie, Cotter was not only very keen, he was also a 'first-class bloke'.[10] Then Hardie apologetically broke the news that he was now planning to travel to England in November, and hence would be unable to join the Christmas rehearsal.

By mid-October Hillary was back in New Zealand, complimenting Riddiford and Hardie on 'dashed good work' in organising the trip, and saying that he was highly honoured at the opportunity.[11] Lowe was also grateful to Riddiford for his immense energy and meticulous preparation.[12] But while there was some useful planning advice from Bill Packard and Noel Odell, numerous questions could be answered only from first-hand experience. (Odell's view that their New Zealand gear would suffice turned out to be somewhat misleading: nailed boots, for example, proved totally inadequate for Himalayan conditions.) Decisions on expedition gear reflected the minimalist approach in New Zealand, where climbers had to carry everything themselves – once the essentials were on board, that was quite enough: tents, sleeping bags, lilos, cooking equipment, boots, ice axes, pitons and carabiners, ropes, clothes, writing materials, first aid supplies, cigarettes … and food of course. By the end of October the party had a complete inventory of items to be organised, and the food list was under way.

Through NZAC stalwart Roland Ellis, double sleeping bags were obtained from Dunedin manufacturer Arthur Ellis and Co. These were to prove excellent, although the climbers' lilos literally let them down by constantly deflating, and their tents did not compare with superior models used by parties from other countries. To protect themselves from extreme weather the climbers were relying on heavy tartan woollen shirts, a hooded parka, scarf, windproof trousers over gabardine trousers, two pairs of socks and windproof lined gloves. Woollen clothing from

Bruce Woollens was provided at half price. Hardie would be responsible for extra purchases in England, such as rope, tents, equipment for the Sherpas, carriers and sacks for the porters, primuses, fuel and cooking gear. In November Riddiford wrote to the Union Steamship Company asking for a concession, or perhaps an arrangement for the party to work their passage, on the cargo ships MV *Wairata* or *Wairimu* from New Zealand to Calcutta in April. An alternative was a P&O crossing of the Tasman to Sydney, linking with a sailing to Bombay, followed by a 2000-mile rail journey across India.

Riddiford pressed for progress on permission, and asked Algie about the possibility of a government grant to help the expedition. At the same time he was in contact with T.H. Braham, the honorary secretary of the Himalayan Club in Calcutta, giving estimated arrival dates and requesting assistance in the engagement of four to six Sherpas plus porters, and access to maps.[13] He also contacted Ludwig Krenek, the Darjeeling secretary of the Himalayan Club, about engaging Sherpas there.[14]

Then came the bad news: at the end of November Wade told Riddiford that Tibet was out of the question, that permission for Sikkim was increasingly unlikely, and that it was altogether not a good time to visit the Himalaya. In reply, Riddiford stressed his determination not to delay. '*We intend to go in April next year* unless prevented by war or refusal to travel in India itself. If we cannot get into Sikkim, we will probably visit the Garhwal area.'[15] Within a week Wade had contacted New Delhi about new plans for Garhwal, and Riddiford was in Wellington lobbying again for a government grant.

Hearing that the sailing date of the MV *Wairimu* was uncertain and there would be no fare concessions, Riddiford booked passages on the Orient Line's *Orontes* to arrive in Colombo on 17 April. As time sped by nothing was getting easier, however. In December a cable from the Ministry of External Affairs informed him that Sikkim had refused permission, and there was as yet no reply about Garhwal. Riddiford also faced scepticism on the home front: many considered his plans over-ambitious and the objectives almost impossible. The timing was also unfortunate for his dream team, with the three others all at turning points in their careers and personal lives. McFarlane, newly married and short of cash, was not entirely convinced they had enough experience and was the first to opt out. Beaven was committed to working in the family business, but wonders now whether he turned down the 1951 expedition because deep down he did not share Riddiford's supreme confidence.[16] Harry Ayres found out his pay would be cancelled if he went on the trip; with a family to provide for that was out of the question. Hardie had left the country on 2 December, working his passage to England where his future wife Enid was teaching. Soon after his arrival he and Enid became engaged; his parlous financial position, together with the news that Beaven and McFarlane had dropped out, were factors in his decision to forgo the expedition and pursue his career instead. Milne, who was not available for the Christmas training expedition, was also a non-starter.

As the numbers fell away, Riddiford was forced to scale down to a party of four. And so it happened: Riddiford had three dedicated climbers – Cotter, Lowe and Hillary – but he had climbed with none of them himself. The only men who had climbed together were Cotter and Lowe.

But Riddiford always looked ahead. With the courage of his absolute conviction, he was determined that a New Zealand party would succeed in the Himalaya. First it was essential that they bonded as a team. During the year it had been agreed that their get-together in the mountains, set for the Christmas holiday period, would centre on Elie de Beaumont via the still unclimbed Maximilian Ridge. With Bill Beaven along for the ride, Riddiford, Cotter, Hillary and Lowe would meet at the Hermitage at the end of December for a crossing of Climbers Col before their attack on Elie from the west. This exhilarating expedition is described in the next chapter.

After their return, however, the minister of internal affairs, W.A. Bodkin, wrote to say there would be no government grant. A shoestring budget and paralysing diplomatic red tape looked likely to stop the expedition in its tracks. Then to their great relief, on 30 January Wade sent news that the government of Uttar Pradesh would not object to a Garhwal party, provided a pass on the 'Inner Line' train service was secured.

At this point, Hillary suggested that the party might be forced to downsize further, as there was no way Cotter could meet his expedition costs of £400. But Riddiford was of a different mind. *Time* magazine was encouraging him in his intentions, and he persuaded Hillary that Cotter should still be one of the party, with various donations subsidising his share of the trip. Thus Cotter's participation was assured: Lowe considered him a 'really good all round bloke' and Hillary, who was 'all for the Maximilian Ridge team', agreed that Cotter's inclusion would be ideal if it could be arranged, possibly by extra cost-cutting. He wrote to Riddiford, 'I think we will be a happy bunch, which to my mind is essential.'[17] Dates were settled for June, July and August in India, and Riddiford re-booked the party, this time on the P&O *Orion*.

The whole project was to be kept under wraps as Riddiford negotiated confirmation of all the necessary permits, since officially there was still no mountain to climb. Then came the first tiny dent in their unanimity: Hillary talked to the press in Auckland. An NZPA release on the planned expedition reported that 'only Mr Hillary has been outside New Zealand on a climbing trip' and that 'George Lowe has climbed just about everything in New Zealand worth climbing, and welcomes the opportunity of taking on the Himalaya.'[18] The news spread. Cotter, back at work in Christchurch, was astounded when he was unexpectedly called into the chief accountant's office to explain why he had failed to inform his employers of his forthcoming trip. As a newly appointed office manager, he was most embarrassed. He had not mentioned the expedition to anyone, including his parents.

In February the NZAC intimated it might provide some financial assistance. However, there was still no advice on target mountains in the Garhwal. Riddiford wrote again to Braham in Calcutta to ask for his recommendations and for four Sherpas, including Pasang Dawa, who had accompanied Packard in 1950. By March, with only two months to go, the party had its final list of personal gear and equipment. Cotter was appointed treasurer, plane bookings were arranged to Sydney, and formalities like passports, income tax clearance and vaccination became priorities.

The pace for Riddiford in Christchurch was becoming frenetic. Bill Beaven's brother Don helped with medical supplies; Cadbury Fry Hudson donated 50lb of fruit-and-nut chocolate and 20 tins of Pascall's Butter Drops; 10 tins of Ovaltine came from A. Wander Ltd and 'Service' biscuits from Aulsebrooks. Finally, at the end of March, a letter from Braham suggested the Badrinath-Mana Pass route to Mukut Parbat (23,760ft) and Nilkanta[19] (21,640ft). Braham pointed out that Pasang Dawa did not speak English, advised that customs duties could be heavy, and warned against rail travel in India. On 1 April, Krenek wrote from Darjeeling to say that he had engaged Pasang Dawa Lama, who spoke English, as sirdar or lead Sherpa, and a letter arrived from Pasang Dawa Lama himself, arranging their meeting at Ranikhet. Riddiford expressed himself pleased that Pasang clearly 'had his head screwed on the right way'.[20]

Then the 1951 waterfront dispute hit. Between February and July 1951, unrest on the wharves culminated in the biggest industrial confrontation in New Zealand's history. At the peak of the dispute 22,000 wharfies were off the job, and the First New Zealand Himalayan Expedition was going nowhere without its 1000lb of equipment and provisions. The *Wairimu* would not be leaving New Zealand in time, but if the dispute were to be resolved there was a chance of getting luggage on the *Monowai*, sailing from Wellington on 20 April. If the wharfies and others did not return to work, the only possibility would be to arrange for a passenger to take the expedition gear as personal luggage. When the *Monowai* sailing was cancelled, things were looking 'bloody grim', as Lowe said in a letter to Cotter on 11 April. He had decided against sending his own case down to Wellington as arranged. 'The only ship to Aust. according to the *Dominion* this morning is the *Wanganella* on April 26 from Auckland. If we can't get our gear on her, we're buggered.'[21] In the last-minute panic, even Hillary's legendary gung-ho courage deserted him: on the same day he cabled Riddiford: 'SUGGEST CONSIDER DEFERRING TRIP NEXT YEAR LEAVING EARLIER STAYING LONGER BETTER FINANCES.'[22]

This hit Riddiford right where it hurt most: the idea that after his gargantuan efforts one of his team could think of scuttling the expedition, right on the point of departure, was unbearable. He came out swinging. 'SHAME ON YOU SUGGESTING DELAY SENDING GEAR UP NEXT WEEK.'[23] At the last a passenger was found who would take their gear as baggage: fellow mountaineer David Gerard was booked on the *Wanganella* sailing. The first step was for Cotter to take the luggage on the Lyttelton–Wellington ferry, with a good number of mountaineering enthusiasts at either end providing the manpower to load and unload, then it was railed to Hillary in Auckland to be loaded on the *Wanganella* bound for Sydney. Riddiford arranged for shipping agents in Sydney to transfer the baggage onto the *Orion*, then booked the party's return passages. Wade suggested it would be a shame not to experience an interesting train trip through India, and advised that the Indian trade commissioner, B. Sanyal, would endeavour to make sure they had no difficulties en route. A chain of official letters followed in May, as officials in the Uttar Pradesh government negotiated for the issue of the relevant 'Inner Line' passes in Garhwal.[24]

A final note from Hillary on 21 April confirmed that all cases had arrived in Auckland. There was a temporary glitch when Lowe turned up in Auckland without the obligatory tax clearance: he had only a receipt for tax paid, which he thought was enough to get him out of the country, but the authorities would not accept it. He was finally cleared after a call to the income tax office in Napier confirmed all was in order. Riddiford wrote a last letter to the secretary of the Himalayan Club in Ranikhet about the engagement of porters and the purchase of food there, and with the envious good wishes of all their friends and climbing companions, the First New Zealand Himalayan Expedition was on its way. In the years ahead, Riddiford was often to say that it was harder to get a Himalayan expedition away than to climb one of these mountains.[25]

Most lives are serendipitous to some extent. For Riddiford, Plan A had centred on the four great friends who were so fortunate in their climbing fellowship. As it happened, it was to be members of Riddiford's 'B' team who contributed so much, not only to the first ascent of Everest, but to New Zealand's golden era in the Himalaya during the early 1950s.

But before we join the team in the Himalaya we will backtrack a few months to the Christmas 'practice expedition' to climb Elie de Beaumont in the Southern Alps.

3. AWESOME ELIE

A feat unequalled for 30 years

As a training ground for the Himalaya, Elie de Beaumont was ideal. Although there are great height differences between the Southern Alps of New Zealand and the Himalaya, the two regions feature similar deep-cut valleys and difficult ice. As George Lowe wrote later, a challenging New Zealand climb carried out in hazardous and isolated conditions similar to those in the Himalaya fitted a man more appropriately for a Himalayan expedition than any testing ground in the Swiss Alps.[1]

New Zealander Dan Bryant had learned this first hand on the 1935 British Everest Reconnaissance:

> Special qualities are required to face the rigours of Himalayan mountaineering. It requires a long apprenticeship in difficult mountains. Physical toughness is the first prerequisite. Icemanship of the highest order, knowledge of weather … the ability to make vital decisions and choose routes … judgement of snow conditions … and the control and leadership of heavily laden porters crossing difficult terrain – all of these are basic requirements. For all these, there is no better training ground than our Southern Alps … Few overseas mountaineers have ever appreciated fully the magnitude of some of our New Zealand climbs, the heavy glaciation and the difficulties engendered by our weather, until they have spent a season or two here.[2]

Majestic Elie de Beaumont, soaring above the Tasman Glacier to the north of Mt Cook, had long been a temptress conquered only from the easier Tasman side. In 1943 Canterbury climber Jack Ede described her as the most beautiful peak in the Southern Alps, though a 'fickle jade', a 'disdainful lady' who gazed in lofty isolation at her suitors before treating them to snowstorms and avalanches.[3] During the wet summer of 1949–50 Riddiford had been similarly thwarted. But now Elie's jagged Maximilian Ridge, plunging deep into the West Coast forest, was set to play a star role in preparing his team for the First New Zealand Himalayan Expedition.

Though only 10,200ft high, Elie de Beaumont is a formidable mountain of looming precipices, steeply angled glaciers and high, difficult passes. As the four climbers, accompanied by Bill Beaven, set off for a 21-day trip over the 1950 Christmas holiday period, they were thinking hard about the challenges they would meet overseas. They would have to carry heavy loads over similar terrain, so 70lb packs went with the deal. Lowe had already carried some stores from Ball Hut to Malte Brun Hut before he met up with Riddiford, Hillary, Beaven and Cotter at the Hermitage. Even so, Lowe and Hillary were surprised by the size of the loads to be carried for their extended journey; unlike the others, they were not accustomed to packing for long trips.[4]

Original plans were for a clockwise route from the Tasman via Climbers Col to the Spencer and Burton glaciers, and from there to the Elie summit via the Maximilian Ridge. The intention was to continue over the Callery Saddle via the head of the Callery River, descend to the head of the Whataroa River, move up the Whymper Glacier and over the Whymper Saddle, then traverse around to Tasman Saddle and finally back down to the Ball Hut. But two hours out from the Malte Brun Hut, the first glimpse of Climbers Col scuppered that plan. The approach was very broken and steep, and it was clear that a combination of avalanche snow, difficult terrain and heavy loads would prevent them attempting that route. Deciding to reverse their trip anti-clockwise, they struggled up to the Tasman Saddle, where they arrived mid-morning in varying stages of exhaustion.

While the others dozed in the sun for a while, Cotter decided to take a look into the Whataroa Valley from the Hochstetter Dome–Aylmer Ridge, which dropped straight down to the Whymper Glacier. The view was superb, but to avoid being branded a 'peak bagger' he turned back 20 feet from the summit of Mt Aylmer. From the ridge, however, he had picked out a possible descent from Whymper Saddle to the Whataroa Valley. (Later, when he pointed out the route from the floor of the valley, it was dubbed 'Cotter's Mistake' because of the icefalls and sheer faces of rock barring the way.) Back at Tasman Saddle, the party roped up in two teams for their descent into the head of the Murchison, gaining the Whymper Saddle (7300ft) by 2.30pm. From there they plotted a direct route down into the Whataroa.

As they descended, the Maximilian Ridge towered above them, a sheer 6000ft above the valley floor, overlooking the Hochstetter Dome. Progress down the glacier was very slow as they negotiated schrunds and jumped crevasses. Beaven remembers that no one really wanted to go first, and they had to watch for hanging moraine rocks at the bottom. In the lower stretches the two ropes took different routes, adding a touch of competition. Riddiford was already learning more about

National Publicity photograph showing Aylmer (top left), Elie de Beaumont (top right), the Whymper Glacier (bottom left) and the Maximilian Ridge (right). Riddiford collection

his climbing companions. As in his days with Hardie and McFarlane, he found he needed to get a 10-metre running start out of the tent in the morning if he wanted his share of the lead. 'When with George Lowe, I would recommend hitching him to a ball and chain as well.'[5]

On reaching the Whymper glacial moraine at 4150ft, they pitched camp close to a water supply. Late the next morning, under a blue-dome sky, they moved off down the loose and unstable moraine. As they made for a high moraine terrace to the left, they faced a greater challenge – a very difficult high lateral moraine wall. To reach the top required their combined knowledge of mountaineering

Bill Beaven jumps a crevasse below the Whymper Saddle. Riddiford collection

Crossing the saddle between the Whymper Glacier and the Callery Valley. From left: Ed Cotter, Earle Riddiford, Bill Beaven. Riddiford collection

technique,[6] but after that they were able to follow a grassy terrace to a pleasant campsite at 3300ft. To celebrate Christmas and 'help the boys forget their packs', Cotter strung the campsite with a large collection of novelty balloons, which successfully kept the colony of resident kea at bay.

The weather had been perfect, but on 27 December it was changing to nor'west and deteriorating. They left 'Balloon Camp' at 8.15am, climbing up a dry creek bed to a grass shoulder at 4600ft. In misty conditions, they were simply guessing that a broken icefall above might lead to the Callery Saddle. At 1pm they reached a ridge beyond which lay a wide snow gully. Heavy mist hid any access to the saddle, so they decided to camp on the ridge. In heavy rain, their 7x7 tent was 'definitely overcrowded'.[7] At about 3am Cotter was sent outside to deepen the trench around the tent, which was in danger of floating away, and he spent six hours trying to mop up water as it flowed in.

28 December was spent in their sleeping bags with a cook-up or two. On the 29th, in a cold southerly, they worked their way up a steep rock wall en route to the saddle, setting up a food dump at the top of the wall. That meant an easier task next morning as they kicked steps up the snow gully for 500ft. By 11am they were on the Callery Saddle at 6400ft, by 1.30pm on the remains of the Callery Glacier, and a couple of hours later at the Burton refuge, a large bivvy rock at the

Outside the Burton bivvy: Ed Cotter, Ed Hillary and Earle Riddiford. Bill Beaven is inside suffering from chickenpox. Riddiford collection

Callery–Burton junction (3800ft). The kea there were the cheekiest and noisiest in the Southern Alps, according to Cotter.

On 31 December they prepared to establish a snow camp on the Burton Glacier from which they could tackle the Maximilian Ridge. They scraped out a tent site on ice at 5800ft, and that afternoon picked their way up a side glacier to get a look at the main ridge. Some steep ice and soft snow gave them a good idea of conditions ahead. On New Year's Day they were off at 3.30am; Beaven, feeling unwell, returned to camp at 4am. When nor'west cloud hit the summit the others followed him, and back at the bivvy rock Beaven was diagnosed with chickenpox. On 2 January in cold, squally weather they declared war on kea, although Hillary had little success with his makeshift bow and arrow. The following morning the weather looked more promising. It was to prove a very long day.

Leaving Beaven behind at the rock, they 'grumbled their way up the moraine',[8] followed their earlier tracks up the side glacier to a rock peak, dropped to the head of the Burton icefall, cramponed up through the breaks and topped the ridge at 9am. Above was the first obstacle, a high rock step, a vertical wall that blocked progress. Lowe 'turned on a good show'[9] by climbing out to the left on the Whymper face and cutting steps to regain the ridge above the wall, and from there gave a first-class lead in perfect weather. Riddiford and Cotter were thankful they had 100ft of nylon for the belay over that section,[10] while ahead of them Hillary and Lowe were cutting steps along a corniced ridge. The climb was exhilarating, with the ridge rising ahead in a series of six big steps. Finally, a shout from Lowe announced the way was clear up a steep and corniced ice slope sneaking through great ice cliffs to the Anna plateau, which they reached at 2pm, after what Riddiford termed 'the most completely enjoyable climb'[11] he had had to date. Another hour took them to the summit.

The task achieved, the problem now was how to get back to Bill Beaven, who in the meantime had spent the day too delirious to get water.[12] None of the climbers was happy about descending the Maximilian Ridge in the few hours of daylight left. The best option seemed to be to traverse to the Malte Brun Hut and return over the Divide the following day. But as they were traversing Mt Walter, Cotter and Riddiford saw what looked to be a way down into the Spencer Valley to get back to Beaven and made a snap decision to give it a go. Hillary declared that he was feeling off colour, however, and thought he was possibly also coming down with chickenpox.[13] He wanted to set off for the Hermitage and home from there. Lowe went with him, taking the news that the Maximilian Ridge had been climbed for the first time. (To some experienced contemporary climbers, splitting the party was a serious breach of mountaineering ethics.[14])

Riddiford and Cotter began the task of heading back to Beaven and all their gear. It was a hectic journey in the evening light, Riddiford wrote, with something of the quality of a dream. The upper Spencer Glacier was the most extraordinary mass of ice cliffs, tributary glaciers and tangled icefalls – the most impressive and fascinating stretch of ice Cotter had ever seen. As they approached the big bend of the glacier, with broken ice ahead, the valley mist came in. For an hour they were jumping crevasses, belaying across others, and waiting for better visibility. Finally, after running the gauntlet of three icefalls, they found a clear path through to more stable ice.

By 8.30pm they were opposite Cox's Couloir leading to the Cerberus Glacier. They had supper near a huge waterfall, travelled along a trough on the glacier edge for another hour, and at 10.30pm settled for the night under an overhanging rock

George Lowe and Ed Hillary en route to the summit of Elie de Beaumont. Riddiford collection

Bill Beaven and Ed Cotter on the Tatare Saddle on the way out to the West Coast. Riddiford collection

at about 4000ft. Next morning they set out at 5am and took five hours to achieve the 1700ft climb over the ridge separating the Spencer and Burton valleys. When they arrived at the Burton bivvy, Beaven was not much improved, and extremely pleased to see them.

Now Riddiford and Cotter faced another enormous task – carrying out the gear for all five members of the party, with the ailing Beaven unable to shoulder a load. Their route took them up the Callery, a 2200ft climb to the Tatare Saddle, and then down over steep, rotten rock. The Tatare kea were shrewd, silent types, stealing Beaven's shorts and, somewhat inconveniently, one boot. But the next day, as Beaven's health improved and the other two tired, Beaven was able to bear some of the burden. In the process he was carried some way down a couloir by a dislodged boulder, but was fortunately unharmed. (Beaven insists he was sliding, not falling.) A beer at the Franz Josef Hotel started to seem very, very attractive, but they had to spend another night in the bush before dropping to the river next morning and arriving at the hotel for a good West Coast meal.

Beaven then took the bus back to Christchurch. His fellow passengers were fascinated by what appeared to have been an unusually vicious encounter with hordes of mosquitoes; they soon beat a retreat to the back of the bus when Beaven told them he had the pox. The gear belonging to Hillary and Lowe was stored at Franz Josef, and for the next four days Riddiford and Cotter built up their strength to re-cross the Divide back to the Hermitage, where Riddiford had left his car.

By chance, Mt Cook guide Harry Ayres was also at Franz Josef, preparing for a crossing to the Hermitage with a female client, M.E. Macaulay. The group combined for an enjoyable trip up the Franz, with the crossing of Pioneer Pass helping to make the day interesting. The next day Cotter and John Morris, second guide to Ayres, kicked steps from the Haast Hut onto Glacier Dome for an attempt on Mt Cook. With Warren Jones and Eric Feasey, who had just climbed Tasman from the Fox, there were seven climbers on three ropes. Conditions on the ascent were ideal, but a cold wind on the summit soon sent them back down. Soft snow on the Linda Glacier hampered progress on the descent, but they arrived back at Haast Hut at 5pm happy and satisfied. Cotter says he climbed Cook just for something to do, but it had been a long, 16-hour day ending in a taxing drop off the Haast Ridge and down the glacier to Mount Cook Village.

When Lowe wrote up the Elie de Beaumont trip he described Hillary as 'not as toughened as he was soon to become', 'labouring at the rear and panting with the effort to keep up',[15] and content just to follow if Lowe could keep on plugging in front. In the only paragraph devoted to the Elie climb in *Nothing Venture, Nothing Win*, Hillary described Lowe as calm and confident, displaying 'boisterous competence'. He also credited Riddiford with tons of drive and ambition, saying that although he was not particularly robust, his climbing and cool intellect were impressive.

For Hillary, at that time, the Elie expedition was 'a happy and successful trip'.[16] By 1999, however, when *View from the Summit* was published after Riddiford's death, Hillary's perspective had changed. 'Earle Riddiford regarded himself as the expedition leader, and he certainly organised permission … but George and I didn't accept him as such in the field. We were the lead pair, we felt, and confident of our ability.'[17] His account of the climb draws heavily on Riddiford's much earlier *NZAJ* article, but completely ignores Riddiford and Cotter's mammoth slog in returning to Beaven and carrying out everyone's gear.

During the trip Riddiford and Cotter had their first introduction to the climbing mindset the other two climbers would take into the Himalaya: they realised that Hillary and Lowe, both North Islanders who had spent most of their climbing time based around the Hermitage, were determined to be the lead pair and had quite a different mountaineering philosophy. For the Canterbury men, sharing the lead was the expected protocol: a 'first to the summit' approach was alien to them. 'Earle and I both noted that we were never offered the lead, as would have been the case within our climbing fraternity,' Cotter recalls.[18]

But Cotter was very fit and relished the challenge of this groundbreaking climb. For him, getting onto the Maximilian Ridge was half the battle. 'Once we got onto the hard stuff, George led most of the way, and I just followed. That was all the training we did, just getting to know each other, and we all got on okay together.'[19] In his diary, he summarised the high (and low) points:

> The first crossing of the Whymper Saddle; a new route over the Maximilian Range Ridge; the comfort of Earle's bivvy rock at Burton junction; huge numbers of keas; Bill catching chicken pox; our successful climb of Elie de Beaumont and our trip down the Spencer Glacier back to Bill; our trip out via the Tatare; watching poor weak Willie sliding down a loose gully in the steep Tatare Ridge; Earle and myself climbing Mt Cook from Haast after a traverse of Franz and Fox and Pioneer Pass; the use of surnames necessitated by the fact that Ed Hillary and I had the same cursed Christian name; and the marvellous photographs taken by Earle and George.[20]

This was an important ascent, described by Philip Temple as one of the most notable ridge climbs undertaken by amateurs.[21] Though the mountain had been traversed from the Spencer Glacier by Carty and others in 1937, the Maximilian Ridge was virtually unknown. The success of Riddiford's party on this difficult route was not equalled for another 30 years.

4. EN ROUTE TO NILKANTA

Indian reality and a steep learning curve

Although there was still some uncertainty about final permits for the Garhwal, the expedition party set off confidently enough knowing they had the full cooperation of the Himalayan Club. Cotter's detailed and amusing expedition diaries began on 3 May 1951, the long-awaited date of departure from New Zealand. Full of flair and feeling, the journals lay gathering dust for 60 years, his family unaware of their existence. He also wrote home, and these letters were later returned to him. Riddiford kept no diary, instead sending his mother lengthy accounts that were passed on to friends and family and preserved. These two sources provide a valuable double perspective on an expedition that undoubtedly influenced mountaineering history.

From the outset, Riddiford's background, including his legal training, was a great advantage not only in communications with authorities, but also in public relations. Just before the expedition left, he was invited to give a lantern-slide talk to the Auckland section of the Alpine Club where Dan Bryant, who had been on the 1935 British Reconnaissance of Everest, made a speech wishing them well. Finally, the party was on its way. After interviews with reporters and photographers[1] the four took off in a flying-boat from Mechanics Bay in Auckland and travelled to Sydney, where more journalists greeted them.

In Sydney the main task was to buy 80lb of tinned ham and 40lb of tinned butter, unobtainable in New Zealand because of the waterfront dispute. As Riddiford wrote to his mother, negotiating a discount was not so easy:

> It took me an hour of phone calls to wholesale firms before I got onto some. I was told we would have to pay full export price for the ham, 7s 4d per pound. I asked the head of the firm for a concession (for business purposes, we were now the first expedition to go to the Himalaya from New Zealand and Australia.) He said they were the biggest wholesale firm in the Southern Hemisphere and I was asking for

something to which I was not entitled: but then he grinned and gave it to me for 6s (4s 6d New Zealand, so that's not too bad).[2]

From Sydney, reunited with their equipment and supplies, they all squeezed into one four-berth cabin for their voyage to Colombo on the P&O liner *Orion*. The ship sailed on 5 May at 11am, a colourful sight with thousands of people lining the wharf holding streamers. As they passed under the Sydney Harbour bridge, out through the heads and past Bondi Beach, Hillary and Cotter sunbathed and the next day were enjoying the swimming pool. Soon they had met three New Zealand girls, and an Australian party of five heading to London.

Shipboard life was exciting. The youngest of the four, Cotter had grown up accepting clear boundaries between girls as friends and girls as potential wives. He had never had spare money for courting, and besides, most of his leisure time was spent climbing with members of the Canterbury Mountaineering Club – definitely a male preserve. There had been a cloudy notion that one day he might get 'hooked up', but that was a very long way off. For the others, the allure of unclimbed peaks and the changing moods of the mountains had also cast a stronger spell than the mysteries of the opposite sex. But the four quickly made an impact on social life on board, with deck games, swimming, dances, pictures, drinks, and late suppers in one of the cabins or on the top deck.

Living the Dream. From left: Ed Cotter, Ed Hillary, George Lowe and Earle Riddiford before their departure. Cotter collection

An unusually close shipboard encounter for Ed Hillary. Cotter collection

Cotter's relative penury was relieved temporarily when he won 26 shillings at Housie one night, but it didn't last long. His ability to walk on his hands along the ship's handrail attracted much attention, not just from fascinated young ladies but also from the apprehensive crew. Even for Hillary, known for his gaucheness in the company of women, the relaxed and lively atmosphere provided an opportunity to socialise easily. He was given the nickname 'Cosmo P' (short for Percival) because of his experiences of ports visited on his trip to London the previous year on the P&O liner *Otranto*. Nevertheless, Cotter later described how Hillary was out of his depth at times:

> There were lots of gorgeous New Zealand girls heading off on their OE. We were four innocents who couldn't really cope with the close-up encounters which necessarily became more revealing as the ship approached the warmer climes of the Equator. Hence the great shot of Ed with the daughter of the editor of the Melbourne *Age*. He looks, and was, quite out of sync with the moment.[3]

The *Orion* next berthed at Melbourne, where more reporters awaited the four climbers. They spent a Jubilee Day holiday touring the city, then sailed to Adelaide where they went out on the town with their new shipboard friends.

En route to Fremantle, despite hopes that the Australian Bight would not be as bad as feared, Riddiford and Lowe were confined to their cabin and dined only on seasickness tablets. From Fremantle they toured Perth, once again with their new friends. There were over 200 passengers on board for the trip to Colombo, and the four climbers relished the novelty and sheer fun of cruising in warmer temperatures. Cotter wrote to his sister Cecily, describing the 'Crossing the Line' ceremony on 22 May:

> Earle was clerk of the court dressed in a white nightshirt, flaxen hair shoulder length, with a megaphone through which he called each of the 19 victims to come forward. After reading the charge … the victim fully clothed was sat in a chair, then I as barber, dressed in long underpants, college sox, boots, moustache and shower cap, lathered up their faces with flour and water and shaved them, and the chief of police pushed them chair and all into the swimming pool. George, as Queen Amphitrite (Poseidon's wife) was suitably attired with the barest necessities. The show was a grand success.[4]

Riddiford did not escape the same fate as those he charged: he was also immersed, nightie, wig and all. It was a very late night with much merriment as they waited up to see the first lights of what was then Ceylon.

They berthed on 23 May. In the immense heat of Colombo they were interviewed yet again by the local papers and visited a native bazaar, impressive mainly for its filthiness. With their shipboard party they hired taxis for a long drive past the beach resort of Mt Lavinia to a restaurant in the middle of a lake at Bogoda, where they enjoyed lunch and drinks in beautiful surroundings before returning to Colombo. Their night train through Ceylon left at 7pm that evening: the young women from the ship came to see them off and there were some rather sad farewells. The next morning a short ferry trip took them across to Dhanushkodi on a hot, dry peninsula on the east coast of India, just 32km across the water from Ceylon. It seemed like the 'end of nowhere'. (Years later, in 1964, a cyclone destroyed the Dhanushkodi railway line, and a relatively thriving tourist town and pilgrimage centre became a ghost town.)

Constant arguments with porters over wages and unexpected extra charges at every turn were to plague Riddiford throughout the expedition. In Dhanushkodi swarms of red-turbaned railway porters were all keen to carry one of their 40 cases to the customs shed, where a trial of patience began with a two-hour session of protracted negotiations. 'They slammed us £16 duty, an awful shock. Then excess baggage through India, another £45, was a terrific blow to finances.'[5]

In Perth: Ed Cotter and Ed Hillary with three shipboard friends. Cotter collection

In India they were to travel to the hills on narrow-gauge rail, a fascinating journey during which they would meet a few of the country's teeming millions of inhabitants:[6] five days on the Madras Express to Calcutta,[7] then another two days to Ranikhet by rail and road. Riddiford wrote home describing the mass of his correspondence to India – making forward arrangements, remitting money and disentangling accounts. 'The trip is costing us £1600 by the way, £400 each less donations. We have over £300 donated from various sources which I think was pretty good and gave us a feeling of the goodwill towards us.'[8] But that money had to stretch a long way in an unfamiliar country.

Cotter recorded events in his diary:

24 May: We passed primitive little villages and at every stop there were more beggars wanting baksheesh. Our first class compartment (four berths with fans) was a big thing in India. If only we could have known that all the way to Calcutta and further up to the railhead at Kathgodam the countryside was all the same:

flat, barren, dry, hot and dirty, each village with a stench, and no cold water to drink, in case of infection. We had been advised to take food and drink only from Spencers, caterers for the South Indian Railways.

On 25 May, after travelling throughout the night, they reached Madras.[9] Cotter's diary describes the city, with a smell all of its own:

> We spent a very hot tiring day there. We decided to visit the market and were met by several volunteers wanting to show us bargains. Earle adopted them while Ed H. and I wandered off on our own. I had a good time bartering for socks and puttees. The boy in the stall offered to toss a coin for the price, and won both times. Meanwhile Earle was out in a rickshaw and was asked if the gentleman wanted a nice English girl, very nice, very clean. We had an instructive walk through the city. One little kid with his sister about nine months was lying on the footpath begging, and an Indian boy with an American accent and a stock of American swear words followed us some way. That evening we hired a taxi for a trip to the beach, and the driver told us about an offer of nice French girls. Said the driver: 'Cost you 30 rupees for one night, then you get one month in hospital free.' He was very voluble on the subject …

From Madras they took the mail train north on a 45-hour journey to Calcutta. There was plenty of entertainment as they passed through villages; at every station hawkers offered local delicacies that did not look very appealing, and Cotter's diary entry details the determined efforts of children trying to hitch a ride on the train:

> 26 May: At one station as we were pulling out a young girl of about five jumped into our compartment with about 30 pounds of rice: we tried to push her out, but she wouldn't budge. She was the beginning of an amusing morning. When she got off she was replaced by a horde of kids with rice sacks. A dozen policemen attacked hangers-on taking a free ride home to the next station after buying rice. They used sticks, chasing off those who were climbing on, and after the train was on the move they whacked the ones hanging on as the train went past. When they got to their station the hangers-on hopped off and ran for their lives, as anyone caught had their rice confiscated. We left our door open at one stop and immediately had half a dozen kids visiting. We chased them off, but one little kid cried all the way as he had spilled some rice. They even climbed under the train, hanging on to the iron framework.

On 27 May they arrived at the Howrah station in West Bengal, the filthiest place so far. They checked in to the Grand Hotel, and that night Riddiford and Cotter went to Princes, an air-conditioned nightclub, where they enjoyed a good line of Latin music, samba as it should be danced, and a glass of beer which they made last an hour. On the 29th the party crossed the Ganges by rail, second class this time, to Lucknow, where the temperature hit 45 degrees. Riddiford and Cotter visited the civil secretariat to discuss Inner Line passes that would allow them entrance to the buffer area 80km from the Tibetan border. By 6pm they had the necessary letters and were off to the station again, where Lowe lost the toss to share a three-berth compartment in a converted first-class carriage. The next morning they arrived at Kathgodam at the foot of the hill country, and from there took local transport to Ranikhet, which had earlier served as the starting point for successful expeditions to Nanda Devi and Kamet. Cotter recorded some unexpected budget woes: 'Tilman,[10] who paid only three shillings to travel with his baggage to Ranikhet 48 miles away, travelled in better days. The local bus service quoted us 58 rupees, (£5), a shocking blow as finances were not what they could be.'[11]

In the cool, beautiful hill station of Ranikhet, which at 6132ft has an uninterrupted view across deep valleys to Nanda Devi (25,000ft) and other western Himalayan peaks, they stayed at the West View Hotel run by a Swiss member of the Himalayan Club, Monsieur Frapolli, and his French wife. Riddiford got on well with both, finding them kind and helpful as well as keenly interested in the New Zealanders' plans. The Himalayan Club had recommended the main objectives of Nilkanta (21,640ft),[12] near the hill town of Badrinath, and Mukut Parbat (23,760ft), a lovely unclimbed mountain near Kamet (25,447ft). Nilkanta has three ridges, all protected by huge pitches of steep rock. Its east ridge was considered unclimbable; there had been an attempt on the south ridge, but the west ridge was thought the most feasible. The New Zealanders decided to attempt the mountain from the Satopanth Glacier, and with Frapolli's help spent a busy two or three days obtaining supplies at the local bazaar, making arrangements with the bank, and obtaining permits for kerosene and sugar.

At the hotel the climbers also met 21-year-old law student Keki Bunshah, a Parsee[13] from Bombay who accepted their invitation to join them as far as Badrinath and proved very useful as an interpreter. 'He is extremely well educated, fond of classical music and well read. Rather a fusspot, and obviously always well looked after, but good value,' Riddiford wrote to his mother.

The four Sherpas who joined the party on 1 June turned out to be highly satisfactory. Riddiford recorded his first impressions:

A day after us, our Sherpas arrived, four hard-looking characters with cheerful grins. Pasang the head man was about 40: the others were his brother Nima, Thundu the cook, and Yila Tenzing, 31,[14] the boy of the party who is always given the dirty work like washing clothes. Tenzing is very athletic and springs about like an 18-year-old. All have a Tibetan cast of countenance, Thundu being more Chinese looking – in fact he looks like one of the crew of a pirate junk. They quickly made themselves very useful with the packing up of gear. They are all excellent, steady and experienced. Pasang is the only one who speaks English.[15]

A letter from Krenek advised that Nima Sherpa had climbed on Nanda Devi in 1939 with the Poles and with Snelson's Garhwal expedition in 1950: he was described as willing and strong. Yila Tenzing had done excellent work in Sikkim in 1939, and Thundu – who had accompanied two other Sikkim expeditions in 1936 and 1942 – was an excellent cook. Sherpa Pasang Dawa Lama not only spoke English but also had greater experience than Pasang Dawa, who had accompanied Packard on the 1950 British West Nepal Expedition.[16] So named because he had been trained as a Tibetan monk (lama), Pasang Dawa Lama had been with the ill-fated American K2 expedition in 1939, when Dudley Wolfe and three Sherpas perished on the upper slopes. Pasang and the American leader Fritz Wiessner had reached 27,400ft, only about 700ft from the summit, when they were held up by bad weather. When they returned to the mountain valley the expedition had packed up and left, believing they also were lost.[17]

It took Riddiford a fortnight to realise his great good fortune in employing this Pasang, who had climbed higher than any other Sherpa: he was an excellent guide, and was the principal reason why Riddiford's expedition flowed comparatively smoothly.[18] It was to be Pasang Dama Lama who provided crucial encouragement as they faced their most difficult decisions. (In 1951 Hillary was reluctant to recognise Pasang Dawa Lama's superior climbing skills.[19] But after Everest, in hindsight he described him as a 'mighty formidable individual'[20] who had proved himself a forceful climber in the Garhwal.)[21]

Coolie porters were engaged locally to carry their gear to Badrinath. Riddiford soon found that great patience was a prerequisite in these dealings:

> We found we had almost 30 loads of 60 pounds each, and arrangements were made with the local government contractor of porters for that number of Dhotial coolies to be ready on the morning of our departure. They were produced for our inspection, a motley collection: a lot of them just boys, and one old man. The

Sherpas Tenzing, Pasang Dawa Lama, Nima and Thundu, taken in Badrinath on the same day as the expedition photograph (front cover). Riddiford collection

The party travels through alpine meadows on the way in. Cotter collection

journey took ten days: they would do about ten miles a day and were loud and long in their complaints if asked to do more – one day there was almost a riot.²²

The journey to Badrinath followed a regular trade route and involved the crossing of three high, parallel bush-clad ranges separated by deep valleys. They passed through pleasant countryside with terraced fields and numerous villages where they were able to buy potatoes, onions, greens and occasionally eggs to supplement supplies. The first trek was to Ramni, a village at 4000ft, almost 15km on from Ghat. Cotter's diary for 5 June detailed some of the lighter moments:

> We had a good time with plenty to laugh at. George produced his trick of placing a coin on his foot and picking it up in his teeth. The No 13 porter tried his skill unsuccessfully, then Pasang came along, grabbed the coin, put it on his own foot, picked it up in his mouth and pocketed it. The porters thought it was a good joke. Rain began when Ramni was still two miles away and Keki had my parka, so I travelled in shorts and tennis shoes only … the men of the village gathered outside the bungalow and gossiped and stared. George got organised and began a pancake session to show the Sherpas how much better than chapatees they were. Then he put on an act for the kids around the place, turning on a haka which impressed even us. I had a joke and a yarn or two with the porters and was reprimanded later for getting too friendly and allowing them to think us

Heavily laden barefoot porters make their way over the stone-strewn path to the mountains. Riddiford collection

soft and so take advantage of us. The boys are probably quite right but I doubt it – the porters are very simple folk who enjoy a joke and always have a smile ready. Karansingh the head man reminds us of a St Bernard dog, as he follows us to make sure we don't overstep the camping spot – we call him 'Watchdog'. Another porter, a tall streak who arrives first in camp every night, is 'Captain Hook', more on account of his headscarf than his nose. With him comes No 13, a solid type who seems a humorous fellow. After the porters had sung around their fire for two hours, he told them to shut up.

Next day their route lay over a range, with a 2000ft climb providing magnificent views. Below them was Kalinghat and, on a ridge beyond, the Kuari Pass at 12,400ft. They dropped down to a riverside camp at 6500ft, hoping the next day to climb another 2000ft to Kalinghat and then to Dhakwani, 2000ft below the Kuari Pass – a 14km day. 'Tilman was correct when he said that nine or ten miles doesn't sound far, but we now appreciate the fact that the crossing of three ranges requires some effort, considering the valleys are at 4000ft and the passes at 9000, 10,000 and 12,000ft.'[23]

On 7 June they set off early. A mischievous Cotter put rocks in the Sherpas' packs to give them something worth carrying because they were 'great boys for parking their gear in the porters' loads'. After two hours they reached Kalinghat, from where the climb was very steep and tiring. After lunch, as Cotter vividly recorded in his diary, a 'screaming mass' of porters became most upset by plans to carry on to Dhakwani, calling the four climbers 'murderers'. When the sahibs called it a day after eight and a half hours and agreed to set up camp under some cliffs, the porters quickly appeared happy again. Cotter wrote:

> How like children they are, depressed one moment, happy the next. We must not give them too long a day tomorrow or there will be a rebellion … In case the Sherpas still had rocks in their packs, I put one in my pack, dragged it out in front of them and cursed everyone in general, George in particular because he was the closest, making out I had carried it all day.

On 8 June the party climbed 2000ft in just over an hour to reach the Kuari Pass, then spent a while taking in the spectacular view of the Garhwal peaks, including their first target, Nilkanta. It was a long way down from the pass, with more altercations between the sahibs and porters. Hillary became so incensed when one fellow shouted at him in Dhotial that he grabbed the porter, who immediately began to tremble at Hillary's size and violent reaction. That night

Lowe and Cotter rest at the top of the Kuari Pass, enjoying the magnificent view that had so delighted Frank Smythe on his approach to Kamet: 'We halted, silent, on the pass. The Himalaya were arrayed before us in a stupendous arc. Our vision swept from the gorges of Trisul to the peaks of Kedernath.' E.P. Hillary, CMC Kennedy Collection

they camped under the trees beside a stream, and there were no cigarettes for the porters owing to their day's behaviour. The following day was a short but hot and tiring journey to their bungalow at Joshimath, 10km down the Dhuali River, a tributary of the Alaknanda River and a major source of the sacred Ganges. They were surprised by the size of Joshimath village and by a group of boy scouts singing a rousing chorus. One 'sincere little chap' impressed Cotter by repeating the scout's law and promise – that he would rather die than tell a lie.

On 10 June scales were employed to weigh loads and revealed the Sherpas' ruse of offloading to the coolies: Sherpa Pasang had 22lb, the sahibs ('the idiots') 35–40lb, and one coolie who had tuberculosis and was supposed to be carrying light loads had 68lb. The carrying capacity of a swingbridge over the Dhuali then came into question, with one coolie finding the raging waters too much for his nerves. The party was now following a pilgrim route to Badrinath, passing many returning old people who appeared to be on their last legs. At the junction of the Dhauliganga and Alaknanda rivers some were bathing in the torrent to wash away their sins. The closer pilgrims drew to the source of the Ganges, the more powerful their purification became.[24] Their dedication intrigued Cotter: 'Old women carried in baskets strapped on coolies' backs, big fat overfed men in coffin-like containers carried by four dandies, over-laden ponies and mules, and poor pilgrims with only a staff and a small bag, all were part of the procession homeward.'

By 11 June, tired after their previous 26km day, they had only 8km to go through attractive scenery to reach Badrinath at 10,200ft. From their bungalow there they had a wonderful view of Nilkanta, 11,000ft above the village: of all the peaks in the Badrinath Range, there was 'none to equal it in beauty of form and grace of outline'.[25] They could also hear a drum that was beaten repeatedly by an old woman to announce the arrival of weary pilgrims, who were of such sour appearance they prompted this from Keki Bunshah: 'If their souls are as black as their faces, then the devil would have an easy task.'[26]

After quite a scene about pay, Riddiford dismissed the Dhotial porters and, with three weeks' supplies sorted for the Nilkanta attempt, engaged a fresh set of 11 men from Mana, a village close to the Tibetan border, whose hardy inhabitants

An elderly pilgrim takes a first-class seat to the Badrinath shrine. Cotter collection

Keki Bunshah (foreground) and Ed Cotter find a high point above Badrinath from which to enjoy the majestic sight of Nilkanta Peak. E.P. Hillary, CMC Kennedy Collection

were a mixture of Tibetan and Hindu. There followed another wrangle over rates of pay. The new crew, who would accompany them to base camp on the Satopanth Glacier, demanded six rupees and food – double the Dhotial porters' pay. While higher rates were acceptable for work off the beaten track in the mountains, the New Zealanders would only move so far. Cotter wrote:

> Of course the French expedition which gave six rupees per day was the cause of this inflation and we cursed them for having so much money to throw about. Just as we were considering carrying everything ourselves or getting mules, the Mana head sherang came back and agreed to accept four rupees.

The next morning they all awoke feeling ill, joining Riddiford who had begun to suffer from dysentery on the way to Badrinath. A rather sad parting from Keki Bunshar marked the day: he had been a cheerful companion, and his invitation to stay with him in Bombay on their way home was gratefully accepted. The Mana men arrived at noon; shortly after the party set off for the Satopanth Valley and that night enjoyed an easy camp in a pleasant meadow. The Satopanth Glacier lies on the northwest side of Nilkanta, below an 8200ft face, and on 13 June as the party moved up the valley to set up base camp at 13,500ft on the glacier, the mountains on either side were 'of the 18,000ft variety'. Nilkanta's majestic ice face gleaming in the sunshine left them gaping. From the camp, the west ridge – their rock route – looked impossibly long and steep; the col at 18,000ft that led to the ridge looked enough of a climb on its own.

The Mana men were discharged with 12 rupees each. On 14 June snow kept the party in their tents, Cotter reading *Great English Short Stories* and Riddiford still suffering from dysentery. Two weeks in the Satopanth were about to educate them in the realities of Himalayan climbing and acclimatisation. On 15 June they traversed a snow basin to the slopes below the face of Nilkanta with thoughts of attempting the peak across its face of ice cliffs. But the weather was packing up again. On 16 June it snowed heavily all night. Cotter wrote:

> Cosmo [Hillary] and George smelled the fleshpots of Badrinath or perhaps Mana village – anyway their reason to us was a trip down for more food and mail … Earle and I went up the valley and climbed up onto the moraine wall. At 12 noon we had reached a point from which we could see the head of the glacier, not very interesting. Then we trudged down the trough. As we neared camp Earle put on a big burst of speed. I arrived back at camp to find him completely done in. He was like that for the rest of the day.[27]

Tea break, location unknown. The four well-equipped Sherpas (facing camera) enjoying a chat over cha with their New Zealand sahibs. Riddiford collection

The next day was one of complete rest. On the 18th Riddiford and Cotter wandered up towards the ridge: the climb did Cotter good and he felt quite fit again. Back at base camp they met Hillary and Lowe, whose trip from Badrinath had taken six hours, but there was no mail. On 19 June after more snow they all set off for an attempt on Nilkanta. Hillary and Lowe headed for a col on the east ridge, reaching an intended campsite where it became clear that snow conditions ruled out this approach. As they traversed back, the others with Sherpas and food supplies caught up. But the col below the west ridge was still a long way above, with steep snow in between. They took three hours to reach the slopes below the col, where the snow was so deep they were forced to traverse right. At 3pm the weather deteriorated: Cotter's diary reflects a tactical blunder in attempting too much too soon:

The snow slopes were very very steep and tiring but we decided to make the col or bust. We did a 300-step plugging effort without a spell, and arrived at 5.20pm. I felt fairly fit and did a fair portion of the kicking, the climb taking nine hours. The col was at 18,000ft so we had done a 4500ft climb with 30lb packs, too much for one day as we later found out to our misfortune.

20 June: All had a good night: still snowing but fairly warm. It cleared later so I put on boots and wandered up the col to try some rock climbing. Earle got the pressure cooker functioning: it proved invaluable. As Shipton[28] said, he'd rather be without an ice axe than a pressure cooker in the mountains.

The morning of the 21st showed promise so they left, as Hillary said (foreshadowing his famous report on Everest), 'to knock off this peak if we do nothing else'. It was heavy work plugging steps up soft snow slopes. By 12.30 they had gained a point at 19,000ft on the ridge, but the summit at 21,640ft was a long way off and they decided to turn back. While they were descending a steep slope a cornice fell off, rather too close. Cotter, 21 June:

George was suffering from altitude headaches. The Nilkanta Ridge looks too much for us – anyway it is out of the question while snow remains on it. Snow avalanches fell continuously all afternoon … it would have been suicide to have been on our route to the valley.

That night, Cotter handed around a mirror. All were shocked. Riddiford commented, 'Jesus Christ Almighty!' Hillary: 'God, that's just how I feel too!' Lowe: 'Hell, what a poor old man!'[29]

On 22 June the snow was much firmer and, in a third of the time, they cramponed up to where they had been the previous day, looking to attempt an adjacent 20,550ft peak. All were tired, although Hillary was doing better than the others. But after 15 minutes a sobering experience quashed further progress along the ridge, as Cotter reported that night:

Suddenly 'Bumph!' And the ridge broke off at our feet. As I jumped for safety I saw George doing the same. Earle had also made it and we were glad to know we had acted instinctively. After this episode we saw that our steps had disappeared for 30 yards along the ridge. A few more steps, a glance at the difficulties ahead, the murky weather and poor snow conditions turned us homewards. There is no doubt that we have not acclimatised, we have no energy or drive. We had to keep

Badrinath, showing its temple and steps down to the Alaknanda River. George Lowe, CMC Kennedy collection

well below the ridge on our way back. We glissaded down to camp, struck camp and left with large loads. Our descent down the snow face was slow and laborious. Masses of avalanche snow which had fallen since our ascent had to be crossed.

Ed H. and George kicked steps down the slopes belaying most of the way. Below the steep gut we sat down to an enjoyable glissade. Then a huge avalanche fan stopped our progress. I was feeling the benefit of the increase in oxygen and hurried across the snow plateau, Ed and George close behind. Then there was a marvellous sitting glissade to the valley. Pasang told us he was not expecting the sahibs, so all he could do was give us the food he had prepared for his boys – dhal soup followed by delicious roast chops and baked potatoes. The Sherpas Nima and Thundu came in some time later. Ed H, who carried 60lbs down, weighed their loads – 70lbs and 80lbs. No wonder Thundu and Nima took the steep slopes slowly, and we had to forgive Nima his grunts and groans.

23 June was a rest day. On the 24th they prepared for the trip down to Mana and Badrinath, and discovered that the Mana men considered their loads of 65lb

to be reasonably light. Dressed in simple homespun woollen garments, the strong, hardy Mana porters usually travelled barefoot over difficult country. As Cotter noted that day, 'There's no doubt the Mana men can show us a thing or two about carrying loads. To see them walk and climb steep tracks with 60lbs on their backs makes the whole thing look so easy and effortless.'

Riddiford was travelling slowly, so the others strolled down with him, admiring the scenery and later the masses of beautifully coloured flowers that had blossomed since their climb up the valley. They were enjoying the diverse alpine flora of the Valley of Flowers,[30] declared a national park in 1982 and now a World Heritage Site. From a sunny resting spot beside a stream they used Riddiford's field glasses to watch some pilgrims on the other side of the river climbing up to a spot below two waterfalls, the refuge of an early saint who had spent years there in contemplation. Near Mana the party came across Thundu and Nima asleep on the track, having put in a fine effort crossing a snow bridge to reach the track ahead of the sahibs. Back in Badrinath the Mana men were paid off again, and 25 June was declared a rest day for the climbing party, who undertook a stocktake, mended lilos, lunched on roast chicken and visited the bazaar.

The New Zealanders certainly were used to roughing it, but not in foreign territory and at high altitudes. Overreaching themselves on Nilkanta was a sobering reality check. Christchurch climber Geoff Harrow, who had helped Riddiford organise medical supplies, says the work Riddiford put into preparation was immense, but it was not enough to protect them from stomach troubles. Riddiford's would plague him for months and, as he wrote to his mother on 27 June, the associated weight loss was a further complication:

> The Himalaya are a tough proposition. Ever since June 17 on the way to Badrinath I have been suffering from an affliction and now I have lost well over a stone. I will not attempt to do any work until the complaint leaves me. I am taking chlorodyne and thalazole[31] without result so far. But we all acclimatised fairly evenly though we were weak at 20,000ft.

From Badrinath, Cotter was able to update his old friends at the CMC on his Himalayan experiences: 'We made a ten-day unsuccessful attempt on Nilkanta. The monsoon had started, and fresh snow hampered us … we were all suffering from altitude and Earle had a touch of dysentery. This decided us to return to Badrinath. So far mountaineering in New Zealand is the ideal – no worries about porters or money.'[32]

Mukut Parbat and Kamet from peak at 20,760ft. E.P. Hillary, CMC Kennedy Collection

5. 'WE LONG WAY COME'

The conquest of Mukut Parbat

While they rested in Badrinath, the four New Zealanders pondered the harsh lessons learned on Nilkanta, learned a little more about the country they were in, and laid plans for their next objective. Much had been written about Nilkanta, only 8km from Badrinath: its impressive proportions and the difficulties it posed had made it famous. But little was known of the group's next target summit, Mukut Parbat, and they were dependent on the Himalayan Club for information.

Cotter's diaries and letters home provide a fresh first-hand perspective on the lead-up to a marathon ascent of what was then the highest unclimbed peak in the Garhwal.[1] There were two possible means of approach: via the Pachmi (west) Kamet Glacier, 20km north of Badrinath; and via the Chamrao Glacier, 5km further on.

> Badrinath, 26 June: George produced hair clippers and we sat in the sun, cutting each other's hair. Ed [Hillary] was active again and by the end of the day had made up 15 loads for our Mukut Parbat trip. The local doctor spent three hours with us, the main topic of conversation Hindus and their religion. The Hindu bible, the Bhagavad Gita, was recommended to us as being a code of living, moral and spiritual. The men about Badrinath in orange robes are holy men, and quite a few hermits are in residence here, each denying himself a particular worldly pleasure.

On 27 June Hillary and Lowe left early to reconnoitre approaches to the mountain. Yila Tenzing, a very strong man, was loaded up with 54lb, Hillary and Lowe had 20–25lb each, and a Mana boy called Gopah Singh carried their food in a 65lb load. Leaving Badrinath, they followed the swift-flowing, glacier-fed Saraswati River up a gorge and arrived at the site of the Ghastoli bridge at 3.30pm, only to find the structure had been taken down for the winter months. They tried to push heavy stringers about 10 metres long across the gap over the rushing torrent, but were unsuccessful. Instead they camped overnight beside a pleasant spring-fed lake, leaving a second attempt to bridge the gap until the next morning. Back in Badrinath, Riddiford and Cotter were catching up with correspondence and absorbing local colour.

> Earle and I spent the afternoon writing letters. The doctor arrived when we were at the Post Office and came to the bazaar with us, with the postmaster insisting that we visit the shop selling Tibetan goods and buy something to remind us of Badrinath. The first item was a long wool-lined coat and a Tibetan fur hat with mufflers over the ears: I was pleased to put it on for the fun. Earle was interested in a heavy wool blanket which he thought would do for his car, but then a similar Tibetan outfit to mine was brought out for him and he had no option but to wear it. No doubt we were a sight. So we left the shop and wandered through the bazaar in our Tibetan rigout – everyone thought it rather funny.

George Lowe tries out his barber skills on Ed Cotter.
Cotter collection

Their Badrinath friends accompanied Riddiford and Cotter to the bungalow, wishing to see the gear used in mountain climbing. A loaf of Thundu's bread was offered, while Riddiford ordered tea. Aware that Hindu protocols were strict, the New Zealanders had been uncertain whether to offer food or not, but the doctor explained that although he was a high-caste Brahmin, in his profession even he was often unable to keep to the rules of his caste. Afterwards, the postmaster admitted this was the first time he had eaten food cooked by a person of another caste or not Hindu.

On 28 June, Tenzing and Hillary retraced their steps down the valley to a point where the previous day they had noticed an avalanche snow bridge across the Saraswati River. Taking up positions opposite Lowe, they were able to breach the 10-metre gap using a 'stone and rope'[2] technique and pull the stringers into position. Gopah Singh with his huge load shuffled across the narrow planks, but

A Mana porter crosses the Saraswati River using the climber's makeshift bridge at Ghastoli (13,500ft). Cotter collection

Lowe was happier to cross 'à cheval', straddling the shaky sagging structure. Safely across, they all hurried on towards the terminal moraine of the Pachmi Kamet Glacier. En route they met the first two Tibetan traders to cross the Mana Pass that year, travelling with 22 longhaired sheep and goats. That afternoon Hillary and Lowe climbed 2000ft, pitching camp at 15,500ft.

Meanwhile Riddiford remained behind in Badrinath at the doctor's suggestion, hoping to recover from the dysentery that had plagued him for three weeks. He would then rejoin his companions. Cotter was delegated to organise the transport of four weeks' supplies to Ghastoli. Though he was assisted by Pasang and Thundu, the language barrier made for an extremely frustrating time getting the 20 Mana porters moving. As usual the porters, later described by Riddiford as 'respecters of nobody', were in no hurry. Cotter had plenty of time to enjoy the scenery as he made his way up from Mana through the Saraswati Gorge.

> Pheasants flew about a mountain stream, black and red as I climbed up the hillside past Mana women doing the family washing. The track led back to the river and

Mana villagers at 10,000ft. Cotter collection

a natural rock bridge took me across an 800ft chasm. The river dropped down through its water-carved cleft with terrific force – I was glad to have it behind me. After following along old banks of moraine accumulation and waiting for the rest of the party on the hillside, I drew a map of the world to explain where I lived: you Mana (and I pointed on my map): me Christchurch.

At Musapani, their usual stopping place on the Mana Pass route, the porters decided they were staying there. Cotter was very annoyed and told Pasang so. But nothing could be accomplished by threat or argument – the porters already had their fire going. 'I watched on as the proper sahib should while my tent was pitched 20 yards below the gang. On Pasang's enquiry re dinner I told him I would leave it to Thundu. I offered them a brew of Ovaltine and biscuits, then found they were not hungry as they had had a meal at Mana – the rotters.'

That night Cotter told Pasang he was disappointed at the men's poor showing. He insisted they had to reach the Pachmi Kamet Glacier to meet the other sahibs. But there appeared to be some confusion over the route to be taken. A 15-minute discussion in which he took no part resulted in the men leaving his tent more satisfied with their own map drawing than Cotter's, and Cotter even more confused about where he was going.

> The Mana men gave a lot of trouble. Although there is no doubt about their superior carrying ability, their laziness and refusal to do anything approaching a reasonable day's work caused us to lose confidence in them. My coolies refused to travel for more than three and a half hours the first day, declaring that the next camping spot with firewood was many miles away. With this precedent established, they took it as their right to do only short marches. We also cursed the delay caused by their 'community pipe' which consisted of five parts each carried by a different man, so that some time elapsed before the pipe was fitted together and puffed by each man in turn.

Cotter's party set out later than he wanted on the 29th, across ground covered by glacial boulders. Soon the track began to lead upwards. He saw an eagle soaring back and forth across a high cliff face and watched marmots running around the rocks. He arrived at a point from which he could see the upper Saraswati Valley, bare and Tibetan-looking, then followed the track down to Ghastoli. But he was dismayed to find that the bridge over the river consisted simply of some rather saggy stringers. Lowe had left a note[3] explaining their efforts of the previous day. Without dwelling too long on what might happen if he slipped, Cotter walked across, balancing one foot on each stringer, then returned and got his pack across. Cotter's diary for 29 June recounts how when the porters finally arrived more than an hour later, they were visibly dismayed.

> Such a cry went up when they saw the condition the bridge was in that it became evident they did not intend crossing it. I ran across and showed them how simple it was – they were not impressed, so I told Pasang I would begin carrying loads across. I was in constant danger of death by misadventure, but once I had got most of the loads over the porters sat down for a smoke and decided they would like to make a really first class job of the bridge for the Tibetan traders who were grazing their flocks until they could travel down to Mana. When an old man began laying 3ft lengths of timber across the stringers and tying them into position, I realised that the New Zealand Himalayan Expedition was being reinvented as a bridge building expedition to consolidate the Mana trade with Tibet.
>
> One smart lad decided there was a lean on the general angle of the bridge, so off came the planks while the stringers were straightened. An hour's argument followed. The Mana men decided they were not interested in carrying our loads any further: Pasang's reply was to leap onto the bridge and begin untying the planks. I decided to let him deal with the situation, because otherwise the Sherpas would have a mighty lot of carrying to do. At 4pm it was decided that the Mana men would continue at least to Khati, several miles upriver, leaving behind four of their number to complete their work on the bridge.

It was late in the day when Cotter met up with the advance party at Khati. After they had crossed the bridge at Ghastoli, Hillary and Lowe had moved up onto the Pachmi Kamet moraine, where they set up camp at 15,000ft. On 29 June they had travelled quickly up the glacier and onto a main dividing ridge at 19,500ft, from which they saw enough to convince them that the Chamrao Glacier would provide a better approach. They had been much impressed by Tenzing, who had carried a 30lb pack all the way. He had collapsed on the ridge, saying, 'No further, sahib,' and smiled with relief when they agreed to stop.

The following day Hillary and Cotter went ahead, aiming for a base camp in a moraine hollow at 16,000ft, below the terminal of the Chamrao Glacier. The porters and Lowe followed, Lowe leaving a note for Riddiford at the footbridge over the Pachmi Kamet stream: 'June 30, 9am: Leaving for base camp up Dakkhni Chamrao. Pachmi Kamet no good. Mana coolies very sluggish.' The Mana men had to be coaxed up the 3km of moraine to the campsite, and Lowe's language was not at all complimentary: he had cursed them every time they stopped.[4] Tilman

A meal break at base camp at 16,000ft in the moraine hollow of the Chamrao Glacier. From left: Cotter, Pasang, Lowe and Hillary. Riddiford collection

had had a similar experience on his earlier ascent of Nanda Devi: 'The Mana men are very independent, and dislike being hurried. The pipe would be passed around before there was any hint at readiness to pack up.'[5] But Ed Cotter was still in awe of their strength:

> The main impression we have gained is their ability to move with a 70lb pack without the slightest effort, even on a steep slope. Whereas we sit and gasp after putting down our 30lb packs, they laugh and chat amongst themselves after dropping their loads.

Nevertheless it was a relief to pay them off at base camp, although they grumbled because they hadn't been given a longer contract. Against Lowe's wishes, an agreement was reached that included baksheesh for some. Riddiford's party arrived at base that evening from Badrinath, having met and shared tea (cha) and cigarettes with some rather cold, disgruntled Mana porters making their way down.[6] On the way up, Riddiford had crawled across the completed Ghastoli bridge. His Sherpa, Nima, was the perfect gentleman's gentleman, carrying Riddiford's pack for him, and even the sheep they bought in Mana reached base camp under its own power.

The Sherpa kitchen: Nima, Tenzing (kneeling), Pasang and Thundu. Riddiford collection

Sunday 1 July was a rest day, but not for the sheep. To save it dying of its own free will, as Cotter put it, it was quickly dispatched before the few remaining Mana men left. In fine weather there was a splendid array of ice peaks visible at the head of the valley, with Mukut Parbat a wonderful sight, a huge wall of rock outlined by a delicate ice ridge against the blue sky. From camp, a route through the ice face looked impossible and any approach to the high summit ridge lay hidden, so a reconnoitre was planned for the next day.

The weather on the following day was not first class, so they delayed their departure until 7am. The four climbers set off up the moraine, reaching the junction of the Uttari Chamrao and Dakkhni Chamrao glaciers at 16,800ft. Riddiford was soon under pressure and dropped out, while Cotter travelled on up the moraine gully below a high moraine wall that Hillary and Lowe were negotiating. Then, sick of boulder-hopping, Cotter simply climbed straight up the wall to a delightful spot on the hillside where he sat down, amazed by the profusion of alpine flowers and butterflies, and waited for the others. Hillary, who had been having stomach trouble, was the first to arrive. Together they carried on up the wall for half an hour to a point where it merged with stony hillside.

While Hillary rested, Cotter climbed onto the spur and sidled around rock-strewn slopes. There ahead of him lay a way through the icefall, which had dropped back several hundred metres on the extreme left; easy slopes now led to a névé above the icefall. When Hillary joined him they discussed the possibility of continuing further, but decided instead to take the good news back to the others at base camp, which they reached at 12.45pm. Having discovered an excellent site for Camp 1 – an oasis of flowers and grass tucked into a corner of the glacier between the moraine wall and the hillside – they spent a cold, misty afternoon sorting out supplies for several days further up.

On the 3rd they prepared to establish Camp 1. Riddiford remained behind to supervise the portage of loads to Camp 1 the following day. In the sunshine Hillary, Lowe and Cotter made good time up the moraine, and Cotter waited for the Sherpas at the top of the moraine wall. Tents were pitched at Camp 1 before an afternoon's rest. With the Sherpas down at base camp, Lowe cooked breakfast the next morning – rather unsuccessfully, as a sticky mass of porridge was served up. Cotter, Hillary and Lowe left at 5am, followed the moraine, dropped several hundred feet to glacier level, then moved over the glacier past the lower icefall. A climb up the snow face took them to the top of the second icefall, the Dakkhni Chamrao Glacier.

They cramponed up a last slope to reach a point at 18,000ft, from which their Mukut Parbat route was visible. This lay to the left of the peak through a doubtful-looking icefall to a ridge at 21,000ft. The steepness of the ice face looked more daunting than its brokenness. Having seen what they wanted, and

Ed Cotter at Camp 1. Cotter collection

deciding that Camp 2 should be as near as possible to the foot of the icefall, they turned their attention to the left-hand branch of the Dakkhni Chamrao Glacier, where a snow peak at 20,330ft invited their inspection. The day was still young, and they were at the foot of the unnamed peak by 9.30am. Then followed a long, exhausting climb to the corniced summit. Altitude was having its effect on all of them: they climbed sluggishly, breathing heavily, and experienced what Cotter called the 'Nineteen Thousand Foot Blues'.[7] The descent took six hours.

> Keeping well down from the dangerous ridge, we traversed the peak knowing that the ridge led down towards our camp. The snow was in very bad condition,

As near as possible to the foot of the icefall, Camp 2 at 19,000ft was pitched on a col between the Chamrao and West Kamet glaciers and commanded a view of both. *Cotter collection*

Two of the New Zealanders ascend a 2000ft icefall leading to the summit ridge of Mukut Parbat.
Riddiford collection

and at every second step we would sink through to bottomless slush. This ridge continued with similar snow conditions for two and a half miles to a rocky peak of 18,740ft above our Camp 1. We traversed across that, then dropped down to Camp 1 at 6pm, tired after a difficult 13-hour day, but pleased to have climbed our first 20,000-footer.

5 July: A fine rest day in the delightful Camp 1 oasis. Below us the daily Saraswati valley mist was racing hell for leather towards Mana Pass. Tenzing made a small boat and sailed it across a small lake Ed [Hillary] had made. Ed, who evidently

controlled the planning of the Lake Pukaki power scheme after spending a winter there, had used a dam of special Hillary construction to hold back a small stream. I began building an outrigger and Ed followed suit. This filled in a large part of the day, and was suitably concluded with a regatta, eight or nine vessels taking part.

On 6 July Hillary was on another of his 'desperation runs', moving well ahead of the others on the moraine wall, but over the spur he slipped at the head of the icefall. He and Lowe waited there for Cotter and Riddiford, who had the rope. In the heat, their trip up the glacier was exhausting. Camp 2 was established at the foot of the Mukut Parbat icefall on a saddle leading to the Pachmi Kamet Glacier. Tents were pitched on a snow terrace, and the Sherpas returned to Camp 1.

The following day Hillary and Cotter left Camp 2 to look at the icefall. They reached the big basin below the main icefall slopes where they experienced blazing heat with no air movement, so quickly retreated back to camp. 'On a clear day at this altitude, 19,000ft, any activity after 10am appears out of the question. We didn't expect to see the Sherpas up today, but they arrived with two tents and food at 2.30pm.'

On the morning of the 8th the pressure cooker gave trouble and it was 4.30am before they got their brew of porridge. The task for the day was to see if the icefall could be negotiated up to the col. Hillary and Lowe went ahead, making good time over the basin to the steep slopes leading to the col, where there was quite a lot of cutting to be done for the benefit of the Sherpas. All four climbers experienced very cold feet and made haste for the sun on the slopes above, where they took off their boots and socks to restore circulation. Using crampons they continued on through a snowfield in the direction of the col, over a doubtful snow bridge then along a ledge, from which Lowe cut 100ft up an exposed ice slope onto the col at 21,000ft. There they had their first view of Tibet – bare mountains to 21,000ft backed by a plain of the same brown hue. Below them a Tibetan glacier remarkable for its evenness flowed from behind Mukut Parbat. The whole panorama gave them an inkling of the sense of accomplishment they would experience after a successful climb. But the knife-edge Mukut Parbat ridge looked long and steep, a tough job ahead.

They sorted out a good site for Camp 3 on an ice ledge a little below the col, but an icy wind soon sent them gasping back along their tracks to the warmth of Camp 2. Cotter decided his personal blackout area was 19,000–21,000ft, as once again he experienced a lack of energy at about 20,000ft. The Sherpas, tired after three relays carrying supplies, struck camp against a rock. The sahibs envied them,

Ed Cotter surveys the daunting summit ridge of Mukut Parbat from an altitude of over 20,000ft. The climbers established Camp 3 on the ice shelf middle left. Kamet can be seen to the right.
Riddiford collection

Setting up Camp 3 on the ice shelf at 21,000ft. *Riddiford collection*

given that their own campsite was poised over a crevasse of unknown dimensions, which produced cracking noises as the snow settled beneath the weight of their tents and bodies.

Owing to poor weather, 9 July was a rest day. 'We racked our brains for a list of alpine books one would have if not spending our money on trips to the Himalaya,' wrote Cotter. They also organised food for three days at Camp 3 at 21,000ft.

The 10th brought a very cold morning as they all set off for Camp 3. The sun kept them warm but the altitude had its effect: all were feeling it, especially Riddiford, for whom every step was a dragging effort.[8] Cotter decided to go first on their rope, hoping the psychological effect of leading might help, and he and Riddiford arrived in the upper basin about noon, half an hour after Hillary and Lowe. The Sherpas were close behind, Tenzing laughing and jumping around. The party made slow progress along the shelf to the new camp, where Cotter was feeling at his worst yet and could not help with pitching tents. Pasang was to have been sent back, but he was very keen to do the climb and looked so hurt when told to leave and come back up the following day that they relented and said he could stay. That meant Riddiford, Cotter and Lowe squeezing into a two-man tent, with Hillary and Pasang and the cooking gear in the other. The camp below the col was on an ice shelf only about 30ft wide: they hoped no one would fall off during the night.

A 'recce' of the peak was planned for the next day, though lethargy made them doubtful about how far they would get. The mood was not optimistic: the ridge to the summit looked dangerous, and as their enthusiasm dropped a little, so did their confidence. It was not a great night anyway: the lilos were faulty and needed to be reinflated frequently. For extra insulation and padding they placed spare clothes in layers under their sleeping bags. Cotter felt he was finally acclimatising, however: 'Life at 21,000ft isn't particularly pleasant but I'm pleased to know that I have taken it fairly well – I've also been good-tempered for the whole trip, even at heights, and that's a personal satisfaction.'

11 July: The ascent of Mukut Parbat. With the promise of a good day, they began preparations with breakfast at 5.15am. Hillary and Lowe left 10 minutes ahead of the others, just as the sun touched their tents at about 8am. The night before, Cotter had hung his snow glasses outside the tent, as there was such a crush inside. The next morning they were gone. Certain they had been mistakenly taken by Lowe, since they were with Lowe's ski cap, Cotter hurried to catch up. By then Hillary and Lowe were kicking up a steep snow face, making for the ridge where they hoped the conditions would be good for crampons. Lowe did not have the goggles, however, and Cotter had to make do by pulling his balaclava over his face. Fortunately the light was not too strong, although he was not to escape snow blindness. What happened to the snow glasses is still a mystery. Cotter says Lowe had been hallucinating and talking incoherently in his sleep that night, and still believes that could have contributed to some confusion the next morning.

Rather than follow the others, Riddiford, Pasang and Cotter on the second rope decided to move left on a difficult traverse of steep soft snow that took them onto the crest of the ridge. At this stage Hillary and Lowe were a little ahead, on snow ideal for cramponing. But for Riddiford and Cotter, Pasang's cramponing technique caused problems: as the middle man, he needed instruction in handling

Riddiford, Pasang and Cotter leave the col for the summit. Riddiford is cutting green ice as a wind of gale force whistles over the ridge. The height is about 22,700ft, the Tibetan side to the left. *Cotter collection*

the rope more efficiently. On some of the steeper sections Riddiford cut steps which Cotter described as a godsend, as Riddiford was at that point travelling much better than he was.[9] But the icy, near gale-force wind over the ridge made the going very unpleasant.

Though all five were climbing in full windproof clothing, they had to stop a number of times to remove crampons, boots and socks and rub their feet to restore circulation. Cotter was glad of his rubber boots, whereas on the other rope Lowe was discovering how relentlessly the cold moved from crampons through nailed boots to the feet. After one such stop Riddiford's rope took the lead, climbing steadily until at about 22,300ft Cotter, who was dragging a little, decided it was time for another foot massage. When he took off his boots he found his toes were blue: Pasang pounded Cotter's feet with his fists and held them to the warmth of his stomach until after 30 minutes he pronounced them okay.[10] At midday Riddiford's rope cut around an ice slope to top a small subsidiary peak at 22,500ft on the ridge.[11] From there they could see the main ridge narrowing to a knife edge, soaring up to the summit plateau in one ice-glittering sweep, with a fall on either side of several thousand feet down to the Tibetan and Pachmi Kamet glaciers. Cotter recorded their initial misgivings:

> Above us was a steep snow and ice ridge unbroken except for several pitches of rock. This slope appeared very long, and the summit far above too high to be reached that day. When the other boys appeared behind us, they held the same view. But Earle wanted to cut across to a little col at the foot of the ridge to gain a better idea of its true angle. I was not very keen about going further, especially when Hillary muttered words to the effect that we'd better try an approach from the Tibetan glacier. I told Earle I thought our chances of reaching the summit were slim and if we went home we would have a chance of being fit on the morrow for another attempt. But I followed him to the col, from which the ridge did not look as steep as it did from face on. Then Pasang joined in, much to my surprise, to the effect that 'We long way come, summit only two hours.' So what could I do but agree to go on.
>
> We cut up from the cornice above the col, making slow progress for an hour. Then, with occasional cutting, we moved faster over several snow bumps at right angles to the main ridge. Next we came to a rock section, clambered over the rocks and began climbing the main ridge, which was very narrow, using our crampons on each side of the ridge. The wind was a lot stronger here, but when Earle questioned whether we should go on I was agreeable, as the summit appeared

A panoramic view of the Mukut Parbat landscape. Riddiford collection fairly handy. At 4.50 we were on the summit plateau, where the wind was fierce and I had a spell. I wasn't very interested in whether I reached the summit, but we dragged across the plateau in soft snow. The final slopes were a b….., the wind seeming to buffet out any air we had in our lungs. But all things come to an end sometime, even the joy and exhilaration of climbing a 23,760ft peak, so that at 5.45pm we trod on the narrow summit.[12]

As the sun sank over the foothills the three exhausted climbers shook hands, sheltered in a snow hollow, and sucked a couple of sweets. (Three photos were taken, but these are untraceable.) In one direction they were looking at Abi Gamin, 24,124ft, very close to Kamet and brick red in the setting sun. Below them a blue Tibetan glacier flowed towards bare hills and yellow plains.

After 10 minutes they turned for home. In what Riddiford termed 'a faultless exhibition of cramponing',[13] Cotter led them off the shoulder and down the steep ridge in a race against time and darkness, and once off the plateau they made steady progress. The wind had reached gale force, the rope was blown taut over the ridge, and much care had to be taken at one spot in particular on the rock section where the wind was howling across a low gap. But Pasang showed himself to be a keen and able climber. As Cotter noted, 'Without his interest and keenness to reach the summit, it is doubtful whether we would have tackled the upper portion of the climb.'

The descent was carried out 'at top speed consistent with safety', Riddiford wrote home.[14] Their worries were not over until they were past the difficult sections and back over the 22,500ft subsidiary peak, but from there they made good time. At 8.30pm they met Lowe, who had climbed up with a torch while Hillary cooked a meal. After a weary 20-minute trudge back to camp they 'crawled and gasped' their way into their sleeping bags.[15] During the night Lowe put cocaine drops in Cotter's eyes to ease the snow blindness that was coming on, and massaged Riddiford's freezing feet and hands. The next morning Riddiford left with Pasang for Camp 1, where his toes and fingers would have a better chance of getting back to normal. Hillary, Lowe and Cotter spent the day resting, Lowe reading aloud to the hapless Cotter, who would be becalmed by snow blindness for two days.

6. MONSOON WOES

'We have not one rupee among us.'

While the New Zealand party had been in Badrinath preparing for Mukut Parbat, the British 1951 Everest Reconnaissance Expedition, led by Eric Shipton, was finalising plans for exploring a new approach to the summit of Mt Everest from the south. The timing of the Mukut Parbat ascent on 11 July contributed to what became a historic confluence of interests.

Hillary, deeply disappointed that he and Lowe had not achieved the summit of Mukut Parbat, was astonished by Riddiford's stubborn determination and tremendous willpower despite being weakened by dysentery.[1] His accounts in *Nothing Venture Nothing Win* (1975) and *View from the Summit* (1999) reveal how galling it was when he and Lowe were stalled massaging their feet and the others moved ahead. But in the matter of timing, these substantially identical versions do not tally with letters and diary entries written by Riddiford and Cotter just after the ascent.

Riddiford's letter home on 27 July tells how his rope took over the lead from Lowe and Hillary after only half an hour: presumably this means from the beginning of the day's 10-hour climb. He reinforces this timing in another section of the same letter: 'The day on Mukut Parbat when I was going almost as easily as at sea level was a very lucky miracle as it was the one day I needed it. I had to lead all the way for nine and a half hours.' The early change of lead is corroborated by Cotter's diary entry for 11 July (though, owing to snow blindness, this must have been written several days afterwards). This records how Riddiford led off after one of the earlier stops. Further on, Cotter makes another reference to how 'some way below them' Hillary and Lowe had stopped once again, as Lowe's feet were giving trouble.

However, in both the books mentioned above, Hillary wrote that the overtaking manoeuvre took place later in the day, at 22,500ft (the height of the subsidiary peak), where he and Lowe had reached a rocky outcrop which provided shelter from the wind while they massaged their feet again; at that stage the others were 'quite a long way behind'.[2] This is a major discrepancy that readers can ponder.

What is clear is that on the day, despite the advantage of being on a more mobile two-man rope, Hillary and Lowe were outclimbed. When they caught up with Riddiford he was moving very slowly on hard ice, but Hillary knew it would not be easy to pass the other team on the ridge, so after a brief discussion he and Lowe arrived at what proved to be a mortifying miscalculation:

> The other team were not as fit as we were and we frankly doubted if they would have time to lead the apparent difficulties of the ice ridge and reach the summit before dark, and meanwhile we would get mighty cold waiting behind them. Shouting across the wind the two parties debated the matter. In the end Lowe and I decided to return while the others went on. All afternoon we watched them high on the ridge making apparently little progress, and then the cold drove us back to our tents.[3]

When Riddiford, Cotter and Pasang got back to camp, exhausted but triumphant, Hillary learned a memorable lesson. 'We had done most of the work on the lower parts of the mountain, but then we'd made a wrong decision.'[4] Cotter still believes that this failure was a personal defeat for Hillary that dogged him for a long time.

The day after the ascent, as Riddiford and Pasang made haste to Camp 1, the highlight for Riddiford was the resounding account of the climb Pasang relayed to the other Sherpas at Camp 2. Riddiford wrote home that Pasang was 'as pleased as a dog with two tails'.[5] Hillary and Lowe spent a day with the blinded Cotter, then made their own attempt on the mountain. Faced with new snow and more intense cold, they soon realised their physical condition had deteriorated badly during the two days at 21,000ft, and had to turn it in. Running out of food, Hillary, Lowe and Cotter prepared to withdraw to Camp 1.

The next day, as they went down the Pachmi Kamet Glacier, Lowe, in the lead, broke through the surface snow of a covered crevasse. His crampons and pack saved him from a long fall, and by lying full length to spread his weight Hillary was just able to see him in the depths below. A rope was lowered, Lowe secured himself, and Hillary helped him out while Cotter belayed them from safer ground. The party roped up, with Lowe leading once more, but had moved only about 10 metres when, with a shout and a roar, he disappeared from sight again. Hillary quickly produced a pick belay and held him, taking the strain in time to arrest Lowe's fall. Muffled shouts of pain and quite a bit of cursing were heard, as the rope had twisted around Lowe's thumb, which then had to take the full weight of his body. But he soon reappeared – mainly by his own exertions, Cotter wrote.[6]

After a day's rest at Camp 1 and reunited with Riddiford, the party agreed to make their way to Badrinath to recuperate for a week at lower altitude. A contributing factor in that decision for Riddiford was his dysentery. At Camp 3 he had found having to get out of bed three or four times a night especially annoying. After the ascent, he was clearly coming to the end of his tether.

27 July: I have been in trouble with d … now for seven weeks, perfectly well and happy otherwise but it has reduced my weight a good deal and weakened me a lot … When we came back here to Badrinath for a rest I was finally ordered to bed for several days with a course of powerful drugs. I am not sure whether they have worked or not but hope for the best … on my climb altitude effects were almost nil, if it wasn't for my damn stomach I'd be 100%.[7]

In Badrinath, Hillary saw a newspaper cutting about the British Reconnaissance Expedition. He 'cheekily'[8] wrote to Shipton suggesting he include two members of the New Zealand party, a proposal that was immediately rejected.[9]

The four climbers had made good friends with the Badrinath postmaster, the secretary of the temple and the local doctor, Misra, and passed their time pleasantly enough playing soccer with the locals, catching up with mail and writing newspaper articles. But after five days Hillary was bored, so he and Cotter moved off with four Mana men to restock Camp 1, from which the two climbers hoped to ascend a 21,000ft peak. Over the next few days in Badrinath, Lowe and Riddiford spent time with six members of a French party straight from the disaster on Nanda Devi (25,645ft) in which they had lost the leader, Roger Duplat, and one other man, Gilbert Vignes. French plans after Nanda Devi had included Mukut Parbat, so they were most interested in the New Zealand ascent. Riddiford found them great company:

They were a first class bunch, friendly and sincere and first class mountaineers. The discussions at table were deafeningly French at times. I enjoyed swinging my mothballed New Caledonian French into action again: only one of them spoke English. They were magnificently equipped. Their high altitude tents are a revelation and they had 100 coolies to carry their stuff into the Nanda Devi basin.[10]

Meanwhile, monsoon conditions had delayed any climbing for Hillary and Cotter. After three days Lowe arrived, and on 26 July, in more doubtful weather, he joined Hillary for an exploratory journey into the Uttari Chamrao Glacier and a rock climb on a 19,560ft peak from which they managed a glorious view of Mukut Parbat, Kamet, Abi Gamin and Mana.

On 27 July the party discharged their Mana coolies, recommending to Riddiford that no baksheesh be paid because of their poor work. After a slow carry to base, the Mana men had refused to carry to Camp 1 unless paid extra: they had also pilfered cigarettes and sweets.

A note from Lowe to Riddiford in Badrinath that day told of their desperate finances and the urgent need to book berths for the return home. 'We have not one rupee amongst us – sorry for the despondent note. Our plan tomorrow is to take a tent and two days' food to North Chamrao in the hope that weather will improve for a trip to Camp 3 and a Mukut Parbat attempt.'[11]

But the next day conditions were again unfavourable. They spent their time rock climbing in the mist, reaching the top of a 19,450ft peak. The following day the weather was even worse: they returned to Camp 1 in a snowstorm. By 31 July Riddiford had joined them there, accepting that with money so short they would have to return home early. That decision was some relief to him: 'I will be quite happy to leave the mountains after another fortnight, as three months in the Himalaya is enough, especially with a misbehaving stomach.'[12] A look at Kamet was mooted, but the belated and strong arrival of the monsoon scotched that idea.

With time, money and supplies all running low it was possible for only two to return to Camp 3, from which Hillary and Lowe were still hoping to climb Mukut Parbat. They made the move with three Sherpas. From 1 August they

Riddiford (left) during a lunch break with Pasang, two other Sherpas, and Cotter in foreground.
Cotter collection

Ed Cotter singles out another peak for the party's attention. Riddiford collection

spent two days storm-bound at Camp 2 then set off for Camp 3, even though deep new snow covered the icefall. After digging out the tents there and sending their Sherpas back, the climbers spent another two days in their tents while the snow fell, the wind blew and avalanches rumbled.

Finally, during a break in the weather, they managed the first of their two objectives – a peak at 22,180ft – and returned to their tent just as a terrific hailstorm struck. Their second conquest was to have been Mukut Parbat, but after studying the heavily snowed-up ridge from which a strong wind was blowing loose snow into Tibet, they decided an attempt would be unwise. As Lowe wrote later, 'The four days which we had spent at 21,000ft had stripped the flesh off us … our appetites were gone, and we were not really fit enough for a long hard day.'[13] The next morning they evacuated camp, facing subsidence on steep snow slopes and the tension of possible avalanche during an agonising descent to Camp 1, where Riddiford and Cotter were waiting for them.

The poor state of their finances spelled the end of further grand plans, but Riddiford was keen to return to Nilkanta for a second look:

> As soon as it clears I am going back for a final pop at Nilkanta as I couldn't leave here without wanting to come back if I didn't climb it. Stomach is OK and for the first time I feel it's really good to be here. On the mend and am feeling very fit. Though goodness knows you need plenty of patience for Himalayan climbing … The other three thought it too much of a lost cause, so we agreed to divide for a week and meet again at Badrinath.[14]

Natar Singh, a Mana headman who had led porters for many Himalayan parties, provides some advice for Ed Hillary (rear) and Ed Cotter (right). Cotter Collection

He took with him Thundu and Pasang. Fresh supplies were easy to obtain: they purchased new potatoes, beans and cooking apples in Badrinath, and the hindquarters of a lamb that had fallen over a cliff were bought cheaply from the shepherds. By then Pasang was invaluable: 'Pasang would act as my climbing companion, and a damn good one as I knew from experience on Mukut Parbat.'[15] Riddiford also engaged Gopah Singh, the coolie who had displayed great courage in crossing shaky bridges.

So the party split up, and Hillary, Lowe and Cotter moved off to camp at 17,500ft on the Uttari Chamrao Glacier before attempting a peak at 20,760ft. That evening they entertained Nima and Tenzing with part-songs, solos and a Māori haka, Lowe proving himself a man of many parts. On the climb the next day, Cotter plugged up 800ft of deep powdered snow to the summit in what he remembers as the most enjoyable climb of the expedition. They were able to peer down through a hole in the summit cornice to see the moraine of the Balbala Glacier, and kept enough energy in reserve to roll boulders down a 3000ft drop.[16]

Back on Nilkanta, with the monsoon at its height, Riddiford was gambling on the possibility of two fine days. Hoping to attempt the north face route, he and the two Sherpas succeeded in finding their way over a vital col in a 'very providential' way. Pasang got into conversation with two sheep herders camped nearby, who told him of a tricky route traversing a series of grass ledges on the great cliff face along the side of the Satopanth Valley. 'No one looking from below could imagine that such a route existed – but except for one bad place the track was quite safe though highly sensational,' Riddiford wrote later.[17] They camped at 15,500ft and enjoyed magnificent views during a brief break in the weather. The north face looked feasible – but heavy rain came in. 'If we could have got those two fine days, I think we would have given it a damned good go. Snow conditions were very bad, soft and unstable, but Pasang and I climbed up to be just under the East Col and far enough to see that the mountain could be reached and probably climbed by this route.'[18]

Meanwhile, the Mana coolies Riddiford had employed to evacuate the Chamroa camp were engaged on a set-rate contract, as Riddiford explained in a letter home:

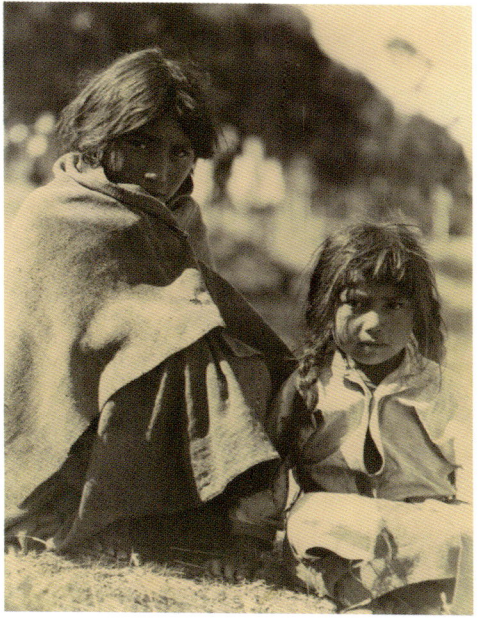

Two shy Mana girls take their portrait opportunity very seriously indeed. The local people often found themselves somewhat puzzled subjects for the sahibs' cameras. Jen Cotter

> This was a great improvement, without incentive to dawdle or grumble, as they covered the journey each way at a gallop. But after the coolies arrived, George and the two Eds left the Sherpas[19] to pack up and went down. The latter disgraced themselves. The Mana men brought up some grog, they all got drunk and the Sherpas threw away quite a lot of good food and supplies so the Mana men went down with light loads. It would not have happened if Pasang had been there.[20]

By 14 August the four had regrouped in Badrinath. Feeling extremely fit by then, and sorry to be saying goodbye to the mountains of Garhwal, Hillary and Cotter made a last dash into the hills near Nilkanta before the expedition party bid farewell to their Badrinath friends on 16 August. On their last night there the New Zealanders enjoyed dinner Indian-style with Dr Misra and the postmaster: 'We had expected the food to be an ordeal but were pleasantly surprised. The quality and the cooking of the rice was a revelation, with all sorts of subtle and

Rain in the Alaknanda River valley. G. Lowe, Kennedy Collection

strange flavours in the various dishes quite an experience, served very late in the usual Indian style.'[21] Riddiford was pleased to hire four ponies at a contract price to take their 500lb of equipment back to Ranikhet. 'Horses have one advantage. As Pasang said, horses no talk. And the horsemen turned out to be a good lot.'[22]

Spirits somewhat dampened by cold rain, the party followed the pilgrim trail back to Joshimath, 30km down the valley. From there, as they headed down the grassy track towards the plains of India, they felt the magnificent mountains receding into memory. 'To say farewell to Joshimath is to say farewell to Garhwal,' wrote Cotter.[23]

On the second day out, however, there was anxious talk of a bad slip ahead in the deep Alaknanda gorge – a common occurrence in heavy rain. A whole hillside had been washed away, and Riddiford declared it a 'hopeless-looking proposition'. The track and bridge across the river had disappeared, and huge rocks and masses of earth were coming down every few minutes. On retreating to a nearby village for a night in a pilgrims' rest-house, they learned that the only alternative was a detour 2000ft higher up, meaning the horses would have to be unladen. The thought of double packing everything on their backs for a whole day through the forest was so repellent the climbers decided to risk the slip route. Next day they left early in the morning; fortunately the rain had stopped and the slip appeared to have settled. But in crossing it they were forced to use considerable ingenuity with carabiners, pitons and lengths of rope, as Riddiford wrote:

> First we had to traverse along a rock precipice before attempting to get down to the river 150ft below. We got out our pitons, carabiners and piton hammer for the first time on the trip – without them the job would have been impossible. I went ahead with a rope and an ice axe, chipping out rough steps in the rock and rubbish and hammering in pitons into crevices in the rock to which the rope was attached … we then got to a point where I could be lowered down into the river. The crossing looked difficult and I had myself swung along the cliff face until I could get onto a conical rock in midstream. There remained a difficult jump of about six feet to the far side … I got the rope slackened off and jumped.
>
> Next thing I knew I was in over my head and being tumbled down with tremendous force by the torrent. I remember the thought clear in my mind, 'Is this the finish?' By this time a large local audience had gathered, good gallery stuff as you can imagine. But I fastened the rope and a flying fox was improvised. This took about three hours and for the human passengers it was quite a sensational journey, suspended in a sling from a rope 100 feet above the river. We thoroughly enjoyed this diversion and I was none the worse except that I noticed my lower left chest out of shape. No ribs broken, but three definitely caved in, ascribed to the weakening effect on bones from loss of weight.[24]

Unsurprisingly, there were no volunteers among the local people to travel by the new ropeway. The New Zealanders carried on down the valley covering an average of 29km a day. After two and a half months at altitude they began to notice the almost undrinkable heat of a cup of tea lower down. In the latter part of their journey they encountered heavy rain as they crossed the high passes en route to Garul, where they caught a bus to Ranikhet and civilisation. On the long journey through the foothills Riddiford finished up as fit as anyone, pleased that he was apparently none the worse for his Alaknanda exertions.

Thanks to Riddiford, the master planner, an expedition many considered impossible was successfully brought to a conclusion.²⁵ Riddiford, Cotter and Pasang had achieved the main goal of Mukut Parbat. Riddiford was especially pleased that no one on the party had suffered as much as a cut finger – 'which is as it should be'. He later said the experience of being the organiser had been exhausting and all-consuming. In India, frustratingly slow business transactions and all the 'major headaches' that went with the portage of food and equipment meant that 'climbing the mountain' was almost an afterthought.²⁶

Every time the party moved from one place to another, there were 33 pieces of luggage to be carried, porters to be engaged, and arguments over wages. By the end of the expedition Riddiford (centre, between two porters) was relieved his task was over. Riddiford collection

7. INTO THE CRUCIBLE

An agonising impasse

As they prepared to leave India the mood was cheerful. Hillary was eager to get back to his beekeeping, Cotter and Lowe were happy to be returning home, and Riddiford was looking forward to spending a few months in England with friends and family. But this state of easy equanimity would not last long after they reached Ranikhet on 25 August.

Eric Shipton had flown in to Delhi on 19 August. Just two days before he left London he was informed of a cable from NZAC president Harry Stevenson, suggesting that the New Zealanders' considerable achievement would qualify one or more of their fit, acclimatised party for inclusion in the British Reconnaissance team. Addressed to Scott Russell, a member of the British Alpine Club committee who was brought up in New Zealand and climbed with Shipton on his Karakoram expedition in 1939, the cable read:

> ANY POSSIBILITY ONE OR MORE NZ PARTY CONSISTING RIDDIFORD COTTER LOWE HILLARY PRESENT SUCCESSFULLY CLIMBING GARHWAL HIMALAYAS BEING INCLUDED FORTHCOMING EVEREST EXPEDITION STOP THEY HAVE NOT BEEN APPROACHED SO UNKNOWN WHETHER EXTENSION LEAVE COULD BE ARRANGED STOP EXCELLENT TYPE CLIMBERS WHO THROUGH BEING ACCLIMATISED SHOULD PROVE USEFUL ADJUNCTS REPLY.[1]

The backstory to this approach is important, as even Hillary got it wrong.[2] The move was sparked by former NZAC president Roland Ellis, who reportedly said to the NZAC committee, 'Why don't you jokers get your president to cable the Alpine Club president asking if some of the NZ Garhwal expedition could join the 1951 Everest Reconnaissance Expedition?'[3]

In the choice of party members for the British Reconnaissance, the Himalayan Committee of the RGS had paid particular attention to potential Himalayan climbers of the future, as Scott Russell explained in a subsequent letter to Stevenson:

Shipton was the obvious leader and his three British companions could hardly be improved upon. A letter from Hillary asking if two of them could join Shipton arrived some minutes before your cable. Seeing Shipton is in complete control of the expedition, I felt the only course was to ask him personally, and in view of the difficulties already experienced and overcome about permits, he felt – and I considered him right – that nothing could be done …

Your cable, which I interpreted as an official request from the NZAC, however made it possible for me to approach those who had already done so much work seeking permits etc. Their attitude was that they were prepared to open up the question of the size of the party with Nepal, in view of the achievements of the NZ party and the NZAC request. Shipton was delighted by this. Last minute alteration of plans and consequent extra work for officials would be unusual unless a case such as your cable could be put to them.[4]

Shipton's change of heart was prompted largely by his huge respect and liking for the tough, extremely competent New Zealander Dan Bryant. 'I have never had a more delightful companion – cheerful, humorous and supremely confident.'[5]

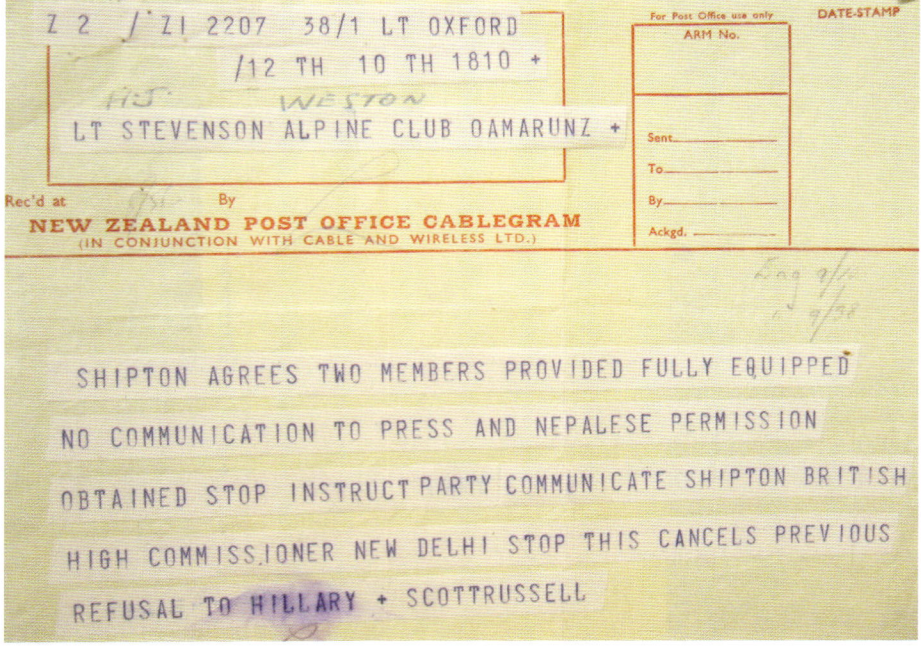

As a result of a direct approach from the NZAC, Scott Russell was able to send news that would arguably change the course of mountaineering history. Hocken Collections

Shipton explained later how a single shaft of memory played its part in New Zealand's epic Himalayan history:

> Two days before we left I received a cable from the president of the New Zealand Alpine Club saying that an expedition of four of his countrymen was climbing in the Garhwal Himalaya, and asking if two of them might join our party. He did not divulge their names. The answer was obvious: I had already turned down several applicants with very strong qualifications on the grounds that I wanted to keep the party small; our slender resources of money and equipment were already stretched, and I had no idea where the two unknown climbers were or how to contact them. I was about to send a negative reply, when in a moment of nostalgic recollection, I recalled the cheerful countenance of Dan Bryant, and I changed my mind.[6]

This most fortunate about-face allowed Scott Russell to send Stevenson welcome news by return cable:

> SHIPTON AGREES TWO MEMBERS PROVIDED FULLY EQUIPPED NO COMMUNICATION TO PRESS AND NEPALESE PERMISSION OBTAINED STOP INSTRUCT PARTY COMMUNICATE SHIPTON BRITISH HIGH COMMISSIONER NEW DELHI STOP THIS CANCELS PREVIOUS REFUSAL TO HILLARY STOP SCOTT RUSSELL.[7]

The good companionship built up over three months of shared experience was to be shattered by the NZAC cable that awaited Riddiford at their Ranikhet hotel:

> PERMISSION OBTAINED FOR TWO OF YOUR MEMBERS TO JOIN EVEREST EXPEDITION COMMUNICATE SHIPTON BRITISH HIGH COMMISSIONER STEVENSON PRESIDENT.[8]

This wording was recorded by Riddiford in 1960 in a *NZAJ* article disputing Lowe's version of the invitation.[9] In his 1959 autobiography *Because It Is There*, Lowe claimed the cable was sent by Shipton. His recollection of the telegram was 'more or less': 'INVITE ANY TWO OF YOU TO JOIN MY PARTY IF YOU CAN GET OWN PERMISSION ENTER NEPAL, BRINGING OWN FOOD AND SUPPLIES.'[10] Over many decades, Hillary reinforced the perception that the invitation came from Shipton. The wording he gave was: 'ANY TWO CAN JOIN US. GET THEIR OWN PERMISSION. BRING THEIR OWN FOOD AND CATCH US UP.'[11]

This invitation for two New Zealand men to join the British Reconnaissance was to shape international climbing history, but it was to end the New Zealand expedition in the worst possible way. Of course all four desperately wanted to go, and a bitter dispute raged throughout the night. It was an agonising impasse, and over six decades there have been varying accounts of how it was resolved. The invitation lit a flame of personal ambition in four climbers with absolutely different value sets, men whose individual reactions revealed deeply embedded personality traits that would shape their futures. The decision that had to be made was summed up by Riddiford in a letter home as 'an invidious choice'.[12]

Each of the four had a claim for inclusion in the British party. Riddiford had organised the expedition and achieved Mukut Parbat with a display of incredible tenacity; he also had access to funds (recently sent by his cousin Dan Riddiford). He may have struggled physically as a result of a dramatic loss of weight due to severe dysentery, but he had shown superhuman mental powers. Cotter had also succeeded on Mukut Parbat, climbing on doggedly where Hillary and Lowe had given up: he was young, highly talented, physically resilient and had acclimatised well. But Cotter could not afford it, whereas Hillary, quick to declare himself the strongest and fittest climber, could find the money easily enough. Lowe was just as broke as Cotter, probably in lesser physical condition than Hillary but fitter than Riddiford, and was driven by the conviction that he had a moral right to be considered.[13]

According to Lowe, Riddiford's first reaction was to announce that he would be going, and that he would decide by the morning who would go with him. Lowe 'burned in silence'.[14] In a burst of purple prose he later wrote that on their return to Ranikhet they had been a happy group ready to sail home and sink themselves into the comparative modesty of New Zealand's mountains. The opportunity to join Shipton, 'mountaineering's Angel Gabriel', turned four amiable New Zealanders into 'four tense tigers, caged, self-seeking, eyeing each other with jealousy … Into a quiet sitting-room of a mountain hotel he had thrown a hand grenade – not killing anyone but blasting our emotions, churning us collectively and individually, and transforming us above all into a set of stony egotists.'[15]

Over the 60 years and more since that terrible night it would be hard to find anyone who would apply the terms 'jealous', 'self-seeking' or 'egotistical' to Ed Cotter. Never one for acrimony, Cotter couldn't stand the unpleasantness that erupted that night. He says the selection process involved each man declaring himself the one to go, and he was shocked by the display of aggressive self-promotion. Somewhat tentatively he suggested they all turn up to meet Shipton; the worst outcome would be that one or two would be sent back, but at least they would all have had a taste of new adventure. But the other three embarked on a marathon of sustained altercation – an argument that has tainted the success of this expedition ever since. Disillusioned, Cotter decided to go to bed 'with more or less grace', as Lowe later conceded.[16]

The battle continued through the small hours, Lowe fighting with all his might to negate Riddiford's claim. Though Riddiford had planned the expedition, Lowe maintained that they had climbed without an acknowledged leader. He also claimed that Dan Riddiford's money had been intended for the expedition as a whole, rather than for Riddiford personally.[17] But Riddiford insisted it was his private family money, and that he was going because he had climbed a higher mountain. Convinced of his ground, he harboured no ill-feeling towards Lowe, whereas Lowe made his bitterness towards Riddiford very clear.

Hillary never for a moment let up on his determination to join the Shipton party. 'I was very fit and there were no arguments about my inclusion,' he claimed in *Nothing Venture, Nothing Win*. 'Earle had climbed Mukut Parbat and he had the money – you couldn't argue with that. George Lowe couldn't see that. Comradeship was forgotten and bitterness crept into the discussion.'[18]

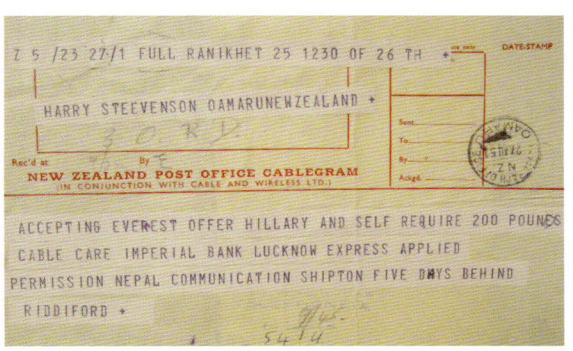

Riddiford's urgent plea for money, sent as he and Hillary raced to catch up with Shipton's party, did not go unheeded. Hocken Collections

Of the four contenders in this woeful situation, Lowe and Cotter became the losers. Riddiford cabled Stevenson from Ranikhet to let him know the outcome:

ACCEPTING EVEREST OFFER HILLARY AND SELF REQUIRE 200 POUNDS CABLE CARE IMPERIAL BANK LUCKNOW EXPRESS APPLIED PERMISSION NEPAL COMMUNICATION SHIPTON FIVE DAYS BEHIND RIDDIFORD.[19]

Shipton could not have foreseen the consequences of his invitation,[20] and later was to express regret at its divisive effect, saying he would have preferred to have all four join the Reconnaissance rather than the acrimony that ensued.[21] Lowe wrote that he and Cotter were 'riddled with envy, flatness and disappointment'[22] as they watched the other two set off on their journey. Cotter described his own feelings as a mixture of distaste and disillusionment of a more serious kind that would completely alter his mountaineering focus. 'I was disappointed that the bond that had held us together on a rope was pretty soon shattered by everyone's egos.'[23] As a youngster Cotter had learned to climb with experienced mentors from the CMC, men whose fellowship was unquestioning. He had spent more years honing his mountaineering skills than any of the others on the expedition, was physically and mentally exceptionally fit,[24] athletic and completely fearless. He had climbed six Himalayan peaks, including Mukut Parbat, and lost far less weight than the others. He had everything in his favour except his own generosity of spirit – and lack of finance. As it happened the NZAC was already fundraising, however. Stevenson had written immediately to Riddiford telling him not to worry unduly, because the NZAC would do its utmost to help.[25] The requested £200 was promptly delivered to Lucknow; the NZAC planned to recoup the funds advanced to the climbers from lectures and articles after their return to New Zealand.

Soon after the debacle at Ranikhet, Cotter wrote home from Ceylon:

> I was a bit too big-hearted in the choosing of two of us to go to Everest. George was in favour of a ballot drawing straws. I wanted to see Ed H. go, considering him the most suitable, so I didn't want a ballot. Earle had a different approach. He said he knew we would have no objection if he was included as his ascent of Mukut Parbat had made the offer possible. He told George he had no drive – imagine George taking that!!! And I was not even mentioned as a contender by the others even though my record was better and I had not suffered weight loss on the expedition – only seven pounds as against their 35lb, 21lb and 14lb. I was pretty disgusted at everyone's intention to be one of the two to get to Everest. Eventually I said I would not take part in the selection, and left them to fight it out among themselves. The next morning George said he would stand down and we left Ranikhet that day for Delhi.[26]

It is tempting to speculate about what might have happened that night in Ranikhet had there been four selfless men in the room. With the turn of a friendly card, it could have been Cotter who became a pivot of the Everest expedition. Long-time climbing friend Geoff Harrow, himself a veteran of the Himalaya, believes Cotter would have bolted up Everest:

> Not only did he have admirable strength and endurance, he had magnificent balance, was a very able climber on rock, snow or ice, and acclimatised very well: just a natural mountaineer for whom extreme conditions and imminent danger

were all part of the deal, to be met and overcome. He just loved the mountains, and would lope along in such an easy-going manner – he could keep it up hour after hour.[27]

Hillary always asserted that he was the strongest of the team: his strength was certainly a huge asset and his energy and enthusiasm were undisputed. However, that didn't mean he was technically or tactically superior. On Mukut Parbat, Hillary and Lowe failed through a triple blunder: misreading the opportunity ahead, advocating a retreat and underestimating the other team. Cotter certainly has misgivings about Hillary's attitude:

> On the day of the Mukut Parbat climb, Ed and George were away from the tent before Earle and Pasang and me; there was no question they intended staying in the lead. But it was Ed and George who decided to call it a day. As we moved above them Ed called out that we would never make it. He later wrote that they took off after us again, but knew Earle wouldn't let them get in front. It was this philosophy, which so differed from the way we had approached our climbs in Canterbury, that disillusioned me about high altitude climbing.[28]

During the expedition Riddiford had arguably been mistaken in failing to insist on being accepted as leader. With such disparate, strong personalities involved he may have been wiser to insist. His democratic approach was laudable,

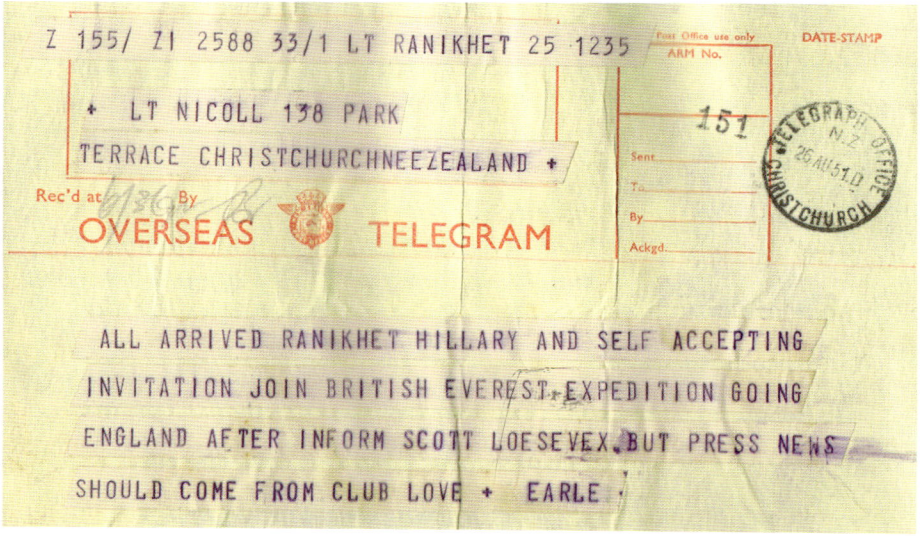

Welcome news: Riddiford's telegram to his mother from Ranikhet. Riddiford Archives

harking back to the companionable complementarity of his dream team, but the dynamics of this party were different. Initially Hillary had been content to follow Lowe's lead, preferring at times not to take part in decision-making. Later, however, Lowe and Hillary on the same rope were allowed to take the lead both physically and psychologically.

In a series of radio talks the following year, Hillary gave a sanitised impression that all was well between the New Zealand climbers. 'On August 26 we arrived back at Ranikhet to enjoy warm baths and clean clothes, and to cap it all, there was a telegram inviting us to join the British expedition – the perfect climax to months of successful climbing and good companionship.'[29] Much later he told a different story: 'There was a great deal of acrimonious discussion before it was reluctantly agreed that Earle and I should accept the invitation. I can still see George's accusing glare as we drove away in the bus.'[30]

Before Riddiford and Hillary could set off on their journey to join Shipton's party, Riddiford had more work to do in Ranikhet: negotiating with the UK High Commission in Delhi for permits from the Nepalese authorities. He also sent a telegram to Shipton at Jogbani, advising that he and Hillary would be joining the party and bringing two good Sherpas with them. In Lucknow, where they heard the way was clear for them to proceed, the two climbers were delighted to be staying very comfortably in a double suite at the Carlton Hotel, and they ate heartily to make up for previous deprivation. Riddiford was also able to visit a doctor for a chest X-ray. The most onerous task – buying food for 100 days – proved very expensive at such short notice.

As they left Lucknow, Riddiford's foresight in obtaining a letter of introduction from New Zealand Prime Minister Sidney Holland paid further dividends. On a number of occasions Riddiford had successfully waved its impressive embossed letterhead at obstructive Indian officials, telling them it requested state employees to facilitate the progress of the New Zealand Mountaineering Expedition. In Lucknow, 'We had a hectic getaway as the officials wouldn't put our gear on the train. I got the stationmaster and showed him our letter from Mr Holland which has been very useful, and he put the fear of God into them and held the train until everything was on.'[31]

It was a 30-hour train journey to Jogbani on the Nepal border where they stayed with the only Europeans there, Mr and Mrs T.G. Law of the Biratnagar Jute Mills. From there it would take three weeks on foot to reach Namche Bazar in the Solu Khumbu district, the gateway to the high Himalaya – and Everest.

PART 2: MAN OF PURPOSE:
Harold Earle Riddiford: 1921–1989

> Though it is natural for each man to have his own aspirations, it is in mountaineering, more than in most things, that we try to believe
> 'The game is more than the players of the game
> And the ship is more than the crew.'
> – H.W. Tilman, *The Ascent of Nanda Devi*, 1937[1]

8. PIONEER SPIRIT

'Determination was the secret of his success.'

The single quality that best defined Earle Riddiford's character was resolve. During his life he was driven by aspiration, both for material success and for conquest of the highest peaks. The physical demands of the Himalaya would take their toll, but his quest to emulate the farming achievements of his forebears through ownership of Orongorongo Station would also exhaust him. At only 67 years of age, he was the first of the dream team to die.

The enormous motivation that lay behind all his ventures sprang from his early days as a scion, though not from the wealthier branches, of the influential Riddiford family descended from Daniel Riddiford (1814–1875), an emigration agent for the New Zealand Company. Daniel's connection with the colony came about after his widowed mother married G.S. Evans, a schoolmaster who later became a barrister and an enthusiastic supporter of the Wakefield colonisation schemes. Through that association, Daniel Riddiford arrived in Wellington on the *Adelaide* in March 1840 with his stepfather and Captain E. Daniell, his partner in an agency business acting on behalf of overseas land purchasers.[1]

Daniel Riddiford's duties included receiving immigrants as they landed and arranging temporary accommodation for any who needed it. But as sheep runs were taken up in the Wairarapa he joined the ranks of pioneer farmers and by 1846–47 occupied Orongorongo Station, with an effective lease from 1 April 1848 over some 7000 acres between the Wainuiomata and Mukamuka rivers.[2] With restricted flat grazing, he soon looked further afield and in 1848–49 leased the Te Awaiti Block – about 30,000 acres – on the East Coast. Daniel, his wife Harriett (née Stone) and their family lived at Orongorongo Station until 1855.

It was no easy existence on the wild and isolated Wellington coastline, with supplies delivered once a year and difficult access by canoe, and in 1855 they moved to their Woburn property in the Hutt Valley. In the course of its eventful history, which included a serious earthquake in 1855, a disastrous fire not long afterwards

Earle's father, Frederick Earle Riddiford, photographed while he was studying law at Cambridge University. Belinda Cranswick

Earle's mother, Helen Easton. Belinda Cranswick

and a huge landslide that engulfed the homestead in 1939, Orongorongo Station was run on and off by four generations of the Riddiford family.

After his father's death, Daniel and Harriett's eldest son, Edward Joshua, took over management of the Riddiford properties. Born at Port Nicholson in 1841, Edward was educated at Christ's College in Christchurch and Scotch College, Melbourne. At 21 he was already managing and developing Te Awaiti, and he continued to extend the family holdings. Later known as 'King' Riddiford, he was an immensely colourful character who reputedly became the largest payer of tax in the dominion.[3]

From Daniel and Harriett's 11 other children sprang a legion of well-known Wellingtonians, including many farmers and lawyers. One influential runholder among the Wairarapa pastoral elite was a grandson, Dan Riddiford, whose home farm, Longwood, was near Featherston. His son, Daniel Johnston Riddiford, took his LLB from the University of New Zealand, joined the Expeditionary Force in 1939 as an officer,[4] and from 1946 ran a legal practice in Wellington where he was later joined by his cousin Earle Riddiford. Daniel Johnston Riddiford later became MP for Wellington Central during the Holyoake government, minister of justice, and attorney-general.

Daniel and Harriet's eighth child, Frederick, was Earle's grandfather. Frederick married Alice MacGregor and the couple had four children, the second being Frederick Earle Riddiford (also called Earle), born in 1890 in Hawera. Frederick Earle trained as a lawyer and was finishing his degree at Cambridge University in England when he met his future wife, Helen Easton. He worked for her father in London, during which time he lived with the Easton family. Helen had a number of sisters who all fell for the 'animal magnetism' of the young man from New Zealand, but it was 16-year-old Helen Josephine who was to be his bride.

Frederick Earle's legal career was abruptly curtailed when he contracted tuberculosis and was forced to return to New Zealand, where he could live in the country. He took work as a farm manager for his cousin Eric Riddiford at Tora, a sheep and cattle station on the Wairarapa coast. Several years later, after he had built a house there, Helen sailed to New Zealand to marry him. The isolation would have come as a shock: in stark contrast with Helen's life in London, it was a lengthy trip by horse and buggy from Tora to Martinborough, with many rivers to cross.

The young couple lived in a rambling homestead with staff to help them, but it was a lonely life and they were effectively cut off from society. During the heady early days of World War I, when most young men were enthusiastically enlisting to defend the empire, the young manager at Tora was regarded with some suspicion. Anna Riddiford, Earle's second daughter and a practising doctor in Nelson, believes her grandfather was classified medically unfit for service in the war because of tuberculosis. 'That didn't stop people sending white feathers and

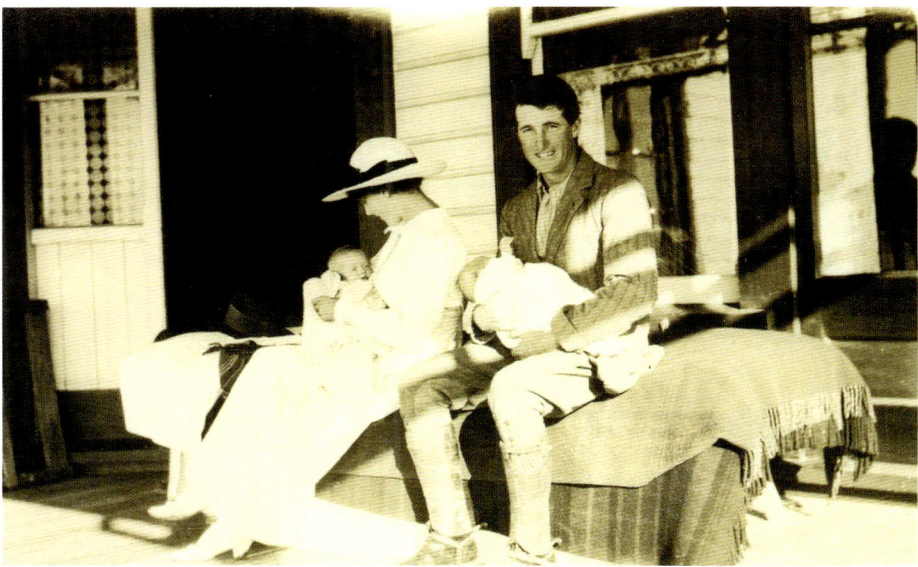

Helen and Frederick Riddiford with their twin girls, Val and Trish. Belinda Cranswick

Staff and pupils of Hadlow School, 1930. Earle is in the front row, second from left.
Belinda Cranswick

not speaking to my grandparents. I think having Tb must have been something quite shameful, turning the sufferers into social pariahs, because my grandmother never told us about it even though she lived with us for a time and she and I were very close.'[5]

After the war and just before a crash in wool prices, Frederick and Helen purchased Hadleigh, a small farm out of Masterton in the Bideford area. This was a lot closer to civilisation. Soon, twin babies Val and Trish arrived. But Earle was never to know his father, a tall, good-looking and well-liked man. Frederick Earle Riddiford died in May 1921 at the age of 33, just four months before Earle was born. His death was caused by a blow to the head from an overhead gate in the Bowlands woolshed, just down the road from Hadleigh, sparking tubercular meningitis. This was a tragedy on many levels for the family, especially Helen. Not only did her husband suffer a slow and painful death, but once he was gone, she found herself in very difficult circumstances. The farm mortgage was temporarily taken over by Vivian Riddiford of Glenburn Station, a wealthy accountant concerned about the fate of the grief-stricken family. In June 1951 Vivian wrote from London to his brother Dan enquiring about their welfare and expressing his intention of taking them under his wing should that prove necessary.

After Hadleigh was sold in a mortgagee sale, Helen and her children moved to Cole Street in Masterton. She worked for a time as a school matron and later ran a boarding house. She also received ongoing support from the wider and more prosperous family, which paid for her children to go to boarding schools in accordance with family tradition. Earle never spent much time with his sisters, as the two little girls were sent to boarding school at a young age. Earle attended kindergarten at St Matthew's College and at the age of five moved on to Hadlow School, a boys' preparatory boarding school in Masterton.

This was a troubled and unpleasant experience in a spartan environment, complicated by a scandal that resulted in the suicide of the school's headmaster. Nevertheless, Earle made some good friends at Hadlow and retained many happy memories of his mother's little villa in Pownall Street, Masterton, a couple of doors down from St Matthew's. He was able to keep a pony and, as the property backed onto a little stream, he also spent many hours in his dinghy. He was close to his mother, and would remain so.

Relationships with the extended Riddiford clan were somewhat complicated for the impoverished young family. After Edward 'King' Riddiford inherited everything from his father, it was accepted that, where necessary, the Riddiford estate would also care for other branches of the family. Dan Riddiford of Longwood sponsored Val and Trish to Nga Tawa Diocesan School in Marton, where the twins proved both intelligent and outgoing, excelling at maths and very keen on sport. Visits to Riddiford country homes, where there was a constant round of tennis parties and picnics, made a big difference to their lives. The girls frequently visited Longwood, and with Earle also had vivid memories of Glenburn Station on the Wairarapa coast, where they were cared for by Nellie and Francis Hewitt, who were managing Glenburn for Vivian Riddiford. Francis Hewitt's grandmother Thomasina was also a Riddiford, another family connection. To this day, the heights of each of the three children – Val, Trish and Earle – are recorded on the office door at Glenburn.

Frederick Earle Riddiford's second sister, Alys, known as Awa, did the most for the fatherless family. Married to farmer Henry Arkwright, 'Aunty Awa' lived at Overton, an imposing Tudor-style house with an expansive garden just out of Marton in the Rangitikei. Helen, Earle and the two girls spent much time there, and Awa was a great friend and confidante for the gentle, well-educated Helen. Henry Arkwright was passionate about cricket, and was also a fairly strict disciplinarian who stepped in as a father figure from time to time. Awa's second child, Rosalind, was so close to her twin cousins that the three were called 'the triplets', and Earle's cousin John Arkwright, Awa's younger son, became his close and life-long friend.

When Earle was about five years old his mother sailed to England to visit her family and was away for some months, during which time Awa stood in as mother.

During his childhood years in Masterton Earle spent many hours in his made-to-measure dinghy.
Belinda Cranswick

Both very spirited people, Earle and his aunt quickly recognised that they shared similar qualities, and this part of Earle's life was very happy. Rosalind remembers Earle as an inquisitive child who never stopped asking questions. On one occasion this so infuriated his aunt that she shut him in the bathroom. His response was to kick holes in the door and most of the walls. John Arkwright recalls that the young Earle had a fiery nature and could throw some spectacular tantrums. 'Later on, that same determination was the secret of his success.'[6]

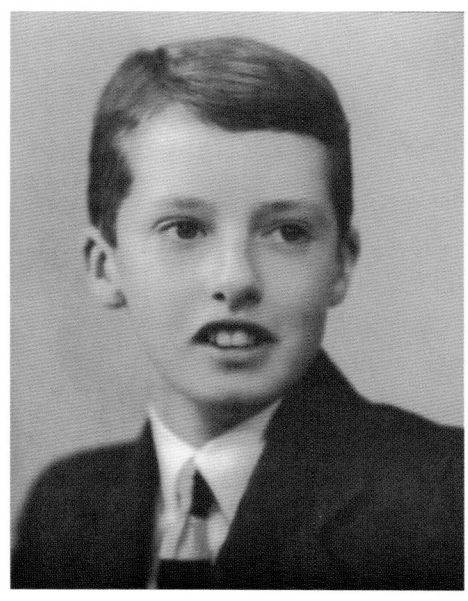

Earle in his Collegiate uniform. Sarah Riddiford

Thanks again to Dan Riddiford of Longwood, Earle was able to attend Wanganui Collegiate from 1935 to 1938. Helen Riddiford was 'thrilled beyond words' by this opportunity,[7] but Earle found Collegiate only a little less grim than Hadlow. Because he never had a strong physical presence he came in for more than his share of bullying. Throughout his life he loathed bullies. His daughter Belinda can still hear him saying: 'A lot of people say their boarding school days were the happiest days of their life, but this was certainly not the case for me.'[8] Academically inclined, Earle played the piano, enjoyed classical music and loved jazz. Letters home to his mother showed he was already setting the bar high. After an interschool exchange with Christ's College, he wrote, 'The Christ's chaps seem a very nice lot. They all seem to speak well, while the standard here isn't too hot ... I have been trying to stuff in as much knowledge as I can for the last few weeks. Everything seems a bit deadly at the moment, including myself – you must write me a moral treatise on how to stimulate the mind.'[9]

He was a keen boxer, and John Arkwright,[10] one year ahead of Earle, watched Earle compete in the school's boxing tournament. 'He wasn't a great athlete, and certainly not a great boxer, so when he came up against a much stronger boy he was battered so badly he couldn't see through the blood. But he kept on and on sparring into thin air, just hoping he would connect. It was a total slaughter – the boys could withdraw then, if they wished, but Earle just wouldn't. It was awful to watch, but he showed tremendous character and spirit.'[11] In his senior years, a school climbing trip to Ruapehu introduced Earle to the mountains, which quickly became a passion.

Most school holidays were spent at Overton, but occasionally Earle and his sisters went to stay at Orongorongo Station, owned at that time by Earle's godfather, Eric Riddiford. The homestead was run in a lavish manner with servants and three-day-long house parties. Such visits gave the three children an entrée into a privileged way of life, and they spent wonderful holidays with their cousins, sharing games and being a part of grand social occasions. Earle developed a keen interest in the Riddiford estates, and the detailed knowledge he built up impressed even Eric Riddiford, who in July 1935 wrote to Helen from Tora with high praise for the 14-year-old:

> I am terribly thrilled with Earle. He is such a nice boy, and full of brains. He asks such intelligent questions, and what he does not know about all the Riddiford properties is not worth knowing … He tells me he is going to be a lawyer, but Helen, I think he should be a sheep farmer: but then again, what prospects? I must come and have a talk to you about him. He has impressed me very much.[12]

The power of positive thinking shared by all three of Helen Riddiford's children was a valuable trait learned from their mother, who had faced many challenges but seldom faltered in her courageous approach to life. During Earle's secondary-school years, Helen met a Christchurch man, Harry Nicholl, on her second sailing back to England. English by birth, Nicholl had emigrated to New Zealand to join the staff of the Bank of New Zealand. With two brothers, he set up as a frozen meat exporter based in Ashburton, then went on to serve on various boards including the United Wheatgrowers' Association and the Lyttelton Harbour Board, and held the presidency of the New Zealand Trotting Conference for 25 years. Described as 'one of the Dominion's outstanding personalities',[13] he was left a widower in 1935. In March 1937 he married Helen Riddiford and she moved to Christchurch. Just before that, Helen wrote to Dan Riddiford expressing her gratitude for the support she had enjoyed from the extended family:

> Besides having been particularly kind and generous to me I feel you are the head of the family and the one to whom I would like to say how much I have appreciated the way you have all considered and looked after me and helped my children, whom I have tried to bring up to be a credit to their name … Earle is deeply interested in and attached to the family to which he belongs, and after the manner of mothers I fondly hope that he will grow up to add distinction to it … with my love and sincere thanks for all you have done for me, yours affectionately, Helen.[14]

Earle followed her south in 1940 and enrolled at Canterbury University College to study law, later working part time for the firm of C.S. Thomas. He joined the university tramping club and proved himself a quick learner as he gained experience in the mountains. Just before Christmas 1941, with Fred Tozer[15] and Bruce Menzies, Earle set off from the Hermitage on his first really serious mountain trip. They crossed the Copland Pass and climbed to Welcome Pass via Scotts Creek, laden with enough supplies in their 70lb packs to take them out down the upper Landsborough and then down to Haast.[16] After pitching tent in the Douglas névé, on 28 December they ascended Mt Sefton by the west route. Later they descended to the Douglas Valley via the Wicks Glacier, climbed Mt Thomson and made the first ascent of the southern Sharks Tooth. They returned to civilisation via the Landsborough, including an ascent of Fettes Peak. This all took an epic three weeks, much of it in rain. In later years Earle enjoyed entertaining climbers with an account of how everything that could conceivably go wrong, did:

> I've never been through anything like it before or since. When we got to the Hermitage, there was an air of doom as Japan had just come into the war. There was almost no one about. The first night we couldn't find the track up to the Hooker Hut, and slept out on the moraine. Then we struck rain. When we pushed up to the Copland Pass, we lost the track to the hut and had to camp out in the bush. On Christmas Day from Scott Creek we lost the track again and had to battle through steep, very difficult bush. From our camp in the Douglas névé we set off for Sefton, when Bruce fell into a crevasse. We got up the mountain and admired the view, but the next day on the way out to Welcome Pass it was an absolute whiteout.
>
> In the evening the mist cleared and we moved out, but that night in the tent below Blizzard Peak was the coldest of my life. The next day we had to find our way out down the glacier. We lugged our gear through to Harpers Rock, then dossed down and slept until four o'clock the next afternoon. Then we got back up onto the Divide to attempt Mt Brunner, but we had no idea what it looked like and never found it, so just climbed a Sharks Tooth instead. We crossed Douglas Pass out to the Landsborough, and the others climbed Fettes but I had frostbite. We went out down the Landsborough on the west side. We roasted a kea, which was quite edible, then at a deer cullers' camp we found a tin of biscuits and some honey and jam left behind, all very welcome. When we got down the gorge to where the cage over the river should have been, it was on the other side. We succeeded in

recovering it, then went down the other side and got the last truck going out of the valley that day. It was a whole boatload of experiences all in one trip.[17]

By now Earle had proved himself a very capable, determined climber. In 1942 in various parties he climbed Mts Davie, Murchison, Harper and Greenlaw, made the first recorded traverse of the Copland Valley via the Sierra Range, and journeyed from the Hermitage to Lake Wanaka. In November 1942 he gave a lecture on the Douglas and Landsborough districts to the Canterbury–Westland section of the NZAC, just before war service interrupted his climbing career as well as his legal studies. He embarked with the 2nd New Zealand Expeditionary Force for service in the Pacific, where he worked in army intelligence and spent time reconnoitring New Caledonia for possible Japanese landing sites. It was a comparatively comfortable wartime experience, as he reflected in letters home:

> I'm still enjoying the existence of a base wallah, and had a taste of even greater luxury when I visited the general hospital for a check up of my eyes. On arrival I enjoyed my very first hot bath for 18 months! I was quartered in a ward but free to come and go. Comfortable beds with sheets, good meals, a hot water system and sisters and nurses looking after our wants combined to make it a pretty comfortable stay. I met Bob Pilgrim, a friend of varsity tramping days. He is a scientist now and has an ideal job working in the laboratory of the hospital, investigating blood samples for sundry tropical diseases. I spent a couple of enjoyable evenings with him and his friends. They lead a pretty good life there, going tramping in the hills sometimes and in the weekends sailing in the estuary.[18]

On his return to Christchurch in 1944 he quickly resumed climbing, spending much time in the upper Landsborough region. In the summer of 1944–45 he joined members of the Otago section of the NZAC in a Christmas camp in the Rees Valley, trail-blazing with a mixed group of young trampers, and with John Gummer he climbed Mts Earnslaw and Leary from the Rees on 4 January 1945.

In December 1945 he climbed with a Dunedin party, Paul Powell, Colin Marshall and John Sage, on a trip to the Mt Aspiring region, which included a first traverse of the Volta and Therma glaciers and a first ascent of Fastness Peak on 27 December. This trip also involved heavy packs containing food supplies and fuel for three weeks. After the ascent of Fastness, which was not difficult, they cached some of their stores on the Waiatoto face of Aspiring, since speed was essential under the mountain's hanging icefalls. As they were doing this a section of ice cliff several hundred feet high broke off and pushed up a huge mushroom

War service included time training in Christchurch: in this undated photo, Sergeants Wederal, Bennetts and Riddiford are pictured at Lancaster Park. Belinda Cranswick

cloud of ice dust on the Volta névé, 'hardly a sight to cheer us on our way around the north-east corner and under its hanging ice!'[19] As the peaks of the Haast Range grew closer, ice avalanches continually rumbled off the Haast Range and from the ice faces of the Therma just below the climbers. Most of the crevasses were easily crossed, but in very soft snow they had a seemingly endless climb up to the northwest ridge of Aspiring. They made their way out via Quarterdeck Pass to French Bivvy, and the next day walked out down the West Matukituki Valley.

By then it was clear to all that Earle Riddiford took his climbing seriously. In 1945 he began a three-year term as secretary of the NZAC Canterbury–Westland section, and through this, early in 1946, he met brothers Bill and Don Beaven. In a party of four, Earle and Bill Beaven climbed Mt Temple near Arthur's Pass in June 1946, and in December 1946, together with Don Beaven, John Gummer and M. Spencer, they lugged 15 days of supplies and equipment over Christopher Col into the Douglas Glacier. In his report for the *NZAJ*, Earle said that even with the most rigorous culling of gear, his pack weighed 59lb on the Hermitage scales before they left.[20]

They planned to cross from the Mueller Glacier to the head of the Twain (now the Douglas), to camp there at Harpers Rock, attempt Mt Brunner, and return over the Sierra Range to the Copland Valley and back to the Hermitage. 'We also intended to try something new – Christopher Col, between Mt Vampire and Mt Bannie, approximately 8000ft high. As a packing route, it was a doubtful quantity.'[21] On the approach to the col they ran into difficulties. One crevasse had to be jumped, so their packs had to be hauled up and across on an improvised rope railway – an annoying delay in intense heat – and steps had to be cut. They were all tired by the time they started up the final slope. Bill Beaven took a turn at the lead. 'I did not envy him. Cutting steps on a hard steep slope with a 60lb pack in a gusty wind after 14 hours' going is no fun. As well, we had the nagging uncertainty as to the route, caused by the thick mist.'[22]

With a gap in the weather, they hurried over the col in a howling gale and ran down soft snow slopes towards the McKerrow Glacier to pitch camp below Douglas Pass at 8.15pm. The next day they moved to Harpers Rock, the worst of the carrying over. 'During the afternoon we made great improvements to the rock. We built a rock wall to keep out draughts, excavated a larger sleeping area, built a new fireplace, and finally a covering of snowgrass made the place thoroughly comfortable.'[23] The following day they climbed the Gladiator for a good view, but once on the summit saw nothing but thick mist. On 29 December, however, a faultless clear morning greeted them for their attempt on Mt Brunner. On this expedition, unlike the 1941 trip, Earle was able to identify his target. On the way up the Thomson Spur they counted 30 avalanches coming off the Douglas in one hour. After some slippery conditions and a tricky ice wall, they made the summit and were back at the rock by 6pm. The next afternoon they crossed Douglas Pass to the head of the Landsborough and pitched their tent on the terraces beyond the Spence Stream.

On New Year's Day they summited the unclimbed Mt Townsend and were not long back at camp before Hardie, McFarlane and David Hughes arrived. They had just carried large packs up the Mueller Glacier and over Fyfe Pass. From there, the Hardie party climbed the Gladiator in fine weather and were able to enjoy the magnificent view of the spectacular ice cliffs of Mt Sefton. Below them, at the Harpers Rock camp, Bill Beaven cooked a huge batch of damper scones for the Riddiford party while they basked in the sun all day. For amusement, they wrote up a hut book for the rock and left it in a tin. On 4 January they left for the crossing of the Sierras to the Copland, but their chosen route up the extreme west end of the Douglas névé caused many problems, with endless rows of crevasses. The traverse of the Sierra Range proved much tougher than in 1942, when snow conditions had been soft.

> Now it was more difficult. A thin and slippery coat of powder snow lay on top of an icy surface beneath … the ridge over Scott Peak gave trouble as we shuffled

our way along the narrow and slippery crest. Soon after, at 7.30, we pitched our tent on Welcome Pass. During the night two or three feet of snow fell around the tent. Next morning the weather was worse. The mist was thicker than ever. It was freezing cold and still snowing. At 11 we commenced a groping traverse along the upper snow slopes of the Tekano Glacier … there were one or two awkward descents down snow-plastered rocks but a welcome break in the mist showed the way down into the head of Scott Creek. Powder snow avalanches began to slide off the steep rocks of the Sierras above, but we were well out of their way.[24]

The route down to the Copland was utterly changed, as Scott Creek was filled with avalanche snow. Once they reached the Welcome Flat Hut they were thankful for a hot sulphur bath and a huge meal. 'We crossed Copland Pass in fine weather, and the Hermitage was a welcome sight after a fortnight out.'[25]

Over Easter 1947 Earle and Bill Beaven also spent four or five days in the Arrowsmith Range, which provided perfect weather for ascents of Jagged Peak and Tent Peak from a bivvy near the head of the north branch of the Cameron Glacier. Jagged gave no particular trouble: the only difficulty was a vertical wall of 40ft near the summit, which was not so easy to get down. They found Tent was a peak that could be underestimated. 'The ascent had been an unexpected strain, but the descent was wholly enjoyable, and we came down the ridge with the pleasant feeling of confidence that two days of rock climbing had brought about.'[26]

The meeting of the Riddiford and Hardie parties in the upper Landsborough marked the beginning of the strong climbing partnership described in the first chapter of this book. To more conservative New Zealand climbers it may well seem presumptuous to have considered unleashing those energies in the Himalaya. There is no doubt that Bill Packard's inclusion in the 1950 British West Nepal Expedition was a major influence on Earle. Packard went to Nepal feeling uncertain about whether his technical ice skills would measure up, but found when he got there that he was as good or better than British climbers, who were pre-eminent on the world scene. If Packard could match their ability at high altitude, so could these Canterbury boys.

Like his pioneering forebears, Earle Riddiford took a giant leap into unknown territory, determined to prove himself to the world one way or another. Once he had done that on Mukut Parbat, he would join Shipton's Everest Reconnaissance knowing that as a fit, skilled, determined and acclimatised climber, his stars were aligned for further heights.

9. THE 1951 EVEREST RECONNAISSANCE

Negotiating the Khumbu death-trap

Of the three Himalayan expeditions in which Earle Riddiford took part, it was Shipton's 1951 Everest Reconnaissance that he found most exciting and personally satisfying. In finding a way through the Khumbu Icefall he made a major contribution to the expedition's success, and was widely acknowledged for his skill and enterprise.

Back in New Zealand there was little coverage at the time. Under a copyright agreement with *The Times*, which was underwriting the expedition, no Everest Reconnaissance material could be used for news articles for a specified period.[1] This meant Riddiford and Hillary were unable to send progress reports to New Zealand newspapers. Relieved of this at times onerous task, Riddiford wrote home as often as he could to his mother and these letters provide much of the material for this chapter. He asked her to keep all his correspondence, which he hoped would provide material for a book. That book never materialised, but the letters have survived to provide his perspective on what he described as 'the real job' in Himalayan exploration.

> Dearest mother
> I am writing this from Namche Bazar, right in amongst the most striking mountain country I have seen. We have reached our base of operations and are within two days of Everest and ready to start on the real job. What a prospect – by an entirely new approach through unexplored country! ... I have just received the most wonderful mail – who would have thought your aerogram postmarked September 6 would have got to Jogbani and then by runner 140 miles through the hills to here, all in 18 days ... It took us three weeks to get here from Jogbani, leaving there September 1. (We caught up with the Englishmen on the 8th at a place called Dingla – but more of that later.) We took with us Pasang and his brother Nima. The first day was thirty miles by truck after heavy rains had been falling and we got stuck twice and had to transfer all our baggage each time ... at the end of our truck ride we arrived at the foot of the hills and commenced our long march.[2]

Meanwhile, NZAC members were busy fundraising to support Riddiford and Hillary. Although NZAC president Harry Stevenson had been assured by the British Himalayan Committee that they would finance the New Zealanders, Stevenson felt strongly that the extra two climbers should pay their way. They had effectively gatecrashed the expedition at the last moment, while other British climbers had been excluded from the party for financial reasons. 'We feel it up to us as a responsible club to shoulder our responsibilities, and by doing so we stand a better chance of having you or Ed or other New Zealand climbers invited to participate in future expeditions,' he wrote to Riddiford.[3]

It was unfortunate that there would be no newspaper payments to offset NZAC contributions. The club hoped, however, that some revenue would accrue from magazine articles, which could be published one month after Shipton's final article in *The Times*.[4] On their return to New Zealand Riddiford and Hillary would also present a series of lectures around the country to help repair the dent in NZAC coffers. (Later, Hillary expressed a different view: 'Harry Stevenson says he considers the NZAC should pay as a gesture to British Mountaineering, or some such cock, and that the whole club is geared to produce it by personal appeals, lectures etc. This is a bloody good show but I think the money would far better go into a fund to send another New Zealand expedition to the Himalaya.'[5])

Hillary and Riddiford were fortunate in the support they enjoyed from home, where Shipton's invitation was perceived as an enormous coup. The NZAC's financial assistance had arrived straight away and money was no longer a problem – a great relief for Riddiford.

On their seven-day march from Jogbani to meet Shipton at Dingla on 8 September, the pair covered 12–16km each day and stayed in Nepalese houses at night. Their main concern, Riddiford wrote, was to stuff as much food into themselves as they could during their brief spell in civilisation, as they had both lost considerable weight. 'We were living like kings, perfectly looked after by Pasang and Nima who were able to buy plenty of eggs and vegetables and usually a chicken for dinner. Plenty of fruit: bananas, an occasional pineapple and several varieties of other fruit.'

The main incidents of the trip to Dingla, for which they had engaged 17 coolies at three rupees per day, involved two river crossings:

> In each case Ed and I had to ferry the coolies across, taking them in batches of four grasping a long pole. It was hard work but quite good fun. The coolies took a lot of encouragement, as they are short and the water was up to their waists. The smallest of them in fact [was] dangling on the pole, hanging on like grim death.

The British members of the 1951 Reconnaissance. From left: Eric Shipton, Mike Ward, Bill Murray and Tom Bourdillon. Riddiford collection

At Dingla they were relieved to meet up with their British climbing companions at last and found them congenial company:

> There are four in the party. Eric Shipton is 44, a big man, grey but fit: rather vague and not at all the 'grasp of detail' type of leader, but of course he knows Himalayan mountaineering 100 per cent. Bill Murray, 38, is lean, rather scotch, quiet and independent, who was the leader of the Scottish Garhwal expedition of four men last year, which travelled around a lot but did not climb very high. Tom Bourdillon is six foot and more, a physicist who works on rockets, like Shipton a married man. Dr Mike Ward, 26, is very light-hearted. Both the latter are first class rock climbers, with no previous Himalayan experience, but very likeable – in fact that goes for all of them, they are a very nice bunch.

However, Riddiford was not impressed by their provisioning:

> The first thing we noticed was the bloody awful food they were eating. Shipton seems more or less indifferent to diet and of course the younger members had been too diffident to say anything. Tom Bourdillon was more or less half-starved.[6]

By a few tactful suggestions, we put the matter right over the next few days and we have been eating well ever since. We had bought almost the same quantity of food for two as they had for four. They had too little sugar, hardly any porridge or milk powder (incredible) and were low on butter and jam. Now that we have pooled our food we are doing well.

The British were carrying a large amount of low-temperature clothing, however, so the New Zealanders were soon better equipped with extra gear. 'The best items we have scored are beautiful nylon down-filled jackets, which we had seen the French wearing, and good gloves. Otherwise our equipment generally compares well with theirs, but our sleeping bags are better.'

Riddiford was delighted when Shipton agreed to take on Pasang and Nima on a permanent basis:

Pasang I know will be an asset. He is the only Sherpa who speaks English and is by far the most capable including Angtarkay, the sirdar, who is most likeable, has an outstanding record and has always been with Shipton, as well as on all the Everest expeditions of the 1930s. However Pasang is a much better organiser, has as good a climbing record, and acts as a sort of unofficial second in command.

Having been involved in most of the Everest expeditions during the 1930s, Shipton was well acquainted with the difficulties he could expect; to him, 'the attempt to climb Everest, once an inspiring adventure, had become little more than a gambler's throw'.[7] His objectives were clear: he was to take a new approach to Everest from the southwest through Nepal, seek a way through the Khumbu Icefall – the death trap between Mount Everest and the Lhotse-Nuptse Ridge – and find out if the slopes up to the South Col were climbable. Just how to beat the monsoon season, when the mountain became wrapped in a blanket of snow, was a vital question.

Shipton had found his decision to lead the expedition a difficult one. Lately emerged from communist China and having been away from mountaineering for some time he doubted his value to the expedition, but found the opportunity to visit the Sherpas' land of Solu Khombu irresistible. He had not made up his mind until July, however, and then had only until the end of the month to ship stores and equipment. It had been a busy and confusing time: all sorts of things were in short supply and ship sailings were infrequent. The day before their gear was due at the docks nothing had even been packed. The NZAC cable asking him to consider New Zealand participation had arrived just two days before he flew out to Delhi.

The New Zealand members of the 1951 Reconnaissance: Earle Riddiford and Edmund Hillary. Riddiford collection

The British party had travelled in from Jogbani, a railhead in North Bihar on the Nepalese border, accompanied by Shipton's sirdar Angtarkay from Darjeeling. By 4 September the expedition had reached Dingla where they were held up by difficulties engaging coolies, then joined forces with the two New Zealanders in what proved to be a happy association. 'They turned out to be excellent men,' Murray wrote later.[8] From Dingla the party walked 10 days in continuous heavy rain but were able to find fairly comfortable sleeping quarters each night, sharing a bedroom with a calf on one occasion. Leeches proved a worry, requiring constant vigilance to prevent them from settling and filling up with blood. As the expedition moved on, Riddiford noticed changes in the local population:

> From Dingla on higher country the people are much like Tibetans and are Buddhists. They are most hospitable and at each place we stop, the people in the best house take it as a matter of course to make room for the sahibs to live and sleep. Most have never seen a European before, and for the last few days when a Sherpa has gone ahead to give news of our approach, large groups of people have taken up grandstand positions beside the track to see us pass. The reaction varies

from blank astonishment to loud mirth. The Sherpas are exceptionally friendly and cheerful. They all live in two-storey houses of distinctive design, stock below, make excellent chang (Tibetan beer) and seem prosperous and well-fed.

Riddiford was in a state of sustained excitement when the party set off towards the terminal of the Khumbu Glacier:

> We will be looking for a possible route up to the South Col. What a fascinating prospect – you have no idea what a stimulus the sight of these big mountains is after the long journey through the foothills. If a route is found, no doubt we will concentrate on an attempt … I am feeling very fit. Ed Hillary has not been feeling well, but he takes a lot of keeping down.

The expedition was warmly welcomed in Namche Bazar, which they left on 25 September with supplies for 17 days. From the village of Pangboche, Riddiford described their visit to Tengboche, situated on a beautiful grassy plateau studded with trees:

> Thyangboche [Tengboche] must surely be one of the most remarkable and beautiful places in the world. On one side of the plateau are grouped several Sherpa houses and dominating them a Buddhist monastery, a beautiful Tibetan-style building rising in three or four tiers with a pagoda roof. But the most remarkable sight is of the enormous mountains which loom up out of the surrounding country. None of us except Shipton had ever seen anything like them. In about five groups or massifs, great walls of ice rise to spires or ridges of ice that look quite impossible to climb.

Shipton, who had lived at 10,000ft for a number of years as British consul in Kashgar, had acclimatised quickly, but the other three British climbers were struggling at altitude. At the Khumbu Glacier terminal they looked for a base campsite, from which the first task would be to forge a way up the 2000ft icefall that blocked the entrance to the Western Cwm. With Hillary still unwell, the acclimatised and confident Riddiford came into his own.

> I was in the lucky position of being the only one fit to tackle the icefall, as Shipton had other jobs. Two days later, after moving base camp again, Pasang and I got halfway up the icefall after a hard day's work zigzagging amongst all sorts of obstacles. Tom Bourdillon and Mike Ward also set out but got hopelessly tangled

up in some ice pinnacles and in any case were very weak at the altitude (no worse than we were four months ago). Everyone seemed quite pleased at our results and two days later we took a light camp up to the foot of the icefall and tackled the job of getting right up it. The party was Shipton, Ed Hillary, Tom Bourdillon, myself and three Sherpas including Pasang. Once again Tom had to turn back owing to altitude, so you can see that up to now Shipton would not have been able to do much without acclimatised New Zealanders.

It was a hard day. One of the complicating factors is the snow conditions. After the monsoon there is a deep accumulation of soft powder snow like sugar. This snow does not consolidate and harden, especially high up where without melting there can be no freezing and hardening. This factor will probably prevent any real attempt being made at this time of year as steps have to be plugged in the soft snow as well as finding a way through crevasses and ice pinnacles. Eventually we got to where there was only a big break separating us from the smooth slopes of the glacier leading into the Cwm. With some trouble we wended our way through the floor of the big crevasse and started to climb up to the crest above us.

When we were almost there, the whole slope cracked and avalanched, and I was in the middle of it. Eric Shipton behind me managed to scramble off. I will never forget the horrible strength of that avalanche as I was carried down, and the feeling of complete helplessness. The rope kept on running out and I thought everyone was going. But the avalanche stopped and a moment later the rope held me. Pasang, who had been step-plugging ahead, had managed to get a secure hold with his axe – good work. I had made frantic efforts to get off the avalanche and later to keep from being smothered, and was left gasping for air. I can promise you nothing like this will ever happen again if I can help it. Then time was up, and we turned for home as fast as we could, very tired.

Described by Shipton as 'a nasty little incident which might with less luck have had rather unpleasant consequences',[9] that mishap on 4 October prevented them from getting a glimpse into the Western Cwm from the top of the icefall. Shipton was satisfied enough with what they had learned about the route up, but was now very conscious of avalanche danger, and determined that the rules of mountaineering should be rigidly observed.[10] He decided to wait for a fortnight in the hope that snow conditions on the icefall would improve. They would spend the time making some journeys into unexplored country to the west and south.

The expedition divided into two parties. Murray, Riddiford, Bourdillon and Ward set off westward from base camp, looking for a pass over the range to the north that could lead to the West Rongbuk Glacier, from which they could

Riddiford (centre) above the crevasse that split the glacier from side to side, preventing access into the Western Cwm.
Riddiford collection

attempt Pumori. They found no such pass, but did cross a col that led them into the upper basin of the Dudh Kosi in a cirque formed by Cho Oyu (26,750ft) and Gyachung Kang (25,910ft).[11] Murray was to remember that journey without much pleasure: 'We had too few Sherpas and the Sahibs had to carry 50lb loads.'[12] Meanwhile, Shipton and Hillary were looking for a way through a tangle of ranges to the Kangshung Glacier, which flows from the eastern flanks of Everest. They crossed the Hongu basin and found a pass leading over to the great Barun Glacier at the foot of Makalu (27,790ft) but did not have enough food to reach the Kangshung.[13]

Although neither party achieved their goal, they learned much about a long stretch of the Himalaya that was previously unknown to them. 'This form of mountaineering, the exploration of unknown peaks, glaciers and valleys, the finding and crossing of new passes to connect one area with another, is the most fascinating occupation I know,' Shipton wrote.[14]

When the party returned to the icefall at the end of October they were surprised to find how much it had changed: the avalanche risk was diminished, though there was still an extreme danger of collapsing ice. Over three attempts the team forced their way to the top of the icefall, only to find one monstrous crevasse blocking the way to the flat Western Cwm plateau. To cross it would have taken many days of hard work and a good deal of ingenuity, and Shipton concluded they were not in a position to do this. Although a route through the icefall had been found, and the route from the Western Cwm up the Lhotse face to the South Col looked feasible, he was concerned about the dangers of taking porters through such an area:

> Though it might be a permissible risk for a party of unladen mountaineers ... we would not be justified in trying to climb it with a party of laden porters whose movements are always difficult to control ... Pasang and Angtarkay made no secret of their apprehension ... they were convinced it would be madness in the present conditions to try to carry loads through it, and unfair to ask the Sherpas to do so.[15]

Shipton decided there was nothing for it but to submit, hoping for another chance in the spring. Riddiford confirms the difficulty of finding a route over which they could reasonably ask porters to carry heavy loads:

> When we came to the wall that had floored us before, we divided into three parties to try different routes. Two turned out to be no good and the route we used

finally, an hour and a half later, was the one cut by Tom Bourdillon (now quite acclimatised) followed by Nima. The route was diagonally up the overhanging lip of a big crevasse, steep and covered with treacherous soft snow: Tom didn't cut steps, he literally dug out a trench clearing away all surface snow. We all followed this route up and although the overhang was a solid buttress of ice, it gave a loud crack at one stage. I have never seen a glacier like this for enormous cavernous overhangs.

Looking back down this route from the top wall I can only describe it as being like some surrealist nightmare. The edge climbed hung above in great blue chasms. However we had got over the wall and at last could look up into the Cwm which stretched away with the South Col hidden around a corner to the left. The triumph was short, for trudging on a hundred yards or so we found that we were completely isolated from the upper slopes by a great crevasse about thirty yards wide and that a series of these cut right across the valley … access to the sides of the valley was pretty hopeless, seracs and pinnacles and great crevasses barring the way … We sat down and had a lunch of sorts. It was now clear that there was not a decent packing route up the icefall and the only hope was that it would be a better proposition in the spring, after winter snowfall had filled in some of the holes.

Riddiford's performance with Pasang on the icefall earned high praise from Shipton, who said the excellent progress they had made in a party of only two at the first essay was highly encouraging.[16] The New Zealanders had proved themselves extremely fit and mountain-hardened,[17] but Riddiford could not help feeling disappointed when conditions at the top of the icefall finally defeated them. He was not alone: Bourdillon and Ward also felt in retrospect that if they had moved everything up to the lip of the cwm and made a full-scale attempt on the crevasse, they might have reached the Lhotse face.[18] In 1987 Riddiford admitted to some 'rage and fury' at Shipton's decision to withdraw totally from the mountain and turn his attention to more exploratory journeys:

On that first trip up the icefall, when Ed Hillary was ill, Pasang and I got a fair way up. The British didn't get far at all – they were just not used to that sort of thing. Then after the whole party went up, Shipton decided we should move on to a reconnaissance elsewhere. So two fully acclimatised New Zealanders, much fitter than the British, had to disperse with the others, right when we would have loved to have gone as far as we could.[19]

Riddiford was beginning to develop reservations about Shipton's leadership:

Bill, Tom and Mike are a really nice bunch and Shipton is a fine mountaineer. On the big day on the icefall, he went like a train and had a lot in reserve at the end of a hard day. But to say that I think he runs the expedition efficiently at all times would not be true.

These reservations were to drive a wedge between Riddiford and Hillary, who had always regarded Shipton as a heroic figure. Both forceful personalities, Riddiford and Hillary were no longer on the same wavelength. The two also failed to see eye to eye about Pasang Dawa Lama, who during the expedition continued to forge a strong climbing partnership with Riddiford, who in turn greatly annoyed Hillary by 'constantly singing Pasang's praises',[20] including suggesting that Pasang's technical climbing skills equalled those of Hillary's great mentor, Harry Ayres. When Hillary downplayed Pasang's skills,[21] Riddiford threatened to knock him down. Hillary's reply to the lightly built Riddiford was, 'You and what army?'[22] These altercations foreshadowed more serious differences that would develop later when three New Zealanders – Riddiford, Hillary and Lowe – were all invited to join Shipton's 1952 expedition, expected to be an attempt on Everest.

However, in spite of his misgivings about the dispersal of the party, Riddiford enjoyed the challenge of the fortnight-long exploratory trip into the Dudh Kosi river valley which he undertook with Pasang, Murray, Ward and Bourdillon. They saw the Nup La, a high pass into Tibet, which was guarded by a big icefall, and, with Pasang and Riddiford in the lead, managed to find a tortuous way through the worst of the icefall until they emerged on the upper slopes. But because the pass was still a day of difficult icework away, and they did not have enough food to take a camp higher, they had to give up on the idea of reaching the pass. However, it was a gratifying excursion. On the icefall, Pasang 'went like a bomb', Riddiford wrote. 'At one stage he climbed a 20ft wall up an ice chimney, the only possible route. I think the icefall was rather a revelation to the Englishmen who had never seen anything like it in the Alps.'

Walking out from this exploratory trip down the beautiful valley that led back to Namche, Riddiford was already having second thoughts about the prospect of another Everest expedition the following year. From Namche Bazar on 24 October he wrote to his mother:

The three Englishmen I found very congenial company, more so than the New Zealand Garhwal party … When next I write, the climbing will be over and I will be on the way home – happy thought. There is almost sure to be a full-scale attempt next spring, May and June 1952. That means two or three months in England and then back here. I will have the chance to come again, all expenses paid, but am in two minds. Pros – the chance to have a go at Everest – magnificent. Cons – the rather big disadvantages of expeditions of this sort, controlled and run by others, and I don't like the leader. After all, mountaineering is only a sport, and all my enjoyment has come from private parties run to suit ourselves, and no messing about! I can't really form an opinion until I've had a spell in England, but will be interested to hear what you think.

His last letter on this expedition, dated 20 November and sent from the British embassy in Kathmandu, gave an account of the final assault on the icefall and his feelings of relief that the expedition was drawing to a conclusion:

Ed and I are both very thin and the dysentery persists at odd times. I will have to have treatment when I get to England – all the drugs I have taken have had no effect. We had to wait three days in Namche for all the gear to arrive down. Ed was keen to get back to the bees as quickly as possible and I was eager to get home, so we planned to take a short cut to Kathmandu via the Tesi Lapcha Pass just south of the Tibetan border, known to be used by Sherpas during the summer months. The Englishmen planned to go up to the Nangpa La Pass, a trade route into Tibet, then head westwards … they wanted to see if there was a route to Cho Oyu. If a route existed it would provide an alternative objective if Everest proved not feasible next year. They did see two good easy routes onto the mountain, so that is a good thing, but that piece of information is confidential as far as the climbing public is concerned.

During their stay in Namche, Riddiford enjoyed two Sherpa dinners followed by dances, highly spirited occasions in both senses of the word, as he quipped:

Sherpa dances are rather good – a big crowd and a row of them line up arm in arm singing choruses, followed by a dance in a clog dance style to some sort of guitar accompaniment. Two of the young Sherpas were arrested while drunk, and the ensuing Gilbert and Sullivan negotiations with the police went on for two days. Pasang seems mainly responsible for getting them out of their mess.

From Namche, Riddiford and Hillary were accompanied by G.N. Dutt (an Indian geologist who had with him four coolies and a dog), Pasang, Nima, nine

Namche Bazar in 1951. Riddiford collection

porters including one woman, another woman on a pilgrimage who appeared to be a friend of Pasang's, and Pasang's 11-year-old son, Gelgun.

> Quite a collection. The pass turned out to be all a pass should be – a great gap in the range surrounded by extensive and beautiful snowfields, and on its left a beautiful ice peak very like the NZ Minarets … droppings in the snow showed that yaks are taken across the pass – rather incredible at that height … we expected an easy walk down the glacier the next day but were in for disillusionment.

The descent proved very demanding and they spent a long afternoon negotiating crevasses and backtracking to avoid difficult sections. Finally three Sherpas found a route down to the foot of an ice wall, and the party carried on in the moonlight to a campsite on flat ground. 'With the technical difficulties behind us, looking back we could see that the icefall behind us was on the grand scale, and there had been much more to the Tesi Lapcha than we imagined.' The next day they had a tiring walk for miles down moraine country at the side of the glacier and out to the first inhabited village, where they decided on a rest day.

During their 10-day trip out they passed through country that no European had visited before, and were warmly welcomed everywhere. Hillary described the Nepalese hill country during harvest season as 'throbbing with music and laughter'.[23] Riddiford, too, was struck by the festival atmosphere at a pleasant village called Malapur: 'When the gathering started singing it was wonderful, quite unlike anything I had ever heard – wild and surging, with a fascinating theme, and the whole effect on this warm moonlit night was pure magic. I would go back to Nepal just to hear them sing like that again.'

From Malapur to Kathmandu took them four days:

This journey home was the most fascinating I have done. Everywhere we stopped, small crowds collected and gaped. Eighteen miles from Kathmandu we picked up a ride from an army truck … with much horn tooting and panic stricken running of chickens it took us into the Kathmandu basin, and we finally reached the British embassy about 9pm (16 November) … There we were made very welcome by the Summerhayes (the British ambassador, his wife and 18-year-old daughter) and began a new chapter, a life of luxury and a round of almost continuous social engagements … we have played tennis, read, listened to Beethoven and Charlie Kunz on the radiogram, been sightseeing and attended parties with the King and Maharajah – what a business. The other four came in five days after us.

At Kathmandu they separated from Nima and Pasang. The latter wrote to Riddiford from Darjeeling with his final thanks and best wishes: 'I do hope and pray to God for your safely reaching your home. With best wishes and Salam from me and Nima – Goodbye to you.'[24]

From Riddiford's final letter home, it appears the two New Zealanders enjoyed a reasonably companionable and accommodating relationship during their journey over the Tesi Lapcha and out to Kathmandu. 'Ed and I were travelling on our own together for the first time since reaching Dingla, and we had long talks as we walked along, comparing notes on the expedition.' But in Kathmandu their memories of a hard-fought reconnaissance mission were to be marred by terrible news that spoiled all their hopes for Everest the following year.

10. CHO OYU

Shipton's folly

The 1951 Everest Reconnaissance had gone so well that Shipton's party was confident they would be returning to Everest in 1952. But as they passed through Kathmandu in November 1951 they were dismayed to learn the Swiss had beaten them to it. Not only did the Swiss have the permit for 1952, they also had an elite team, a sizeable budget and, to cap all that, the knowledge obtained from the British Reconnaissance.[1]

The news sent the British into a state of shock. After recovering from a sense of umbrage, the Himalayan Committee tried to persuade the Swiss that the British had the moral high ground for Everest. When that failed, they offered the opportunity of a joint Anglo–Swiss attempt with Shipton as leader. The Swiss were interested in Shipton, but only as a co-leader. Shipton was happy enough with that, but on condition that two New Zealanders would be included.[2] (How much New Zealand owes Shipton!)

Frantic negotiations ended in a stalemate. On 5 January 1952 the Himalayan Committee issued a press release saying both the Swiss and the British believed a combined expedition would prove unwieldy and unworkable.[3] With some urgency a new plan was plotted. The British Himalayan Committee would apply for Everest in 1953, but in the meantime would mount a preparatory training expedition with Shipton as leader. In spring 1952 he would take a party to Cho Oyu, at 26,750ft the world's sixth-highest mountain, the unclimbed 'Turquoise Goddess' straddling the border between Tibet and Nepal 20km west of Everest. The objectives were to summit Cho Oyu, to train up a pool of climbers who could acclimatise well at 24,000ft or more, and to investigate oxygen apparatus through experiments at high altitudes.

The 1952 British expedition to the Himalaya would prove a difficult, unhappy affair: 'one of the great black holes in the history of post-war mountaineering'.[4] After a series of tactical blunders, Shipton's hold on leadership foundered. The expedition also turned into a personal nightmare for Earle Riddiford. Friction between the New Zealanders (Riddiford, Hillary and Lowe) on Cho Oyu intensified to such a degree that in 1953 the NZAC faced difficult decisions about the composition of its own 1954 Himalayan expedition.

Riddiford's misgivings about Shipton's leadership were to prove valid. Shipton was an inspiring, charismatic personality, but he was uncomfortable with the 'grossly unwieldy and inconvenient'[5] scale imposed by the Cho Oyu expedition, and reluctant to engage in organisational detail. In his view, a shortage of funds dictated extreme economy and simplicity: he spent just one afternoon drawing up lists of food and equipment.[6] The British turned to Riddiford for assistance. (After the Reconnaissance he had cancelled his ticket home to New Zealand and with Michael Ward had travelled instead to England, where he was living on the outskirts of London with Norman and Enid Hardie.)

When Riddiford took over he was horrified to find that virtually nothing had been done. He set about ordering and packing food and equipment, solving problems and circumventing bureaucratic obstacles. Each morning he and Hardie took the train into the city, where Riddiford was based at the expedition office. In the evening, on the return commute, Riddiford would regale Hardie with the difficulties of procurement and his frustration at Shipton's casual attitude. Shipton was hardly ever around to be consulted and frequently could not be found at all. Riddiford immersed himself in lists of clothing, climbing equipment, travel formalities, food supplies, and medical, scientific and photographic gear. His enormous contribution was duly acknowledged in Hillary's *NZAJ* report: 'Due very largely to fine organisation by Riddiford, the expedition was arranged, equipped and transported to India according to schedule.'[7]

Shipton's selection of climbers for Cho Oyu was equally cavalier. Before Christmas 1951 he had written to Hillary saying that if a British party went to Everest, Hillary and Lowe would be going – he included Lowe solely on Hillary's recommendation. A fortnight later Hillary received a cable inviting them both to Cho Oyu.[8] Bourdillon and Riddiford had performed well on the Reconnaissance, so were sure of their place. Murray had struggled at altitude, so was not included, and Mike Ward was unavailable. Somewhat surprisingly, Bourdillon's wife Jennifer was allowed to accompany the party. Experienced British climbers were turned down, but Shipton was persuaded to take Charles Evans, who had been with Tilman on Annapurna in 1950. He also insisted on taking an old friend, Campbell Secord, who had climbed with Shipton and Scott Russell in the Karakoram in 1939. Two others – Alfred Gregory and Ray Colledge – were both new to the Himalaya although they had impressive records in the Alps. Shipton had met neither of them.

The final member of the party was another wild card in his carelessly assembled

En route to Cho Oyu. *Riddiford collection*

pack – the colourful, unpredictable and eccentric Griffith Pugh, a redheaded 42-year-old doctor and physiologist working for the Medical Research Council. From the late 1940s Shipton had urged the British Himalayan Committee to take more interest in physiological research at high altitude, and this expedition offered an ideal opportunity. Many revered climbers regarded the use of oxygen as unsportsmanlike,[9] but British failures on Everest were mounting up. It was now high time for the Himalayan Committee to pursue professional advice about how oxygen could be used to advantage, so Pugh's participation was approved – although the bulky, heavy equipment Pugh took was bound to be a constant nuisance to a leader who preferred to travel light.[10]

The first contingent of seven, including Riddiford, sailed on 7 March on the *Canton* from Southampton to Bombay. Shipton, Secord and Pugh flew out later and the whole party met up at Jaynagar railhead on the Nepalese border

Situated at 12,300ft on the route from Namche Bazar to Cho Oyu, the Sherpa village of Thame (Thami) was occupied in summer. The roomy stone houses accommodated stock below and families upstairs. Riddiford collection

on 29 March. During the 17-day march to Namche Bazar the weather was unexpectedly bad with numerous heavy snowstorms. Most of the team suffered in varying degrees from stomach problems as a result of sloppy hygiene, and throat infections contracted from the runny-nosed local people. When Pugh told the climbers early on that he was shocked by their complete disregard for hygiene, he invited scorn: even Evans, the expedition doctor, described Pugh as 'bellyaching' about their water supply.[11] But Pugh had trained in the war years, had been a doctor in hospital camps in Bombay, Iraq and Iran, and was well aware of the dangers of contaminated water. In vain he urged Shipton to intervene. As he predicted, most of the team were soon sick, and sleeping in lice and flea-ridden Sherpa houses added to the misery.

At the village of Chisapani at the edge of the foothills they engaged over 50 coolies. On 7 April, from the village of Okhaldunga at 6000ft, they moved into higher country, catching memorable glimpses of the Everest massif, Makalu and ice-topped Cho Oyu. On arrival in Namche (11,286ft) on 16 April they learned that the Swiss had left the previous day for the Khumbu Glacier. In Namche high-altitude gear was issued, including rubber-soled boots, down jackets, trousers, hoods, gloves, double-thickness windproof trousers, parkas, lilos, reindeer skins and efficient Canadian sleeping bags.

On 19 April they set off up the Bhote Kosi River for Thame (12,300ft), Chule and finally Lunak (17,500ft), a small settlement southwest of Cho Oyu below the Nangpa La trading pass. Shipton established his base camp at Lunak, and almost immediately sent parties out to reconnoitre approaches to Cho Oyu suggested by the Reconnaissance team. This meant climbing at further altitude, and 10,000ft in three days[12] was too much, too fast, for climbers who were not in the best shape. Shipton himself always acclimatised easily, and he failed to recognise that others of his party would be more severely challenged.

Pugh was not so blasé – back in Namche Bazar, recognising his own symptoms, he decided to take his time, and undertook the final part of the trek on 24 April with his Sherpa, Da Tenzing. When he later rejoined the party at Lunak, he noticed in them all the signs of 'the depressant effect of oxygen lack', with a 'striking reduction in conversation, gaiety and general activity'.[13] As the expedition climbed higher, worsening headaches, temperatures and irritability would make the climbers even more impatient, not just with their leader but with each other.

Hillary and Lowe left on 24 April to cross the Nangpa La to assess an approach from the northwest. Evans and Gregory were sent over the ridge between the Nangpa and Ngojumba glaciers to explore prospects from the south. But on 26 April, when Evans and Gregory arrived at a point from which they could see the

Contemplating their options: from left, Hillary, Lowe, Evans, Shipton, an obscured climber and Pugh. Riddiford collection

whole south wall of Cho Oyu, they were dismayed by an unbroken barrier of ice and snow thousands of feet high, stretching as far as Gyachung Kang (26,089ft), 10km away. They spent a 'corker morning' wandering easily at 19,000ft among the highest mountains in the world – though not one of these except Everest looked remotely climbable – and returned the next day to Lunak with their discouraging news.[14] Hillary and Lowe arrived back on 28 April; they reported that the west face route was formidable, but still a possibility if ice cliffs halfway up could be climbed, and that it would be necessary to establish at least one camp on the Chinese-occupied Tibetan side of the Nangpa La.

This was unacceptable to Shipton, who worried about the possible consequences of meeting a Chinese patrol.[15] As British consul-general in Kunming, China, he had witnessed first hand the Chinese Revolution of 1950. He knew that if Chinese soldiers got wind of their presence they could be denounced as spies. Not only was Shipton acutely aware of the danger to his men, he was also nervous that an international incident could derail the Everest attempt in 1953. For all those reasons, he ruled out any camp on the north side of the Nangpa La. Before he made his decision, however, a raging argument was allowed to develop among climbers upset by the dilemma they found themselves in, and further stressed by the effects of altitude.

Bitterly opposed views were thrashed out over a whole afternoon, with

Riddiford, Secord and Hillary lobbying hard for an all-out approach.[16] Riddiford and Secord forcefully opposed Shipton's stance, something Hillary later attributed to their reluctance to accept any of Shipton's ideas on principle.[17] Hillary and Lowe, on the other hand, felt some loyalty to Shipton, but also desperately wanted to proceed; they expressed confidence in their ability to outrun Chinese soldiers. Bourdillon sympathised to an extent with Shipton. Words flew, morale plummeted and Shipton vacillated until evening, when he reluctantly settled on a compromise position: he would put a camp just short of the Nangpa La and send a small, more mobile party to attack from the Tibetan side (the standard route today), so that if Chinese soldiers were sighted the camp could be quickly withdrawn. As a result, Pugh's physiological work would be scaled back.

Hillary recorded the group's reaction:

Fond though I was of Shipton I did not think he handled the situation well. By arguing all afternoon he demoralised us. Campbell Secord on his return to London did his best to destroy Eric's reputation over this incident. I think we all understood that any chance of reaching the summit of Cho Oyu had evaporated.[18]

Secord had been a firm friend of Shipton's. He and Mike Ward were initiators of the Reconnaissance and it was Secord who had suggested Shipton lead that expedition, but he had completely changed his mind about the leader.[19] In his expedition notebook Secord wrote a list of candidates who should be discarded in 1953: they included himself, Riddiford, Bourdillon and Shipton.[20]

New Zealand esprit de corps had also disintegrated. From early on it proved disastrous to have Lowe and Riddiford in the same camp. Before the fateful night in Ranikhet there had been no open hostility between the two, but the grudge Lowe bore Riddiford for 'squeezing' him out of the Reconnaissance never abated, and somehow he took Hillary along with him. When they were climbing, Lowe was determined to better Riddiford at all costs;[21] when they were not, both Hillary and Lowe ostracised him. Riddiford got on well with the British climbers, and ate and tented with them rather than with his fellow New Zealanders.

During the following week nearly everyone was unwell to some degree: Shipton and Bourdillon with pharyngitis, Secord with a paroxysmal cough, Riddiford with his dreaded diarrhoea, Hillary recovering from two days' fever at Chule, Colledge suffering from exhaustion. But stores were taken up to Jasamba at 18,500ft, south of the Nangpa La: this was to be their advanced base camp from which they would send a smaller assault force. On 30 April, Shipton and Bourdillon moved down to Thame so they could recover from their serious throat infections; Pugh, battling lethargy, followed soon after.

With Hillary and Lowe left in charge at base camp, no one was happy. Serious trouble was brewing as they cooled their climbing heels. Hillary was bored, and others were bordering on mutiny. Riddiford, who had made it clear to Shipton that he was ready to risk crossing into Tibet, was intensely frustrated by Shipton's absence. He lobbied from tent to tent, advocating an attempt on Cho Oyu without Shipton, but no one was so bold. Lowe and Hillary did leave camp to attempt a peak close to the Nangpa La, but were caught out by Shipton as he returned on 5 May. An incensed Shipton excluded them from his climbing party, though he later relented.

When they regrouped at Jasamba, Shipton and Colledge were still unwell and Riddiford was suffering from sciatica. On 6 May the remaining six climbers (Secord, Bourdillon, Gregory, Hillary, Lowe and Evans) and 18 laden Sherpas set out for Cho Oyu. After crossing the Nangpa La they made their way up the Kyetrak Glacier (also known as the Gyabrag Glacier), making a camp at 19,500ft. The next day they reached their highest camp, on a ridge at 21,500ft. From this desolate spot they dismissed all but six of the Sherpas. There followed some unsuccessful forays up the ridge in appalling weather with poor visibility and strong winds, and Evans, ill with laryngitis, retreated to Jasamba on 9 May, escorted by Secord. Things there were not much better: paralysed by diarrhoea, Pugh was getting on Shipton's nerves, while Riddiford, still at odds with Shipton, faced all the frustrations of forced inactivity and his relegation to a minor role in the expedition.

The assault was now left to four climbers who were short of food and fast losing confidence. In a last-ditch attempt on 10 May, Gregory, Bourdillon, Lowe and Hillary got to 22,500ft on the edge of an ice gully, from where a huge ice cliff many hundreds of feet high barred the way forward.[22] It was obviously no route for laden Sherpas and, recognising the danger from poor snow conditions and overhanging ice, Bourdillon and Gregory insisted the team turn back. They retraced their steps gloomily. Hillary was mortified: 'We had been a miserable failure and no one said a word as we retreated to the ridge camp and over the glacier.'[23] The expedition was now such a humiliating flop it led Hillary to reappraise Shipton as leader: 'In retrospect it would have been better to have abandoned Cho Oyu before dissension divided the group.'[24]

On the Nangpa La they met Riddiford and Shipton coming up from Jasamba with more supplies, planning to join the party on Cho Oyu. But bad conditions and poor provisioning had already taken their toll: after giving up at

Alf Gregory, Charles Evans and Griffith Pugh. Riddiford collection

disappointingly low altitude the group was utterly demoralised. Shipton decided to bail out of the Cho Oyu attempt, virtually telling his men they could do what they liked. Lowe and Hillary went off to climb some peaks to the north of the glacier, where they faced miserable conditions; the rest went back across the Nangpa La to Jasamba. There was considerable illness; Evans wrote: 'Gregory, Shipton and I had respiratory infections, Bourdillon had only just recovered from a similar complaint, Riddiford was lame with sciatica but still pushing himself on, and Pugh was weak with diarrhoea.'[25] Disgusted by the turn of events, Riddiford was at an impasse. As well as hurting his back while rolling rocks down the mountain with the Sherpas, he had lost all motivation after the organisational shambles that followed the retreat. He decided to call it a day and set off for New Zealand.

Unfortunately, the letters written to his mother from Cho Oyu are lost. Norman Hardie confirms that Cho Oyu was an unhappy expedition for Riddiford: quite apart from the mishap in which he damaged his back, the differences with George Lowe kept stirring a disturbing undercurrent.[26] But while Lowe's hostility was unsettling, the general discord cut even deeper. Riddiford was certain that

The Cho Oyu party came in for close scrutiny from the local people. Rear from left: Colledge, Hillary, Shipton, Pugh, Riddiford, Lowe. Front: Secord, Gregory, Evans, Bourdillon. Unidentified news clipping, Riddiford collection

Shipton was quite the wrong person to be in charge. His feelings came across loud and clear to Shipton, who responded, 'Maybe Earle is the sort of chap we want to climb Everest – so determined, dedicated, thrusting and bloody-minded.'[27] Friend Roger Peren says Riddiford was a wreck on many levels when he returned to New Zealand, and was hospitalised for a time.[28]

Once the rest of the party had reassembled in Lunak on 16 May, Shipton split them up again. Shipton, Evans and Gregory headed away for explorations in the Menlung area to the west. Lowe and Hillary made a tough first crossing of the formidable Nup La pass, which Hillary described as their best trip, even though they did not climb a single peak. 'It was quite a tricky bit of work finding a safe route up three thousand feet of broken icefall, and it took us five days from the bottom of the icefall to establish a camp on the Nup La.'[29]

Meanwhile, Secord, Bourdillon and Colledge went into the Pangbuk Valley for oxygen experiments with Pugh – little enough, since Pugh had been promised two weeks in the Everest area with a full complement of climbers as experimental subjects.[30] Throughout the expedition Shipton, who was well acquainted with the scope of Pugh's research, had failed to support him, and had done little to impress on his Cho Oyu team the importance of participation and co-operation with Pugh's work. Shipton knew that Pugh was an experienced skier – a former member of the 1936 Olympic ski team – and a passionate ski-mountaineer who had climbed frequently in the Alps, but failed to share this information also with his climbers. Assuming Pugh was a complete novice, most of them adopted a rather patronising, impatient attitude to the oddball scientist who wore pyjamas to prevent sunburn and travelled festooned with instruments and 10 bulky pieces of luggage.[31]

Pugh was made to feel an outsider, which made his work that much harder. Most of the Cho Oyu climbers were reluctant subjects for his experiments, and while Secord and Bourdillon did co-operate, Bourdillon also made journeys back down the mountain to see his wife Jennifer at Namche, upsetting the acclimatisation programme.[32] When Hillary and Lowe proved to have low haemoglobin levels following their descent from the Nangpa La, Hillary condescendingly pronounced the results baffling: 'At this point my confidence in this aspect of high altitude science disappeared never to return.'[33] Despite so much scepticism, Pugh was never less than forthright. In the end, however, no one reached 24,000ft, so his experiments were stymied.

The Cho Oyu expedition was effectively disbanded, although in June, Hillary and Lowe joined Shipton and Evans for a relaxed exploration of the Barun Valley, after which Evans travelled towards Darjeeling and the three others to Kathmandu. The expedition had met none of its primary objectives. In his first dispatches to *The Times*, Shipton had made it clear that his main aim was to conquer Cho Oyu.[34] But Cho Oyu had defeated them.

11. FALLOUT

Ripple effects from a frightfully British bungle

The collapse of the Cho Oyu team had a profound twofold effect. In Britain, Shipton's reputation was very publicly blown to smithereens. In New Zealand the Dunedin-based NZAC Overseas Expedition Committee was left grappling with the composition of its own 1954 Himalayan party as they factored in a serious rift between their foremost climbers.

The strong, often silent Shipton had been such an icon, such a source of inspiration, that the revelations about his disappointing leadership came as a shock. Although guarded in his public assessment of Shipton,[1] Hillary was explicit in his private correspondence and his Cho Oyu diary, as in this entry for 15 May 1952:

> In my opinion Eric is now quite unsuitable as an Everest leader as instead of a powerful combining and shaping factor in the expedition, he disturbs people's confidence, saps their enthusiasm and fills them with doubts entirely, because he has now little or no confidence in his own judgements, so [is] jealous of the positive judgements of others.[2]

From the P&O *Strathmore* on 19 July he wrote home to Jim Rose: 'I don't think there's much doubt that Eric is far from the ideal big party leader – he realises this himself.'[3] Hillary also confided in Norman Hardie, 'Our party was a bit of a hotch potch collection and we had a lot of ill health … Shipton, apart from a spell of climbing in the Tesi Lapcha region, wasn't fit enough for anything much until we finally came out from Namche Bazar via the Barun glacier.'[4]

Whereas stories from the Reconnaissance had been received with waves of public and media enthusiasm, this muddled and fractious expedition seemed eminently forgettable. In his report to the Royal Geographical Society (RGS) on 22 December 1952, Shipton conveyed an impression of 'carefree days of sheer enjoyment' without a hint of dissension or illness.[5] In his autobiography he gave the expedition only passing mention; Lowe wrote only two lines about Cho Oyu in *Because It Is There*; Hillary hardly mentioned it in *High Adventure* except to say that Riddiford decided to go home; and there were no books or *Times* supplements. In a 1953 report for the *NZAJ* Hillary wrote that the party had no hesitation in declaring the route under the ice cliffs quite unjustifiable. (He later contradicted this in *Nothing Venture, Nothing Win*, where he said the others insisted he stop cutting steps.) In *View from the Summit* he devoted a couple of pages to the Cho Oyu trip, in which he reflected on how the experience was clouded by bad weather, ill health and unimaginative food, the idiosyncrasies of his companions, the depressing atmosphere at base camp, and the shame of giving up so easily. In a frank interview many years later he expressed his opinions much more forcefully, referring to the expedition as 'one of the biggest cock-ups of all time'.[6] It seemed the only enjoyment to be salvaged from this expedition had come at the end, after the party split in different directions.

Ironically, the first ascent of Cho Oyu was finally made in 1954 by two Austrian climbers with Pasang Dawa Lama, the sirdar so highly praised by Riddiford.[7] This was a spectacular climb without oxygen on the northwest face. Pasang Dawa Lama went on to reach the peak a second time in 1958 with an Indian party.

Riddiford had realised his own lack of fitness on Cho Oyu, but never imagined this third expedition would be the end of his climbing in the Himalaya. After news that the Swiss had abandoned Everest, he did not discount the possibility that he might join the 1953 British expedition; if that did not eventuate, his dreams of the colossal, incredibly difficult Kangchenjunga could take him there instead. But in England, the Cho Oyu debacle marked a turning point for the Himalayan Committee. A letter organised in Shipton's name by Bourdillon called for a rethink of the way British expeditions were run, stressing a need for better training and the importance of oxygen work.[8] Secord reported back with complaints about haphazard equipment and hygiene, the lack of resolve and wasted research opportunities – all criticisms backed up by Pugh, whose report was scathing; Gregory, who described the expedition as 'a balls-up';[9] and Riddiford, who vented his feelings in a letter to the RGS.

Adding to evidence of Shipton's inept team management was his decision to go exploring with Hillary, Lowe and Evans instead of returning home immediately to front up for a sorry effort on Cho Oyu. The mumblings and grumblings of disaffected members of the party forced the Himalayan Committee to digest the unpalatable truth that Shipton had failed miserably, and his absence made the

With two Nepalese (left and centre), Ed Hillary, A.E. Lombard (geologist for the Swiss Expedition) and George Lowe relax in Namche Bazar. Riddiford Collection

failure even more difficult to swallow. He finally returned on 19 July, following a month disporting in the Barun, and was called to account on 28 July. At that stage he was still considered the leader for 1953, but as his inefficiencies and inadequacies came to light the argument for his removal became more compelling. Cho Oyu had been a testing ground for Everest, not only for the climbing party but for the leader, and Shipton had failed. The Himalayan Committee announced that the 1953 expedition would be led by John Hunt.

It was Hunt who, with no ties to New Zealand, later turned down Riddiford's application for 1953. Bill Packard, who had approached the committee on Riddiford's behalf, wrote to Riddiford to break the bad news:

> The change of leadership was particularly ineptly carried out by an aged and vacillating Himalayan Committee. I gather the volte face was basically about Shipton's bad routine book and paperwork, his apparent lack of drive to climb Everest, and his desire to make the party up largely of New Zealanders! Shipton was quite rightly very angry indeed, but being the gentleman he is, has done nothing angry.[10]

Meanwhile, the increasing profile of New Zealand climbers had given the NZAC such a confidence boost it was planning its own Himalayan expedition (to the Barun area) for 1954.[11] NZAC minutes attribute this decision to recommendations made by both Riddiford and Hillary.[12] Riddiford had written to NZAC president Harry Stevenson from London in March 1952, prior to Cho Oyu:

> It is grand having three of us from New Zealand in the party – I only wish Bill Beaven and Norman Hardie could be in it too … I think it is now generally realised in England that New Zealanders can make a very strong contribution to an Everest attempt. I hope we can get a full-sized New Zealand expedition away later to attempt one of the big peaks – Kangchenjunga has always been my idea of a good ice objective for a New Zealand party![13]

In July–August 1952 Riddiford was in hospital having treatment for his back, but in response to a request from Roland Ellis[14] he submitted a number of recommendations to the newly formed NZAC Overseas Expedition Committee, describing himself as an experienced if somewhat disillusioned lobbyist after all the frustrations he had experienced with Himalayan permits.[15] But although the achievements of Riddiford's 1951 expedition, and those of Hillary and Riddiford on the Reconnaissance, were widely appreciated, the NZAC was on a mission to make sure other climbers had their turn. As early as December 1951, Harry Stevenson had written to the Alpine Club (UK) expressing the hope that the NZAC might at least be consulted on the suitability of club members for inclusion in future expeditions. 'Because Hillary and Riddiford were in the Everest Reconnaissance, it didn't mean the NZAC could not field a stronger team for a full-scale attempt.'[16] Scott Russell of the Alpine Club replied that climbers were selected largely by the leader, and suggested the NZAC should make its views known to the Himalayan Committee.[17]

Spearheaded by the much-respected Stevenson, the NZAC was determined to choose its 1954 party very carefully in an effort to avoid the sort of problems that had arisen between Riddiford and Lowe. They also had reservations about the ways climbers were positioning themselves for further trips. Some of those reservations related to funding. The club had already managed donations to the 1951 expedition, and had sent Riddiford £365 towards Reconnaissance costs, after which club members were asked to subsidise the same climbers for Cho Oyu. (One committee member complained about financing a club member who 'wanted to go on an overseas holiday' while the club's huts were in their death throes.[18]) In early

February 1952 Stevenson had written to Roland Ellis on the NZAC Overseas Expedition Committee, enclosing a copy of Riddiford's letter about looming Cho Oyu expenses:

> The whole committee should be notified of developments … I felt under a moral obligation to help the Everest show but I don't feel very inclined to help Earle and Co on a second expedition … we are being asked to send at least one man whom I wouldn't consider for a moment. Apart from Lowe's unsuitability temperamentally, he hasn't treated the club very well.[19]

Days later Stevenson sent Himalayan Committee assistant secretary Tom Blakeney a carefully measured response to the composition of the 1952 British Cho Oyu team:

> We are particularly pleased that Riddiford and Hillary proved themselves last year. We note that Lowe has been included in addition to the other two. We realise the difficulties in selecting members for a party but we must say we would have liked very much to have had the opportunity of naming possible climbers from whom Shipton or whoever is selecting the party could have made his choice.[20]

After Cho Oyu, the NZAC Overseas Expedition Committee (Stevenson, Ellis and Phil Cook) consulted extensively with Riddiford, whose experience in making applications, planning equipment lists, engaging the local people and coping with the demands of high-altitude climbing was invaluable. In choosing New Zealand climbers, Riddiford advised they look for a proven ability to travel over rough and difficult mountain country quickly and safely, rather than a preponderance of Hermitage-based climbs. 'The combination of travel and high climbing is of course ideal – I can still say that Beaven, Hardie and McFarlane are the strongest party I have climbed with, both technically and in general mountaineering ability.'[21]

In November 1952 Basil Goodfellow, secretary of the Alpine Club and joint secretary of the Himalayan Committee, wrote to Stevenson with advice on applying for permits. There was a queue for Everest, with the French booked for 1954 and the British for 1955; Goodfellow was arranging for an NZAC application for the Barun area in 1954.[22] Strong leadership would be crucial. As the NZAC proceeded with its planning, Roland Ellis, who had been instrumental in winning the New Zealanders' invitation to the 1951 Reconnaissance, was in close correspondence with Hillary. Considering his private view of Shipton's shortfalls as a leader, Hillary's letters to Ellis a short time after the Cho Oyu debacle were somewhat disingenuous:

> I received a shock today in a letter from Shipton in which he said he wouldn't be going next year and that a chap called John Hunt had been asked to lead it. Shipton doesn't know if there will be any change of personnel but intends doing his damndest to see that the three New Zealanders still go.[23] Eric Shipton has been a jolly good friend to New Zealanders I consider. Everest without Shipton wouldn't be quite the same![24]

Several months later he wrote again to Ellis with the surprising suggestion that if Shipton was at a loose end he might fill the top spot for New Zealand:

> Shipton is pretty cut up about the whole miserable business and considers the Himalayan Committee has treated him rather badly … his preference for New Zealanders has been one of the points a little resented by some of the old buffers on the Himalayan Committee. Why not ask Shipton to lead the NZAC Makalu Expedition in 1954? As Shipton has been ditched because of his New Zealand preference among other things, I think he might consider it.[25]

The NZAC were not looking in that direction, however. They were seeking a leader with both organisational and leadership skills. Committee member Frank Newmarch advocated an 'older type' with whom it was 'almost impossible to have a row, and whose judgment was respected', in preference to someone like Hillary who was forthright in his outlook rather than diplomatic.[26] Harry Stevenson was considered ideal, but it was not possible for him to go. Harry Ayres was also a strong contender.

In the meantime, because the NZAC felt indebted to the British for the two places on the Reconnaissance, they suggested inviting the British to send two men on the 1954 expedition. On 12 February 1953 Hillary wrote to Ellis expressing his surprise. He had formed a low opinion of some of the Cho Oyu party, which, as he put it in a letter to Jim Rose,[27] included several 'deadbeats' taken more on past virtue than present ability. 'I do not think we should just accept any that the Himalayan Committee may decide to send us. A couple of unsuitable types can prove a decided nuisance – we saw this only too well on the Cho Oyu trip and I have serious doubts about the ability of that august body the Himalayan Committee to choose a couple of climbers that would fit in both temperamentally and technically.'[28]

When the NZAC finally decided on a combination of leader and climber for 1954, they opted for Hillary, whose position in the 1953 British expedition boosted their confidence. On 24 February Ellis wrote to Hillary saying the club wanted him to take on the organisation of the party as well as active leadership in the field. But two days later, 'in strictest confidence', Ellis informed Jim Rose (later Hillary's father-in-law) that several climbers had said they would not be starters if Hillary was leader, whereas they would welcome Harry Ayres. He also spelled out very clearly the potential for cronyism:

… whilst I think Ed will make a good leader, we want to make absolutely certain that in picking his team he does it fairly and without bias. It was no doubt Ed's efforts that got George Lowe into the Everest expeditions, because this never came from the NZAC committee, so if Ed could work for his cobbers in one expedition he could perhaps do the same on this one … You, as president of the club, should watch that aspect very closely.[29]

Hillary accepted the leadership, but the 1954 Himalayan expedition was to be his fifth in four years, and from Everest on 4 May 1953 he wrote to Rose saying he had reconsidered. 'Quite frankly I don't think I will be able to afford to go. I feel rather strongly that I'm letting the club down … I hope you will not think too harshly of my decision.'[30] The NZAC then approached Harry Ayres, who declined because of his lack of Himalayan experience. Vice-president Doug Dick thought Riddiford should be sounded out, but made his position on Lowe very clear in a letter to Phil Cook:

Regarding the difficulty his party had, I sometimes think lack of discipline personally and selectively led them into a few arguments. George Lowe was thoughtlessly outspoken and was the prime cause of minor disagreements. At the outset the party failed to recognise the official leader. I think Ed and Earle mutually respect each other, but when George is present, Ed and George form the pair, and Earle is left out … Earle and George should not be in the same party unless there was a senior and competent leader. George hasn't applied to go with the NZAC expedition. I certainly think that under no circumstances should George be appointed leader. I have had personal experience of George in the mountains. No doubt he will have matured since, but my comments stand.[31]

All committee members were canvassed for their opinions, with interesting and mixed results. Mavis Davidson said that in a choice between Riddiford and

Lowe it should unquestionably be Riddiford, whose organisation and meticulous attention to detail led to success in the Garhwal:

> I understand that Shipton recognised this quality and cashed in on it. Where judgement was required, Earle's inspection of the final ice ridge on Mukut Parbat, which Hillary and Lowe said could not be climbed, indicated how tenacious and purposeful Earle was. Though he is outspoken, rather I think the outcome of an analytical mind that insists on facts, the same companions have featured on successive trips, so he must have been able to get along with people. None of his contemporaries, including Hillary and Lowe, seem to have shown such qualities of leadership.[32]

In comparing Riddiford with Lowe, Jim Rose (who succeeded Stevenson as NZAC president) admitted to Ellis that his notes were coloured by Hillary's opinions. The gist of those notes was that Riddiford was inclined to be conceited and give orders, which caused some resentment in the Garhwal, and that something similar had happened on the Reconnaissance, when Riddiford even told Shipton what to do. According to Rose, neither Hillary nor Lowe thought Riddiford's mountaineering judgement good: they considered his ideas about routes on Nilkanta were dangerous, and that with no safety margin on the Mukut Parbat climb the party would have been in a bad way had there been no one to receive them.[33] On the other hand, Lowe lacked drive – 'all right with a peak in front of him but not so good slogging in at low level and putting in camps. All right with someone else to egg him on. Technique far better than Earle, also judgment. Not really a natural leader but is perhaps a better choice than Earle.'[34]

In the end, after the successful Everest expedition, Hillary changed his mind and agreed to lead the 1954 expedition after all.[35] He set off for the Barun Valley, as did George Lowe, even though the NZAC suggested Lowe stand down as he had already had three seasons in the Himalaya.[36]

Riddiford was mistakenly named as a reserve in the Christchurch newspapers, whereupon he wrote tersely to the NZAC pointing out that he had never been an applicant. With that line drawn very clearly in the sand, the New Zealand trio from Cho Oyu would never again climb together.

12. NEW DIRECTIONS

The joyous adventure into marriage and fatherhood

Earle Riddiford was a highly ambitious climber, but after Cho Oyu his Everest exploration was effectively over. When Hunt replaced Shipton, membership of the 1953 party was reviewed. Hillary and Lowe were included because they had been on Shipton's 'curtain-raiser' expedition in 1952 and because of their New Zealand ice experience. Ayres was refused because he was a professional.[1] Norman Hardie, with no Himalayan experience at that time, was also turned down; Hunt told Hardie there was already enough opposition to having New Zealanders in the party. Riddiford's cable asking to be included drew a reply from the Himalayan Committee saying that after most careful consideration, the NZAC had been informed that New Zealand participation would be restricted to two.[2]

Meanwhile, Riddiford's long-deferred legal career was taking off: he was offered a position in Daniel Riddiford's Wellington practice with a view to partnership. Letters to his mother show he was quickly adapting to the challenges of city life:

> When I arrived at the office Daniel was rather businesslike ... The scheme is that I am to work for the firm for a probationary period of six months. Then he would be willing for me to go into partnership on the same terms as himself with [Rawdon] Beere ... Colonel Beere is 73 and taciturn to a degree, but doesn't seem to be a bad old stick ... I don't feel rusty at all. We do a lot of agency work, a good line of business but rather dull. The premises are good, with loads of room for expansion.[3]

By October 1952 he was feeling like a true Wellingtonian and beginning to like the place.[4] For a short time he lived in a boarding house in Boulcott Street and saw a lot of his sister Trish and her husband John, with whom he attended Hillary's lecture on Cho Oyu. At weekends he was able to visit his Aunt Awa at

Overton and enjoy the busy social life there. Often he was pressed to share his Himalayan experiences. At Huntly School in Marton he lectured to a mob of fidgety schoolboys, but 'piled in as much blood and thunder as I could, and they gave me three rousing cheers at the end'.[5]

His passion for climbing was by no means spent. Through Norman Hardie he kept up to date with the Shipton/Hunt controversy and ensuing decisions about the composition of the Everest party:

> I must admit your news stirred me up a bit and made me wish I was back at the RGS at the present time … Shipton I expect was not unduly perturbed at having a good reason to leave me out, but of course I was not expecting to be included and in addition not really 100% keen under what I thought was half-hearted leadership. We have got strong representation in Ed H. and Geo … and I have done my very best to get Bill B. included.[6]

In the same letter he said his six-week rest treatment in hospital had worked well and he was back to normal, making plans with Bill Beaven to tackle Malte Brun from the unclimbed Murchison side. This trip took place over Christmas 1952, with Beaven, Ian Ogilvie Gibbs and Hugh Tyndale-Biscoe.[7] On Christmas Day they toiled with heavy packs under a relentless sun, up the Murchison valley to a camp at the terminal of the glacier. It was a great pleasure to be climbing again with Beaven, and the two others made up a 'competent and congenial party'.[8] Malte Brun made them work very hard. On their first attempt on 29 December they were stopped by a large crevasse and retreated to the Malte Brun Hut. Success finally came on New Year's Day:

> Beaven did a long gruelling spell up the final pitch of snow ridge … but the hour's ice traverse to the summit was delightful … hardly a breath of wind, a cloudless sky and a magnificent view on all sides. Two days later we were on our way up the Haast Ridge bound for a Grand Traverse of Mt Cook when a large chunk of the ridge fell on me and broke three bones in my foot. I can see that an accident broadens one's experience, but it is an experience I could well have done without.[9]

Riddiford had to be carried back to Ball Hut, but was soon sufficiently recovered to be dancing at cabarets in spite of a plaster cast, and with a surge of new business his professional life was on the move. Standing at a city intersection one morning he was introduced by a mutual friend to Roger Peren, then working

Earle's companions on the Malte Brun climb, from left: Hugh Tyndale-Biscoe, Ian Ogilvie Gibbs and Bill Beaven. Riddiford Collection

in the Department of External Affairs. Peren, educated at Otago, Victoria and Oxford universities, was to become a lifelong friend, always in touch throughout a diplomatic career during which he was head of mission in Singapore, Jakarta, Geneva and Tokyo. After his retirement in 1987, he came home as foundation director of the New Zealand Centre for Japanese Studies at Massey University. A long sequence of amusing letters between the two friends reveals their great mutual respect.

It was not long before Peren invited Riddiford to share a flat at 49 Moorhouse Street, Wadestown. Peren found his new flatmate a talkative chap who was always physically active. He soon became acquainted with Riddiford's insistence on open windows and fresh air, and his frenetic driving style – he was always more interested in getting where he was going than the management of the vehicle, Peren says, recalling an occasion when Riddiford took delivery of a new car and immediately took it up to 100mph (160km/h) on a stretch of road in Upper Hutt. Riddiford brought his extensive collection of LPs to the flat and greatly enjoyed Wellington's smorgasbord of cabarets, ballet and theatre, with ski trips in winter to Ruapehu to balance the city lifestyle. The pair also shared a number of expeditions to Taupo where they occasionally met up with Ian Gibbs, then stationed at the Kinleith sawmill in Tokoroa. Sailing on Gibbs' yacht *Snark*, the only one on Lake Taupo at that time, proved an excellent way to explore the western bays.

A flurry of correspondence with Pasang Dawa Lama reveals that Riddiford's

Himalayan aspirations were still ticking over. Pasang was delighted to hear he had recovered from his back injuries on Cho Oyu, writing, 'my joy knew no bounds'.[10] He was also pleased to learn that his friend was considering an expedition to Kangchenjunga in 1955, and promised he would make himself available.[11] In June–July 1952, Pasang was sirdar for four months with Jan de Graaff's successful Himalayan party. He was able to send glowing references from de Graaff[12] as he negotiated remuneration rates with Riddiford, who was also assisting Athol Roberts in engaging Sherpas for his private New Zealand expedition in May–June 1953. In the end Pasang was unable to accompany Roberts as he was engaged by a German party, but did organise an experienced team for him.

In February 1953 when Bill Beaven left for overseas, Riddiford felt the loss of 'a real sheet anchor, an absolutely first class bloke'.[13] Consolation arrived in the form of 23-year-old Rosemary Johnston, a friend of the Peren family in Palmerston North. 'She really is awfully nice and most intelligent as well, and I hope to be seeing some more of her,' Riddiford told his mother.[14] The relationship deepened as he introduced Rosemary to his family and also to his great love of climbing; she reciprocated with invitations to family occasions and beach holidays shared with friends. In April, Earle joined the Wellington NZAC committee and was busy with many lectures, requests for articles and photographic material, work on a new map of the Mt Cook region and his article on the Malte Brun trip for the *NZAJ*.

Riddiford's public lecture on the Everest Reconnaissance in the packed concert chamber of the Wellington Town Hall on 12 May was attended by 1000 people, including Governor-General Lord Norrie and Lady Norrie and many other dignitaries. With the Everest expedition so much in the public mind, his graphic descriptions and almost continuous slide show were to help the NZAC considerably in fundraising for their 1954 expedition.[15]

Then came the Everest conquest. Riddiford's message to Hillary and Lowe was a generous one:

> Congratulations to you both on your wonderful achievement, and to you particularly Ed for your supreme effort. I was delighted to hear the news. Having some idea of what is involved in getting to the top, I never expected success, but you've certainly proved the pessimists wrong, and it is difficult for me to express my admiration and congratulations for what you have done. Everyone in New Zealand has been immensely pleased and proud.

Riddiford's own contribution did not escape notice: one telegram he himself received read 'Congratulations: NZ and Hillary really owe this to you.'[16]

After the ascent there were many more requests for Riddiford to oblige public interest with radio interviews[17] and speaking engagements. While praising Hillary's mountaineering skill, he paid tribute to John Hunt's wise and courageous leadership, and the magnificent effort by Bourdillon and Evans in reaching the South Summit. 'Knowing them well, I am personally sorry that they or some of the other Englishmen did not reach the summit as well as Hillary.'[18]

In London Bill Beaven was revelling in the Everest aftermath and sending regular dispatches:

> The most important point seems to be the use of oxygen. It is only a matter of time now before all the big peaks in the Himalaya are climbed, for with adequate supplies of oxygen it appears that all technical difficulties high up could be overcome.[19] Norm and I have applied to go on the next trip ... What do you think of Sir Edmund? The papers here have been full of Ed's pictures and other bull, and if you know London evening papers you can guess at the sensationalism.[20]

Beaven said it was hardly possible to credit the adoration and respect Hillary had earned with his climb and subsequent knighthood. He spent some time with the members of the Everest expedition, visiting Eric Shipton's Outward Bound school in the Lake District.

> Norm and I went rock climbing with Tom Bourdillon and the other rock kings. The English boys who had had to put up with a certain amount of abuse over their ice climbing on Everest were trying to get some of their own back – Ed and George were wise and stayed behind canoeing on the lake with Eric ... When we all went canoeing down the flooded Esk River, nearly all the canoes capsized and George lost his teeth, much to everyone's amusement.[21]

Midway through 1953 Riddiford was told that Hillary could not go to the Barun in 1954 and that he himself might be asked to lead the expedition. But when the news filtered through that Hillary had changed his mind, Riddiford wrote to his mother that he was fairly unmoved about the matter either way.[22] There were other priorities. In Rosemary, he felt happy he had the right girl, 'if she'll have me'. However, she had plans to travel to England, meaning he had to move fairly quickly. 'She says it will only be for six months and that time is a good test in these matters, which I don't find consoling,' Riddiford wrote to his mother. 'I certainly don't have any doubts – she is very sweet as well as extremely attractive, and has lots of character.'[23]

In September a radio broadcast about Everest attracted many listeners. Riddiford found it a balanced report, but his old climbing friend Bruce Gillies thought it extraordinary that neither Hillary nor Lowe had one gracious or grateful word to say about Earle or about the NZAC, which had negotiated the invitation in 1951 and given so much financial support. 'Bruce said he thought Hunt should have had a knighthood and all the rest of the party a lesser decoration – and that seems to be the general opinion in the mountaineering world. It is scandalous that Ed has a better order than Hunt,' Riddiford wrote.[24]

Around this time Helen Nicholl received a somewhat flustered letter from her son: Rosemary's trip to England was off, and Earle and Rosemary ('Rodie') were engaged. 'I am a very lucky man indeed. Rodie is a wonderful girl and we are very much in love. It is highly exciting and I still can't concentrate on my work properly.'[25] The next letter listed a series of cocktail parties and celebrations, but also mentioned his unsuccessful attempt to get permission for a New Zealand party to climb Kangchenjunga. The Indian government turned it down on the basis that Kangchenjunga was a mountain sacred to the Sikkimese. Riddiford described that as 'eyewash', but was not surprised by the refusal, since the British were planning a similar expedition (though from Nepal, not India).[26]

In late October, Riddiford visited Athol Roberts, whose private New Zealand party had just made the first ascent of 23,507ft Chamar in the Nepalese Himalaya,[27] and enjoyed his movies of the trip and the Nepalese music he had brought home. Then the film *Conquest of Everest* arrived in Wellington. Earle declared it visually first class but found the soundtrack disappointing:

> My attention was constantly distracted by the commentator. His commentary was fatuous and stupid, and the music more so and I really don't think those words are too strong. Neither composer nor announcer had ever been near a mountain, I should say, but the film itself is good. George Lowe did a particularly good job from the South Col, I thought.[28]

As Hillary and Lowe toured the country post-Everest they were invited to tea by Riddiford's mother, who gained the impression that while Hillary was exhausted by so many public appearances, Lowe was thriving on them. Her son agreed:

> I heard them lecture here and thought Ed was good. George to be perfectly frank I found fairly nauseating, obviously very pleased with himself, and playing to the gallery. I think his sense of humour is pretty poor … I was most offended by his

poking fun at the Hindu and Buddhist religions – this just displays ignorance and bad taste. But Ed on the other hand is quite unspoilt, and has a genuinely funny sense of humour. I was much amused by his remark to the press: 'Some people have mothers-in-law – but I have George!' Ed was good, but if the public thinks George is witty and entertaining, all I can say is My God, one expects something better from a mountaineer.[29]

In January 1954, after a memorable farewell party, Roger Peren left New Zealand for his first posting, to Washington. He sent Riddiford a postcard from his air-conditioned hotel there: 'Even fresh air fiends here appreciate this is winter: Wake up, Moorhouse St!'[30] Another candid letter in February described how Hillary and Lowe 'shambled' into New York, where the Everest party lunched with the National Geographic Society, before a high-profile civic reception. Somewhat casual and uncouth, their manner brusque and bored, the New Zealanders seemed at ease only when talking about mountains. Hillary seemed too tired to put his story across well, and his 'dinkum Kiwi' accent also created difficulties for some Americans.[31] In sharp contrast, Peren found Evans impressive:

> Charles Evans is delightful, quite the nicest and most intelligent: I told him at once that I had lived with you, and thereafter saw him frequently in such a way that we could wink behind the solemnities … Charles Evans now [tells the story] from Base Camp to the Lhotse Face, and is quite the best: logical presentation and a delightful dry wit, which Americans do not at first understand.

Peren also recalled 'the drinking bouts of carefree bachelor days', and regretted the loss of the sessions of Nat King Cole and the Goodman Trio he had shared with Riddiford. 'But one thing you would really enjoy here: Satchmo[32] has just come to town and is playing at the Basin Street!'[33] In a more serious mood, he congratulated Riddiford on the momentous occasion of his forthcoming wedding, apologising for not being there to make a 'diversionary' speech, and hoping that someone had given Rodie a good collection of expendable crystal glasses.

Earle's marriage to Rosemary began what Peren called 'a joyous adventure'. Before the wedding there was a flurry of activity as Riddiford positioned himself to support a wife and family. The hunt for a house was followed by the acquisition of everything they needed to go in it. Fortunately Rosemary was also able to contribute, which made it possible for the young couple to afford a new car to get them from the city to their new home in Espin Crescent, Karori. The car would also save them a lot of honeymoon travel expenses, Riddiford pointed out to his mother, as he asked her for a loan. They had a small 'Rehab' furniture advance plus wedding present cheques to look forward to. A highlight for Riddiford was the 'best stag party possible': cousin Daniel hosted a dinner at the Wellington Club.

> It really was a magnificent show. A couple of drinks beforehand, then we went in to a superb five course dinner better than anything I had in London or Edinburgh, with good wines for each course followed by coffee and the best cigar I have smoked. We then retired to a private room and conversed and drank whiskies and brandies (with a dimly remembered supper served sometime.) So you can see it was something to be remembered and a very fine effort on Daniel's part. All parties were much the worse for wear.[34]

Wedding of the Year, 1954, from left: Ed Cotter, Ian Gibbs, John Arkwright, Earle and Rosemary Riddiford, Judy Tennant, Jennifer Will, Gillian Peren. Belinda Cranswick

The men in the wedding party – Earle, Ian Gibbs and Ed Cotter – stayed with the Peren family before the wedding on 24 April 1954: Bill Beaven, still in England, was very sorry to decline an official position.[35] After the big occasion at All Saints Church in Palmerston North and the reception at the Palmerston North Club, their honeymoon took the couple first to the Ohingaiti Hotel and then on to Taupo, Rotorua and Tauranga, concluding with Riddiford's attendance at a Maori Land Court hearing in Hastings. 'Weddings may be hectic but I don't think it will come near a Himalayan Expedition in the final stages before departure,' he wrote to his mother.[36]

The young couple enjoyed an active social life, out four or five times a week or entertaining at home. Rosemary, who was very fashion conscious, relished the life. During the day she threw herself into gardening, a lifelong interest (and into cooking for her new husband: she made him a different pudding for every night of the first year of their marriage!)

Once in partnership with his cousin in the Wellington firm of O. & R. Beere & Riddiford, which merged with Smyth Johnson & Stevens in the 1970s, Riddiford displayed what Peren described as a genius for friendship.[37] He developed an unusually wide circle of friends and, in his profession, approached problems with enthusiasm and vision. He was generous with his time and effort, and paid great attention to detail, which built his reputation as one of the best conveyancing lawyers in the city. The practice expanded with a new branch in Lower Hutt.

He kept in touch with progress on the NZAC Barun expedition through Hardie and Beaven, and received the confidential information that Hardie would be joining Charles Evans on the Alpine Club expedition to Kangchenjunga the following year. Hardie wrote saying his opinions about Lowe were too strong to put into print, and expressed further exasperation with the Barun party:

> I wonder if you had all these birds taped before the party ever sailed – I can't see what the committee was thinking about. I have all words of praise for Bill and Jim [McFarlane] – strange how the fellows with whom one could bear more than one consecutive trip seven years ago are still more than palatable … I thought Ed [Hillary] did a difficult job fairly well, and I was very sorry for him at the end.[38]

Beaven was bitterly disappointed that the bungled rescue of the badly frostbitten Jim McFarlane from a crevasse[39] had set the expedition back considerably. 'Norm and I have been very keen to try Lhotse II but there is so little drive in the expedition there was never much hope, I'm afraid. The approach to Makalu II is fairly difficult, so [I] shouldn't be surprised if we don't climb it with this team.'[40]

Earle and Rosemary (centre) visiting Ed Cotter (rear) in Fiordland, with friends. Belinda Cranswick

From Kathmandu on the way out he wrote that he thought they might have been more successful had Hillary not fallen ill, needing to be carried out.

> It was a problem getting him down all right, requiring all manpower, Sherpas and Sahibs, however we should never have taken down all the high camps or pulled out completely. It was old George that persuaded everyone it was necessary. Norman and I were highly browned off but there was nothing we could do. You have probably read of the Baruntse climb, it was in all the papers. I will correct you on a few points – it was not George Lowe's climb. He was completely useless on the mountain.[41]

From Burwood Hospital in Christchurch, where he was making only slow progress with skin grafts, McFarlane also sent Riddiford his perspective on the expedition: 'I must say I got fairly browned off with the mucking about involved with such a large party, plus its attendant array of porters.'[42] The ever-cheerful McFarlane received frequent visits from fellow mountaineers, but he would not return to the hills for a year, and his climbing would always be limited by the loss of the front halves of both feet.

In Washington, Roger Peren was delighted to hear that Rosemary was expecting: 'I'm looking about already for cowboy outfits: in this country, all children wear them regardless of sex.'[43] The couple's first child, Belinda, was born in February 1955. Riddiford wrote to his mother describing his feelings: 'It's a wonderful experience becoming a father – the most exciting and dramatic thing that has happened to me ... She has been more sweet and charming and beautiful every day.'[44]

He was a very affectionate father, always full of enthusiasm, and Belinda was close to him from a very early age. Riddiford would race home from his office in Lambton Quay to their house in the hill suburb of Karori during his lunch hour, just for that extra time with his daughter. Peren wrote his congratulations again, picturing the mountaineer–father dichotomy: 'I can just see you fighting the gales up there on the South Col, pegging down the stove, lighting the house inside a sleeping bag, throwing the ice axe out with the bath water, then being unable to chip ice off the baby except with a bottle-opener ... all in glorious Kodachrome.'[45]

Earle with baby Belinda in Karori. Belinda Cranswick

So it was almost against Riddiford's paternal inclinations when climbing friends persuaded him to spend a weekend in the Orongorongos where, in spite of some torrential weather, he thoroughly enjoyed the dense beautiful bush on either side of the Orongorongo Valley. No matter how reconciled he might be to Wellington, he still hankered for the Southern Alps. With Beaven back in New Zealand from January 1955 there were murmurings of a quick trip to the Arrowsmiths, but Beaven's life was soon complicated by his engagement to Gay Hall: 'A wonderful girl, a first class skier and a jolly good climber as well, altogether "Just the job" as Ian Gibbs would say.'[46]

Over the winter Riddiford represented the FMC on the committee running the New Zealand Antarctic Expedition to lay depots for the Commonwealth Trans-Continental Crossing, and travelled to Christchurch and Dunedin with Hillary to interview personnel. He advised Harry Ayres to apply as a dog handler, since apart from Hillary there would be few places available for 'purely mountaineering types' on what was a designated scientific expedition.[47] In June he wrote to Hardie to ask if he was interested in applying for the Antarctic party as a surveyor, and to congratulate him on his historic ascent of Kangchenjunga.

The lawyer, 10 February 1955. Anna Riddiford

'What an absolutely bloody wonderful effort, and you have my most envious and admiring congratulations.'[48]

These five golden years of New Zealand's exploratory trips to the Himalaya were marked by a special occasion masterminded by Dan Bryant. All the climbers who had taken part were invited to keep their memories alive by sharing a weekend together in Christchurch in September 1955. And what a roll call it was, from Odell, Bryant and Packard to almost all the other big names from later expeditions.

More memories flooded back for Riddiford when he was contacted in early 1956 by Keki Bunshah, who had joined the 1951 trek to Badrinath. Since qualifying as a solicitor Bunshah had been working in his father's firm, but was now planning a climbing expedition to Trisul Peak in the Garhwal Himalaya and was seeking guidance on clothing, equipment, food and medicines. He urged Riddiford to hurry back to the Himalaya: 'Ama Dablam ought to offer you a challenge, but at the rate peaks are going it will not remain virgin for long.'[49] (Two years later Bunshah wrote again, describing the glorious time he had on the Trisul expedition and his plans for Cho Oyu and possibly Pumori with a team of Indian climbers and Pasang Dawa Lama as sirdar.)

Riddiford was prominent on the Ross Dependency Research Committee established in 1957, and was of considerable assistance to Griffith Pugh of Cho Oyu days, the organiser of the English end of an Anglo–American physiological expedition to Antarctica. In the early 1960s he served as president of the FMC for two years, at a time when the Deerstalkers' Association and the Lands and Survey Department were in furious dispute over the classification of deer, chamois and thar as vermin.

By then three more children had arrived – Richard in November 1956, Anna in October 1958 and Sarah in May 1963. Family life was busy with four children, all brought up to be ambitious and independent. Belinda remembers a life that was never dull with her father around:

The 1955 Himalayan Dinner. From left, back row: W.B. Beaven, B. Wilkins, P. Bain, H.E. Riddiford, E.P. Hillary, H.J. Harrington, M. Bowie, L.R. Hewitt, R. Chapman, K. Suter, N.E. Odell, L. Krenek, J.B. (Jock) Harrison, G. Harrow, R.H. Watson, S. Conway. Front row: W.P. Packard, E.M. Cotter, G. McCallum, H.T. Milner, L.V. Bryant, W.E. Hannah, J. (John) Harrison, C.J. McFarlane.
David Ellis

I adored my father, though he could be very impatient at times and he had very high expectations of us. But there were endless lively conversations around the dinner table: TV and telephone calls were banned. As children we were allowed to express our opinions fairly freely. He took a great interest in everything we were doing at school, he delighted in taking us to pantomimes and other cultural events, and he was very keen for us to exercise and get plenty of fresh air in the outdoors.[50]

For many years Earle had dreamed of taking over Landsborough Station, by now part of Mt Aspiring National Park. He looked at Westland properties and made a few offers, his favourite objective the Cron run at Haast, along with the Landsborough grazing lease, which he called 'The Cron Jewels'. All this was most unsettling for Rosemary, who was somewhat relieved when his attention turned to Orongorongo Station, once owned by his great-grandfather. At least it was a little closer to home, but finance was still a major obstacle. Earle, however, was determined to put the family 'back on the map' by taking possession of the grand former Riddiford property, and he pleaded with his reluctant wife to release

Belinda, Earle, Anna and Richard on the fence at Jubilee Road, Khandallah. Anna Riddiford

funds she had at her disposal. A family story tells of how she refused to sign the documents, locking herself in the bathroom to avoid argument. When Earle thrust the papers and a pen under the door, she wrote a strongly worded refusal. A few weeks later she relented.

13. ORONGORONGO STATION

Living another dream

On 13 October 1963 Earle and Rosemary took possession of the 3850-hectare Orongorongo Station, which had been out of the family for a decade. Earle was now able to indulge his great love of wild country. He was confident he could strike a balance between the law office, his beloved Wellington Club and the demands of station ownership. Orongorongo – which included a significant portion of Māori leasehold land – gave him plenty of scope. Financially, however, they lurched from crisis to crisis.

For many years the family enjoyed an enviable lifestyle, living in Wellington during the week and spending wonderful weekends and holiday times at Orongorongo, with parties in the ballroom and hair-raising 4WD rides over

The homestead at Orongorongo Station. Riddiford collection

steep farm tracks, usually with a picnic thrown in. The three girls on their ponies delighted in riding around the station, and Earle was always keen to hear about the new routes they found. He once or twice removed a transistor radio from a daughter's pack, telling them they should be listening only to the birds and the natural sounds around them.

These were happy years, with much entertaining. The record player was constantly belting out the Beatles, Ella Fitzgerald, Mozart, Louis Armstrong, Beethoven – Earle's preference for jazz and classical music predominated, but Belinda remembers he took delight in some pop music as well, especially if it had a good beat. He must have thought himself a good dancer too, because he often told her, 'Just watch me if you want to know how to dance.' Belinda's close friend Caroline Kraayvanger spent much time with the family, finding Earle a 'softie' with a twinkle in his eye who always enjoyed a joke and had a slightly left-field sense of humour: 'He was not one to be bothered with mundane day-to-day requirements – he always had much larger tasks to attend to, and there were many times when he needed to be reined in.'[1]

Earle's children look back on some extraordinary years when, despite not being typically fatherly, he showered them with the benefits that flowed from a wonderfully positive approach to life. Sarah recalls his fast and furious driving

From left: Anna, Sarah and Rosemary Riddiford at Orongorongo. Anna is holding Twiggy, the family cat that travelled from Wellington to Orongorongo every weekend. Riddiford collection

From left: With their friend Mandy Treadwell, Anna and Belinda return from a ride at Orongorongo. Their younger sister Sarah is walking alongside (c. 1971). Belinda Cranswick

style, especially one day when he passed three buses on the dangerous Kapiti Coast road; even when her father was teaching her to drive he would tell her just to put her foot down. Later, when she decided her ideal husband would be a man who talked intelligently, laughed a lot, liked to travel and enjoyed dancing, she realised she probably had a father fixation.

Rosemary Riddiford showed extraordinary patience in handling her impulsive, almost hyperactive husband. He was forever hatching plans for altering the homes they lived in; sometimes the builders had only just left when the next renovation or move was mooted. He had a good eye for architecture, and built up a strong and lasting friendship with Wellington architect Daryl Cockburn, who managed numerous projects for the family. Cockburn found that Earle's horsepower occasionally affected his clarity of vision, but he greatly respected Earle's intelligence, his ability to establish good working relationships, and the results he achieved.[2]

The couple shared a well-developed sense of humour; when things went wrong laughter often saved the day. John Arkwright describes Rosemary as a gentle and gracious lady and the couple's relationship as extremely happy. The two also shared a great love of gardening – Earle thrived on the discipline of trimmed edges – and strove to make the Orongorongo grounds as beautiful as possible. Whenever they were there for a weekend, their gardener Gerald would

Hardies and Riddifords converge on the Beavens' bach at Bealey Spur near Arthur's Pass, 1971. From left: Richard Riddiford, Bill Beaven, Norman Hardie, Jane Hardie, Belinda Riddiford, Derek Cook (shouldering son Edward), Sarah Riddiford, Anna Riddiford, unknown child (obscured), Ruth Hardie, Enid Hardie and Rosemary Riddiford. Riddiford collection

Rosemary and Earle at Orongorongo, c. 1975. Riddiford collection

come for Saturday morning tea to discuss plans for the week ahead.

Both Rosemary and Earle took an open-hearted approach to those around them, genuinely connecting with all visitors with style, charm and generosity of spirit. Earle was interested in everyone and keen to share the homestead and its gardens with visitors and groups undertaking charitable projects. The annual New Year's Day party was always memorable. While most family holidays were spent at Orongorongo, the children once enjoyed a South Island jaunt visiting their father's old climbing friends, staying with Norman Hardie in his bach at Cora Lynn near Arthur's Pass, and roping up together in crampons on Franz Josef Glacier. When they called in to see Mick Sullivan, he looked the once skinny mountaineer up and down before observing 'My, you've been in a good paddock.'[3]

Earle often told his family his forties were the best decade of his life. Spending easily and living high, he had escaped the constraint that characterised the generation that lived through the Depression years. Presenting well was important to him, and he set high standards whenever he entertained. He had a broad view of the world, was politically aware and read widely; and nothing gave him more pleasure than poring over a map.

In 1971 the Riddifords hosted Sir Edmund and Lady Louise Hillary, with Tenzing and his wife Daku, on a visit to Orongorongo Station. From left: Earle, Graham McCallum (vice-chairman of the Wellington section of the NZAC), Tenzing, Daku and Hillary. Riddiford archives

Regular guests at Orongorongo – some of them very distinguished indeed – grew to accept that he would seize any opportunity to give them an adventure. An overland trip in his Landcruiser would sometimes end nerve-rackingly close to a cliff face near the air strip, from which there was a magnificent view across to Wellington and out to Cook Strait. Sometimes the gin-and-tonic suitcase went with them – though Earle was not a heavy drinker himself, it was an excellent excuse to stop somewhere and admire the sunset. On several occasions he took a well-dressed party of friends over to the Pencarrow block some distance away from the homestead, where there was a good chance of getting stuck in the mud. There would be frantic attempts to dig the vehicle out, and if that failed a party would walk to Baring Head to raise the alarm – not so much fun in a howling southerly.

The day-to-day farming was left in the hands of farm managers. Earle was not cut out for full-time farming: sheep he found uninspiring. Yet for 20 years he was engrossed in extending the boundaries and increasing the carrying capacity of the run. He revelled in the joys of road building along Orongorongo's high rocky ridges, and the hard work of clearing scrub. Under various government development schemes he undertook improvements to steep hill country, and relished the pyrotechnics of burning scrub before over-sowing with grass. He constantly had exciting development plans in mind to further indulge his enthusiasm for the environment.

Earle stands beneath the portrait of his great-grandfather Daniel Riddiford at Longwood.
Belinda Cranswick

But the pace was hectic and the demanding lifestyle took its toll. Earle suffered a massive heart attack at Orongorongo in 1975, followed by a series of smaller episodes, which restricted his activities – although not his enthusiasm or optimism. He stepped back to become a consultant to the law firm and increasingly involved himself in station activities. But ill-health and an over-dependence on managers eventually stretched the viability of the farm enterprise too far. Earle became somewhat irascible: in retrospect his family understood the stresses he faced in combining a legal career with the stewardship of Orongorongo, but were also staunch in their defence of the long-suffering Rodie, who at times had been unable to prevent her husband over-reaching himself financially. Finally, in 1986, Earle was forced to sell up, to a business group which turned the homestead into the Orongorongo Lodge.[4]

Earle Riddiford never got around to writing the book that should have cemented his pioneering status in New Zealand's climbing history. But he kept in touch with his climbing friends and travelled south on many occasions to join them on climbs. Although he felt out of practice, after a 1961 South Westland climb with Hardie, Beaven, Derek Cook, Jock Montgomery and Ian Gibbs he wrote: 'I was really slogged at the end of it … but I felt there was no better place to be and that I had been missing something over the years.'[5]

Two years later the same party regrouped to climb Mt Pollux in Mt Aspiring National Park, and in January 1968 Earle climbed Mt Rolleston via the Rome Ridge with Hardie, Beaven and Cook. Some years later, Hardie recalls, though he has been unable to find a record of the journey, Earle pressed for another trip into the Landsborough. Hardie, Earle, Brian Hearfield and Bob Cawley were helicoptered to Mueller Pass, then went up the Landsborough and out via the Karangarua. Hardie says that although packs were lighter than in the past, Riddiford struggled, but the party did climb Mt Strachan.

Riddiford's membership of the NZAC was abruptly terminated in 1976 after he was nudged once too often about his overdue subscription. On 12 July he wrote to the club:

> Twenty-five years ago today I led the first ascent of Mukut Parbat, still the highest peak in the world climbed by a New Zealand party. Ed Hillary turned back half way, because he said it was too difficult. I also organised the first New Zealand expedition to the Himalaya, and invited Hillary and Lowe to join it. I got the expedition away despite considerable difficulties, and again Hillary wrote to me

Earle with Norman Hardie before their climb of Avalanche Peak, 1987 or 1988. Belinda Cranswick

suggesting that the expedition should be abandoned because of these difficulties. As a result of the success of this expedition, New Zealanders were given the opportunity to take part in the British expeditions to Mt Everest and other mountains. It could be argued perhaps in one sense that the Club owes me more than I owe it.[6]

In 1986 Earle suffered severe angina attacks that limited his activities, but in these later years he loved to walk around Wellington, sometimes disappearing for two or three hours at a time. He delighted in his role as grandfather, though the family noticed he was becoming more difficult to predict, and sometimes irrational. Earle had inherited the Riddiford resistance to giving up, and keeping track of his impetuous and sometimes unwise decisions became increasingly worrying for Rosemary.

Despite his health concerns Earle was still keen to initiate more mountain schemes, and in 1988 was delighted to succeed on Avalanche Peak with Hardie and Leaven, despite having to count steps to fifty and then stop to rest. 'I climbed Avalanche Peak last February – slowly, but it gave me a thrill to get amongst the glaciers again,' he wrote to Mavis Davidson in his 1988 Christmas message.[7] The following year, on 26 June 1989, he finally lost the battle and died in Wellington Hospital. At Earle's funeral in Wellington Cathedral on 29 June 1989, Roger Peren paid tribute to his old friend:

> Thinking of Earle, and his style and achievements, I have felt that there was someone who was very firmly based in certain tried and tested standards and virtues, who always knew where he stood on matters of ethics and behaviour, self-discipline and duty, and as a consequence proceeded through life with great confidence and self-assurance, the blithe confidence of our own early pioneers, perhaps. In many ways he was a rather old-fashioned chap.[8]

Earle's unwavering self-confidence could be exasperating and certainly got him into trouble, Peren conceded, but was the very quality that had made it possible for him to plan and lead the successful 1951 expedition against great odds. 'That expedition, his first great adventure, called for vision, energy, organisational skills and sheer determination, as well as prowess in the mountains … and I have heard the warmest tribute to Earle's initiative and his dogged courage in the face of debilitating sickness on the Everest Reconnaissance. Of course he would dearly have loved to get to the top of Everest, but he was well pleased with the climbs he achieved and never lost his enthusiasm for Nepal or the mountains.'[9]

At home in the hills: Earle looking towards Mt Rolleston from the summit of Avalanche Peak, 1987 or 1988. Belinda Cranswick

Although Lowe, and to some extent Hillary, had treated him so poorly on Cho Oyu, Earle Riddiford was a gentleman and never referred to this in public.[10] His opinion of Lowe has remained private until the publication of this book, but he was generous in expressing his respect for Hillary's good qualities. In 1953 he wrote a gracious letter not only to Hillary and Lowe, but to Hillary's parents, congratulating them on their son's great achievement.

Hillary showed no such restraint. When *View from the Summit* was published in 1999, 10 years after Earle's death, Anna Riddiford was stung by Hillary's criticism of her father: 'I respected Earle's dogged determination but I can't say I liked him – none of us did. On no occasion did I share a climbing rope with Earle and I had no wish to do so.'[11] Nearly 50 years after Cho Oyu, this horrified many who knew and respected Earle. As well, it was simply not true: although Cho Oyu was miserable for everyone, Riddiford had got on well with the English climbers. This is made clear in a letter from Tom Bourdillon, who wrote after Everest saying he wished Riddiford could have been in the 1953 party, and insisting that he visit him in England to share some of the 'very good rock' to be had there.[12] Hillary's assessment effectively excluded Riddiford from some notional A-team to which Hillary, and presumably Lowe and possibly Shipton, belonged.

Like the rest of her family, Anna Riddiford was at a loss to understand why Hillary would write so unpleasantly and provocatively about her late father. The four Riddiford children had grown up strong-minded, and as they battled their sometimes intractable father the family dynamics were not always easy – but they knew Earle's high standards of behaviour and loyalty, and saw those qualities reflected in deep and permanent friendships. Some friends, like Daryl Cockburn, found it hard to credit that Earle could make an enemy. Ed Cotter, who valued Earle's friendship highly, was unable to recall any major eruptions that could have accounted for Hillary's comments.

Bill Beaven, who probably knew Earle Riddiford best of all, found it difficult to accept Hillary's denigration of a man to whom he owed so much. With Norman Hardie and Ed Cotter, Beaven wrote to Hillary pointing out that Shipton's high praise for Riddiford[13] was at odds with Hillary's portrayal. Their letter was never acknowledged. At a subsequent NZAC dinner Beaven asked Hillary why he had never replied and suggested that he make amends in some way, but Hillary responded that it was just the way he saw things at the time.[14] Beaven was well aware of George Lowe's resentment towards Riddiford. En route with Lowe from India to join the Barun expedition in 1954, after listening to one too many rude remarks from Lowe at Riddiford's expense, he had challenged Lowe, who was unrepentant: as far as he was concerned, Riddiford deserved everything he got.

The strength of Rosemary Riddiford's attachment to her husband was undiminished through their later trials: she always appreciated the entrepreneurial, risk-positive nature of the man she married, and remained loyal and loving to the man and his memory until her death in 2013. She too was shocked by the hostility expressed by Hillary in 1999. In 1971 she had hosted Hillary and his wife Louise, who brought Tenzing and his wife Daku with them to Orongorongo, and Rosemary had always considered Hillary and her husband to be friends.[15] She was incensed that Hillary should attack Earle's reputation after his death, when he was no longer able to defend himself. Rosemary took an opportunity at a book signing to slip a note into Hillary's pocket, asking what had happened to his conscience. It was her last direct contact with him.

In 2003 when Hillary unveiled his bronze statue outside the Hermitage as part of celebrations marking the 50th anniversary of the Everest climb, Ed Cotter was there. For a few moments before dinner, Cotter spoke to Hillary of their 1951 expedition, and mentioned how much his unkind portrayal of Earle had hurt Rosemary. Hillary conceded that he should not have written that way, a sentiment he agreed Cotter might convey to Rosemary.[16]

Film-maker Richard Riddiford plans to make a documentary about his father as a way to redress the injustice. In 2004 Richard and Anna produced a short film celebrating Earle's role in New Zealand mountaineering. *Stepping Stones to Everest* was filmed in Bill Packard's crib in the mountains and took the form of shared conversations over lunch between Hardie, Cotter, Beaven and Packard, reminiscing about the thrilling days of exploratory climbing in the postwar years. The excitement of first ascents, the joys of traversing country seldom if ever visited, and the sense of camaraderie shared by the group – all these had forged lifelong relationships based on mutual respect. In the film Hardie recalls how much in debt he was as a student, and how it would have suited him if Earle had delayed the trip for a while, but how Earle, greatly encouraged by Packard's experience, was all for going at the first opportunity.

George Lowe, who was visiting New Zealand at the time, was also interviewed for *Stepping Stones*. In 2004 he was still sticking to his version of the night in Ranikhet: 'I think that we got on well enough before, but this was a difficult

Flanked by Norman Hardie (left, in red jacket) and Ed Cotter (right), Sir Edmund Hillary pictured at Mount Cook in 2003 after the unveiling of his own statue commemorating the 50th anniversary of the first ascent of Everest. Cotter collection

thing to deal with and it definitely split us apart when Earle said he was going and someone else could go with him. Later on Shipton was really concerned about what happened. He said he never really gave his message any proper thought.'

The reunion for this filming helped to put on record just what the mountains had meant to these climbers. Ed Cotter had no regrets about not returning to the Himalaya:

> Just being in the mountains was always the joy and reward, taking you away from your ego. You are able to live exactly there, the outside world is forgotten and you become totally involved in the experience. And it doesn't have to be on high summits.

Norman Hardie said simply looking at vistas from high places made it all worthwhile: 'I still get a great thrill out of getting above the bushline.' Bill Beaven believed success in life was all about giving it a go and experiencing complete satisfaction; while Bill Packard said mountaineering was about living much more intensely, enjoying a special friendship and rapport with companions.

Unfortunately Riddiford was not there to hear his old friends. Packard's assessment of the 1951 Reconnaissance was that Hillary and Riddiford had cemented their right to be there by proving extremely competent on the Khumbu Icefall, with ice work that was well beyond the experience of all the others, except possibly Shipton. Riddiford had led the way, although the importance of that has been overshadowed by the actual conquest. The film reaffirms the 1951 Garhwal expedition as a vital link in a chain of New Zealand successes in the Himalaya.

The credit owed to Earle Riddiford for his 'brave, independent journey from New Zealand to Garhwal' was recognised at the time of the Everest conquest by an editorial in the *Press* on 3 June 1953, entitled 'The Path to Everest':

> From the moment in July 1951, when two New Zealand climbers with their head Sherpa stepped on to the summit of 23,670ft Mukut Parbat in the Garhwal Himalaya, it became virtually certain that New Zealanders would have some part in future British attempts to climb Mt Everest.[17]

PART 3: SPUR OF THE MOMENT:
Edmund McCarthny Cotter: 1927–

We are the Pilgrims, master; we shall go
Always a little further; it may be
Beyond that last blue mountain barred with snow
Across that angry or that glimmering sea.
– James Elroy Flecker [1]

14. BORN FOR ADVENTURE

At home in the hills

Ed Cotter was never cut out to be the accountant his father hoped for. Being confined to an office would have stunted the soul of a man whose life has been dominated by a love of spontaneous adventure. Any adventure would do, on land, air or water, but always it was the mountains that came first.

The influences that shaped him began with wandering Irish forebears. Ed's great-grandfather, Edmund Rogerson Cotter (1833–1908), emigrated from Bandon, County Cork, to New Zealand where he became a police constable then gaol warden in Lyttelton. In 1868 he married Martha (Marolin) Shaw Glover. Just over nine months later, their son Edmund Glover Cotter was born in Lyttelton.

Later the family moved south, where Edmund Rogerson worked as chief warder at the Timaru gaol. Edmund Glover attended Timaru Public School, and in May 1894 married Victoria Violet Wallace. Their second child was Edmund (Ted) Wallace Cotter, who in 1926 married Dulcibel Minnie McCarthny (Dulcie), and their first born was yet another Edmund: Edmund (Ed) McCarthny Cotter. Ed and his wife, Jennifer Allen, named their first son Guy, boldly breaking the chain.

Ted was living in Greymouth with his family and working as a law clerk when he was called up for the 18th Reinforcements for the NZ Expeditionary Force during World War I.[1] As a member of a machine gun detachment he was hit by shrapnel, suffering serious arm injuries that saw him hospitalised overseas for over a year. On his return home he met Dulcie, his future wife. The couple lived for some years in Auckland, until Ted Cotter opened a Reuters advertising agency in Christchurch, where he also worked in newspaper advertising. During World War II he also trained Home Guard recruits and acted as quartermaster in the Christchurch office. In later years, after moving from the suburb of Cashmere to Hills Road in Shirley, where he had a few acres of land, he set up with some success as a daffodil grower and breeder. (The daffodil *Narcissus* 'Judy Cotter' was named for his elder daughter.)

Ed Cotter had two younger sisters, Judith (Judy or Jude) and Cecily, and a younger brother, Ralph. Until Ed was five, the Cotters lived in Auckland with the wider McCarthny family. Ed retains only hazy memories of this time: shadowy impressions of a house on a hill from which they could hear lions roaring in the zoo, a long walk down a hill and across a creek to get to his first school and, hanging over the bedroom doors, swathes of voluminous bloomers belonging to his three aunts, Rita, Cora and Vera.

But from the time he was five years old, there were signs that he would resist authority and seek freedom and adventure instead. The first manifestation of this independent spirit came when he wagged school as a relatively new entrant. Rebelling against the long trek from home, he decided to play instead in the gully, floating pieces of wood down the stream. Then he found a marvellous hiding place. For nearly a week he simply stopped going to school, amusing himself all day until he thought it was about time to go home. When the school followed up on his absences and he had to own up to his crime, a memorable interview with the headmaster resulted:

> I remember that as though it were yesterday. My mother was beside me when he climbed up on a chair, reaching up to a top shelf and, pulling out a strap, gave me two on each hand. Of course I cried, and my mother cried too. Back home I hid under a double bed because of my Aunt Rita … She was a hard thing, and I knew she wouldn't like what I did either. Sure enough she dragged me out from under the bed and belted me.[2]

When the family shifted to Christchurch, Ed went to Addington School for a year until they moved to Dyers Pass Road below the Port Hills, from where it was a long trek up a steep and winding road to Cashmere Primary School. On his first day Ed was taken up on the tram, which ran past the school to the Sign of the Takahe, but remembers getting lost after school when he tried to find a shortcut home.

Though the family was now closer to Greymouth, where Edmund Glover Cotter was an importer,[3] Ed recalls only one family visit to his grandfather's house – where he blotted his copybook: 'I loudly asked who the funny man with all the hair was …'

His father worked hard to support the family but there was little money to spare, something young Ed learned early on:

> Once I went to the phone booth across the road to make a phone call for my mother. It was a penny for a phone call. Something went wrong and I didn't get through, but I couldn't get the penny back. When I told my mother she had a bit of a cry, simply because I had lost that coin.

Judith, Dulcibel, Ralph, Cecily and Ed Cotter at Dyers Pass Road. Jude Horn

At school the Cotter children would sit next to someone who had a textbook rather than ask their father for money. Ed recalls Saturday mornings spent hiding behind a gorse bush at the foot of Dyers Pass Road, waiting for someone to come along and damage a huge billboard advertising Steelite Green paint. Why? A warning notice promised a £25 reward for any person helping to convict someone of damaging the sign. To his great disappointment, no one ever obliged.

When Ed was in Standard 5 the annual school trip to the Industries Fair caused another money crisis. Ed took to his claw-toothed Post Office Savings Bank money-box with an axe, producing six shillings and sixpence, and at the fair had more money than anyone else. But when his father found the wrecked money-box there was trouble. 'He dragged me outside into the yard, gave me a beating and threw me down on the coal heap. He was a hard man, badly affected by his wartime experiences.' Ed's sister Jude believes Ted Cotter's unsympathetic attitude stemmed from his own tough upbringing, but gives credit to her father for never being out of work in spite of his damaged arm. She also remembers him as a clever man, able to recite from memory all the poetry he learned at primary school.[4]

Ed always got on well with his two sisters and younger brother, all gentle children, and their two-storey Cashmere home provided many happy times with its large section and an empty paddock next door. When he was still small, Ed would set a tennis ball off down the gutter from the top of Dyers Pass Road. Then he would simply run as fast as he could to beat it to the bottom several kilometres away. Already he was showing considerable athletic ability, and while still at primary school he began to accompany his father, a keen member of the Canterbury Mountaineering Club, into the hills:

> My father started taking me up to the head of the Waimakariri River where the CMC had their first hut, the Carrington, about four hours walk up from the road bridge at Bealey. On one of our first outings we were heading up to the hut when it started to rain and the river was coming up fast. We had only been going about an hour and a half. My father decided to cross the river and get onto the other bank. Once we got there, it was too dangerous to carry on, so we camped the night there in the open. A thunder and lightning storm broke out, but we had a fire to keep us warm … that was a most memorable experience, which whetted my appetite for adventure.[5]

Ready for adventure: Ralph and Ed Cotter.
Cotter collection

Jude says their father often recounted the drama of how the river had overtaken their original position, and Ed's pleasure in the experience. 'It was then, I believe, that Ed's lifelong interest in the mountains began.'[6]

At the age of 10, Ed went to see *Mutiny on the Bounty* with a group of CMC climbers, and from then on always felt very much at home with them, whether on a working party, a social get-together or a climbing trip into the hills. Many of Ted Cotter's own trips were explorations, some recorded in the CMC's *Canterbury Mountaineer*, including a first ascent of Mt Stoddart in January 1941.[7] When CMC members came to pick up his father for a weekend trip, Ed, who had already achieved fame at school for being able to cover half the length of a football field walking on his hands, remembers walking down the stairs of their two-storey house on his hands just to show off.

His inclusion in so many CMC activities from such a young age certainly provided the platform from which to launch himself into new challenges, building up the immense stamina that later became his hallmark as a mountaineer.

Church also played a large part in the Cotter children's life, with choir

The hub of much CMC activity: the bar at the Dew Drop Inn. Ted Cotter is standing second from left, Harry Walker extreme right. Cotter collection

practices during the week as well as services, Sunday School and delivering church newsletters. Dulcie's family occasionally came to visit, arriving by ferry in Lyttelton often around Christmas, meaning lots of fun, and sometimes they would all go into the Grand Theatre in Cathedral Square and watch a film – always a special occasion. On the Cotter side, Ed had a number of aunts and uncles from Edmund Glover Cotter's two marriages, first to Victoria Wallace and later to Ann Hindmarsh. Ted's stepbrother Harry Cotter, a market gardener near the Cashmere Tuberculosis Sanatorium, employed Ed when he was a primary school pupil, giving him two shillings and sixpence for planting a thousand lettuces. Ed remembers him as an unusual man, a former boxer who came to see them one day with his hand heavily bandaged: he had cut off his thumb in order to avoid active service during the war.

In 1938, when Ed was 11, his mother became ill with tuberculosis. From then until her death 24 years later she was in and out of the Cashmere Sanatorium, never again living permanently at home. The effect on family life was devastating. For the first three years most weekends centred on visits to 'the San', a 25-minute walk up the hill.

At first Dulcie recovered well. The doctors believed she was well enough to go home, but they needed an x-ray to confirm that she was clear. Tragically for

Dulcie, in 1941 all supplies of blank x-ray plates had been sent overseas for the war effort. She remained in the San and her condition steadily deteriorated; a collapsed diaphragm with further complications eventually meant she would never regain her health.

At the sanatorium, set high on the Port Hills, exposure to sunlight was the core treatment. Most hopes for a long-term cure rested on a combination of isolation, sunshine, fresh air, rest and healthy food. The middle hospital admitted only women, who were accommodated in small detached huts. On the highest level was the Fresh Air Home for Children, which provided care and schooling for children whose parents had the disease. Ralph and Cecily, the two younger Cotter children who joined their mother for two years on 'Hospital Hill', both later developed Tb – Cecily[8] after she started work, and Ralph during his fifth-form year. Both were themselves treated at the San, Cecily for six to eight months and Ralph for several years. Ralph has never forgotten the consequences of this disease. As a young child he was upset when Dulcie came home from the San and he was not allowed to get into bed with her; in the street people walked by with handkerchiefs over their mouths.

Ted Cotter's army and Home Guard activities meant he was often away from home during the war years. For some time the family had a housekeeper, Muriel, who kept their home spotless and managed frugally on three pounds a week. When Jude was 14 she stepped up into the housekeeping role. She sometimes annoyed Ed by laying down the law, often about not being at home enough. But he would never argue with her: his way of dealing with disputes was simply to walk away.

Ralph believes that Ed was probably the one who suffered most in the absence of Dulcie's calming influence on her husband:

> She was such a nice person, tall and very placid, whereas my father was quite a martinet. But you have to forgive him for much of that, he had such a hard life himself. His injuries had left his arm hanging by a few shreds of flesh. Amazingly, they rebuilt it, joining up the tendons in what was a very ambitious operation in those days. But then he came back to the Depression, and though he did reasonably well in advertising, after that the family finances were always difficult.[9]

Ed attended Christchurch Boys' High School, biking there and back every day from Cashmere. He passed his university entrance exams and played hockey – captaining the second XI – as well as cricket. He was a well-known tuck-shop assistant, which probably entitled him to a free lunch, but his greatest claim to fame was his party trick of walking up and down the school's feature staircase on his hands.

He took the general course, often coming top in English.[10] He was a member of the photography group, an interest that persisted throughout his life. During compulsory military training he was a platoon commander; his most vivid memory is the embarrassment he felt when his voice broke as he gave the order to stand to attention. Geoff Harrow, a fellow pupil who became a lifelong friend and a frequent companion in the mountains, recalls Ed as bright and gregarious, the sort of boy who made friends easily.

Ed knew a lot about the Waimakariri Valley from times spent there with his father, and before long he was encouraging his friends into the hills. Harrow's first mountain experience with Ed came in the third form, when he and Ed and Robin Johnson, another third-former, rode their bicycles up to Mt Grey in the Canterbury foothills one school holiday. On the summit Ed found a dead possum, which he took home, but his father was enraged because in those days possums were protected animals.[11] The next year the same group went into the Waimakariri Valley, and they would sometimes bike round Banks Peninsula, stash their bikes in the bush and walk over the tops and around to Akaroa. On returning to the bikes they would spend the night on the roadside in their sleeping bags, before cycling back to Christchurch. Ed recalls these as great days spent with mates who were to be friends for life.

> … by that stage we had joined the CMC ourselves and were going out on journeys with them in the weekends, as well as helping with hut building. We were involved with some very interesting characters. Many of them were real hard cases who had been away to war and made the most of any opportunity to get back to the mountains. There were some women trampers around then, but they usually didn't go into the CMC huts because the returned servicemen looked on the mountains as a male-only domain. To get any women out of the huts they would start telling wartime stories that were not very polite, which usually resulted in the women's rapid departure.

The active and fiercely independent CMC was pivotal in shaping the man Ed Cotter was to become. In 1931, six years after the club was founded, it was invited by the NZAC to become a local branch; the CMC declined, preferring to retain its less hierarchical structure.[12] The club's first hut, the Carrington, rebuilt in the early 1940s, became the main training ground. Before the rebuild there was a practice build: a hut was erected at the Anti-Crow, halfway between

A happy band of CMC stalwarts gathered over Christmas 1943 to renovate the Anti-Crow Hut. Nui Robins and Ted Cotter standing, leaning against rock; Ed Cotter standing extreme right.
Cotter collection

the Carrington and the Bealey. War restrictions meant it was built from various odds and ends, and the pig-netting bunks were 'pretty awful'.[13] Over Christmas 1943 there was a big push to improve the Anti-Crow: a party of what T.T. (Nui) Robins described as 'men-mules', including Ted Cotter and 'Ted Junior', dragged a heavily loaded trailer up the riverbed to the hut and then back to the Bealey. The two Cotters were then dropped over to Arthur's Pass to catch the train home, while the others walked back to the Anti-Crow to get on with the renovation.[14]

Another of Ed's early building trips was to the high-altitude site of the Barker Hut at the head of the White River, far above the bush line and an eight-hour trip from the road. An old truck was used to take the materials as far as possible, after which it was a matter of carrying everything in, with river crossings adding to the challenge. A 45-strong team of young and old members performed this feat and the hut went up in record time.[15] As Robins pointed out, 'The main thing about building a hut isn't about building it at all. It is carrying it to where it will be erected.'[16]

Tom Newth, another veteran, recalled a flying visit to Christchurch to pick up young Ed Cotter and Bob Roberts to assist with carrying in materials for a couple of bivouacs. The older men had opened up the Mingha Track to allow for men carrying timber, and then themselves carried burdens beyond men of their mature years:

> Harry [Walker] looked and no doubt felt as though he had consumed his last rum, and Nui had a knee popping in and out of joint with sickening thumps … so the two boys gave us valuable assistance during the next two days, with the packing of the rest of the material.[17]

On one of Ed's more taxing adventures, he and Robin Johnson were driven with their bikes up to the Cameron River at the end of the Lake Heron road to help CMC members carry new mattresses in to a hut up the Rakaia Valley. The boys hid their bikes, loaded a mattress each on top of their packs, and walked up the Rakaia to a bivvy and on to the hut. From there they climbed a sizeable mountain, came back down to the hut just on dark, and next morning had a four-hour tramp downriver to their bikes before riding home to Christchurch. 'We only did that once.'

A young Ed Cotter (centre, with Tom Newth seated behind him) in an unidentified summit party. On the right are Malcolm Stewart and Robin Johnson. Cotter collection

A CMC work party at the Mingha Bivvy, Goat Pass. From left: Ed Cotter, Robin Johnson, Tom Newth and Andy Anderson. Cotter collection

During excursions with his father, Ed also got to know the young Jim McFarlane, whose father was a frequent visitor to the Cotter home and companion in the high country. The two fathers and their sons sometimes stayed together in the Canterbury University lodge at Cass.

The senior members of the CMC had cut their teeth on exploratory climbs in the 1930s. 'Very little detail was known of our river systems and mountain valleys back then,' says Ed. 'People wanting adventure turned to newly formed tramping clubs and by the mid-1930s were exploring and mapping the valleys and the mountains.'

Postwar, these explorer mountaineers led a whole new generation into the hills, leaving a deep and lasting impression. Ed Cotter came into climbing on this wave of enthusiasm. Not only was he gaining valuable climbing experience, he was also learning a lot about life from men hardened by war and the outdoors, many of them strong, silent characters for whom it came naturally to retreat to the mountains with friends who had shared similar experiences. Fellowship was unquestioning. The adventures they shared were an escape from mundane working lives, and the mountains also afforded them the odd dose of adrenalin.

As they worked together to build and expand facilities, they imparted their values to junior members.

These men were highly organised, and there was a strong discipline imposed. Unwritten rules governed the way you treated people, the way you talked to them and what you shared with them. As Ed learned, when you saw someone coming you put the billy on, you respected other people's equipment, and you complied with what the older members expected of you – or suffered the consequences. All club members were expected to set an example to others in their treatment of huts and equipment as well as their behaviour in the mountains. Safety rules were emphasised, as well as careful preparation for big trips.

Every Easter the club held a training camp based at the Carrington Hut. Experienced climbers gave lessons in step-cutting in ice and snow, extrication from crevasses, the use of crampons, the use of ropes in crevassed areas, belaying with axe and rope on snow and ice, route-finding and assessing avalanche danger – skills Ed found invaluable. Provisioning was fairly basic, he recalls: 'We would take in some meat and veges, collect firewood, and have a cook-up over the fireplace.' Lessons on river crossing were also important. 'Usually a crossing was obvious enough, but once the rain came and the river rose, it wasn't that

Road end and the start of another mountain expedition. The car, which belonged to John Sampson (seated third from left), provided vital transport to remote places that for younger climbers would otherwise have been unattainable. Ed Cotter (third from right) used Sampson's generous transport on scores of climbs. Cotter collection

Ed Cotter, second from left, with a group of his regular climbing companions. From left: Alan Evans, Cotter, Robin Johnson, Jim Shipman, John Sampson, Eric Pilgrim. Cotter collection

easy. Often we used a rope to send the strongest member of the party across in advance of the others.'

The aim was to get members fit enough to do big climbs safely, and after training, experienced elders led younger climbers on climbs from the Carrington. 'Often we would just fit in a climb of one of the mountains at the same time as some hut work, and it was all good learning.' In 1946, when most members who had served overseas were back in their native hills, almost 80 people attended the Easter Camp.

The camaraderie experienced on CMC trips cemented in Ed Cotter a lifelong loyalty to the CMC. The greatest benefit he reckons was being steeped in the prevailing unselfish mountaineering philosophy. 'Climbing to a summit was a bonus you might enjoy, but not the reason for any trip, and no one would have wanted to be labelled a "peak-bagger". We understood that just being in the mountains was the ultimate.' Team spirit was paramount, and that was to make a lot of difference to the way Ed climbed.

At the end of the sixth form he was told he would be a school prefect if he returned for the seventh form. His father said there was no chance of that – it was time to get out and earn his living. And so, at 16, Ed Cotter left school.

15. REACHING FOR THE SKY

To the high Himalaya

With a thorough grounding in mountaincraft and a deeply rooted identification with the CMC ethos, Ed Cotter had committed himself totally to the mountains: fiercely, romantically, innocently.

In 1945 he took up his first job, as office boy for hardware firm John Burns, where he worked alongside half a dozen office girls – a situation he found interesting but also rather daunting. A year later he left to become a cadet accountant in the Public Trust Office, in a multi-storey building beside Christchurch's Avon River. His main duties turned out to involve sorting the mail, so, not surprisingly, young Ed sought light relief from the boredom. His transgressions began with harmless lunchtime escapades driven by comparative poverty. Approaching people on the riverbank, he would bet them a shilling he could cross the river and back without getting wet – a safe enough wager, as he had worked out a way through an especially shallow section. Another trick was walking around the building's high parapet on his hands.

In the strict working environment of the Public Trust his behaviour soon raised eyebrows. One of the other young staff members was law student Frank Haden, later to gain fame as an outspoken journalist. Nearly half a century later Haden recalled the exploits that had helped relieve the boredom of processing piles of legal files:

> The most indelible memory I have of [Ed] back in 1947 is climbing out through one of the windows of the cafeteria on the top floor, walking along the parapet like Spiderman, stumbling over a ring-bolt, then getting back in through another window.[1]

A further career setback came when Ed failed to show up to work for three days after the Godley–Whataroa crossing of the Main Divide led by Stan Conway over Christmas 1947, during which the party battled torrential West Coast downpours. The morning he reported back to work he was still horribly hungry, and grabbed a chance to cook up some bacon and eggs in the tea lady's kitchen on the top floor:

> Unfortunately I hadn't realised how the smell of the cooking would travel all the way down the lift shaft to the ground floor where people were making their wills and enquiring about their estates. So I was called to see my boss, Joe Hinchey (the Gestapo!). He was very, very displeased and wanted to suspend me twice in one day, once for my absence and then for the stench.

Ed's time at the Public Trust was running out. In 1948 he moved to Skellerup Rubber, where he spent a few happy years handling office communications to the many branches around the country. He was then transferred to Marathon Rubber in Woolston, where at 23 he was put in charge of the office with about four staff.

All the while he was studying at night school towards a bachelor of commerce. He passed four subjects before giving up, greatly disappointing his father. His sister Jude feels it was the correct decision for Ed, however: 'You could never have imagined Ed as an accountant in an office, and by that time he had mustered the courage to face up to our father. I remember a huge scene when he was about 17. For Ed it was probably a trigger point in his life, when he decided he could stand up for himself.'

Ed was relaxed and outgoing, popular for his easy manner and his sense of humour. His brother Ralph says Ed had so many friends he was rarely home before 11pm. Like Geoff Harrow and other young climbers, Ed was too poor to afford any serious investment in the opposite sex – but no one worried about what they were missing because they were too busy climbing. Jude recalls that austerity ruled their lives. 'Ed never spent much on frivolities. He never smoked, and he biked to work every day. We earned very little really – after paying board, there was almost nothing left.'

About this time, Ed acquired some homing pigeons and built a walk-in cage for them. He would sometimes take them on the train to Arthur's Pass, releasing them some way up the line. But injuries from shotgun pellets, deaths from canker and the objections of neighbours soon spelled the end of that enterprise. He bought a 1928 Indian motorbike with a sidecar. Ralph recalls staying home from school to help fix it, the reward being a trip in the sidecar – only to have Ed power off up the road while the sidecar stayed still: a fairly typical Ed Cotter practical joke.

Weekends and holidays were reserved for the mountains. Most Fridays Ed and his friends would leave their bikes at the Christchurch Railway Station and catch the 6pm 'Perishable', the goods train to Arthur's Pass (cost 12s 6d), arriving at 2am. They would do their best to avoid paying the fare with various ruses such as stretching out in the luggage racks and hiding among the packs. It didn't always work. The young climbers would spend months planning for bigger trips over the holiday periods. These were usually serious attempts on unclimbed peaks of the Southern Alps, which took them over the Main Divide and down a West Coast river. 'All that planning just engrossed us. The idea of getting away from the city and having an adventure was a real enticement. We were young and very fit, and it was our way of escaping from a hemmed-in environment where we worked for a pittance.' Ed recalls one trip with Bruce Menzies, a lawyer in the Public Trust:

> He was a lot older than me, but decided he wanted to go to the Easter Camp and climb Mt Rolleston on the way. This turned out to be a very drawn-out exercise, as he was older and slower. But we eventually climbed Rolleston and descended via the Waimak Col to sleep that night in the Waimak River bivvy. The next morning we travelled down the river to reach Carrington and the rest of the party. They probably thought we were mad.

Ed counts himself fortunate to have been on two alpine crossings led by John Sampson, a regular climbing companion. Their routes took them up the Rakaia, through the Godley and beyond, and on each outing they climbed good summits and explored a number of West Coast valleys. 'John was a very competent leader and would have measured up to any mountaineer in the world I ever came across.' A trip over Christmas 1946 included Sampson, Robin Johnson, Eric Pilgrim, Jim Shipman, Alan Evans and Cotter. During the climb, after being hut-bound at the Lyell Hut, Johnson and Ed left the group on Christmas Day and headed for the Armoury Range between the Rakaia and Rangitata watersheds. They summited Amazon, The Warrior, Spearpoint, Bardolph and Pistol peaks, glissaded down the slopes and got back to their bivouac just after 9pm, very satisfied with themselves.[2] The next morning they rejoined the rest at the Lyell Hut, and later suggested several more gladiatorial names for features in the area. The rest of the trip took them via the Strachan Pass through to Hari Hari on 7 January.[3]

From 1946 Ed Cotter's name began to appear regularly in the 'Ascents' lists of the *Canterbury Mountaineer*. In addition, many articles recorded the fresh and daring challenges he and his friends sought, such as climbing 7037ft Mt Franklin near Arthur's Pass in time to catch the return trip by the Perishable.[4] (Two other names beginning to feature in the climbing journals were those of E. Hillary and G. Lowe, older climbers from the North Island who had come south to test

On the summit of Seymour: Stan Conway, John Sampson and Ed Cotter. Cotter collection

their skills.) In 1947, at the age of 19, Ed climbed Mt Greenlaw, regarded as a difficult peak. The group included Stan Conway, who with Tom Newth and Frank Gillett had planned a Himalayan adventure before the war intervened. Conway's attempts on Greenlaw were already in double figures before this trip, so he was determined this time. Conway's 'assault force' met at the Anti-Crow and, climbing separately but roped up on their way to the summit, in favourable conditions they made the top about 3pm. On the return Conway waited until darkness for Ed, who had decided to make a quick ascent of Mt Gizeh as well, as Conway wrote for the CMC:

> Ed demonstrated how fit a climber should be ... The next morning it was a pleasant trip to rejoin the others at the Anti-Crow, to end a good trip in the hills. Greenlaw, more than others, the last of the major peaks left for us to climb in the Arthur's Pass National Park, will always be foremost in my memory.[5]

In early December 1947 Ed and school friend John Ennis met at Arthur's Pass to attack the Otira face of Mt Rolleston, a climb that had not been attempted since 1936. Belaying was necessary up a steep snow couloir, and a deep avalanche groove made for awkward step-cutting. They managed to gain the safety of a rock ridge running parallel to another deep snow-filled couloir that ran the height of the mountain. At the head of the couloir the top snow began sliding away to expose hard frozen snow, so they took the alternative route to the summit, kicking steps to the col between the middle and high peaks, and descended via the Bealey route.[6]

Over the Christmas holiday period of 1947–48 Ed joined Sampson, Johnson, David Hall and George Lowe on the Godley–Whataroa crossing, led by Conway. There was much interesting climbing, plus a chance for Conway, Cotter and Sampson to sunbathe for three hours on the top of Seymour Peak on 3 January. The next day Lowe, Johnson and Cotter climbed Mts Moffat and Livingston. On their reconnaissance of a possible route out to the coast Cotter and Sampson employed some 'precarious acrobatics', as David Hall wrote,[7] but eventually proved astute pathfinders. With dwindling food supplies and heavy rain, the wet and cold party finally made it out to the Whataroa Hotel on 15 January.

That trip occasioned the frying-pan episode in the Public Trust tearoom, mentioned earlier. It was also the first time Cotter had climbed with George Lowe. He well remembers Lowe on the last day telling them that all they had was a prune each to eat on the way out. They were advised to eat the prune flesh for breakfast, suck the stone for lunch, then break open the stone and chew it for afternoon tea.

George Lowe and Ed Cotter in French Ridge Bivouac. After a 2.30am start they crossed the Bonar Glacier and reached the summit of Mt Aspiring at 10am. Archives New Zealand: AAQT 6401 A16595

As soon as they made it out to Whataroa, both made a beeline for the sweet shop, gobbled far more than their starved stomachs could handle, and together rushed out of the shop to throw up. Cotter said to Lowe, 'What a way to spend your birthday!' Lowe replied, 'How did you know it was my birthday?' Cotter's reply: 'No, it's mine!' Lowe: 'It's mine too!'

The following Christmas, 1948–49, Cotter, John Sampson and three other CMC stalwarts went in to the Barker Hut to carry out some repairs. Finding snow up to the windowsills, they climbed Harper and Speight instead.[8] A later hut-repair exercise featured an evening climb of Mt Murchison, when Cotter took up Sampson's challenge for an 'evening stroll'. They left the hut at 7.30pm and, taking the mountain straight up the glacier, reached the summit at 9pm. Navigating without lights, they were back at the hut by 11pm.[9]

In December 1949 Cotter, Lowe and Geoff Milne acted as guides for an attempt by 22-year-old photographer Brian Brake – one of Ed's former classmates at Christchurch Boys' High School – to make a 'cinematic poem' for the National Film Unit of a climbing expedition to Mt Aspiring. The art team included composer Douglas Lilburn, painter John Drawbridge and scriptwriter James K. Baxter, then just 23. Brake withdrew his team from the mountain when bad weather hit, but Baxter's notes later evolved into the much-loved poem 'In the Matukituki Valley', and in 2005 a Gibson Group documentary, *Aspiring*, used Brake's silent footage to tell the story. The climbers stayed on to make an ascent via the southwest ridge rising from the Bonar Glacier, which had been climbed only once previously, and descended down the more frequently used northwest ridge.[10]

For something to do in winter, Cotter and his climbing companions also took up skiing. Geoff Harrow knew the Arthur's Pass area backwards, having worked on Flock Hill Station and hunted deer in the Craigieburn Valley. Recalling the huge snowfalls and massive avalanches of 1944, he suggested Craigieburn as a valley that would be likely to hold the snow. John Sampson was very keen; unlike the others he had transport, so in July 1947, after some very heavy snows, they took off in Sampson's car on a reconnaissance trip, with Jude Cotter along for the ride. They left her at the car and scratched their way up the streambed until they could climb a hill and follow the ridge to have a good look down into the basin. Their impression was that it would make a great skifield. Harrow described the descent back to the car:

> It was our first time there in the winter, and there was just so much snow. To get back we had to drop down a long gut. Ed went first, then Johnny, sliding on the snow. I came last, and by then they must have worn the snow down. I felt a sharp jag as my trousers ripped. The rocks really opened me up and there was blood all over my backside when we made the car, where Jude had been waiting for seven or eight hours.[11]

The basin they located was quickly to become the Craigieburn skifield. CMC member Alan Evans was a passionate advocate, and in August a work party of 30 enthusiastic CMC members was enlisted to help Harry Walker, who was surveying the track using beer bottles as survey pegs. Over two days a benched track was forced as far as a big bluff halfway up the valley. The bluff looked impassable, but Walker and his helpers managed to blast a way past it, and by December the track went all the way through the beech forest on the south side of the valley above the creek to a selected hut site. In early February 1948 a 73-strong group packed in over seven tons of building materials.[12]

Brian Brake's film *Aspiring*, left unfinished as a silent sequence, was reincarnated as a documentary screened by the Gibson Group in 2006. Archives New Zealand: AAQT 6401 A16588

Gear for the Brian Brake expedition being packed up French Ridge to the bivouac. In the background are Mt Avalanche and the Maud Francis Glacier. Archives New Zealand: AAQT 6401 A16593

A climber watches fog clearing over Mt Avalanche during the Brake expedition. Taken from French Ridge, this photo shows how steeply Mt Avalanche falls away. Archives New Zealand: AAQT 6401 A16596

Three climbers on French Ridge during the Brake expedition. Above them is the Quarterdeck; Mt French is to the left. Archives New Zealand: AAQT 6401 A16592

Building parties carried on until Easter, when the hut was completed. Geoff Harrow was one of the staunchest: between July and April he spent 40 weekends working on the track. John Sampson organised installation of the 215m rope tow. The season opened at King's Birthday Weekend with much on-slope chaos and hilarity. The indulgent club executive was proud of 'about the best ski hut in the country, and an excellent access track, all in a few months!'[13] President Nui Robins suggested there was no limit to what the skiing section of the club could achieve – except win the New Zealand women's championship (the CMC was still an exclusively male club).

Aspiring Hut, Christmas 1949: Geoff Milne, Lois Aldridge, George Lowe and Ed Cotter. Cotter collection

The young climbers who decided to try skiing were all seriously fit and looking for ways to burn up their energy – and new opportunities for ski touring and ski mountaineering. Ed recalls that few of them actually knew how to ski. They used hickory skis with cable bindings, and nailed wedges of leather to the insteps of their tramping boots so they wouldn't buckle in the bindings. Unfortunately when wet the bindings didn't give much support, and broken ankles were not uncommon. 'When we started, we just liked the idea of getting down the hill quickly. I thought the whole point was to go straight down as fast as possible. But then people started slowing down and weaving around the slope, and we realised they were learning to turn.'[14]

The newly initiated skiers would leave Christchurch on Friday night, park at the end of the gravel road and hike up the track, arriving at the hut around midnight. That trip could take several hours as they carried up four-gallon (15 litre) drums of petrol, ski gear, and other fuel required for what became known as legendary parties. When Geoff Harrow wrote up the first successful season, he said the new ski tow allowed skiers to do as much downhill running in a weekend as they previously did in a season.

The first club championships were held in perfect weather. Ed Cotter didn't feature in the results: according to Harrow, he decided early in the downhill race it would be more interesting to burrow underneath than ski on the surface.[15] It was definitely a mixed sport, however, and the CMC's 'men only' rule was now under threat, though a number of old hands strenuously resisted the 'female invasion'. They also feared that as John Sampson improved the tows and the money started to roll in, the club's ski section might overwhelm its climbing section. As a result, in 1954 the Craigieburn Valley Ski Club was established, to which women were admitted.

Climbing took over again in summer. Equipment in those days was basic and consisted of crampons, rope, snow goggles, a waterproof jacket, a pack, warm clothes and an ice axe. Fitness, not gear, was the greatest asset on the mountains. Food was also basic: on one occasion Cotter and Barry Owen resorted to Etagone tablets, supplied to the armed forces during the war years in case of food shortages. They decided that for their attempt on McClure Peak at the head of the Havelock River they would try to use the tablets and very little else, which helped to keep their pack weight down to about 15lb each. They didn't make the top of the mountain, and by the time they drove home on Sunday afternoon they were ravenous. Later, dehydrated food made provisioning much easier.

Arthur's Pass was their favourite launch site: for young climbers with no transport it was easy to get to. As they sought new challenges in the area they became familiar with the terrain of the present-day Coast-to-Coast race: a tough weekend could involve getting off the train at Bealey, just before Arthur's Pass, heading up the Mingha River (at night) to Goat Pass, a break at the top then a scramble down to the West Coast side to climb a peak or two. They would then follow the river down to the railway track and make for Otira in time to catch the Perishable home on Saturday night. They were young, very fit and lived only for the mountains, '… so we did become a bit obsessed'.

In 1950 Cotter's world suddenly opened up when Earle Riddiford asked him to speak to the New Zealand Alpine Club. The subject was climbing in the Godley Valley, and the lantern-slides he used were part of a large collection collated by W.A. Kennedy, patron of the CMC until his death in 1950. Cotter took a light-hearted approach and the talk was enthusiastically received. As he sat down, Riddiford asked him if he would like to go to the Himalaya and do some climbing.

'I said, 'Yes, that sounds amazing.'''

And so to Mukut Parbat, and all that.

16. SOUTHWARD BOUND

Time out in the magnificent Hollyford Valley

The break-up at Ranikhet had been unsettling: Cotter's youthful naivety and ideal of comradeship had taken a severe knock.

In recovery mode he returned to Christchurch in September 1951– not envious and dejected, as Lowe suggests,[1] but out of a need to settle back into everyday reality: a man in his mid-twenties with exciting adventures under his belt, now forced to earn a living and work towards a future that might not involve soft rock and hard snow. After resuming work at Skellerups he was soon transferred to their Cotton Brothers wholesale section as a sales rep, travelling the east coast from Nelson to Otago selling all sorts of rubber products, including clothing and sports shoes, and even compering fashion shows for retailers.

Mountaineering was once again restricted to weekends and holidays. Nevertheless, there were still some fine ascents and memorable experiences with old friends. In October 1952 he and Peter Bain joined a party of 12, led by the wily veterans Stan Conway and Jack Pattle, to climb Tent Peak in the Arrowsmiths. They all reached the summit and returned to their hut in high spirits. A few weeks later the same group took an abortive look at the east ridge of Arrowsmith before returning down the Cameron River to Lake Heron, taking turns bumping down the rapids in a one-man inflatable rubber dinghy.

In January 1953, after climbing Mt Haidinger, Cotter was overnighting in a snow cave with Swiss mountain guide Hans Bohny while they helped build Pioneer Hut at the head of the Fox Glacier. Tasman was beckoning, so in what became known as a 'Tasman Before Breakfast' breakout, they set off at 1am on 2 January in clear conditions up the centre of the Marcel icefall, onto the Marcel Col, over Lendenfeld Peak then Engineer Col and up to the summit of Tasman (11,475ft) by 6.25am.[2] After a quick descent through West Coast cloud they were back around 8am. When the others awoke, they asked where the pair were going. 'Nowhere,' said Cotter. 'We've just been.'

At the old musterers' hut in the Cameron Valley, October 1952. From left, back row: Bob Watson, Ray Chapman, Russell Dawson, Stan Conway; middle row: Bill Hannah, Ed Cotter; front row: Roger Christmas, Allen Kelly, Jack Pattle, Ian Smith, Murray Harris. Peter Bain

The following Christmas he headed off with Conway, Bain, Harrow, Chapman and Bill Hannah on a training climb for the 1955 New Zealand Karakoram Expedition – essentially a CMC venture targeting Masherbrum (25,660ft) that was to be led by Conway. The trip into the Erewhon Col area began with a dodgy crossing of the Rakaia River to Manuka Point Station, followed by two days of heavy swagging up the Rakaia River bed. They crossed the Whitcombe Pass, arrived at Erewhon Col and set up camp on the ridge between the Ramsey Glacier and the Bracken Snowfield. Bain remembers three glorious successive days as Cotter's rope partner as they climbed the Amazons Breasts, Lauper Peak, Erewhon Peak, Mt Whitcombe, the Snow Dome, Red Lion Peak and Mt Evans. 'I still find it barely credible that we climbed in three days mountains that many had attempted and failed over the years. That we did so was largely due to Ed's sureness of foot, speed, balance, quick judgment and route-finding ability.'[3]

On New Year's Eve they opened a surprise package of whisky, cigars and nuts from a fellow climber, Bob Watson. The following day an Auster aircraft appeared over the ridge and dropped supplies intended for another group in the Garden of Eden, 45km south. There were 'delirious shouts of delight'[4] from the unintended recipients, who on the plane's return with another load were still sober enough to write a message in the snow redirecting the surprised pilot to the correct group. Then a nor'west storm sprang up, forcing them to abandon their tent and transfer to a snow cave. There they stayed for three days before descending to the Whitcombe Valley, where the infant Whitcombe River was in flood. Bain recalls Cotter's uncanny river-crossing skills and their hazardous trip down the riverbed:

> Once we were safely across to the desired bank, three of the party decided to camp in the bush, but Geoff Harrow, Ed and I pushed on in gathering darkness and torrential rain. More than once I was tempted to give up, but Ed encouraged me to carry on under and over huge rocks and through deep pools, waterfalls and tangled bush. I took a tumble down a house-sized rock, stoving in the pressure-cooker in my pack, but about 2am we smelled wood smoke and reached the dubious shelter of Cave Camp. There we dried out and decorated the river flat with overdue New Year balloons while awaiting the arrival of the other three.[5]

After the three-day tramp out to Hokitika, Cotter concluded that a journey home down a West Coast river valley after success on a Main Divide peak had completed an ideal mountain holiday.[6] It had been a wonderful trip with major climbs achieved in some lucky weather, though by the end they were all getting

Ed Cotter at Cave Camp, Whitcombe Valley, New Year 1954. Peter Bain.

thinner and thinner, restricted to one pound of food a day including an experiment with dehydrated meat, which provided some excellent stews. Though not as young as the others, Conway, like Earle Riddiford, was a meticulous planner who would cut the handle off a toothbrush to keep the weight down in such conditions.

Back in Christchurch, Cotter felt unsettled and uncertain of his direction. Still considering further climbing in the Himalaya, he wrote to Riddiford saying he would prefer a quiet exploratory trip to a large-scale expedition.[7] He was also tiring of city life: many of his close friends were returned servicemen who spent a lot of time partying.

> I fitted into the party scene easily enough I guess, but eventually I sickened of the frivolity and wanted something more real in my life. It wasn't women at that stage, although I was already 27. I knew that once you had a permanent girlfriend that meant marriage and children, a huge commitment. That was a scary prospect, because I knew I couldn't cope with it emotionally or financially. The alternative was to escape to the outdoors.[8]

Had Cotter decided to join the 1955 CMC Karakoram expedition he would have been the only one with sustained Himalayan experience. But during the planning stages in 1954 he withdrew his name, explaining to Riddiford that the unwelcome prospect of returning to New Zealand penniless – again – and having to settle down again to a job at £12 per week weighed more strongly than his desire to attempt Masherbrum.[9]

At this time jetboats were being developed and tested by the Hamiltons at Irishman Creek, and Cotter's climbing friend Guy Mannering was involved in some of the early trials. Cotter was offered a job there, but while he was thinking about it he heard of a cattle farmer in the lower Hollyford Valley, in Fiordland, who had a vacancy for a musterer. On the spur of the moment he decided that would be his next move.

Soon he was on the train south, loaded up with a Skellerup rubber mattress because he knew he would be sleeping rough. He was about to meet the legendary Davey Gunn, who battled isolation and difficult terrain running cattle on leased land at Martins Bay, the southernmost cattle run on the West Coast. Born at Hakataramea, Gunn had left his wife and children in Oamaru and moved to the Hollyford in 1926. For 30 years he toiled in the bush, his annual draft of 70–100 cattle yielding a meagre income. Supplies were delivered yearly to Martins Bay or Big Bay by the lighthouse steamer; Gunn's nearest neighbour was George Shaw at Elfin Bay on Lake Wakatipu, 80km away. The challenges of farming amid

Ed (right) learns the art of a cook-up in Davey Gunn's open-plan kitchen. Cotter collection

the rainforests, lakes and rivers of the Hollyford, Pyke and Kaipo valleys were compounded by atrocious weather that caused all sorts of setbacks: washed-out tracks, impassable fords and bridges and huts swept away.

But Gunn seems to have relished his lonely, frugal way of life. A quiet man of immense physical strength, he was guiding trampers and climbers through the district from the early 1930s. Gradually he opened up the area, cutting one track up the Pyke River and another south towards Milford. He spanned rivers with cages and cables and welcomed all who tramped the tracks, climbed the mountains, studied the wildlife or simply came to admire the magnificent scenery.

On 30 December 1936 a fatal plane crash at Big Bay catapulted Davey Gunn and his beloved Hollyford into newpaper headlines. Invercargill journalist Sutton Jones lost his life, and Gunn played a huge part in the dramatic rescue of the four survivors. Already in his late forties, he made a 21-hour dash on foot and by dinghy to raise the alarm from the Public Works phone at Marian Corner, 90km from the beach via Martins Bay, Lake McKerrow and Hidden Falls, a journey that normally took four days.[10] This astonishing feat captured everyone's imagination

Mustering days: cattle at the top end of Lake Alabaster with Mt Madeline in the background.
Cotter collection

and made him an instant folk-hero. He was subsequently awarded the Coronation Medal and a memorial stone was erected at Marian Corner.

Publicity around the Big Bay rescue attracted more adventure seekers to the area. Gunn offered them a trip down Lake McKerrow on a converted lifeboat called *Fiordland*, and a unique 'pioneer experience' at Deadmans Hut and later at Hollyford ('Gunn's') Camp. As more people came, he enlarged the sleeping quarters around his huts at Deadmans, Hidden Falls and Martins Bay. It was all still rather primitive, but that was part of the attraction. The visitors loved their outback experiences, and interest kept growing. World War II put a stop to all that until 1945, but in the summer of 1950 more than 300 walkers went through.

When Ed Cotter met Davey Gunn, the tough old legend was 67 years old and still living mostly by himself, apart from the men who came for his twice-yearly musters. Gunn called the Hollyford 'The Land of Doing Without' and had little time for 'modern inconveniences'.[11] Jack Jenkins, who also worked in the Hollyford with Cotter, described Gunn as 'made of horse-shoe nails and whipcord'.[12]

When he first arrived at the ramshackle Gunn's Camp by bus from Te Anau, Cotter wrote to Earle Riddiford with his first impressions of the weather-beaten, gruff old stockman:

> Dave Gunn is a real old-timer, very kind and jolly good company, but contrary to the point where one could scream at him. He builds everything from the bush, will spend ten minutes straightening a rusty nail, and on the subject of huts is convinced that a mud floor is better than tongue and groove – so there are difficulties. His son Murray (30) is here, a likeable bloke, and the idea is that Murray and I will take over the tourist and cattle business.[13]

The camp was rudimentary. It consisted of one main building with a corrugated iron fireplace and chimney, plus a couple of workers' huts for Ed and for Jack Jenkins, who would arrive later. Jenkins was very experienced; Ed Cotter certainly was not. When three weeks of bad weather kept him at camp doing nothing, he became very lonely and bored. Gunn suggested he go to look at the Hidden Falls Hut 10km down the track.

> I was given a horse called George to carry my pack and food, but after riding half an hour I decided it would be more comfortable walking. I dismounted and sent George on ahead. That was a mistake, because an hour later when I got close to

him, he just trotted off. Two hours later, with our destination not far away, he had still not allowed me to catch another ride. Even worse, all that time he knew where he was going, and I didn't.

In the corrugated iron Hidden Falls Hut, Cotter prepared a fern bed and attempted to heat some food by candlelight. Within minutes all the mice in the hut had appeared to sit on the table and share his meal. 'The next day I returned to Gunn's Camp holding George by the bridle.'

The muster could take from two to four months as the men followed a trail along the coastline and up the valleys looking for cattle in the bush. It was dangerous work as the cattle were half wild; Gunn's team of dogs would seek them out in the dense bush while the musterers on horseback stuck to more open country. The autumn muster from February to April concentrated on identifying, castrating and marking cattle, and in the spring muster (October to December) they would select about 100 animals to sell.[14] Once the stock were mustered, getting them across the Hollyford River was another hurdle. The men would drive them to the mouth of the lagoon, cross it and continue upriver until opposite the hut, at which point they would stampede them into the river so that they crossed and came out downstream.[15]

On the annual drive out, the musterers went from Martins Bay to the Pyke River and out to Gunn's Camp. From there they had a 100km trek to Te Anau and on to the Mossburn Railway Station, where the cattle would be dispatched to the Lorneville saleyards near Invercargill. Gunn enjoyed stopping with farmers on the way who provided a paddock to put the cattle in overnight. Cotter remembers Johnny Chartres from Te Anau Downs, who brought out a bottle of whisky. The next night Gunn picked up the same bottle and invited Chartres to have one on him, as if it were his own.[16]

Occasionally Cotter had to take to a tree to escape a marauding cattle beast. On one occasion at the end of a long day Murray Gunn forgot to secure the fences around the camp and during the night about 20 cattle escaped, as Cotter recollects:

> We had to chase them downstream, round them up and chase them all back again. There was a tricky moment when I was trying to dig out an animal that had fallen into a two-metre-deep trench. I was trying to take out the end of the trench, but he decided to go for me instead of for freedom, and I had to run for cover as fast as I could. That was pretty close.

Gunn relied heavily on horses and dogs in conditions that were swampy, sandfly-ridden and often dangerous. A lot was expected of the horses, but they appeared to have a sixth sense for finding their way around. At night Gunn would lie along his horse's back; when the horse stopped he knew he had arrived at the next hut. One night Cotter was riding a horse called Charlie when his mount stopped in the pitch dark and refused to move. A huge tree was blocking the track. Cotter could see very little, but eventually found a way around it, after which Charlie led him to the hut.[17] Gunn's dogs were always well cared for and were devoted to their master. Cotter acquired his own sheepdog from Te Anau and called it Scenario – he thought it gave a very ordinary-looking animal a bit more class.[18]

Many of Cotter's vivid memories of Gunn's Camp relate to food. 'We lived in the most basic conditions you can possibly imagine. It was really a broken-down hovel of a hut, where we ate porridge and venison, surrounded most of the time by sandflies.' Once a week they would make a round of bread in the camp oven. There were occasional fish, which they caught in the lagoon at Martins Bay, but

Davey Gunn and Ed at Hollyford Camp before the start of a muster. Cotter collection

Ed at Martins Bay. Cotter collection

their meat was frequently flyblown. Gunn would brush the maggots off before cooking it. On one occasion after they had been roughing it for some days he asked Cotter if some fruit would be a good idea. Cotter agreed it would, so Gunn sprinkled a few sultanas onto their porridge.

Davey Gunn was notorious for stinting on food – and just about everything else. Over time, his clients began to expect more, and Cotter found it embarrassing when he was asked to take tours through and show them their fern bunks and draughty huts.[19] He saw scope for greatly enhancing the tourism side of the operation, as he wrote to Riddiford:

> The tourist business is at a low ebb on account of the state of the huts and a lack of advertising. The cattle are left year round without much attention, and the deer cause a lot of trouble during winter months when grass is in short supply. Both businesses could be built up considerably: the valley is very scenic, with Mt Tutoko and Mt Madeline handy and in sight, and with Milford well known and close by it should be possible to attract more tourist business as well as improving the amenities and patronage.[20]

Jack Jenkins (left) driving cattle up the lower Hollyford River. Cotter collection

Cotter's work also involved mountain guiding, helping clients like Ruth Chartres of Te Anau Downs in her 1954 ascent of Mt Eglinton, and the potential for such guided tours was huge. In the early months of 1955 he was thinking seriously about an operation in the Routeburn Valley. 'The track up to Harris Saddle is neglected, so I'm after a contract this winter to clear it and open it for organised tours.'[21] Meanwhile Gunn was losing money and tiring of the whole operation, and in June 1955 he agreed to sell to his son Murray, Cotter and

A hunting party at Pyke River. On the left is Harry Walker of the CMC; Ed (back to camera) is saddling up his horse. Cotter collection

Jenkins: Jenkins would run the farm while Cotter and Murray Gunn looked after the tourists.[22] From Cascade Creek, Cotter wrote to tell Riddiford the news: 'Three of us are supposed to be taking over the Hollyford. Dave Gunn wants £10,000 payable in ten years, interest 5%, annual income £3500 including tourist £1000 – all pretty run down, and I'm the same after nine months down there.'[23]

The sale plan foundered, however, when Gunn Senior imposed too many conditions. An undeterred Cotter continued to investigate other options, telling Riddiford that Arch Scott, Riddiford's sharebroker friend, had taken him under his wing:

> He is keen to build a hotel at Manapouri, a classy 50-bedroom tourist joint, and I'm to look after all the outside activities: everything seems set to go, the Tourist Department having given their blessing. I'm running a six day fishing, hunting and shooting trip this summer from Lake Wakatipu to Mavora Lakes: there are so many likely opportunities here, it's difficult to know what to take. I almost

applied for Antarctica: but this country is good enough, very lonely though. I talked so much in Christchurch about coming down here that I just can't go back now.[24]

At that stage Gunn agreed to give Cotter first option on the tourism business.[25] He spent a weekend with the Riddifords in Wellington, delighted by the small Belinda and Rosemary's excellent cooking, but he could report only poor bookings for Mavora. Plans for the Manapouri hotel had been shelved until the Tourist Hotel Corporation could find sufficient funding, and a climbing trip to the Hermitage area with clients was a write-off owing to fresh snow. That was how things stood when, on Christmas Day 1955, Davey Gunn and three others left Hollyford Camp for Pyke Hut. At the lower ford just before the Hidden Falls Hut Gunn's horse, Dick, went down in the swift current and Gunn was swept away along with Warren Shaw, the 12-year-old schoolboy mounted behind him.

Gunn's body was never found. Cotter, in Queenstown for Christmas, was contacted with the bad news and an invitation to join the search party, which he declined. The lower Hollyford was a big, broken, very challenging river, and he felt Davey Gunn was probably where he would want to be. But he says his time with Gunn helped shape the way he has thought since: 'I picked up a lot of his ways and his thought processes, things like making do with nothing and fixing whatever needed fixing, even if you had nothing much to fix it with.'[26]

After Gunn's death, Cotter found himself moving to Gore in typically serendipitous circumstances. While driving one night he hit a tree not far from the Gore Railway Station, and had to leave his van there. The next day, during a chance conversation in a sports shop, he heard that Gore had the best 'golden mile' in New Zealand – for making money.[27] Two months later when visiting Gore again to sell boats for a friend, he returned to the store. Almost immediately he found himself signed up as tenant of a new shop just being built. The only problem was he had nothing to sell, but photography was a possibility, as he was a keen cameraman and was used to helping out a photographer friend in Queenstown. For three months until the building was completed he took a job in Christchurch with the photographic equipment supplier H.E. Perry, where he was able to learn more about his intended new profession.

During this time he picked up whatever opportunities he could to climb. One of these was a Mt Cook weekend escapade with Brian Hearfield, Allan Foot and Jack Ede, who aimed to be the first party to climb the mountain over a weekend. An unofficial competition was under way, governed by a gentlemen's agreement ruling that contestants were not to leave Christchurch before 5pm on

In Christchurch with Scenario: Ed (left) with his sisters Judith and Cecily and brother Ralph.
Jude Horn

Friday and had to be back at work on the following Monday morning. As Ede describes it,[28] their attempt was a highly memorable outing. Hearfield borrowed a decrepit Commer truck with a defective cooling fan, a fragile canvas canopy and an open back that sucked in the dust, and when the team picked up Ed Cotter he brought an extra climber to the party: Scenario. Travelling on the back with Cotter and his dog, Ede found any sleep impossible. In the early hours of the morning they pulled into Unwin Hut just out of Mount Cook Village, where they slept briefly before Hearfield woke them for the drive up to Ball Hut. Some time was lost when Cotter discovered one of his boots was missing and they had to make a quick detour to the Hermitage to borrow another pair. From Ball Hut it was another four hours before the combined company reached Haast Hut, with Scenario having to be coaxed over some of the obstacles. Steps were then kicked to the top of Glacier Dome, overlooking the Linda Glacier, to provide a suitable trail for the morning.

For their attack on Cook the party left the hut at 1am, climbing up their steps over the top of Glacier Dome and down across the Grand Plateau, past Teichelmann's Corner and into the crevassed Linda Glacier. With access to the top of Zeubriggens Ridge cut off by a large schrund, Cotter began cutting up Greens Couloir. But by noon, the deadline before retreat, they were still well below the icecap, and the lack of sleep was taking its toll, so they turned their backs on the mountain. It proved to be a hot, tiring evening as Cotter coaxed his exhausted dog down with him. There was a nightmare diversion in the dark a little too close to the Hochstetter Icefall before they finally made it by torchlight through the moraine to the truck at Ball Hut, where they found a group of kea had ripped the canopy to shreds.

After a couple of fords on the way back to the Hermitage the brakes failed and the truck collided with the hotel front porch. Scenario leapt out to accost elegant hotel guests, and bar patrons were astonished by the ghoulish, dust-covered occupants. Worse was to follow. Hearfield, the driver, fell asleep on the way back to Pukaki and the vehicle veered across the road, flipped and flung Cotter, Foot and Scenario onto the road verge with a pile of ice axes, crampons and packs. As oil poured out of the engine, the climbers tried to right the vehicle, a job that took another hour. Cotter and Hearfield walked to the (closed) Pukaki petrol station where they commandeered some cans of oil that were outside, leaving their names and addresses for the sleeping proprietor. Taking turns to drive back to Christchurch, the men were all equally smelly, and no doubt the canine member of the party was too, but they were only half an hour late for work. A fortnight later, Hearfield and Foot returned with John Harrison and Wynne Croll in a more reliable vehicle, and dogless, and made the ascent within the official time limits.

Cotter's new photographic venture got off to a shaky start. He had just £100 to invest in stock and not enough change for the till. But he was to spend 10 years as a photographer in Gore, working at weddings, parties and dances. It was a job he enjoyed, though he certainly didn't make his fortune.

17. THE 1964 NEW ZEALAND ANDEAN EXPEDITION

Alpamayo by accident

Although still dedicated to the mountains, Ed Cotter was too busy for serious climbing – let alone a serious relationship. But through a friend in the Southland section of the NZAC, in 1959 he met Jennifer Allen. Ed found her attractive and easy to talk to. 'She was smart and bright, with lots of confidence, and somehow it just happened.'

From a well-known family who farmed near Lake Hauroko, inland from Tuatapere, Jen worked in Invercargill as a doctor's receptionist. She says falling for Ed was easy:

> Ed's defining feature was charm. As soon as I met him, I just adored him. He was gorgeous looking, absolutely delicious, and very, very funny, which was a huge draw. During that first party he just performed all night, involving everyone who was there, and had everyone in fits. He would have been marvellous on stage. He was just so different, and I fell madly, madly in love with him.

Ed also charmed her parents, Sydney and Doris Allen, and was invited to stay at the farm at weekends. The romance blossomed at a great pace. Jen's brother King recalls how any expedition involving Ed would be a lot of fun. On one occasion, Jen, King and Ed went to a ball in Dunedin; when

Ed and Jen not long after they had met early in 1959. Cotter collection

the ball finished at 2am Ed decided it would be a great idea to walk the track into Doubtful Sound. They piled into a vehicle, drove through Balclutha to the power station at Manapouri and struggled to the top of the pass where the snow was

The wedding day, 31 August 1959, All Saints Church, Invercargill. Cotter collection

six feet deep – Ed still in his dinner suit. That rather rugged experience was one of the few times Ed and Jen climbed together.

During the months before they were married on 31 August 1959, Jen experienced a number of 'Cotteresque' adventures, which culminated in a honeymoon in a Catlins crib where they were overwhelmed by the stench of crayfish. The owner, a friend Ed boarded with in Gore, had failed to tell them that locals often tailed their catch on the beach. The next day the newly-weds headed for Christchurch in Ed's old V8, which kept breaking down – Jen had to push while Ed steered. When they finally returned to Gore the flat they were expecting to live in was nowhere near ready.

In quick succession they had three children: Jacqueline, Elisabeth and Guy. Ed took on a travel agency for South Pacific Airlines of New Zealand (SPANZ, a forerunner to Ansett), which he ran in conjunction with the photography shop. Those years with his young family were enjoyably busy. Ed played a part in the establishment of the Eastern Southland Search and Rescue Organisation, lending his experience to rescues and building up a network of good friends, including one who owned an aeroplane and was able to help Ed organise climbs for groups of visitors. Such expeditions gave him some freedom from routine.

Jen was pregnant with their fourth child when Ed's old friends Mike and Jean Nelson invited him to climb in South America. Ed had met Mike through CMC climbing trips when the latter was a student at Lincoln University: in the early 1960s, while employed by a research institute in California, Nelson had been posted to the Argentine for two years and had climbed extensively in the Andes. Ed failed to see any reason why he should not accept his invitation for 1964, and Jen, who was to give birth just a few months before the trip, was adamant that if Ed went, she would too. Around the same time the bank manager summoned Ed into his office to tell him he was in overdraft. The only money they had was

1964: Guy, Jen, Anton, Jacqueline, Ed and Elisabeth. Cotter collection

£180 that Jen had been saving for a washing machine. To complicate matters, Ed had no idea who would look after the shop. His Andes aspirations were saved by a young woman who walked in off the street. She had worked for Kodak, and agreed to look after the business as well as their house.

According to Jen the final decision was swayed by her parents' offer to pay for her fare and for baby Anton to be cared for by a Karitane nurse while she was away. Guy went to Ed's sister Jude; Elisabeth and Jacqui stayed with friends on a farm just out of Gore. As Ed and Jen flew out on a DC-3, Ed persuaded the pilot to fly off course so they could wave goodbye to the two girls. There was snow on the ground, which made picking out the house difficult, but as they zoomed over the farm, sure enough, there were the two little girls running outside in their pyjamas to catch a last glimpse of their parents.

Before Ed left New Zealand a piece of doggerel published in the local newspaper showed he had quite a following:

I notice that Ed Cotter now
Is headed for the Andes;
No doubt he's taking pemmican

And dried fruits, sweets and candies.
He'll climb the Andes with a team
Of expert mountaineers
And of their safety I have not
The slightest doubts or fears.
The climbing may get hot at times
And other times still hotter.
But that should never worry such
  An expert as Ed Cotter.[1]

The writer was wrong. In Peru, Ed Cotter was to spend the longest, most horrific night of his life clinging to an ice face after his climbing partner suffered a traumatic accident. As that slow-motion drama played itself out, Ed thought his number was up. But there was a happy outcome after a heroic rescue during which Ed had to draw on all the survival strategies he had absorbed over the years.

The 1964 New Zealand Andean Expedition, as it became known, was a private venture, though minor assistance was given by the Everest Foundation, NZAC, CMC and various New Zealand suppliers and manufacturers. The party planned a month in Bolivia targeting Ancohuma (21,000ft) and surrounding peaks in the Cordillera Real.[2] This would be followed by another month in Peru with an assault on more serious objectives in the ice peaks of the Cordillera Blanca,[3] Peru's chief climbing attraction, where the highest peak, Huascaràn (22,205ft), gives its name to the national park that surrounds it. But probably Peru's best-known mountain is the dramatically ice-fluted Alpamayo (19,511ft), widely regarded as the world's most beautiful mountain.[4] The first attempt on Alpamayo was made by the Swiss in 1948, and its first ascent in 1957 was by a German party that included Günter Hauser, who praised Alpamayo's overwhelming visual appeal:

> From one side it looks like a symmetrical pyramid, its flanks covered with gigantic cornices, but the other aspect of Alpamayo, the trapeze-shaped south-west wall, is even more beautiful: here the noonday sun scorching down on it almost perpendicularly combines with currents of damp air rising from the jungle to cloak it in a mantle of fine powder snow that gives Alpamayo the appearance of a white cathedral.[5]

The New Zealand party was aiming high, but they had much combined experience. In July 1959 Mike Nelson had led a CMC party to within 300 feet

of the summit of Chopicalqui, at 20,846ft Peru's fourth-highest peak. In 1960 he and his wife Jean (née Adams, sister of Ruth Adams who was rescued on La Perouse) had joined John Tothill and Christchurch climber Don Mackay to form the First New Zealand Andean Expedition, when the Nelsons and Mackay had achieved a notable success by climbing Huascaràn. Mackay was also to be a member of the 1964 party, his third climbing trip to the Andes. For some time he had been organising things from the Christchurch end, in collaboration with Nelson, an economist then working in Buenos Aires.

With so many incredible mountains to climb, Ed found the prospect of joining this party irresistible. He had always enjoyed Nelson's company and found him an engaging easy-going man who laughed a lot and never got rattled. The group also included Harold Jacobs, a 32-year-old park ranger from Te Anau.

Knowing only too well that 'mañana'[6] was the order of the Latin-American day, Mackay went ahead in April to battle local customs and other government departments. The Cotters sailed to Panama, then flew to the Peruvian capital of Lima with Jacobs. There was excitement even before they landed, because the authorities had forgotten to turn on the landing lights for their 2am arrival. The plane circled for 40 minutes, then flew several hundred kilometres to an air force base where they spent the rest of the night.[7] While Mackay organised stores and equipment, the Cotters spent a week visiting Inca ruins in Cusco and Machu Picchu before most of the party assembled in La Paz, the administrative capital of Bolivia, on 19 May. Their crossing into Bolivia involved an all-night journey across Lake Titicaca, followed the next morning by the glorious sight of the Cordillera Real.

With Mike Nelson yet to arrive, the party trucked its gear across the Altiplano to Warizata, a hill village under Ancohuma. There they made contact with the Aymara Indians from whom they hoped to hire donkeys to move equipment to a base camp at 14,000ft in the Chearucu Valley. These Indians, traditionally rebels against authority, were most suspicious of strangers they believed to be prospectors. But Pacho and Edgar, two Bolivian members of the Club Andino Boliviano[8] seconded to the expedition to act as interpreters and as guards at base camp, were useful negotiators. They were able to arrange a burro team, which arrived with its *arrieros* (donkey drivers) at 3am on 28 May and left the village fully loaded. During a trying day's travel over a 15,500ft ridge, however, the Aymara teamsters stopped intermittently to demand higher payment. Finally, at 4pm, they mutinied and departed with their burros. Still 5km from base camp, the party pitched camp on the shore of Lago San Francisco. The next day Jean Nelson, who had developed symptoms of pulmonary oedema, left with Edgar for

Harold Jacobs at their high camp on Ancohuma, Bolivia. Mike Nelson

Warizata. She returned to La Paz by truck to await her husband's arrival, by which time she had recovered.

Meanwhile Mackay, Jacobs and Cotter, with the help of some local Indians and their horses, repacked the gear and established a base camp at 14,000ft against a moraine wall in the Chearucu Valley, from which they explored possible climbs. Their first trip was to the glacier at the head of the Chearucu, and they also climbed to 17,000ft on Ancohuma. In anticipation of the Nelsons' arrival, they moved into a high camp at 16,000ft. The next day, 2 June, they climbed their first Bolivian peaks, Kasiri Oeste (18,900ft) and Kasiri Aguja (19,000ft), both first ascents, but abandoned the summit ridge to Kasiri itself (19,200ft) owing to fatigue and heavy fog.[9] The next day they made another first ascent of an unnamed peak at 19,300ft, for which they suggested the name Arichiri (the Sharpener). With the Nelsons' arrival, they packed back to base camp to rest.

The team planned to improve their acclimatisation before attempting Ancohuma, then re-establish their high camp. But when Pacho and Edgar did not return from a visit to Warizata, Jean and Jen agreed to remain at base camp, which would otherwise have been wide open to herders and their llamas. By now the weather was settled, and it stayed so for their remaining 20 days in Bolivia. On 6 June the four men left at 7am for another attempt on the Kasiri peaks.

Mackay and Jacobs cramponed up an 800ft face to reach the Kasiri summit before midday, its second ascent, while Cotter and Nelson settled for an easy climb of Kasiri Aguja. The next day Nelson, Jacobs and Mackay completed an exhausting slog on high snow peaks to enjoy a panoramic view from a twin-peak summit they named Taparacu (Butterfly Peak). After this they packed up their high camp to move back to base and were met halfway by Cotter, who relieved them of some of their burden.

Mackay, Jacobs and Cotter had already sorted out a suitable Camp 1 site on the edge of the ice at 17,500ft from which they could launch their assault on Ancohuma, Bolivia's second-highest mountain. On 9 June the climbing party packed food and equipment to the site, a gruelling 3500ft climb. On their return to base they found that Edgar had made a brief reappearance and then vanished again after two days. The New Zealanders realised the whole expedition would have flowed more smoothly without the two Bolivian rascals.[10] Once again, Jen would have to remain behind as 'base camp wallah'. On 10 June, Jean moved up with the climbing party to Camp 1 with the intention of climbing further, but for the second time was affected by altitude and returned to keep Jen company at base camp.

A spot for Camp 2 was chosen high on the glacier under Ancohuma. After an 800ft climb in firm snow, the four heavily laden men struggled up the seemingly endless glacier under hot sun on a perfect windless day. They dumped their burdens at about 18,700ft, but the repeat performance the next day left Nelson 'in a condition where I was ready to retire from mountaineering on the spot'.[11] At a very low ebb, they were in their sleeping bags as soon as the tent was standing. 'I was unable to assist in either the preparation of the camp or the meal, but lay quietly in the sack and meekly accepted whatever food and drink was handed out,' Nelson wrote.[12]

On 13 June they set off at 8.30am through soft snow towards Ancohuma's knife-edge west ridge. Soon steeper crampon conditions led them across a hard snow face, and they were on the ridge at 10am. By midday they had reached a broad snow shelf at 20,500ft where they stopped for lunch. Then Mackay took the lead, consolidating steps in unstable snow until they reached the wind-swept summit at 2pm. This was the mountain's third ascent. They could see Lake Titicaca, the blue, yellow and brown altiplano, and lazy spirals of smoke in the valleys below, but the view over the Amazon forest was obscured by haze. A shortcut on two ropes enabled the party to return to camp in two hours.

The next day a stiff crampon climb took them to the shoulder and then the

Ed on the approach to Ancohuma. Mike Nelson

On the summit of Ancohuma: Harold Jacobs, Ed Cotter and Don Mackay. Mike Nelson

summit of Huachana (20,900ft, its second ascent) and back to camp in six hours. Jacobs then persuaded Cotter to undertake another climb of a 19,500ft peak, but 200ft from the summit they turned back because of the time-consuming work required to cut across intervening ice flutings. On 15 June the team moved back down to the glacier, loaded up the rest of Camp 1, and headed down to the Chearucu Valley camp. The Nelsons then climbed Arichiri while the others watched from base. The same day, burros arrived for their carry-out to Warizata, a journey that went smoothly. The Cotters were able to spend a few days in the delightful hillside town of Sorata before rejoining the group in La Paz and flying out to Lima.

The process of transferring everything to a base camp in Peru took longer than expected. Mackay left by truck with the expedition gear bound for Huaraz, nestled 500km north of Lima in the fertile Santa Valley between the Cordillera Negra to the west and the Cordillera Blanca to the east.[13] The others went by service car. On 25 June they set off together from Huaraz by hired truck with their equipment and two porters, Jacinto and Alberto, for the town of Caraz at 7000ft. There they were offered 10 burros for immediate departure and left in high spirits, pleased to be quickly away from the dirty, fly-infested town.[14] They took a 3000ft climb by bridle path to the village of Cashapampa where they settled for the night on the porch of an empty hacienda, to the annoyance of the

A burro team from Caraz climbs 3000ft by bridle path. Ed Cotter

Don Mackay, Mike Nelson, Jen Cotter and Harold Jacobs sample *chicha*, the Peruvian corn beer. Ed Cotter

drunken caretaker who arrived later. Nelson argued with him in Spanish for two hours before the impassioned custodian was eventually silenced by a cash offer.

Ed Cotter called this shot 'The Burro's Revenge'. *Ed Cotter*

In the morning they moved up the Santa Cruz valley through an impressive canyon, and by 4pm had established a comfortable base camp at 13,000ft. Next day they paid off their *arrieros* and spent some time identifying objectives: unfortunately the only guide they had was Kinzl and Schneider's map drawn in the 1930s. As they would soon find out, the German map was wrong. Nelson would later confess that the members of the expedition spent much of their time in a haze as to their exact whereabouts.[15]

From a reconnaissance point on a rocky ridge at 16,000ft they were convinced that they had identified access and routes to three objectives: Artesonraju, 19,767ft;[16] Quitoraju, 19,816ft;[17] and a virgin ice peak at 19,000ft. The mountains looked terrifying, however, and there was considerable uncertainty about the climbability

Moving up the Santa Cruz valley. *Ed Cotter*

Taking a break in the Cordillera Blanca. From left: Mike Nelson, Don Mackay, an unidentified local and John Ireland. Ed Cotter

of fluted ridges that rose sheer from the upper glaciers. At this stage a young English climber, John Ireland, wandered into base camp and was invited to join the team, and Jean returned to Buenos Aires.

The party established two camps en route for an attempt on the virgin: Camp 1 at 15,000ft on the edge of the ice, three hours from base, and Camp 2 on a 17,000ft col east of the summit, from which they expected to see the superb ice peak of Alpamayo. Instead, a sheer 3000ft drop onto a steeply sloping glacier confronted them. Reasonably well acclimatised, the four decided to settle in at Camp 2.

1 July was a perfect climbing day. Cotter and Jacobs were to tackle the east ridge of the virgin and perhaps push for the summit; Nelson and Mackay were to crampon down to the glacier, reach the basin on the north side and examine the north ridge. As soon as they set off Cotter and Jacobs realised what a huge task they had been set. Just 3 metres from camp they began a steep crampon climb up onto the narrow ridge, Jacobs climbing strongly with Cotter belaying him on each section, while they yodelled to the others fighting their way through the slots on the glacier far below. At 3.30pm Nelson and Mackay finally gained the north ridge at 18,300ft, but Alpamayo was nowhere to be seen, and owing to this and other map anomalies, at 4pm they retraced their steps in some confusion. During the day they had last sighted Cotter and Jacobs about a third of the way along the

Harold Jacobs, lost on Alpamayo. With the benefit of hindsight, members of the 1964 NZ Andean Expedition recognised this as the east ridge of the world's 'most beautiful mountain'. Ed Cotter

east ridge, and so assumed they had returned to Camp 2. As Nelson and Mackay approached camp just on darkness they yelled to the others to get a brew on: but there was no one there.

At 4pm when Cotter and Jacobs were deciding whether to turn back or not, they opted to descend the unknown south face of the mountain. They made

Alpamayo in late afternoon, about an hour before the accident. Ed Cotter

their way down steep snow and ice slopes until the light failed, not knowing their height above the glacier or their exact position. Visibility was so poor that when Nelson and Mackay called out, they shouted back that they would spend the night out. As they set about finding a bivvy site on the slopes below, snow conditions provided good shaft belays and for an hour they made some progress. Then came a calamitous sequence of moves.

Held from above, Jacobs double-roped down an ice-coated gully that apparently offered access to the lower slopes. Then, belaying Cotter from below, Jacobs suggested he make his descent face inwards, using his pick as a belay. But the slope was too severe, and with great difficulty Cotter returned to his former position. A fixed belay from above was essential. Jacobs climbed back up, with the help of Cotter's belay. Then Cotter double-roped down to Jacobs' previous belay position and made sure of a shaft belay for his partner's descent. Jacobs sidled over the lip of the ice chute, kicked in his front points, descended another step, and then fell off the slope. He hit the ice about 6 metres above Cotter, then shot past in the darkness. The belay pulled him to a stop near the bottom of the gully, but on the way through Jacobs had already yelled that his leg was broken. He wrote later that just how it happened was unclear:

> I descended three feet, crampons hardly scratching the surface. What happened next is rather vague. There was a bang and a sudden dull pain, I wasn't sure where. I fell head first for an instant, then before the rope came tight I knew by the way it swung round that my leg was broken. My first feeling was of damnable annoyance. Thank goodness I still had the axe in my hand. As Ed hurried down to me, doing well in the dark, I abused him for taking so long as I felt I couldn't hold on to the axe long.[18]

As Cotter recalled,

> There I was clinging to an ice face hundreds of feet above the glacier, with Harold dangling fifty feet below me. If the belay hadn't held, we both would have shot a very long way down. As it was, I had to talk him into getting over onto his stomach and trying to get his ice axe in, which would enable me to take the tension off the rope, all the time hoping he didn't black out before I got down to him.[19]

With extreme caution, Cotter withdrew the shaft belay and edged down to Jacobs. Mindful of the danger from falling ice, he lowered the injured climber another 5 metres on a belay and moved him to one side of the chute, where he whacked a seat out of the slope. Their only option was to attach themselves to the steep snow face and shout very loudly.

Today, Nelson still marvels at how, back in camp about a mile away, he managed to pick up the desperate cries over the noise of their primus. He wriggled out the tent door and yelled, 'What the hell is going on?' There was not a cloud in the brilliant starry sky, not a sound nor breath of wind in the frosty air, but at first he wasn't able to make sense of the replies. Then, as Mackay was scrambling through the sleeve of the tent, the message from Jacobs came loud and clear: the unwelcome words, 'I … have … broken … my … leg.'

After an hour and a half of preparation, Nelson and Mackay set off with thermoses of stew and cocoa, first aid supplies and sleeping bags. They were anxiously awaited. Jacobs was secured to a shaft belay from his waist and also his chest, his most comfortable position achieved by placing the other ice axe under his thigh and allowing the injured leg to hang free. Cotter used his own down jacket to wrap the injured leg, and given the circumstances Jacobs was reasonably cosy. But Cotter was forced to take a standing position beside and facing Jacobs, roped onto the same axe. He had been unable to remove his frozen crampons, and the cold was intense. They had no food, and desperately hoped they would be off the mountain that night.

For a while torch lights moved infinitely slowly towards them, but then they disappeared. By 1am, Nelson and Mackay had reached a point about 100 metres below Cotter and Jacobs, and for two more hours tried in vain to reach them. They shouted the message that they would wait for daylight, and bedded down in a filled-in crevasse. With the rest of the night to endure, Cotter and Jacobs began to worry that rescue the next day might also prove too difficult. With no jacket, Cotter kept his circulation going by swinging one arm at a time against his body, and stamping one foot at a time on the ice step. He did this for hours without stopping, while Jacobs got through the night surprisingly well, even dozing at times.

A tepid sun appeared at 8am and they were encouraged by periodic calls from below. Mackay and Nelson had renewed their attempt at 7am, and by 9.30 were at their sides with hot food, and sedatives for Jacobs.

Then it was a matter of getting everyone down before exhaustion set in. Nelson and Mackay engineered Jacobs' traverse across 60 metres of deep dry snow by digging a channel along which he could sidle, with assistance. That was followed by a roping-up procedure that allowed Nelson to descend with Jacobs to the foot of the snow face with a belayed and controlled descent of the rock bluff below, Mackay and Cotter both holding running belays. As he struggled down the bluff, Cotter realised that only incredible perseverance from Nelson and Mackay had made their rescue from the face possible: even so, it took four hours to get Jacobs down to the névé. Mackay finally double-roped down the rock step, using Jacobs' ice axe as an anchor. The axe had to be left behind, a sacrifice that was decided on the basis that Jacobs was the one who had no further use for an axe. Even in his drugged state he put up a feeble protest, however.

Once they reached the névé Cotter left for base camp, while Mackay and Nelson moved Camp 2 to the foot of the face and made Jacobs as comfortable as possible. Next morning, at daybreak, Cotter, Ireland and Jacinto reached them with stretcher materials. With Jacobs strapped into the makeshift stretcher, they started on a carry out to Camp 1, but in inconsistent snow conditions were soon sledging, using a plywood pack frame as the runner. Nelson wrote later, 'Over the crevasses and ups and downs of the glacier it was still hard work for the "horses", but we arrived in Camp 1 at 4pm.'[20] Mackay then remained with Jacobs while the rest immediately set off for base camp 3000ft below, where they arrived after dark.

The marathon continued the next day, when Nelson and Jacinto left at 5am to recruit carriers from the village of Capiakhueita two hours away. With Jacobs' condition deteriorating, it was imperative to get him to hospital. The stretcher was carried in a gruelling, near non-stop direct descent of the 1500ft moraine wall. The hardy mountain men who helped them down, including a leader they later nicknamed King Kong, were invaluable and displayed incredible strength and endurance. One walked down the moraine wall in bare feet, then continued down the steep valley in the same manner over cactus, bog and rock. On the valley floor, packs were transferred to a burro and the carry continued. Once base camp was reached, Jen took over patient care while the others, including the coca-chewing Indians, celebrated with cheap rum. The next day, Jacobs was loaded onto a burro for a two-day journey to Caraz and transfer by car to the hospital at Yungay, which he reached five days after the accident. Jen went with him to accompany him by air to Lima and see him safely off to New Zealand.

Returning to their base camp, the remaining climbers were very aware they had not yet gained a single Peruvian peak. Still hopeful of success in the week they had left, they planned a camp on the col at the foot of the west ridge of the virgin. Nelson and Mackay left early on 9 July to explore this approach. Seeing them move successfully onto the 18,200ft col, Cotter and Ireland set off in pursuit

Harold Jacobs on his way out of the Santa Cruz Valley. Mike Nelson

Approaching the summit of Quitoraju. Ed Cotter

with packs and enough food for four days, and they settled into a new Camp 2 at 17,500ft. On 10 July, however, while they were resting on the col assessing a new panorama, the 'awful truth' about their whereabouts began to dawn. 'Wasn't that face of the virgin above us the same as the well-known ice-fluted face of Alpamayo?'[21]

Stunned, they realised it was indeed Alpamayo that they had spent so much time reconnoitring and falling off. They had walked three-quarters of the way around and attempted two ridges of the same mountain. According to Cotter, 'Had we seen that well-known face earlier, rather than the unknown approaches, the whole mountain pattern would have solved itself. Our whole problem of orientation had been brought about by the incorrect positioning of Quitoraju on our map.'[22] They quickly changed tack, deciding on a snow peak at the head of what they now recognised as the Alpamayo Plateau, believing it was the virgin they had been looking for. Finding himself unacclimatised, Ireland returned to base camp and the others immediately set off to achieve their virgin summit. They later discovered it was Nevado Loyacjirca, 18,400ft, already twice climbed.

There remained just one climbing day before they went their separate ways. On 11 July they turned their efforts to the sprawling mass of Quitoraju. In a six-hour climb they ascended the 2000ft north face and gained the summit at 2pm. Cotter wrote that it was a satisfying climax for him, it being the same day on which he had climbed Mukut Parbat 13 years earlier:

> The superb summit view was soon lost to sight by swirling cloud, which remained with us on our careful descent to the plateau. As daylight faded from the scene, the sun's last rays pierced the heavy valley cloud to play on the ice-fluted face of Alpamayo, providing us with a sunset display on the face of the mountain itself. This magic display held us awe-bound till we saw the red sun dip into the horizon.[23]

Mackay's account of the Peru climbs for the *Press* also described the view from the spectacular pyramid of Quitoraju, a climb that provided an enormous sense of satisfaction at the end of a very memorable expedition.[24] Jacobs, already back in Christchurch as the expedition drew to a close, wrote up the dramatic Alpamayo accident for the same paper. His most fortunate survival had earlier hit the headlines in Peru after he was interviewed in Caraz en route to New Zealand. '"*Solo un milagro me salvo de morir sepultado entre las nieves eternas de la Cordillera Blanca*", declaro el andinista neozelandes.' (Only a miracle saved me from being buried alive in the eternal snows of the Cordillera Blanca, said the

New Zealand mountaineer.)²⁵ Typically, Cotter never represented his actions as anything exceptional, let alone heroic. It took Jacobs to spell it all out for readers of the *Press*:

> Ed handled the situation like the veteran he is. He tied us both to a good belay, then cut me a seat on the slope and himself a place to stand. Thinking of the possibilities of frostbite, he very generously sacrificed his own jacket and wrapped it around my immobilised leg. Then he stamped his feet all night, while I kept the toes of my good foot moving.²⁶

In the Cordillera Real of Bolivia, Cotter, Jacobs and Mackay had made the first ascent of Arichiri and Arichiri Este, and the first ascent of Kasiri Aguja and Kasiri Oeste; Jacobs, Mackay and Nelson achieved the first ascent of Taparucu; and Cotter, Jacobs, Mackay and Nelson made the first traverse and third ascent of Ancohuma, and the second ascent of Huachana. In the Cordillera Blanca of Peru, because eight days were lost to the accident, Cotter, Nelson and Mackay climbed only Loyacjirca and Quitoraju.

Philip Temple believes this 1964 expedition marked the end of an era in the Andes. 'No more great virgin peaks remained to be climbed and it was the end of a period of intense New Zealand activity, when expeditions from this country claimed first ascents of many of the greater mountains.'²⁷ Half a century on, Guy Cotter considers his father's Peruvian expedition a considerable achievement. Today, climbing Alpamayo via its beautiful chutes is much easier to undertake than the ridge route on which Ed's party found themselves, which Guy describes as desperately difficult, dangerous and unstable, with double cornices and horrible terrain.

Jen Cotter found the Andes trip a questionable adventure. It was the sort of off-the-beaten-track travelling she thought she wanted to experience, but her long days as camp warden were very tedious. 'How we longed for a hot bath, fresh vegetables and a glass of cold, fresh milk!'²⁸ In halting Spanish she managed to get along with the more friendly Peruvian Indians, and found Peru much more pleasant and peaceful than Bolivia, where life was cheap and the locals more primitive, more suspicious, less friendly and less trustworthy. Writing home from the base camp in the Santa Cruz Valley to her sister-in-law Jude, Jen described watching 'the boys' slogging their way up the massive mountains:

> It makes me very nervous and rather worried, I must admit. These mountains in Peru are terrific things. They are very steep, high and sheer, quite startling, very

Photo opportunity in the Antarctic: Ed Cotter centre, McMurdo base behind. Cotter collection

impressive and magnificently spectacular, but they horrify me when I think of Ed climbing them. He has promised me to be extra careful.[29]

In retrospect she has mixed feelings about those three months away from her small children, saying, 'I did miss the children immensely, and I was very ready to come home when it all ended.'

Before Ed and Jen could leave Peru, they needed more help from their long-suffering bank manager. They had left home with only one-way tickets and were close to broke. On their return to Gore Ed found his business on the Golden Mile in Gore had foundered in the face of stronger opposition. 'I had no money in the first place, and then of course I came home to no money.' Looking back, he says this most memorable trip to South America was certainly one of the worst decisions he ever made.

In June 1965 Ed was invited through the NZAC to spend a month in Antarctica training American scientists to handle the environmental challenges of an ice-bound region. He jumped at the chance of a temporary escape from his financial problems. With a team of other mountaineers, including Derek Cook and Jack Ede, he flew down to the ice in August.

Our job was to teach the scientists and other field staff about icecraft and how to cope with problems that might occur, because obviously gathering scientific data in such extreme conditions could be hazardous. It's a continent of huge white expanses and a vast amount of flat country, but it was constantly changing with the weather, so cross-country safety was a matter for some concern as they moved about with dog teams and all their equipment. Crevasses posed the main danger, and training in how to get out of them was essential.

They were based at McMurdo Sound and went out each day on snowmobiles to find crevasses suitable for training purposes. Each group of scientists would have two days' instruction in glissading, snowcraft, icecraft, and how to climb a rope with the aid of Prusik slings. With 76 trainees, the programme was a streamlined one. The weather did not always co-operate, and a few blinding blizzards restricted them to base and made it difficult to move from one building to another.

During that brief interlude in frozen Antarctica Ed found dealing with the cold the main challenge. The social life was another. He enjoyed mingling with American crews there for the summer, and after one particularly convivial Halloween party he arrived back at his hut, which he shared with Ede, a non-drinker, and proceeded to snore for seven hours. The next day Ede gave Ed an earful of his own. Ed suggested an ingenious solution: Ede should tie a string to Ed's big toe so that if the offence was repeated he could immediately give the string a hefty tug. But Ede found the string dangling in front of his nose rather annoying and tied the loose end to the bed. Next morning when Ed jumped out of bed the string arrested his fall so that he ended up on his back on the floor with his foot in the air. 'It would have been edifying to have had a tape-recording of that incident,' Ede wrote.[30]

All too soon, it was time for the Hercules trip back to civilisation. When Ed arrived home, everything was about to change. Again.

A rider pauses beside the Hollyford River, just below Gunn's Camp. Cotter collection

18. TRAILBLAZING THE HOLLYFORD

Heroic failure

Just as Ed Cotter returned from Antarctica and was wondering how to boost his problematic finances, a chance opening led him back to the Hollyford. From the perils of the high Andes to frozen Antarctica to a visionary new tourist venture on the wild West Coast, his adventures were always consistent with his spur-of-the-moment, 'just do it' philosophy.

His experiences of mustering and guiding in the Hollyford and the special role he played in the 1960s in laying the foundation for the world-renowned Hollyford Track have assured Ed Cotter a permanent place in local history. On 16 July 2014, 50 years after he set up his own Hollyford tourist trail, he was flown in to Martins Bay as a guest of honour to attend the official launch of the Hollyford Conservation Trust by the minister of conservation, Nick Smith.

Davey Gunn had no concessions in law for his outback tours.[1] His was a cowboy operation in more ways than one, and confusion over who exactly owned the huts he built on the leased land was never resolved. After Gunn's death his son Murray arranged a formal lease for six of his father's hut sites[2] but by the mid-1960s he was running into trouble and out of money. When a jet-boat he organised for tourists on the Hollyford River sank he was unable to afford the salvage, and was so cash-strapped he had no option but to give up the lease.[3]

The way was clear for Cotter to pursue his own long-imagined Hollyford tourism venture. He had already missed out on earlier opportunities, including the attempt to take over Gunn's business in 1955, followed by an application in December that year to build a fishing lodge at Martins Bay.[4] Even as he was operating his business in Gore, he was always mindful of the Hollyford's huge potential. As an agent for Milford Track tours he sold more trips than any other agency, and he knew first hand that Davey Gunn's tours had satisfied the appetite of adventurous trampers seeking ever more remote and pristine parts of the country. He believed the Hollyford would make a very attractive alternative to the Milford, and was certain it would repay his investment. Late in 1964 he laid his plans, backing himself to succeed without any financial support in a courageous but risky undertaking.

The Hollyford, now a World Heritage Area, has a fascinating history. A huge glacier carved out the spectacular valley 20,000 years ago, leaving behind the Donne Glacier on the eastern face of Mt Tutoko in the dramatic Darran Mountains. Lake McKerrow, running out towards the coastline, was originally a fiord until cut off from the sea by sedimentary deposits at Martins Bay.[5]

As a low-altitude track through rich beech forest, the Hollyford can be walked all year round – but it is much more than just a hike in a national park: it is a chance to follow in the footsteps of early Māori and later intrepid pioneer explorers. Between 1650 and 1800 Martins Bay (Kotuku) was settled by Māori, who found a plentiful supply of food in nearby lakes, sea and forest, as well as pounamu for ornaments, tools and weapons. In 1861 Southland runholders David McKellar and George Gunn[6] traversed the Greenstone Valley to Key Summit, from which they were able to look down into the long Hollyford Valley.[7] In 1863 the gold prospector Patrick Caples went up the Routeburn Valley from Wakatipu, crossed over the Harris Saddle and followed the Hollyford[8] all the way to the sea, the first European to do so. That trip was reversed soon after by Otago provincial geologist James Hector, who travelled from Martins Bay up through the Hollyford to the Greenstone, Mavora Lakes and Queenstown. The township of Jamestown on the shore of Lake McKerrow was surveyed in 1870, and a few families settled there before being driven out by isolation. The McKenzie family raised cattle at Martins Bay from the turn of the century until 1926 when they sold the leases to Patrick Fraser and Davey Gunn.

In early 1965 details of Ed Cotter's proposed 'Adventour' were submitted to the Government Tourist Bureau for inclusion in its record of available tours. The package was outlined in the *Southland Times* on 22 March: between 28 December and the end of February, parties would set out with a pack team to Hidden Falls and the Lower Pyke clearing, take a launch trip on Lake McKerrow, and visit the Martins Bay lagoons and seal and penguin colonies at Long Reef on the coast. From there they could take a plane to Milford, or make the return journey to the Lower Pyke, catch a jet-boat to the head of Lake Alabaster and walk out to the road.[9]

Jacqui Cotter recalls a summer trip into the Hollyford with her father and sister Lis when Ed was in the initial stages of organising his huts:

> We were very young, but it's still very clear in my memory. When we made it in to Pyke Hut we were savaged by sandflies while he was really busy chopping down trees to use for the hut. Then on the way back to Te Anau the car broke down and he had to knock on the door of a nearby house. We had to stay there

for a couple of days with this young couple until the parts came through for the car. They ended up family friends as well as surrogate parents.

Ed's 'Cotters Travel and Tours' brochure promised a Hollyford panorama with sublime views. The vision included cabins built of unbarked larch slabs and a staff of one horse-packer, two guides and a launchman. Bedding, shower facilities and meals of venison and fish with table wine would be provided.[10] On the first stage trampers could visit the spectacular Humbolt Falls, then stay the night in Madeline Lodge at Hidden Falls, beside beech forest under the slopes of the beautiful Mt Madeline; the second day would take them via a forest trail to the Little Homer Saddle, with a commanding view of Mt Tutoko. Lunch would be provided at Alabaster Lodge close to the Pyke River, before trampers crossed the Pyke on a swingbridge to walk down the river to the head of Lake McKerrow, followed by a launch transfer to Tutoko Lodge, only 5km from the Tasman Sea.

On the third day fresh flounder would be served for breakfast at Martins Bay. During a launch trip to McKenzies Lagoon tourists would learn about the hardships of early settlers, then enjoy a rabbit pie dinner and a barbecue supper. On the return trip to the Lower Pyke they would visit the site of Jamestown, and at Alabaster Lodge enjoy a shower, sherry and dinner accompanied by the roar of the Pyke River rapids. The following day, a jet-boat ride up Lake Alabaster would provide a bush, lake and mountain panorama as spectacular as any in the world, before the return to Hidden Falls and the Adventour Camp near the road end. All this, for only £18.18.0.

The brochure was tantalising, but living up to the glossy promises proved difficult. In October 1965, just two months before the tourist season began, Ed finally received word that he had been granted his concession. That meant he could build his own huts in the Hollyford Valley and take people through what was now Crown land. It was a shot in the arm. The problem was, he had already taken bookings even though he had no huts built …

> Rather foolishly I decided to get started right away. Anticipating that I was going to get the concession, I had already advertised through the Government Tourist Bureau, and by the opening of the tourist season I already had about 50 people on my books. But I decided that even though it was so close to Christmas, I could still get some huts built and take a party down.[11]

Ed's enthusiasm was boundless but it was a scramble to get everything ready:

> Trying to put all this into effect would prove an absolute nightmare. I had to design three huts, find someone to build them and have them flown in by float plane. I also had to get horses to transport supplies to the huts, and find boats to use on the lake. From memory I had about eight weeks, which was absolutely ridiculous.[12]

His first hut, Hidden Falls, was to be sited 8km from the end of the Te Anau road. The second, Pyke Hut, was another 8km downriver, and the third was at Martins Bay at the south end of Lake McKerrow, about an hour from Long Reef on the coast. These would each sleep up to 15 people and offer sleeping bags, gas cooking facilities, toilets and running water.

A local builder pre-cut the three huts, hired a float plane from Mt Cook and flew in the Martins Bay hut from Lake Gunn on the Te Anau road. The others were taken downriver by jet-boat, each journey an adventure in its own right. In the midst of this Ed drove to Blenheim and bought a lake boat, a 19ft fibreglass runabout, and parked it at home on the lawn. Jen looked out the window, and asked how on earth he was going to pay for it.

Work on the huts was painfully slow because of heavy and almost continuous Fiordland rain and the time it took to float materials down the river. Ed was fast losing the race. Some memorable moments stand out for Ed today, like when he bought a couple of horses in Gore and borrowed a trailer to get them into the Hollyford. Almost immediately, one of them lay down in the back of the trailer and kicked the side out. Once Ed had loaded them with supplies to take into Hidden Falls, one fell off the track and tumbled some way down through the bush. Fortunately it wasn't injured and he was able to reload and carry on. But all too soon the trampers beguiled by his brochures began to arrive.

The first clients were warmly welcomed at the road end by Ed's chief guide. At Hidden Falls, however, weary hikers expecting a comfortable lodge were not impressed by the 'original' musterers' hut, authentic right down to the mattresses of fern. Meanwhile, Ed still hadn't got the boat up to Lake McKerrow. He had only two days in which to take the runabout up the coast from Milford Sound, around the heads to Martins Bay, then to the head of the lake.

In Gore he asked around for someone to help and found a willing recruit, a student on holiday from England. They drove to Milford, put the boat in the water and motored down Milford Sound and up the coast towards Martins Bay, where they hit rough seas. Making little headway, Ed decided to divert towards a nearby fishing trawler, where they were welcomed on board and stayed overnight.

An Adventours group greeted by a Martins Bay penguin (left). Cotter collection

Next morning, in improved weather, they set off to meet the first tramping party at the head of the lake. Meanwhile, as the trampers neared their meeting point at the lake a chopper flew overhead carrying a heavy load – the building materials for their beds for the night. Shortly after they arrived at the head of the lake, a dot appeared in the distance and slowly drew closer. It was the promised boat. The trampers climbed aboard, but with such a heavy load it was a very slow trip down the lake, and well after dark by the time they got to Martins Bay. There they discovered an unfinished hut, and bunks that still had to be assembled.

It was a shambles, Ed recalls:

They asked where the toilet was, and I said we didn't have one but the hole had been dug. This was right on Christmas, and I was still trying to run the shop in Gore – I must have been bloody mad. I thought it was going to be a breeze, but it wasn't. Luckily some of that group were from Gore, so they didn't get too snaky with me.

Jen and Ed didn't talk much about the Hollyford venture because she also had her hands full. Ed's vision for the future appealed, but her young family was equally important:

> My father and my uncle, who was a bank manager, had done their very best to talk Ed out of the venture, but it was already too late. There was a fair bit of shouting in our house. I had four babies, so most of my shouting was along the lines of 'Help me!' But Ed's position was that if I shouted too much, he would just go off on his own down the Hollyford. He was on a roll, and that was it.

The unwelcome surprises kept coming for Jen. The lino in the children's playroom disappeared one day – gone to be used in the Hollyford huts. Ed was away so much the children got quite used to life without him: one morning when he had turned up overnight, Jacqui asked him, 'What are you doing here?'

When Anton was still very young the whole family trekked down the valley to Hidden Falls, but the sandflies were ravenous. Anton was covered with bites, including his small bald head, and the older children who used the long-drop toilet were initiated into the tenacity of Hollyford blowflies. Jen's brother King Allen says that if you travelled with Ed, your accommodation expectations had to be pitched fairly low:

> When he started out, the brochure promised hot and cold showers … [this] turned out to be a big mistake. One woman didn't see the funny side when after a long tramp she found four poles with a bit of polythene around them, a can with holes drilled in the bottom, and a tour operator who asked her to shout out whether she wanted hot or cold water.

King recalls a memorable jaunt with Ed into the Hollyford in a rickety old van chugging along on three cylinders. They got past Davey Gunn's camp to a Ministry of Works hut where they had hoped to find something to eat but were disappointed. Ed was sure there would be something at Hidden Falls, but there was only a half-gallon of sherry, so they had a mug of that. The next leg was the hike into Pyke Hut, by which time King was 'well and truly knackered'. That didn't stop Ed loading him up with a tin of petrol for his boats. After King fell over in the mud, weighed down by pack and petrol can, Ed offered to go ahead and get their boat started, as it was 'just around the corner'. Almost two hours later King

Adventours hikers cross one of the many streams that drain into the Hollyford River. Cotter collection

A tour group relaxes on the shores of Lake McKerrow. Cotter collection

emerged from the bush after their 30km 'walk' – Ed had deliberately left him behind because he knew King would have no choice but to follow. Fortunately King was fairly handy with motors, and once they had bailed out and refloated the boats he managed to get one outboard going, at which point they tied onto the other boat and headed down the lake.

> It was black as pitch, the middle of the night, and when we got down near Martins Bay Ed yelled out to a group of pig shooters who were camped up there. I stopped the motor, a fatal move because I couldn't get it going again. They came out and helped us in, but there was only one spare bunk. Ed stoked up the fire and slept on a sack – he was just like a dog the way he could sleep anywhere. Then at five o'clock he was up getting breakfast, and we finally got to Martins Bay. Tough! If I was ever going to get lost, I decided it would be with him. As well as being immensely fit, he had great survival skills.

Over three difficult seasons, Ed ran the shop in Gore as well as promoting the Hollyford venture. Demand was mainly over the summer holidays, and finding and paying the extra staff to cope with the unpredictable numbers was difficult. Occasionally the trampers themselves were able to help with cooking, but there were never enough clients to make the business profitable in the face of strong competition from the Milford Track. By 1968 it was all too much: the only way out was to file for bankruptcy.

Adventours closed down. Like the most delicate snow-bridge, Ed's Hollyford dream had collapsed under a burden of good intentions. He lost his boats and his investment, and the Cotters' house went up for sale. Ironically the way was clear again for Murray Gunn to set up the Hollyford Tourist and Travel Company in 1968 with Invercargill partners Jules Tapper and Viv Allot, building on the tour options Ed had developed.[13] Murray was only involved for the first year, then withdrew to concentrate on running Hollyford Camp. The Hollyford Track enterprise has changed hands several times since, but is still essentially the same business. In 2003 it was bought by Ngāi Tahu Tourism, which invested heavily in a refurbished lodge at Pyke River and a new lodge at Martins Bay.[14] Today, the Hollyford Track enjoys high status as a World Heritage Walk that offers excellent accommodation in purpose-built lodges, from which well-to-do trampers can enjoy thrilling jet-boat rides and scenic flights.

As a trailblazer for a unique wilderness experience, Ed contributed much to the Hollyford's human history. Today's more pampered visitors, as well as freedom walkers who tramp to the sea and back via the difficult Demon Trail, can read about Ed Cotter's contribution to their experience in interpretive displays that explain how he turned Davey Gunn's outback experience into an imaginative guided walk.

Guy Cotter believes the Adventours venture was always going to be a step too far for Ed because of limited tourist spending at the time, and the region's remoteness:

> It was too tough and too hard. To be successful Ed needed a partner to do the organisation, leaving him to be the motivator and provide the inspiration. But he never got to the point where he could afford that. The Hollyford is an amazing part of the world, but it still struggles today because of where it is geographically. Ed had a real affinity with it, but there was a lot of bad luck too.

Numbed by his crash into the mortifying abyss of insolvency, Ed had no option but to take any job he could find. The Cotters rented a house in Invercargill, where

The Cotter family on one of their trips into the Hollyford Valley. From left: Jen, Adrian Roberts and Jacqueline (standing), Guy and Elisabeth mounted on the horse. Cotter collection

Ed had been promised work as a life insurance salesman, and soon the children were enrolled in school there. So began five years of knuckling down, during which Ed learned new lessons in survival: 'During my time there I had a very, very short spell selling life insurance, a season in the freezing works at Lorneville, and some years as a ceiling insulation worker, none of which I enjoyed.'[15] There wasn't much climbing, though he relaxed occasionally with NZAC friends. Jen worked as an artist and copywriter with the DIC department store in Invercargill, a job she loved, and before too long they were managing reasonably well and were able to buy another house of their own.

Invercargill proved a wonderful place to bring up children – the swimming pool, art classes and ballet were all within easy reach. Most weekends the family would take a trip somewhere: out to the coast diving for paua, or digging for toheroa at Oreti Beach. There were many happy days spent on outdoor activities instigated by Ed, the occasional holiday on Stewart Island and visits to the Allen farm in Western Southland. Lis Cotter describes the family's Invercargill phase as stable and happy, with two parents who were committed to their family:

> They renovated houses and Dad did all the vege gardening while Mum was the flower, tree and shrub expert. We always had chooks and pets, dogs, cats and

guinea pigs, and Dad would often rescue little things from danger. I never heard my parents argue in those days. I had a lot of freedom when I was a young tomboy, mostly with boys and brothers on bikes, and we had a fantastic climbing tree in Louisa Street, Invercargill, a beech that is still there. Today I still dream about it.[16]

But though the family had settled so well in Invercargill, Ed hankered to return to Christchurch. Once again, the climbing fraternity came to his aid. Among his many climbing friends who had enjoyed visiting the Hollyford was Wyn Harris who, as manager of electrical equipment importer A.R. Harris and Co., offered Ed a position in the Christchurch office, and a company house with it. Ed went ahead to check out the situation, and the family followed.

After about a year with the company Ed moved into the sales department, which gave him access to a company car, and in 1973 the Cotters bought Vailima, a character villa situated on the rocky promontory above Sumner Beach and named after the last dwelling place in Samoa of another adventurer, Robert Louis Stevenson. Accessed via 130 steps from the main Sumner road and with a superb view over Shag Rock and the Pegasus Bay seascape, the property was perfectly matched to its new owners. The boys attended Redcliffs Primary School, later following their sisters to Linwood High School. Jen took a job at Christchurch Hospital as a hospital chaperone, then worked in a Christchurch bookshop.

The Cotters' paua team at Greenhills, near Bluff. From left: Elisabeth, Guy, Jacqueline, Anton, Ed and Jen. Cotter collection

Don Mackay, their climbing friend who was living in Christchurch at the time, introduced the Cotters to Jim and Ann Wilson. Jim had an extensive climbing background including Himalayan expeditions between 1963 and 1966. The Cotter family spent a lot of time with the Wilsons and shared many parties, movies and outdoor activities. Jim and Ann admired the way Ed and Jen gave their children so much freedom, and used the Cotters as role models in bringing up their own.

Ed remained with A.R. Harris for 12 years until he retired in 1984. Jen pays tribute to his tenacity in a job he never really enjoyed. But his tendency to absent himself during some difficult times when the children were teenagers caused increasing family tension. In 1979 Ed and Jen separated, amicably enough, and have remained friends and shared family occasions ever since.

19. VAILIMA AND BEYOND

From the mountains to the sea

For 35 years Rhondda Pope has been a still point in Ed Cotter's turning world, first as his partner and, in more recent times, as a deeply committed, ever-present friend.

In the early 1980s, when Rhondda was newly separated with a young family, she and Ed moved in the same Sumner social circles. Though she was 16 years younger than the 54-year-old mountaineer and adventurer, they were soon spending much of their spare time together. In 1982 Ed bought a 22-foot trailer sailer, and the two often headed out from Scarborough over the bar to sail around Banks Peninsula. Many of their adventures were not 'plain sailing': on a trip to Lake Brunner the mast toppled and missed Rhondda by a whisker. The voyage that spelled the end of their sailing together was an excursion in the Marlborough Sounds when they hit terrible conditions and had to be rescued several times.

Rhondda's three children, Jeremy, Katie and Julian Mitchell, adored the easy-going and impulsive Ed and the exhilarating change he brought to their family life. Taking off with Ed on a whim proved to be a lot of fun, though there was sometimes a downside. On one typical occasion Ed was keen to take Rhondda, 10-year-old Julian and his friend Simon on a trip to the Cameron Hut to assess some storm damage, describing it as 'a bit of a stroll'. Before they set off Rhondda had no idea what was in store, such as heavy packs and multiple river crossings. She didn't even know trampers wore their boots into rivers until Ed asked why she was removing hers. Then he couldn't find the hut, because it had been moved from its previous site. By the time they got there, very late in the evening, Rhondda and the boys were exhausted. To cap it off, Ed had forgotten the primus. Rhondda decided she hated every moment of the experience.

From 1980 to 1983 Ed was president of the CMC. With a steady membership of about 400 the club was in a relatively quiet phase, but end-of-year gatherings at Vailima were always lively. Ed kept in close contact with many old friends, and reminiscences of times past were supplemented by ongoing club activities, especially in hut maintenance and instruction courses. He is modest about his

Ed's interest in photography never faded, and Rhondda's family were frequent subjects. From left on the Sumner foreshore, 1993: Julian, Jeremy with his son Jethro, Katie with her daughter Aimee, and Rhondda. Ed Cotter

own years of service, saying it was little enough because of the debt he owes the CMC for his own climbing success and his desire to see the club passing on its ethos to future members.

After retiring from A.R. Harris in 1984, Ed worked for a year in photographic processing with Mike Perry, a CMC climbing friend, and later took on some casual gardening. Around this time Rhondda sold her home and moved to Vailima with her children. But it was hard work living on the hill with the garage on the main road at sea level and access to the house up a steep zigzag track. Rhondda was used to order, and found chaos. Though she and Ed started into some renovations, it was not long before she suspected this new family might not work out for Ed, who liked his own space and plenty of independence. Her younger son Julian was devoted to Ed, however, and relished the many yachting and tramping experiences they shared. Though Ed could sometimes set a high bar, Julian was never put off, and still attributes his pursuit of fitness and sporting excellence to Ed's example.

In retirement Ed had time for more sailing, often with fellow mountaineers who, in the tradition of the great Bill Tilman, found new adventures in deep-sea sailing. In 1986 Rhondda moved back into a house of her own; Ed rented out Vailima and joined friends from Invercargill days, 'Snow' Ross and his wife Joyce, who planned to sail to California in their 45-foot yacht. This trip featured what was probably Ed's most fortuitous sailing triumph, when he 'found' Tahiti with the aid of a transistor radio.

The voyage began from Whangarei, but a severe and sustained nor'west storm blew them well offshore and the navigation system broke down. After a number of near calamities Ed's faith in the team's navigational ability was shaken to the extent that he decided to take over their direction finding. He fiddled with the tuning of his old portable transistor radio until he brought up a broadcast in French. Knowing that transistor radios give sharpest reception at right angles to the direction of the transmitter, when satisfied that he had the best reception he took a compass bearing at a right angle to its face and steered hopefully in that direction. A few days later the high peaks of Tahiti appeared over the horizon, and soon they were safely in the harbour. But the whole voyage (to California) was supposed to take only two months, and it had taken four or five weeks just to get to Tahiti. Ed had had enough and decided to fly home.

Reluctant to put his tenants out of Vailima, he stayed with Rhondda until he regained access to his own home, where he turned the ground floor into a self-contained flat for himself and made the upstairs rooms available to a succession of temporary occupants. One was teacher Steve Aiken, who was intrigued by Ed, an 'older gentleman' who seemed very much in tune with younger people. Steve vividly remembers hiking over the Copland Pass to Welcome Flat and lying in the

The campsite at Ngawhakawhiti Bay, Tennyson Inlet, 1988. Standing, from left, Jim Wilson, Ann Wilson, Ed Cotter. Jim and Ann Wilson

Don Mackay, Jim Wilson and Ed Cotter on board the Wilsons' yacht *Kororo* during their circumnavigation of the South Island 1991–92. Ann Wilson

hot pools with a wine, enjoying some of Ed's 'reflective wisdom'.[1] Another short-term resident was documentary-maker Gus Roxburgh, who referred to Ed as 'a prince among men, a great free spirit'.[2] Similarly impressed was Amanda Power, who also fell in love with Vailima:

> It was incredibly special, and I felt exceptionally grateful to be living there. We were living pretty free and easy and carefree and Ed was an amazing man, as young at heart as the rest of us. I loved his wit and humour, and the way he always kept active and had more than one trip or adventure planned in the future.[3]

Once her children left home Rhondda moved back to Vailima, but often sought refuge in her campervan from the constant stream of visitors, and eventually shifted into another home of her own. In retrospect Rhondda views Ed as a man who was happier with fewer expectations and less commitment than a permanent partnership entails.

Always up for spontaneous adventure, Ed was haphazard in his preparations. When Ann and Jim Wilson and some friends hatched a plan to sail to a remote spot in Pelorus Sound, Ed agreed to come along with his R-class yacht. He had a catalogue of small disasters on the way: separate tows for his trailer and then his car over the Hundalees Hills; a lengthy delay while he stopped at a house to make a phone call and then returned the favour by mowing the lawns; the loss of a trailer wheel that was repaired by a farmer to whom Ed gratefully presented Ann's precious box of apricots; a very late arrival in heavy rain at Duncans Bay, where he slept under his trailer; and a collision with a wharf during which Ed dislocated his shoulder.

Several times Ed and Jim Wilson joined Don Mackay, their old climbing and sailing companion, to sail around the Marlborough Sounds and to Nelson, and Ed also crewed for Wilson on passages along the coastlines of the North and South Islands. In the summer of 1991–92 the three friends spent two months circumnavigating the South Island in the Wilsons' 30-foot Lotus 9.2, navigating by compass and by bearings to prominent land features when visibility allowed. Around the southwest coast they sailed up fiords, disembarking and climbing through the forest up and around waterfalls. Wilson recalls it as a fantastic trip, in part because of the good company provided by Ed, a great raconteur who could tell stories all night.

Ed swaps climbing stories at Chancellor Hut with visiting British climber Chris Bonington (left), shortly before Bonington was knighted for his services to the sport. Bob McKerrow

But the mountains were never forgotten. Over that same summer Ed spent some time in South Westland working as a glacier guide, a job he was offered through mountaineer and writer Bob McKerrow,[4] who was living in Franz Josef. McKerrow describes Ed as an iconoclast who has lived a remarkable and unconventional life, a mountaineering icon whose trademark is humility and who was easily able to reinvent himself: 'There are few men who at the age of 62, as Ed was then, would still have sufficient mountain and icecraft expertise to take on the responsibility of guiding large parties of 50 to 70 people in glacier terrain.'

McKerrow invited Ed to join him climbing McFetrick Peak, tucked in among surrounding giants at the head of the Tatare River. Ed was keen to revisit the region from which he and Riddiford had made their epic trip out to Franz Josef in 1950–51. They were joined by Mike Browne from Fox Glacier Guiding and one of his guides, Chris Jillet. The party battled whiteout conditions as well as a badly crevassed slope, but fortunately the cloud lifted for a successful summit. 'That night, it was one of those peerless Westland evenings. No one spoke. Ed Cotter sat alone on a rock as the sun turned the high mountains pink.'[5] The next day brilliant conditions encouraged them to summit another unnamed peak from which they could see the Tasman.

Ed also shared a number of holidays in South East Asia with Rhondda, who says he never needed to be asked twice and was the perfect travelling companion. Closer to home, he frequently spent time in Wanaka, where his son Guy was

Ed Cotter (left) in California with Maggie Stafsnes and her husband Donald McPherson.
Cotter collection

based, and where his daughter Jacqui lived for some years with her partner Phil Penney, also a mountaineer and mountain guide. On one visit to Jacqui's home Ed decided to fly a kite. He found a bit of orange tape – the type used on electric fences – to use as a tail, but unfortunately it blew into the high-tension wires across the corner of the property. There was a great flash of light and a buzzing sound as the power went out across the whole town to the Treble Cone skifield, which closed for a couple of hours. But that wasn't the end of the story: a few years later when Ed recounted the tale at a dinner in Queenstown, he found he had outed himself to one of the power company bosses, who said, 'Oh, was that you?!'

After his spell at Franz Josef, Ed guided for Browne at Fox Glacier for two seasons. At 64 he still considered it easy enough to equip tourists with poles and boots, walk with them up the valley and cut steps onto a safe part of the glacier. One of the clients he met there, Maggie Stafsnes from San Francisco, became a firm friend. She had been leading backpacking trips through the US since the early 1980s, and had escorted parties to Nepal. On a tour of the West Coast to see how New Zealand glaciers would fit into her company schedule, she invited Ed to discuss the best options – and the following year employed him as glacier escort for her tour. Browne and Ed convinced her to add a trip to Chancellor Dome to her itinerary, and Ed accompanied her groups for three of those trips. Maggie recalls,

> [Ed] was on a number of the trips I led in New Zealand, and in 1995 he led my husband Donald [McPherson], me and a New Zealand woman I'd met on the Routeburn Track in 1982 over the Copland Pass. We made quite a stir when we arrived in Fox with the equipment Ed had given us. Much of it was similar to that displayed in the museum at Franz Josef.[6]

In 2000 Ed travelled to the US to visit Maggie and her husband for what was to be the first of several joint ventures. He joined her group climbing in Yosemite and at 73 greatly impressed them when he hiked up Half Dome and Clouds Rest (3025m) in one day. The trio drove to Mono Lake in California's Eastern Sierra, travelled through Death Valley, climbed Wheeler Peak in Great Basin National Park in Utah, backpacked in Cirque of the Towers in Wind River Range, Wyoming, and hiked in the Grand Tetons. The couple then sent Ed off on a nine-day trip to the Grand Canyon with a group called the Green Tortoise, a low-budget tour popular with young trampers. As they dropped him off in San Francisco he looked somewhat glum – not only was he the oldest by about 40 years, but all the meals were to be vegetarian. The tour visited the Canyon de Chelley National Monument in Arizona, the Valley of the Gods in Utah, the Navajo National Monument and the Bryce and Zion National Parks on its way to the Grand Canyon, and when Maggie picked Ed up nine days later he was grinning from ear to ear, the obvious favourite of his fellow travellers. Phone calls poured in from young friends who wanted him to join them again, and he even admitted that the vegetarian food was delicious.

In January 2007 Maggie and Donald provided an 80th birthday surprise by joining Ed on his annual rafting trip on the Waiau River, and in 2010 the three made another trip to the Pacific Northwest: Mt Shasta, Crater Lake, Mt Saint Helens, Mt Rainer, the Washington State Cascades and the Oregon Coast – the eastern side of the Pacific Rim volcanoes. Their last adventure together was in August 2011, when the three met up with Mike and Carrol Browne in Ketchikan, Alaska, and spent 15 days on a sailboat circumnavigating Revillagigedo Island.

Taking the watery way from the mountains to the sea, for many years Ed joined rafting trips with Rangitata Rafts, a company operated by the Acland family. His confidence was always an asset and a bit of white-water exhilaration from time to time suited him well. When Grant South formed Hidden Valleys adventure specialists in 2000, after 10 years working with Rangitata Rafts, he put together an 'aged rafters' trip and invited many of the people who had inspired him over those years to come along – Ed Cotter being one of them. Ed joined South's doughty band right up until 2014, when he turned 87, and always contributed

Grant South (aka Southey) helps Ed celebrate his 80th birthday during a rafting trip on the Waitaha River. Grant South

Ed (right) with George and Mary Lowe at Vailima. Cotter collection

much to the good company and hilarious evenings.

Ed renewed contact with George Lowe when in 2001 George and his wife Mary, after many New Zealand holidays, bought a bach at Diamond Harbour on Banks Peninsula. In 2005, when the Nelsons invited Ed to crew with them in the Adriatic, the Lowes offered to take him from the UK to Croatia in their campervan. They picked Ed up at Heathrow and delivered him to Split in Croatia with three days to spare. The sailing group first travelled north to the Kornati archipelago then south to Dubrovnik, before going their separate ways.

In 2006 Ed spent three weeks camping in France with the Lowes, and in 2007 they explored Scotland together. Two years later the Lowes showed Ed around southern Ireland, and he accompanied Mary Lowe to Estonia in 2009, to the Cevennes in southern France in 2010, and to Hungary in 2011.

Mary believes Ed's visits were very important to George, especially when George was in a nursing home in his final years. She says Ed was one of the last people George recognised. For his part, Ed says he will always remember the way George's hand closed over his during their final meeting. He is grateful he was able to be there with someone who had shared the days when they were young and full of glorious ambition, and his great love for the mountains of New Zealand.

20. EVEREST AT LAST

The son lives the life the father imagined

In 2013 it was a thrill for Ed and Guy Cotter to share the spotlight as they were each awarded life membership of the NZAC, the first time a father and son have achieved the honour. Ed, at 86, was commended for his special contribution to New Zealand's climbing reputation during the late 1940s and early '50s, and Guy for his leadership and participation in 30 climbing expeditions and development of one of the world's leading guiding businesses. Guy's role as director of Adventure Consultants, a company that runs 70 different trips worldwide, including climbing expeditions in all seven continents, is a huge source of pride to Ed.

Guy attributes his affinity with the outdoors to his earliest experiences up the Hollyford Valley. Those memories stuck, even though many early family tramps turned out to be near disasters: not for nothing did the children later call their father Captain Chaos. When they asked 'How much further is the hut?', the answer was the classic 'just around the corner'. Needless to say, it often turned out to be some hours and countless corners away. Many years later, in the Himalaya, Guy was able to exact his revenge.

When the family moved to Christchurch there were greater opportunities for Ed to take his children into the mountains, as his father had done with him. This was a crucial time for Guy, for whom the First New Zealand Himalayan Expedition was ancient history long before he was born, and who was in his infancy at the time of the Peru trip. The constant stream of visitors connected to his father's climbing past sparked Guy's interest in the mountains, and when he was 11 and Anton nine, Ed took them up Mt Rolleston (7463ft), a prominent peak in the Arthur's Pass region, which they summited via the Otira slide. It was a remarkable ascent for two young lads. Looking back, Ed is not particularly proud of his high expectations:

Anton, Ed and Guy Cotter on their ascent of Mt Rolleston in 1975. Cotter collection

> ... the boys were simply amazing. It was probably crazy to take kids up there because once we were climbing up a steep section onto the ridge leading to the summit, it was quite exposed and there wasn't much to hold on to. I said we would rope up before moving up to the summit, but Anton didn't want the rope. They had no special climbing gear, they were just following me, but eventually we summited and then descended by the same route.

On the descent Ed went ahead to see if there was an easier way down, telling the boys to stay put until he returned. Guy remembers stopping on a patch of hard frozen snow, then being bumped over the edge when Anton slipped behind him. 'I was on my backside sliding down feet first, and under some sort of control, but I was certainly heading towards the rocks when Ed just managed to jump out and catch me as I went past.' That was Guy's first major climb, with tragedy only narrowly averted. There was another close call on Mt Fyffe when Anton was nearly lost down a huge scree slope. Both boys survived Ed's initiation, but only Guy was tempted to go higher.

By the time his grandfather Ted gave him a scrapbook full of cuttings about young Ed for his birthday in 1976, Guy was already climbing confidently. From his first experiences with his father, he took quickly to rock climbing around Banks Peninsula and exploring the mountains around Arthur's Pass. Sister Lis led the way: she climbed enthusiastically and from the age of 13 was allowed to go to Arthur's Pass by herself if she had the company of capable climbing friends like Nick Cradock or Hugo Young. From the age of 12 Guy joined her on these weekend excursions: on one occasion Lis even drove the Arthur's Pass train while the driver spotted deer. She had little money for the trips, borrowed climbing gear, boots and packs, and became adept at climbing out of the train's toilet window onto the roof until the train had passed Rolleston, when she could be sure the ticket collector had passed through the carriage.

Sometimes Lis would be away climbing all through the school holidays. It's not surprising that with such a lead, Guy quickly became very independent. He might be able to bludge a dollar for the fare but never enough to go both ways, so he often used the same ruse on the train to escape detection. 'After you got back into the carriage you'd be covered in black stuff, but if you got away with it, you had enough money to buy a pie.' These were formative expeditions for both youngsters as they made the most of the considerable freedom allowed by their parents. Guy considers himself fortunate always to have had a clear focus on what he wanted to do; unlike his friend Peter Hillary, he never had to live in his father's shadow. In fact, he deliberately adopted a totally different style from Ed's. The unplanned nature of Ed's trips had the effect of turning Guy into a much more systematic climber: his aim was to be the complete professional. 'I was determined I would always know exactly where I was going and always have everything organised and sorted.' He was also much more cautious than Lis, who was highly talented but a risk-taker; after some serious falls she made the difficult decision to give up.

In 1977, at the age of only 15, Guy took on a traverse of the Southern Alps from Arthur's Pass to Mt Cook. With 16-year-old Rob Hall, Mike Woods and Chris Todd, he travelled via the headwaters of the Waimakariri, Rakaia and Havelock rivers to the Godley, Murchison and Tasman glaciers through to the Hermitage. Ed assisted by taking in supplies and meeting the group at the Mt

Cook end. This was Guy's first big expedition: he found it a valuable introduction to the logistical planning required for ambitious trips.

As a fifth former at Linwood High School, Guy was not without academic leanings, but was thwarted by an unsympathetic principal whose idea of punishment for wagging school was to keep the School Certificate candidate cooling his heels outside his office for a whole month before exams started. As a result Guy left school at the end of that year and moved away from home to work at the Hermitage, writing to his mother that he had learned 12 ways to lean on a shovel for the Ministry of Works. At 17 he made his first ascent of Mt Cook via the East Ridge, in a 14-hour return trip from the plateau that included a one-hour sleep on the summit. While still based at Mt Cook, in spring 1979 Guy joined his father climbing for the last time, when Ed came down with Don Mackay to the Tasman Saddle Hut, and did some 'hiking around', Guy recalls. But father and son had a vastly different approach, and it showed:

> There was some potential for disagreement. For example, Ed never went winter climbing, whereas we would go looking for steeper ice routes. But things just weren't done the same way any more, so there wasn't much to discuss. That was good for me, because I was doing my own thing in a different way, discovering answers for myself rather than being in some sort of apprenticeship. Our interest in the mountains could have provided a way to spend more time together, but it didn't work out that way.

After that, Guy went to Australia, did some building in Melbourne, got his crane operator's certificate and spent his winters working on ski resorts, with spring and autumn climbing at Arapiles. Back in New Zealand the following year he made the first solo ascent of the left-hand buttress on the south face of Hicks, at 19 years of age. Then he moved on to the United States, did a great deal of climbing, had a little manufacturing business making clothes and took up speed skiing. According to his mother Jen he was always an adrenalin junkie – rather like his parents. In 1984 he returned to New Zealand to work towards professional guiding qualifications. He undertook many climbs in the Cook area and parapenting became a favourite sport. Basing himself in Wanaka, he soon began working as a heli-ski guide and a part-time stonemason.

Guy first summited Everest on 12 May 1992 with Rob Hall and Gary Ball. This was Guy's first time guiding in the Himalaya, and he enjoyed leading the group to the top. Gary Ball died tragically in Nepal the following year after succumbing to pulmonary oedema on Dhaulagiri. Hall continued to build the Adventure

Consultants brand until the tragic events of the 1996 Everest expedition: on the descent from the summit Hall was trapped with a client and both died, as did mountain guide Andy Harris and another climber. Guy Cotter was on Pumori Peak near Everest leading a team of climbers from Malaysia when Hall radioed to say he was in trouble. Guy left his party to take over rescue efforts from base camp, which included persuading the Nepalese Air Force to fly a helicopter in to Camp 1 on the Western Cwm to rescue the survivors.

Guy Cotter climbing in California in 1982. Guy Cotter

In June 1996 Guy bought Adventure Consultants from Hall's widow, Jan Arnold. The company was based on a sound philosophy and a strong reputation, and 20 years on Guy employs a staff of internationally qualified guides who operate throughout the world. His personal record is dazzling. He completed his Seven Summits quest by climbing Kilimanjaro, Elbrus, Denali, Kosciusko and the Carstensz Pyramid – all in 2005. More recently he has led ski trips to the South Pole and Antarctic Peninsula. Of the six 8000m peaks he has climbed, he counts his ascent of Makalu as his most memorable, because the summit was elusive until the last few metres.

As Guy points out, mountaineering today is vastly different from in his father's day. Many opportunities now exist that were not available then, and differences in gear and technique make any debate about relative skills and talents irrelevant. He is in no doubt about the special skills that took his father to the top of Mukut Parbat so long ago, however:

> He was an incredibly athletic young man who achieved great things without the recognition that others around him enjoyed. A very talented climber, a free spirit who was physically very able, who obviously got to the Himalaya because Riddiford

appreciated that prowess. In 1951 Ed was very young and quite unconventional … But I learned from Ed that you should never think you know it all. You have to be humble in the mountains.[1]

Guy is still most impressed by his father's 1950 ascent of Elie de Beaumont via the Maximilian Ridge, and the way Ed and Earle went back to help Beaven via the 'tiger country' of the Callery while the others returned to the Hermitage:

It was a massive effort, but in a way they relished it. That's just different personality traits emerging, as they did in the Garhwal. On Mukut Parbat, Riddiford decided to carry on to the summit, and that would not have been in the plan Hillary and Lowe had. Hillary would certainly have been very annoyed that they didn't wait for them, and that might have been a cause of dissension later on. But on that day in 1951 it was simple enough. Ed and Earle were performing better, and seemed to have few problems with the altitude, so when they decided to carry on for a recce they just kept going until they got to the summit.[2]

During his working years Ed Cotter gave up any dreams of further Himalayan summits. Through Adventure Consultants, however, in his retirement he has been able to join a number of expeditions there, soaking up some authentic Himalayan experiences. In 1989, after travelling to Northern India with Nick Cradock, Anna Cook and Brian Dyson, Ed joined Guy on a trip to Pakistan. Guy recalls walking out of the crowded terminal at Delhi Airport to see a couple of bent, bearded souls waving him over. Ed and Anna, sporting fake beards, were pretending to be Sadhus (holy people). On that expedition Guy's party was the third group to summit the Uli Biaho spire, a dangerous 6400m rock needle in the Karakoram Range. Ed and Anna joined them on their trek to Base Camp up the Baltoro Glacier, then moved up to Concordia at the confluence of the Baltoro and the Godwin-Austen Glacier before trekking out. Ed then accompanied Anna Cook and Nick Cradock on a ski-touring expedition around the Nanda Devi sanctuary.

Some years later Guy helped plan a leisurely trip up to Everest Base Camp for his father, accompanied by Steve Aiken, that allowed them to stop at Nepalese villages on the way, talk to the local people and explore the valleys as they adjusted to the altitude. During his father's visits, Guy has also had the opportunity to get his revenge for the seemingly never-ending treks he endured as a youngster. A couple of days from Base Camp, Ed plaintively asked where the next village was. Guy, who had waited so many years for payback time, was delighted to be able to tell him it was 'just around the corner!'

En route to Everest Base Camp, 2008. Cotter collection

Dinnertime was never like this in Ed's day. Ed Cotter, Suze Kelly and Guy Cotter at Everest Base Camp, 2008. Cotter collection

Ed has always found it difficult to sit on his hands, and on one trip in 2008 he became lost several times after wandering off on his own. Knowing how easy it is to get disoriented, Guy put two Sherpas in charge to make sure Ed got down safely to the lodge. A couple of hours later Guy was himself heading down and ran into his very sheepish-looking Sherpas. He said 'You've lost my father, haven't you!' They said they were very sorry. They had stopped at a tea-house, and while they were inside Ed had taken off again, making a right turn instead of a left. That night the father was sternly reminded that unless he stayed close, he would turn out to be a very expensive guest.

In 1951 Ed had shown an ability to adapt to high altitude without ever knowing he was blessed with a type of 'extreme altitude gene'. In 2008 his nephew Jim Cotter was with Ed and Guy at Everest Base Camp undertaking research into altitude tolerance, at the nearby Pyramid Lab located at 5050m between Lobuche and Gorak Shep. Both Jim and Ed exhibited a Sherpa-like 'dampened response' to hypoxia (lack of oxygen). Jim explains: 'While this doesn't help at moderate altitudes, it is thought to be advantageous at very high altitude, since there's still ventilatory reserve available at such altitudes, and breathing is less strenuous before that point.' On the way up to Base Camp, Ed spent several nights with his nephew at Pyramid Lab; Jim says that over the course of his research, Ed coped

Ed shares some time with Ang Dorje of the Adventure Consultants team, at Base Camp in 2008.
Jim Cotter

Guy and Ed ready to roll on the world's biggest mountain. Suze Kelly

Guy and Ed with Ama Dablam in the background. Suze Kelly

with the altitude far better than some other participants a quarter his age.[3]

Thinking back to Mukut Parbat, Ed's most intense memory is of the huge struggle up the narrow ridge above a 5000ft drop, with one boot on each side of the ridge for about 800ft. After that Garhwal expedition, adding further peaks to a list of ascents never interested him: to him a trip into the mountains was only pleasurable if it was spent with others who were compatible. 'To have achieved Mukut Parbat was exhilarating, I suppose, but for me the main thing was always to be with people you wanted to be with, rather than counting summits.'

Over the years Ed has delivered many addresses to mountaineering and community groups, and he finds himself surprised by the way 'history' has quickly absorbed quite recent events in which he has been peripherally involved. During an interview, journalist Nancy Cawley once asked if Ed ever regretted standing aside when the bombshell Reconnaissance invitation came. He replied, 'No, I didn't want it to be me. For me the mountains are about being there. I have never thought it was about popularity or adulation. Having to be a public figure because you climbed a mountain would never have suited me.'[4]

Bill Beaven believes Ed's affable and accommodating approach was always a key factor in why he never received the credit he deserved:

Though I did not climb with him a lot, he was as good a climber as anyone I've known. He had wonderful balance and was always very fit. But he was never one to push himself forward, and that meant he did not often lead. That reluctance to promote himself dogged him all his life, and I think he knows he was not always good at making decisions.[5]

Colin Monteath, freelance photographer, writer and mountaineer, recalls Ed's surprise when his name appeared in the dedication of Monteath's comprehensive publication *Under a Sheltering Sky*.[6] Monteath credited the members of the Garhwal expedition with setting the pace and style for Kiwi mountaineers in the Himalaya:

He asked me why I had put his name first – actually the names were in alphabetical order – but this was effectively a bunch of amateurs who showed just how much could be achieved with light resources. The expedition was run on a shoestring, the antithesis of Everest which was really a commercial expedition, but it set the pattern for later low-key expeditions in the Himalaya and the Andes which all helped to consolidate the excellent reputation of New Zealand mountaineers. Ed

Guy, Jim and Ed Cotter at the Pyramid Lab. Suze Kelly

Ed Cotter just above the settlement of Lobuche, with Taboche behind. Guy Cotter

Cotter played a large part in this, and climbs like the Maximilian Ridge of Elie de Beaumont were ground-breaking, but whereas the other three all went back to the Himalaya, Ed Cotter didn't, and I believe he felt that quite acutely. He was always such an engaging, congenial, eternally youthful character, but that laconic approach to life, totally the opposite of Ed Hillary, meant that he was never able to push himself forward.

When Gerald (Charlie) Carrington initiated the Christchurch Tramping Club in 1925, which later became the CMC, some unwritten rules were laid down:

> To be cheerful at all times, under the most adverse conditions; that at all times a spirit of friendship should exist among club members; that each should overlook the shortcomings and idiosyncrasies of the other; and that all should love the mountains, enter their fastnesses with respect, and vigorously carry out their exploration.[7]

Some might say that Ed's lack of ego meant he never had the forcefulness needed to be the man at the top, as Riddiford and Hillary both strove to be. Others would say those qualities made Ed Cotter exactly the right man for any climb: a fearless, reliable mountaineer dedicated to his team and also thoroughly trained in mountaincraft. Those qualities and abilities stemmed from his earliest days in the CMC. For him, climbing was all about learning to understand the mountains: competition with others was never a driver. 'We felt we were on an apprenticeship, and we were prepared to wait our time, doing Divide crossings and just climbing mountains on the Divide rather than rushing off to the Hermitage.'[8]

He has welcomed a return in recent years to mountaineering for mountaineering's sake: good honest times in the mountains on trips that last longer than a chopper ride to a specific challenge; a return to exploration rather than just high summits, and opportunities for 'non-mountaineers' to enjoy unique experiences in quite extreme locations, 'though there's also a place still for the elite climber with superlative technical skills, the small cadre who will attempt the ultimate'.[9]

Through his friendships Ed has been able to revisit many wonderful experiences:

> It's like an extended family. Once a mountaineer, always a mountaineer. Even though you're not climbing … you read everything that comes through, and feel that common bond.

Vailima after the February earthquake: the view over the Avon-Heathcote Estuary remains, but the room with the view has gone for good. Lyn McKinnon

In later years, George Lowe broached the subject of an apology he said he owed Ed: the overture was interrupted, and whether it was over the lost goggles Ed has never been certain. But their association spanned more than 60 years, and during Lowe's terminal illness, a squeeze of the hand indicated Lowe still felt the bond.

Life goes on for Ed Cotter, last man standing of the 1951 expedition party. By now it's a familiar story – it has been six years and thousands of tremors after the initial earthquake inflicted serious damage on Christchurch and its infrastructure on 4 September 2010, miraculously with no casualties. That was followed by the more serious quakes on 22 February 2011, with the loss of 185 lives, another wave in June, and untold billions of dollars in rebuild costs. When the vicious February quakes hit the coastal suburbs Ed was in his lounge in Vailima, high above Shag Rock, reading the newspaper. The ceiling started to cave in, but he kept on reading. Then he thought he'd better get up and have a look around, and perhaps go down to the Esplanade in Sumner to see how Rhondda was getting on. He had difficulty getting out the doors, which were all jammed, but climbed out a window and made it down the rock-strewn hill to report 'a bit of damage'. His house was quickly red-zoned.

For four years he rented a small flat a few blocks back from Sumner beach, visiting Rhondda most evenings for dinner. One rainy night in mid-September 2014, when she delivered him home, he slipped and fell, breaking his left femur. After three months between Christchurch, Ashburton and Burwood hospitals, he moved over the road from his flat to Edith Cavell at Sumner, a rest home from which he can remain connected to his family and close friends. Christmas get-togethers and birthday celebrations bring his family to his side, though he finds it rather hard to keep track of six grandchildren (Elmo, Lillian, Nina, Jess, Leila and Tintin) and four great-grandchildren (Theo, Sidney, Ziggy and Caspar). Faithful

The Dog Tuckers group meets again, this time in 2010 at Quail Flat in the Clarence Reserve, North Canterbury. From left: Peter Bain, Limbo Thompson, Norman Hardie, Ed Cotter, Bill Beaven, Geoff Harrow. Peter Bain

mountaineering friends are also a great support as they call in to catch up and relive the good times.

Peter Bain says his own interest in mountain travel over more than six decades is due in no small part to the example set by Ed, who has been a much-loved member of the 'Dog Tuckers' group, a loose confederation of retired and semi-retired mountaineers, farmers and others united by a love of the South Island high country. The group has regularly taken an annual three- or four-day trip into the hills, where they have indulged to the limit of their abilities in climbing, tramping, fishing, art and natural history, and evenings devoted to food, drink, music and storytelling. Venues have ranged from Marlborough to the Ahuriri and as far west as Fox Glacier, and there has never been a shortage of volunteers to search for Ed Cotter's missing hearing aids. As Bain tells it, Ed's status as one of New Zealand's leading mountaineers and his entertaining personality have always made him welcome on these outings.

From time to time Ed is jolted into real awareness of what a lucky man he has been. Always the great philosopher, he wrote along those lines to the Moores in Anchorage: 'I guess I have always lived for the Now (and the consequences) because life is short, but it can be very sweet.'[10] Like Scott Russell, whose exploratory climbs of the Southern Alps showed the way, Ed Cotter always dreamed of being freed from narrow horizons. Only then was it possible to recapture 'the art of real living, which is adventure'.[11]

CONCLUSION

Putting the record straight

If an offence come out of the truth, better is it that the offence come than that the truth be concealed. – St Jerome[1]

Six decades on, misconceptions about the 1951 First New Zealand Himalayan Expedition may seem relatively harmless, but selective history can become entrenched and, in the long term, may be seriously misleading. Just like spindrift obscuring a mountain's true form, some versions of this expedition have resulted in a set of half-truths becoming accepted as fact. My own purpose, as a sort of ghost writer for Earle Riddiford and an advocate for Ed Cotter, who has travelled his own journey without bearing any grudge, is to help right a few wrongs.

Sir Edmund Hillary's lifetime achievements far surpassed his youthful ambitions of scaling the highest mountains. His high-altitude climbing career was in fact brief: he effectively gave away the top peaks in 1954 after the crisis on Makalu Col. From the Barun Glacier on 26 May 1954 he wrote to Roland Ellis: 'I'm recovering from a rather bad spell … I stupidly persisted and it finally resulted in all the efforts of the expedition to carry me down. They'd probably be up on the col now if I'd only learned to stand clear and let someone else have a go.'[2] But no matter how brilliantly other climbers perform, or how skilled they become, it is Sir Edmund Hillary's name that continues to resonate.

Guy Cotter believes that the media focus on 'the most iconic climb of all time' in 1953[3] has made it more difficult for New Zealand climbers to shine and be celebrated for fresh achievement. For some others, admiration of Hillary's great success is tempered by reservations about the way he achieved it and the way he wrote about it afterwards.[4] In the matter of the First New Zealand Himalayan Expedition and its significant contribution to New Zealand's mountaineering history, this book is an attempt to give more credit where credit is due.

The success of Riddiford's Garhwal expedition was all about timing. In hindsight it is clear that if New Zealanders were to have a shot at Everest, the

Ed Cotter handwalks across a makeshift bridge during the Garhwal expedition. In 2003, at the time of the fiftieth anniversary celebrations of the ascent of Everest, Napier man Martin Yeoman wrote to *Hawkes Bay Today* about how Ed Hillary's feat of walking on his hands on a plank across a ravine had shamed the frightened porters into carrying their loads across the makeshift bridge. He said that after learning that, he knew nothing would hold Hillary back. But Yeoman was quite wrong about which man had set the porters such a challenge, and later apologised to Ed Cotter.
E. Hillary, CMC Kennedy Collection

1951 expedition had to be successful: if Riddiford had listened to Hillary and postponed it, no New Zealanders would have been invited on the Reconnaissance. In later years Hillary failed by numerous omissions to acknowledge what he owed to both Riddiford and Cotter. He largely ignored Cotter, who was never a threat, although after Everest he suggested to Cotter that if he were to prove his fitness and climbing ability, he would consider inviting him on the Makalu expedition. Cotter, amused by the condescension, turned on his heel. But Hillary's perspective on Riddiford grew increasingly negative, and Cotter has always felt acutely that lack of generosity towards Riddiford.

Over the years it has assisted the bigger story of New Zealand mountaineering to gloss over the failure of Hillary and Lowe on Mukut Parbat, and internet searches reveal any number of articles that continue to perpetuate the myth that they completed the climb. The March 2013 obituary for George Lowe in *The Times* states that Lowe and Hillary were 'part of the first New Zealand expedition to the Himalaya, including a first ascent of Mukut Parbat in Garhwal, India'. Ed Douglas in his obituary of Lowe for the *Guardian* creates the same impression: 'Grand plans of reaching Everest proved overambitious, but their reduced group of four managed instead a perfectly respectable first ascent of Mukut Parbat (23,760ft), in India's Garhwal region.'[5] Close, but not correct.

Lowe himself was partly to blame: in *Because It Is There* he wrote, 'We were a quartet of highly elated climbers, having achieved not merely the summit of Mukut Parbat but five other mountains exceeding 20,000ft.' By omission, Lowe also implied Hillary and he were the organisers of the 1951 expedition, leaping from a conversation about the Himalaya with Hillary straight into the 1950 Elie de Beaumont pre-expedition climb.[6] In his biography of Hillary, *Life of a Legend*, Pat Booth tells how 'the four' climbed their prime objective, Mukut Parbat, and five other peaks. In *View from the Summit*, Hillary wrote that it was Lowe who set off the spark that led to the Himalaya, even though Riddiford had begun organising long before. Many established mountain writers have ignored Riddiford's initiatives, among them Stephen Venables, who wrote that Lowe and Hillary decided to organise a Himalayan expedition, and with advice from Everest veteran Noel Odell chose a mountain called Mukut Parbat.[7] Huw Lewis-Jones, during the promotion of Lowe's *Letters from Everest*, was still broadcasting the notion that it was Hillary and Lowe who took the 1951 expedition to the Himalaya and succeeded on Mukut Parbat, after which Hillary was fast-tracked to Everest.[8] Peter Steele, Shipton's friend and biographer, also got it wrong when he wrote that the whole party had 'narrowly failed to climb' the mountain, rather than just Hillary and Lowe.[9]

Misinformation about this expedition has been perpetuated over a very long time. Roland Rodda, a committee member of the NZAC in 1951, was infuriated when Hillary, in his obituary for his father-in-law, Jim Rose, wrote that Rose was responsible for the invitation for the New Zealanders to join the 1951 Reconnaissance. It was, of course, Roland Ellis who had suggested that Harry Stevenson send a cable to the Himalayan Committee. In August 1991 Rodda (then resident in the UK) wrote to Murray Ellis, 'I am very sorry and indeed extremely angry that this particular one of your father's great deeds has been attributed to someone so unworthy – and by the incredibly indebted beneficiary himself!'[10] After meeting Hillary at the 40th Everest Anniversary Alpine Club function at the RGS in London, he wrote again on 3 October 1993: 'I told Ed I had laughed like a drain when I read the obituary.'[11]

Harry Stevenson also vented his feelings in a letter to Murray Ellis:

> The whole credit for the inclusion of New Zealanders on the Reconnaissance expedition is due to your father ... Earle Riddiford did all the organising of that expedition and I guess more than his share of paying ... Earle was put in an awkward position as the club put it over to him to make the selection and no doubt Ed [Hillary] and George would be pushing themselves. Of course they turned back on Mukut Parbat leaving Earle and Ed Cotter to complete the climb. My opinion of Ed [Hillary] is that he has always been after the main chance and is happy to accept everyone's hospitality etc without so much as a thank you, even to your father who was so generous and through A. Ellis and Co supplied so much to Ed and others. I acknowledge Ed's many good points ... but Earle Riddiford never received the credit he deserves ... He made the main effort to open up the icefall in the Western Cwm.[12]

In a review of Lowe's autobiography *Because It Is There*, Norman Hardie expressed his disappointment at Lowe's extremely sketchy handling of the 1951 expedition:

> H.E. Riddiford provided the inspiration for this important venture and he did most of the organising. He also provided more than a fair share of the finances, although Mr Lowe's judicious omissions tend to obscure this fact. So far as the clubs which gave support were concerned ... Mr Riddiford was the [expedition] leader. I understand that the NZAC was able to arrange for the inclusion of two New Zealanders in the Everest Reconnaissance mainly on the strength of the climb of Mukut Parbat, and there is no doubt about the leader of that climb. No

matter what the exact truth is about their disagreement, I had hoped Mr Lowe would have forgotten the differences of nine years ago ... To his own inclusion in this First New Zealand Himalayan Expedition, Mr Lowe owes all his subsequent invitations. All New Zealanders who shared in the great Himalayan harvest of the last decade owe, in some measure, a debt to Riddiford ... the healing of an old sore could have made this a much worthier contribution to the literature of adventure.[13]

In a personal letter to Riddiford he was more explicit:

I thought Lowe's book was ... written for the glorification of Ed [Hillary], for it is in Ed's reflection that his own claim to glory lies. His treatment of you is just as one would expect from him – no credit, no thanks, just grizzle. I had a long talk to Doug Dick on the subject of the differences in 1951 and their consequences, before we knew George was going into print, and Doug suggested your complete version should be written and placed somewhere deep in Club Archives for a few years. Ed will probably have a few biographers 30 years hence, and there could very well be a full book on New Zealanders in the Himalaya. Your part has never been acknowledged in getting us all started, and I want to see the picture emerge clearly someday.[14]

Lowe's obfuscations in *Because It Is There* greatly upset Riddiford. He prepared a press statement for the *Dominion* but decided against it because he felt publication would only give Lowe's story additional oxygen. He replied to Norman Hardie, 'Even if true, this type of criticism in a book is below the belt, but in this case it is a gross distortion of the truth.'[15] He was reluctant to let Lowe's version of events pass unopposed into climbing history. Jim Wilson, editor of the *NZAJ* in 1960, agreed to publish a letter in which Riddiford disputed Lowe's account of the argument at Ranikhet:

The first suggestion I made was that Ed Hillary should go as he had been outstandingly fit throughout the expedition ... I said we should decide the matter amongst ourselves on the merits. Next morning still no decision had been made ... I asked the party whether they thought it would be fair if Ed Hillary and I went. There was no agreement and discussion virtually came to an end. [Eventually] George Lowe said that if Ed Cotter would agree to stand down, he would do the same ... Lowe also states that the party did not have an acknowledged leader ... Records and correspondence show that the initiative and planning of the expedition came from me and that the other members joined the expedition at my invitation. We took the climbing decisions amongst ourselves in the usual way: although I did lead the climb of Mukut Parbat, 23,760ft, our main climbing objective. These facts are not recorded in [Lowe's] book.[16]

In New Zealand the Mukut Parbat story had hit the headlines briefly. On 20 August 1951 an editorial in the *Press* had praised 'a tale of modern adventure as exciting as anything in a storybook', and the ascent had provided the cover story for the *Weekly News* on 3 October 1951. Very soon, however, Mukut Parbat was eclipsed by the Everest Reconnaissance and the milestone of the Everest conquest. In *Everest 1953: The epic story of the first ascent*, Mick Conefrey wrote that the Everest expedition assumed an importance far greater than anyone had ever anticipated.[17] In the process, Edmund Hillary became the poster boy for colonial Britain. As the world marvelled, New Zealand was quick to adopt a legend that showcased Kiwi courage to the world. The result was iconic status for Hillary that blotted out any other mountaineering triumph before or after.[18]

To restore balance to the history of New Zealanders in the Himalaya we should celebrate the dogged efforts of the three men who climbed Mukut Parbat and so provided the catalyst for further Himalayan exploits. Dan Bryant later wrote that it was a pity the New Zealand expedition did not have a non-climbing leader who could have made a dispassionate choice about who should go to Everest:

> It must have been a bitter blow to the secret ambitions of Lowe and Cotter … to be left out. As far as Lowe is concerned, his turn came later, but Cotter can be counted decidedly unfortunate to have reached the summit of Mukut Parbat and to have been so close to inclusion in the Everest team, and yet miss selection. His consolation will be in the fact that he took part in a glorious expedition, that he performed very well, and that two of his companions went on to do so amazingly well in the final Everest assault.[19]

In a review of Paul Little's *After Everest: Inside the private world of Edmund Hillary*, Shaun Barnett, editor of the *FMC Bulletin*, describes as 'preposterous'[20] the claims that Edmund Hillary was the best climber in the world and George Lowe the second. Barnett notes 'a baseless insult' to Ed Cotter along the lines that someone who walked away from the discussion at Ranikhet probably wouldn't have made it to the top of Everest: 'On the contrary, Cotter had proved he had the ability and drive to climb at altitude to summit Mukut Parbat with Earle

Riddiford, when Hillary and Lowe hadn't.'[21] In another review, this time of *First to the Top* by David Hill and Phoebe Morris, Barnett makes the point that in its account of the major events of Hillary's life there has been a major oversight. 'Inexcusably, the 1951 Garhwal expedition is omitted.'[22]

During his time guiding at Franz Josef, Cotter spoke to mountain writer Bob McKerrow – without bitterness or rancour – about how he was cut out of the Reconnaissance. McKerrow believes Hillary was 'let in the door' because Ed Cotter was so self-effacing. Cotter was highly regarded by those who climbed with him, as a technical climber who had plenty of notable successes with never an adverse comment. He was in many ways a superior climber to Hillary, whose failure on the Barun trip to raise Jim McFarlane from 20 metres down a crevasse, despite having two 30m lengths of rope and the assistance of five Sherpas, exposed a gaping hole in his mountaincraft (see Appendix 2). Hillary's own response to the bungled rescue attempt was 'an awful sense of shame',[23] but the incident revealed that he did not have skills that many would assume were a prerequisite for Himalayan climbing, probably because much of his early climbing was with guides. As climbing contemporary Geoff Harrow later commented:

> [Guide Harry] Ayres … was a magnificent iceman, a world-beater so superb at step cutting and belaying that he never worried too much about getting the clients to take on much responsibility. He was just being paid to get them up a mountain and down again safely. Hillary would have picked up a lot from him, but Ayres was never going to teach him the sorts of things he would have learned at climbing courses, like crevasse instruction. Hillary didn't have a clue – he just tied a rope around his waist and went down, and when the Sherpas pulled like hell they broke his ribs.[24]

Hillary and Lowe put much emphasis on Riddiford's lack of fitness, but Norman Hardie insists that when it was really required, Riddiford could always get there: 'On Mukut Parbat, Earle was true to form: he climbed none of the lesser peaks but was out in front on the biggest and best.'

> Earle had very real leadership qualities. He may not have been quite as strong in load carrying or in cutting steps as some of the others, but we all acknowledged that he had the ideas and the writing ability, the contacts and the organisational talent that you require in a leader. The rest of us got on very well indeed with him, so Hillary's criticisms were in my opinion quite unwarranted.[25]

Like Hardie, Bill Beaven also has high praise for Riddiford's abilities as someone who had tremendous drive and stamina beyond what might be expected of a person of his physique, and was a good route-finder. Beaven found the Elie de Beaumont climb illuminating in that right from the start, Hillary and Lowe clearly decided their role was to be in front. According to Ed Cotter, Hillary always had his own agenda; possibly his quest for fame stemmed from a search for something that would give his life greater substance:

> He sometimes talked of the importance in life of doing something, of having a goal and making a difference … In many ways he had an unusual upbringing, and he was fairly insignificant at school. After service in the Pacific there was a gap in his life that being a beekeeper didn't really fill. When he announced the 1951 expedition to the press, we all thought he was jumping the gun, but of course it meant his name came forward first. It was Earle's expedition, and Earle had it under wraps for a reason, because as yet we didn't have a permit. But Hillary decided to take the spotlight. It's interesting that later on he really did the same thing in the Antarctic, where he pushed on to the Pole against the strategy of the Fuchs expedition, and so he got his name up in lights again.[26] That is just the sort of person he was. He was looking for meaning in his life, and this is how he found it.[27]

But as he turned his face to the camera, Hillary seemed to turn his back on some of the friends who had helped him on the way to fame. Diplomat Roger Peren certainly gained that impression when he was stationed at the embassy in Washington and saw quite a bit of Hillary in his later years:

> He knew that I knew Earle well, but never brought the subject up, though he himself gained membership of the Everest expedition only through Earle's efforts … As with many men, inevitably the patterns of friendship change as people go in different directions … once Hillary was included for Everest, there was nothing more Earle could do for him.[28]

Author and photographer Mavis Davidson, a life member of the NZAC and member of the first all-women team to ascend Mt Cook in January 1953, climbed extensively in the Southern Alps gathering material for guidebooks. In January 1998 she wrote to Rosemary Riddiford expressing her anger at the hype surrounding Hillary:

… the adulation is sickening … Ed Hillary was not within a bull's roar of being the outstanding climber of his day – the best (amateur) climbers of his day were livid about this. Ed had the best guide in the country for his climbing – Harry Ayres – who told me Ed was always willing to plug steps because he couldn't lead … Earle was the pioneer of our Himalayan expeditions, and to me he is the unsung hero of New Zealand participation there … I have never ceased to be aggrieved at the treatment Earle received.[29]

Rosemary Riddiford quickly replied:

I very much appreciated your letter … Earle had a high regard for Harry Ayres and it was good to see your reference to him. Some years ago you mentioned the likelihood of Earle's input into Himalayan mountaineering being overlooked, but having received your letter I feel more confident of his endeavours being acknowledged, now I realise your respect for his effort, which no doubt you will pass on to others.[30]

The following year, in a review of *View from the Summit,* Philip Temple made his views clear:

Ed Hillary gives credit to the crucial help some fellow climbers gave him early in his career, such as George Lowe and Harry Ayres, but bears a lasting grudge towards Wellington climber Earle Riddiford. Riddiford has been dead a dozen years, but clearly this intellectual and rather weedy lawyer from a pioneer landed family got right up our no-nonsense egalitarian hero's nose … things happen on climbing expeditions, but why Riddiford cannot be given his due half a century later is a mystery. As Hillary admits, he has not always been 'thoughtful and kind', and since Riddiford's contribution towards Hillary reaching Everest was important, the record needs straightening a little. On the First New Zealand Himalayan Expedition in 1951, Riddiford climbed their major objective, Mukut Parbat. Hillary and Lowe did not. Riddiford's contribution to Hillary's place on Everest was seminal.[31]

Temple believes that although many people continue to regard Hillary as a paragon, he had his faults.[32] His driving determination, for example, sometimes became plain stubbornness, evidenced by his long refusal to admit he was no longer able to cope physically at high altitude. Temple has also found that anyone who even obliquely criticised the great man could expect some flak. On one occasion in Auckland, when he pointed out the disparity between the tributes accorded Hillary and those received by Tenzing following Everest, Temple came in for quite a grilling from the Hillary fans – 'what you might call a sort of closing of the clan against any adverse opinion'. In 2003 in a review of a reprint of *High Adventure*, first published in 1955, Temple was surprised by Hillary's praise at the time for Riddiford, which was in stark contrast to his later 'less than complimentary' accounts.[33]

In his memoir *In This Short Span*, surgeon and mountaineer Michael Ward who, with Riddiford, took part in the 1951 Everest Reconnaissance, wrote of meeting Riddiford and Hillary for the first time in Dingla, where the two gaunt New Zealanders soon set about proving how well acclimatised and mentally attuned to expedition work they were. In Ward's opinion, Riddiford was in his element as they attempted to get through to the Nup La:

> Though only lightly built he was supremely fit and able both to carry heavy loads and play a leading part in route-finding. It seemed to me that the two New Zealanders were much more mature and experienced in their approach to this particular form of mountaineering than the European-trained members of the party.[34]

During the 1953 Everest expedition, for which he was medical officer, Ward heard Lowe's version of Ranikhet, and his determination to achieve some sort of payback:

> George told me Eric's telegram had turned the four friends into a disharmonious quartet and gave the lie to those naïve beliefs that only high motives and unselfish instincts flourish above the snowline. In 1952 George together with Earle Riddiford and Ed Hillary joined the Cho Oyu expedition, and George went with the avowed intent of climbing Earle Riddiford into the ground.[35]

Over many decades Dunedin's Ellis family, including Roland Ellis, his son Murray and his grandson David, made an important contribution to NZAC activities, and in the early years Roland and then Murray were closely involved with the Hillary camp. In 2003, following publication of an article in *The Climber* magazine, in which he acknowledged Riddiford's Himalayan endeavours, David Ellis wrote to Rosemary Riddiford:

I am pleased you were happy with the article. I had great delight in giving Earle the credit he deserves for being a true visionary for New Zealand's climbing in the Himalaya. His part in Hillary's final Everest ascent needs to be acknowledged and his story told. I believe with time he will get the credit he deserves. If my article is a small catalyst to this it would make me tremendously happy … My father Murray is a very loyal person but over time he has become embittered by Ed's lack of acknowledgement to the people that really helped him along the way. He feels those that have toiled to help get Ed the successes he has achieved have never received the recognition they deserve from him.[36] Although Ed comes across as extremely humble, it is the quiet trumpet of a single man, and it has never included the team he had around him. I think this is unfortunate.[37]

Overseas, Riddiford's contribution did not go unnoticed. As Scott Russell wrote for the British *Alpine Journal* in an article celebrating the centenary of the New Zealand Alpine Club: 'In the record of New Zealand's achievement on Mount Everest, Dan Bryant and Earle Riddiford deserve to be remembered.'[38]

For the last word on balance, we return to the universally respected 1951 NZAC president Harry Stevenson, who in NZAC correspondence now stored in the Hocken Collections in Dunedin, left an undated note for climbing posterity:

For the record both Hillary and Lowe have left the impression in various publications that it was their own efforts more than anything that led [to them] being included in the Everest Expedition. In fact Earle Riddiford, as the organiser and driving force behind the Garhwal Expedition, was primarily responsible. He was not given credit for his influence, which is a pity. This may have been through jealousies or personality clashes. Riddiford was a fine and determined climber and had he not been so affected by altitude he would have been on the expedition to Everest. He did a tremendous job helping the expedition as well as putting New Zealand before the public by climbing Mukut Parbat.[39]

APPENDIX 1

Return to Mukut Parbat
by Evangeline Riddiford Graham

Although my grandfather Earle died some years before I was born, I grew up hearing his name. Earle's personality reverberated down the years and through all family stories – Earle the wonderful dancer; Earle the charming flirt; Earle the fastidious gardener; Earle the terrifying driver hurtling down gravel roads; Earle the maverick, buying back the family homestead, only to lose it again; Earle the intrepid and terrible, marching his four children through the hills of Orongorongo, with the injunction that one must never stop, but there was nothing wrong with slowing down. Earle the feckless young lawyer. Earle the mountaineer. Earle the returning hero, courting my grandmother – an achievement that I personally will always view as his greatest, most visionary triumph.

My mother Anna, the storyteller, inherited Earle's obsession with maps and planning. When this book was planned, she began to dream of a Himalayan journey of her own, one retracing the steps of the 1951 Garhwal expedition – the journey on which Earle, Ed Cotter and Pasang Dawa Lama summited Mukut Parbat.

My mother's expedition party in September 2015 included me, my younger sister Oonagh (15), our uncle Richard (Earle's second child), Richard's sons Freddy (21) and Sam (18), and Anna Cook and her husband Dave McFall. Anna Cook is a New Zealand guide and alpine skier. While she acted as lead organiser, we also travelled with two Indian guides – Mayank, who worked for World Expeditions India, and Badri, a local guide, the last known person to have been up on the Chamrao Glacier approach to Mukut Parbat. Our cooks were Jeet, Padam, Sontos and Veejay.

Following a journey by train and car from Delhi to Rishikesh, the first trek was over the Kuari Pass from the damp town of Ghat to Joshimath. Kuari Pass is a beautiful alpine trail through woodsy villages and beautiful country: dark and handsome forest with silver beech, rhododendrons and a moss carpet, broken up by rock paths shining with mica, and bare green hillside that doesn't roll so much as bounce – up and down, up and down. In September–October the land is bountiful. The terraced farms of the villages are abundant too – bright with beans, tomatoes, corn, cabbages, peppers and millet. The crops allow the villages to be self sufficient, trading produce for power. In the winter, in the snow, many villages are vacated.

Our luggage and supplies were carried on Kuari Pass by a team of mules and ponies accompanied by a group of local horsemen. From Joshimath we drove to Badrinath, pilgrim city, and from there to Chamrao Nala, camping there before walking up to the base of Mukut Parbat, assisted by 22 porters. We stayed at our 'base camp' for three nights, making day trips out from there.

I didn't fully understand what the journey meant until we came face to face with the mountains themselves, the range stretching from the mighty Nilkanth in the north to Nanda Devi in the southeast. It was late morning and the mountains were shockingly blue and white – and vastly high. We sat on the grass and tilted our heads back, like an audience in the front row of a 3D movie. Badri, waving his long walking stick, named the peaks for us: You are Nilkantha, you are Arwa Tower, you are Kamet, you are Ghoni, you are Ghoda, you are Hathi, you are Barmai, you are Sona Ganghri, you are Rishi, you are Dronagiri, you are Kalanka, you are Nanda Devi …

And where is Mukut Parbat? we asked.

Badri squinted. There! Peeking out behind Kamet's left shoulder, over a long white bib of glacier, was our parbat – the mountain Earle, Ed Cotter and Pasang had climbed first. Their mountain.

The mountains, out on their morning parade, felt utterly foreign to me. Not an alienating foreignness – an awe-inspiring one. Like mountains everywhere, including ours in Aotearoa, the Himalayan peaks have distinct identities. Nanda Devi, in particular, is special. She is the patron deity of the Garhwal region. Gazing up at the mountain, Dave reminded us of the ill-fated Nanda Devi expedition of 1976, on which a young woman named after the mountain goddess died 300 metres from the summit. Anna Cook, standing next to me, recalled that she and Ed Cotter were luckier when they skied together in the region in the 1990s, with the mountain looming large in their view, when the sanctuary was still open.

At that point, my feeling changed. The stories I had heard were alive here in the generations standing beside me. I felt a flooding of profound pride. In the highest region in the world, in the heartland of the world's oldest living religion, these New Zealanders – largely self-taught enthusiasts – had led big lives. These were my grandfather's friends, the names on the backs of my grandmother's photographs.

APPENDIX 1   299

The return to Mukut Parbat. From left, Anna Riddiford, Freddy Riddiford, Richard Riddiford, Sam Riddiford, Evangeline Riddiford Graham, Oonagh Riddiford Graham. Anna Cook

They had known the peaks and ridges of the Himalaya intimately. They had spent hours exploring routes. In the Himalaya, their names mean something.

Although I often found myself breathless and irritable in the thin air, the Kuari Pass trail is easy enough – at its top, cousin Freddy declared the pass 'a walk in the park'. Not so Mukut Parbat. Up at 5000 metres, the notions of 'walk', 'mile' and 'hour' began to shift and give way, rather like the rocks beneath our feet. While the 1951 mountaineers walked along the valley floor from Mana to Chamrao Nala Glacier, we drove over a rock road winding high above. Even so, we set up our own base camp far below where theirs must have been pitched. Our camp, a silt bed enclosed by a ring of peaked sand dunes, might have been a crater on the moon. The moraine stretched in undulating peaks and troughs across the starkly shaped valley, all the way back to the foot of the mountain. When we compared the valley before us to the photographs from 1951, Dave and Anna hypothesised that the glacier that had formed it had retreated significantly in the last 50 years. Traversing the moraine, we could take hours to cover one kilometre. And those hours started to feel much more exhausting, at least to me. At a mere 5000 metres, I was a spent husk of a mountaineer's granddaughter.

After three days floundering on the moraine, the sight of Mukut Parbat's icy col began to seem still more ridiculous than it ever had before, and Earle's climbing of it more outlandish. He had chosen this place, and organised an exploration of it – on next to no information. There was no Google, no GPS, no World Expeditions India. There was no one they knew who had been here. Out of one German map, Shipton and Tilman's accounts and his own mountaineering experience in New Zealand, Earle conjured the Himalaya – and conjured a desire for them in himself, and in the people around him.

I knew Earle adored the mountains. But it wasn't until we started up the moraine that I understood that loving the mountains is not a pleasure, but a necessity of being in them: an option only in the sense that survival is an option. Love is the only condition in which you accept the mountains, and the mountains accept you. Looking up at Mukut Parbat's treacherous ridgeline, I realised that while they were up there, Earle, Ed, Ed and George must have loved it too. It's true that later things fell apart. But up there, in the thin air with the loose rocks rolling and tiny red and purple alpine flowers breaking under their cold and heavy hobnail boots, they could only have loved it.

On our last day up the moraine a heavy fog fell as we made our way back to camp. The effect was unsettling. We could have been anywhere. As we neared the campsite, however, we saw the flickering of light. There was my mother standing on a high dune waving her headlamp to guide us home – much as George Lowe

In glorious conditions, quite unlike those in which their father made the first ascent of Mukut Parbat more than six decades ago, Richard and Anna Riddiford follow in his footsteps. Anna Cook

Freddy and Evangeline use the same map taken into the Garhwal by their grandfather in 1951.
Anna Cook

waited for Earle and Ed, shining a torch in the darkness. Then en route back to Delhi we stopped in Ranikhet, in the same hotel where the 1951 boys had received the infamous telegram.

As we trekked, all our smaller experiences amplified the larger ones of the '51-ers'. The 'Ganga Ice Shark' that sliced open cousin Sam's feet in a frozen river crossing echoed the madness of Earle's muddy near-drowning. Our tense relationship with our portable toilet throne was a sedate version of Earle's crippling six-week 'affliction'. The question of the weather window, the trade of sartorial insults, the bells of the cows and ponies, the local women bent double under towering baskets of grass, the rivulets of chatter and silence in accordance with the steepness of the hills – I think we shared all that with them as well.

We were very happy. And in June 1951, I think they were happy too.

APPENDIX 2

What Happened to the Dream Team?

Hardie, Beaven and McFarlane, whose enthusiasm had fuelled Riddiford's Himalayan dream, all went on to climb in the Himalaya on later expeditions.

Norman Hardie, QSO: 1924–

As Riddiford was finalising plans for the Garhwal expedition, Hardie left for London, working his passage on the *Rangitiki* as a steward. His impending marriage to Enid Hurst, who was teaching in Kent, plus the news that Beaven and McFarlane had decided against the 1951 climb, put an end to any immediate Himalayan intentions. He took a job with a structural engineering firm based in London, married in March 1951, and the newly weds were soon sharing a house with Bill Packard and his wife Geraldine, another of the Merivale flatmates.

Through Packard Hardie was introduced to the Alpine Club where he met Charles Evans, who had been on the Annapurna expedition with Packard. In July 1952 Ed Hillary exhorted Hardie to apply for the 1953 Everest expedition, telling him Shipton was talking of a party of four English and four New Zealanders and had a habit of getting his own way.[1] With the change of leader, Hardie's application was unsuccessful, though he was asked to assist the expedition by helping with administration through the Royal Geographical Society office, and expedition secretary J.H. Emlyn Jones told Hardie in confidence he was likely to be considered for a second attempt after the monsoon season.[2] The mountain was conquered in May, however, and during the subsequent media storm Hillary and Lowe stayed with the Hardies in their London home. In 1954 Hardie joined the NZAC Barun Himalayan Expedition, and in 1955 became Evans' deputy leader for a first ascent of Kangchenjunga, described by John Hunt as the greatest feat in mountaineering, with dangers of an order even higher than Everest.[3] When Evans and Hardie were organising the expedition they were given permission to operate on the Nepalese side, but the actual summit was on the frontier of Sikkim. To the Sikkimese, the summit was sacred and should remain untrodden for religious reasons. The expedition leaders took that on board, and though they had climbed from Nepal they stopped 'five feet from the gods', as Hardie put it.[4]

Over 1954–55 Hardie contributed significantly to the mapping of a highly complicated part of the Everest region, earning him a reputation as an outstanding mountaineer and surveyor.[5] In December 1955 the Hardies moved back to New Zealand; in 1960 Hardie declined Hillary's invitation to join the 1961 attempt on Makalu, but agreed to join Griff Pugh's medical research expedition in Nepal for three months. In the summer of 1962 he spent five weeks in Antarctica assisting with training on the ice.

Throughout the 1960s Hardie continued climbing with Beaven, Riddiford and others, and in 1966 during a search and rescue mission to find four climbers missing on Mt Rolleston, he was in the same tent as John Harrison and John Wilson when an avalanche struck. Hardie and Wilson were lifted out, but Harrison, tragically, could not be resuscitated. In 1967–68 Hardie joined Hillary's mapping, geology and climbing expedition to the Mt Herschel area in Antarctica.

In 1973, as a member of the initial Himalayan Trust board, he went to Nepal to help explore the possibility of a national park in the Mt Everest area, and in 1974 was back in Nepal leading a trekking party of 12. Based in Christchurch for many years, the Hardies spent much time in the mountains, and Hardie served on the Arthur's Pass National Park Board. He worked in Christchurch as a consulting engineer until 1983, the year in which he was appointed leader at Scott Base for the summer season. Following that, he became supervisor of a construction project near Nelson. Back in Christchurch, he was involved in setting up experimental vineyards with some mountaineering friends including Don Beaven, and in 1988, after 22 years of service, he resigned from the Himalayan Trust. Retirement years have since featured many trips around the world, often to attend mountaineering functions and commemorative events. Two autobiographies record his life: *In Highest Nepal: Our life among the Sherpas* (1957) and *On My Own Two Feet* (2006).

Jim McFarlane, QSM: 1926–1997

McFarlane's love of the mountains began with trips into the Canterbury high country with his father Alex, a keen fisherman and teacher who became a well-known entomologist. It was on one of those trips that he met Hardie. The two young men served together on the University Tramping Club committee. During one vacation they walked from Whitcombe Pass to Arthur's Pass, and the following year from the Rakaia to the Hermitage and on down the Landsborough, including a new climb of Mt Dechen. With Beaven and Riddiford, the quartet continued to develop their skills in a series of challenging climbing expeditions, including one where McFarlane and Hardie climbed Mt Cook from a snow cave near the Empress Hut site. This trip was unusual, as it was the first time any party had gone there and back along the three-summit ridge in one day.

During his time working in Timaru McFarlane joined the New Zealand Alpine Club and the Tasman Ski Club based at Timaru – one of the first three ski clubs established in the South Island in 1929. On moving to Invercargill he served on the Southland NZAC committee and climbed extensively in Southland and Otago.

Following marriage to his wife Nola, a supportive and capable climbing companion, he was unavailable for the 1951 expedition, but was still enjoying enough success in the mountains to be an obvious choice for the NZAC expedition in 1954. It was a trip with long-term consequences for McFarlane. On 24 April he set out with Hillary and Wilkins from base camp in the high reaches of the Barun Glacier, planning to reconnoitre the approaches to Lhotse II and Makalu II. Five Sherpas accompanied them. After two days they moved to the west of Makalu, the next step an ascent of a 20,244ft peak from which they could look into a five-mile-wide glaciated area. Terraces above the glacier took them to a campsite at the head of the Barun. The following day they climbed another peak at 20,145ft, with McFarlane climbing strongly as he acclimatised. He and Wilkins decided to move on while Hillary elected to return to camp.

On their return from the col they descended a snowfield that narrowed into a glacier. Halfway down the glacier, roped together, they turned to avoid crevasses. At around 2pm McFarlane suddenly saw Wilkins' red hat disappearing into the ice. He braced for the impact, but the ice was too hard for his ice axe: he was able to slow Wilkins' fall, but was dragged in after him. Sixty feet down, he apologised to Wilkins: 'What a helluva mountaineer I am.'[6] McFarlane was having difficulty moving, and Wilkins knew he had to go for help. After a tenacious effort, using a slim ramp of ice attached to one crevasse wall and cutting steps in the walls of the crevasse, Wilkins manage to flounder out onto the surface snow. His escape took two hours, and it was 5.30 – an hour before dark – when he reached Hillary's tent.

Hillary, who was not in a good state of health, mobilised the five Sherpas and the party reached the crevasse in 45 minutes. Hillary tied two ropes around his waist and the Sherpas lowered him, but not far enough to reach McFarlane. When Hillary shouted the order for them to pull him up again the Sherpas moved back too quickly, causing the ropes to cut deeply into the edge of the crevasse. As the ropes rode up his ribcage, Hillary was trapped under the lip with such force that three ribs were broken, and he had great difficulty getting out. A further attempt to lift McFarlane out on a rope proved fruitless and the concussed and injured climber was left overnight, unable to get his feet into the sleeping bags provided because of his crampons, which he had been unable to remove.

The incident was marked by a sequence of errors of judgement, possibly due to altitude effects. Norman Hardie suggests that though Wilkins was exhausted, it was a life-and-death situation and Hillary might have insisted that Wilkins returned with the rescue team to oversee the Sherpas, who panicked at the point where Hillary was left dangling. There was plenty of rope – the crevasse was 18m deep and all expedition ropes were 30m long. Hillary could have left one looped section free to use as a stirrup to take his weight while he was lowered, with the chest rope tied on as a safety measure. That would have meant he could attach McFarlane to both ropes in a similar manner so he could be lifted to the surface; then both ropes would have been lowered again for Hillary's extraction. The grooves in the ice above could have been prevented by placing an ice axe or a pack under the ropes.[7]

Hillary later acknowledged the mistakes he had made and the shame he felt after the failed rescue attempt that left McFarlane facing crippling frostbite and possible death.[8] The next day Wilkins descended via the same route he used to escape and tied a sling around McFarlane who, with great difficulty, was lifted over the edge of the crevasse. Given the questions raised in many quarters about the mismanagement of the first rescue attempt, Hardie's obituary for McFarlane decades later was both tactful and restrained.[9]

After an agonising three weeks being carried out by porters in a cut-down tea chest, McFarlane returned to New Zealand to endure a year in hospital that included amputations to the front halves of both feet and a series of skin grafts. He resumed work in Invercargill and went on to a highly successful engineering career, including a term as national chairman of the Association of Consulting Engineers. In the 1960s he was among a group of committed conservationists who led successful protests against the government's plans to raise lakes Manapouri and Te Anau for the purpose of generating electricity. In 1970 more than a quarter of a million New Zealanders signed a petition to stop the flooding, and in 1973 the Kirk-led Labour government honoured its election pledge to protect lake levels. McFarlane was one of six appointed guardians of lakes Manapouri, Monowai and Te Anau.

Though his own mountaineering career was finished after the 1954 Barun trip, he maintained his alpine interests and served a term as chairman of the southern section of the NZAC. Sailing on the southern lakes and in the deep waters off the Southland coast became a passion, and in 1990 he retired to the Nelson area, where Beaven and Hardie occasionally joined him on the water. He passed away on 18 July 1997 after several years of failing health.

Bill Beaven: 1926–
Born and educated in Christchurch, as a boy Beaven took to exploring the Port Hills. At 14 on his first trip to Arthur's Pass he climbed Avalanche Peak with his brother Don and friends John and Bob Cuthbert. He was greatly impressed with the Crow icefall on Mt Rolleston and the endless mountain ranges stretching north and south. Thereafter on regular trips to Arthur's Pass, mostly by train, he climbed more peaks and tried skiing, then settled on deer shooting, an activity that financed all the gear he needed for the mountains. He studied engineering and commerce at Canterbury University for six years, joined the Canterbury University Tramping Club in 1945, and by living at home was able to afford many mountaineering trips.

Following his encounter with Beaven in the Landsborough in 1946, Riddiford arranged for Bill and Don Beaven to join the survey party for the proposed gondola at Mt Cook, and they were able to climb all the low mountains around the Hermitage. Bill Beaven went on to climb with Riddiford for nearly 40 years. The La Perouse rescue was unforgettable: years later, Harry Ayres would say that Tom Newth, Norman Hardie, Neil Hamilton and Bill Beaven were the outstanding climbers on that most demanding mission.[10] After all the new routes and unclimbed major peaks that Riddiford's dream team explored together, Beaven opted to pursue his career and withdrew from the 1951 expedition, but 1952 was crammed with climbing and ski mountaineering, and on 6 January 1953 he took part in a notable north to south grand traverse of Mt Cook. He then travelled to the UK in 1953, where he worked in engineering factories and climbed in the Lake District and Wales.

After the triumphant 1953 Everest expedition, Beaven and Hardie attended a number of post-Everest events in London and joined members of the successful Everest party at Shipton's Lake District Outward Bound school for a week. Beaven and Bill Packard were also able to liaise with the Alpine Club about NZAC aspirations for the Himalaya. Visits to France and Switzerland brought more climbing in Chamonix with Norman and Enid Hardie and John Morris. He and his brother Don attempted Mt Blanc in hard ice, and climbed the Aiguille de Midi. In 1954 Beaven joined the NZAC Barun Expedition and, with George Lowe, made the second ascent of Baruntse – two days after his expedition companions Harrow and Todd, because Lowe had been 'too shattered' to climb that day. As a result of a boyhood accident Lowe's left elbow was permanently set at an angle of 90 degrees, with limited flexibility each way. He had been manpowered into teaching during wartime because he was unable to stand at attention.[11] His impairment made it difficult for him at high altitude to cut both zigs and zags, and fellow climbers sometimes had to compensate for this. On Everest, Charles Evans had been unaware of this when he assigned step cutting on the Lhotse face to Lowe – a task Lowe later described as 'a study in go-slow'.

When Hardie, Dawa Thondup and Lowe were roped together cutting steps up a relatively hard ice face towards the summit of a 22,080ft ice peak above Camp 3 on Makalu, Lowe was able to take the lead only briefly. On Baruntse, Harrow noted that Beaven always seemed to be in front when he was roped to Lowe. The reason for that was simple – Lowe had said to Beaven: 'You'll have to go first – I have a crook arm and can't cut steps on that sort of slope – you'll have to look after me as I'm not too good at belaying.'[12]

Later, Todd and Beaven joined forces for a first ascent of Nau Lekh. In January 1956, following his return to New Zealand, Beaven married Gay Hall, a nurse from Hororata and a South Island women's ski champion, with whom he had shared some adventurous ski mountaineering. They had three children, Jeremy, Anthony and Susan. Beaven continued climbing major peaks in Otago and Westland with the 'Footloose Fathers', his old climbing friends. In 1970, in partnership with Derek Cook, he bought a bach at Bealey Spur that became the base for many mountain experiences with family and friends, and over the years has been closely involved with the Arthur's Pass Association and various skiing organisations. His career entailed working for Andrews and Beaven Ltd as factory manager, director and then managing director for six years. He served for four years as a director of Repco NZ and various other manufacturing companies. He retired from his directorships at 72.

Of the three mountain-mad young engineers who were unable to accompany Riddiford to the Garhwal, any one of them would have been a worthy candidate for Everest: theirs was an extremely skilled, unfailingly compatible partnership. Astute, careful and courteous men, Hardie and Beaven know better than anyone how much New Zealand mountaineering owes Riddiford. As experienced mountaineers who also climbed with Hillary and Lowe in the Himalaya, they have done what they could to correct distortions and misrepresentations. Both have given their support to this publication and have welcomed it as another opportunity to set the record straight.

APPENDIX 3

British and New Zealand Expeditions to the Himalaya 1950–55

1950: The British West Nepal Expedition (British Himalayan Committee)

Leader: Harold William (Bill) Tilman

Members: Charles Evans, D.G. Lowndes, Jimmy Roberts, Emlyn Jones, Bill Packard (NZ)

Sherpas: Gyalgen, Pasang Dawa, Norbu, Da Namgyal

Altitude sickness so affected the party that most dropped out of the attempt on Annapurna IV (24,688ft). At 24,000ft Packard was in a position to attempt the summit alone, but turned back, recognising the dangers of solo climbing at such altitude.[1]

1951: The First New Zealand Himalayan Expedition to the Garhwal Himalaya (private)

Members: Earle Riddiford, Edmund Cotter, Edmund Hillary, George Lowe

Sirdar: Pasang Dawa Lama

Cotter, Riddiford and Pasang Dawa Lama successfully climbed the target summit of Mukut Parbat (23,760ft) on 11 July.

1951: The British Reconnaissance to Mount Everest (British Himalayan Committee)

Leader: Eric Shipton

Members: Bill Murray, Tom Bourdillon, Mike Ward, Earle Riddiford (NZ), Ed Hillary (NZ)

Sirdar: Angtarkay

The party successfully found its way through the Khumbu Icefall and established a possible route from the Western Cwm up the Lhotse Face to the South Col.

1952: The British Expedition to Cho Oyu (British Himalayan Committee)

Leader: Eric Shipton

Members: Charles Evans, Alfred Gregory, Tom Bourdillon, Ray Colledge, Griffith Pugh, Ed Hillary (NZ), George Lowe (NZ), Earle Riddiford (NZ), Campbell Secord (Canada)

The expedition failed in its attempt on Cho Oyu (26,906ft).

1953: The British Expedition to Mount Everest (British Himalayan Committee)

Leader: John Hunt

Members: Charles Evans, Alfred Gregory, Tom Bourdillon, Edmund Hillary (NZ), George Lowe (NZ), Charles Wylie, Michael Westmacott, George Band, Wilfred Noyce, Michael Ward, Griffith Pugh, Tom Stobart (cameraman), James Morris (journalist)

Sirdar: Tenzing Norgay

Evans and Bourdillon made the first ascent of the South Summit of Everest (28,700ft). Hillary and Tenzing Norgay ascended Mt Everest (29,029ft) on 29 May 1953.

1953: The New Zealand Chamar Expedition (Wellington-based, self-funded)

Members: Athol Roberts, Graham McCallum, Phil Gardner, Maurice Bishop

Sherpas: Namgyl, Nima, Sarki and one other[2]

The party ascended Chamar (23,545ft) on 6–7 June.

1954: The New Zealand Alpine Club Barun Valley Expedition

Leader: Sir Edmund Hillary

Members: Charles Evans (deputy leader), Bill Beaven, Norman Hardie, Geoff Harrow, Brian Wilkins, George Lowe, Colin Todd, Mike Ball (UK), Jim McFarlane

Sirdar: Dawa Tenzing

Wilkins, Ball and Hardie ascended Pethangtse (22,014ft) on 26 May 1954; Harrow and Todd made the first ascent of Baruntse (23,389ft) on 30 May 1954, followed by Beaven and Lowe two days later.

1954: Oxford University Exploration Club Expedition to West Nepal[3]

Leader: John Harrington (NZ)

Members: Colin Todd (NZ), I. Davidson (UK), M. Arnold (UK), J. Murray (US)

Sherpas: Mingma Tsering, Ang Temba

The party climbed a number of peaks to 22,000ft.

1955: The British Reconnaissance Expedition to Kangchenjunga (British Himalayan Committee)

Leader: Charles Evans

Members: Norman Hardie (NZ, deputy leader), George Band, Tony Streather, Joe Brown, Tom MacKinnon, John Jackson, Neil Mather, John Clegg

Sirdar: Dawa Tenzing

Band, Brown, Hardie and Streather made the first ascent of Kangchenjunga (28,169ft) on 25–26 May, but stopped just short of the summit as a mark of respect.

1955: New Zealand Masherbrum Expedition (private, Canterbury Mountaineering Club)

Leader: Stan Conway

Members: Peter Bain, Ray Chapman, Bill Hannah, John Harrison, Rod Hewitt, Alan Morgan, Maurice Brown, Bob Watson, Jahan Zeb (Pakistan), Aslam Khan (Pakistan)

After eight weeks at high altitude the party abandoned its attempt on Masherbrum (25,659ft) owing to poor conditions and portage problems.[4]

APPENDIX 4

Pasang the Indestructible
Pasang Dawa Lama, 1912–1982

The four New Zealanders owed much to Pasang Dawa Lama, who joined them in the Garhwal in 1951. The party knew little of their Sherpa team, though Cotter's diary notes that Yila Tenzing had been with the 1935 Everest expedition when he was just 17, and Pasang on the American expedition to K2 in 1939. But although the New Zealanders did not initially have a high opinion of his skills with crampons, Pasang Dawa Lama was already a veteran of many expeditions, including the ascent of Chomolhari in 1937 with F. Spencer Chapman.[1] The New Zealanders were able to depend on his organisational skills and local knowledge; when it came to climbing, he proved himself strong, able and highly motivated.

Sherpas have often been the unsung heroes who enable their sahibs to achieve their climbing ambitions, but the special contribution and engaging personality of Pasang Dawa Lama have been celebrated in Herbert Tichy's *Cho Oyu: By favour of the gods* (1955).[2] Because the book is rare (and expensive), Tichy's high opinion of Pasang is worth inclusion here. As explained in Chapter 4, Pasang's efforts on Cho Oyu were widely acclaimed. But it is his undaunted confidence, loyalty and dedication to his sahibs that Tichy portrays most vividly.

The foreword to the English edition was written in July 1956 by John Hunt, leader of the successful Everest expedition. He describes Pasang Dawa Lama as his old friend of three small expeditions between the wars: Pasang was with him on Nepal Peak and two reconnaissances of Pandim. According to Hunt, after Cho Oyu Pasang was at the summit of his powers: 'He has set a new standard for human performance, for what the body can achieve when driven by a ruthless will. To him mainly is due the climbing of the world's seventh highest mountain.'[3]

In 1953 Pasang accompanied Tichy to western Nepal where they climbed several previously virgin summits over 20,000ft; it was Pasang who suggested to Tichy that they attempt Cho Oyu the following year. So in August 1954, after accompanying the Argentinian expedition to Dhaulagiri, Pasang joined the Austrian party of Tichy, Josef (Sepp) Jöchler and scientist Helmut Heuberger, bound for Cho Oyu. In Delhi, Pasang was resplendent at a party given by the Austrian ambassador: 'Pasang, in corded silk trousers of a striking brown-red colour, with the bronze 'Tiger' medal pinned on the breast of his blue shirt, talked to ambassadors and excellencies, was photographed and interviewed, just as if it was all in a day's work.'[4] At that stage, Pasang had only ever had one sip of alcohol. That was soon to change, as he became an easy victim of chang beer.

Tichy was somewhat daunted by the experiences of Shipton's party on Cho Oyu in 1952. 'But Cho Oyu took us unawares. It laid itself open from one camp to the next; the problems set by each day had such obvious solutions that we simply had no choice but to go on.'[5] The British had concluded it would take two weeks to make the icefall at 22,000ft passable for Sherpas. 'Such experienced Himalayan climbers as Hillary, Lowe, Evans and Gregory would never regard an obstacle as insurmountable if there were any way over it,' Tichy wrote.[6] But in the event, Tichy and his party – three Austrians and eleven Sherpas – negotiated the icefall in one afternoon. 'I could hardly grasp it; in an hour we had overcome the great obstacle. We had never dared to hope we should negotiate it so rapidly and with so little difficulty.'[7]

But at Camp 4 at 23,000ft, with the promise of an easy summit the next day, an icy tempest struck. Tents were flattened: Pasang shouted that all would die. In the mêlée Tichy's mittenless hands were severely frostbitten and the party was forced back down the mountain. There they met the Swiss party, who agreed to delay their bid for the summit until the Austrians had made a second attempt. The Austrians had to wait at Camp 4 for Pasang to arrive with life-giving supplies, however: he crept in just in time, his face grey and lined with the strain he had been through. '"Have the Swiss reached the summit?" he asked. "No," we replied. "Thank God for that," he panted. "I would have cut my throat."'[8]

The Austrian assault team was to have been Pasang and Jöchler. Tichy wrote, 'Pasang had never been in better form in his life and he if anyone deserved to scale the peak.' At the last minute Tichy joined them – the prospect of staying safely in the tent was so distressing he forgot the pain in his hands.

> Higher and higher. We moved like robots. Suddenly there was no further ascent. Pasang was coming towards us: his ice axe was in the snow with the flags of Nepal, Austria and India waving from it … Pasang embraced me. The tears that ran down his cheeks were blown away into eternity as crystals of ice. He had been sirdar for 20 years and intent on a 'very high' mountain. He nearly had his wish

on K2 and Dhaulagiri, but it just eluded him. Today the great ambition of his life was fulfilled … He was too happy to speak: he could only sob over and over again, 'The peak, sahib, the peak.'[9]

Jöchler and Heuberger also give their impressions of Pasang's remarkable performance in those last few days. According to Jöchler, Pasang 'the indestructible' was sure of the summit, and in such tremendous form it was always going to be a huge effort to keep up with him. Heuberger wrote that they were all in 'pretty good shape' but Pasang was bursting with strength, energy and impatience:

> Pasang lost no time in climbing down and rushing up to us. 'Very lucky day, very lucky day …' All three had reached the summit. Pasang, the stern, impenetrable oriental, threw his arms around my neck.[10]

In the last chapter Tichy reveals the most about the heroic and passionate Pasang Dawa Lama. On their return to Camp 1 Pasang agreed with Tichy that one day they would go for another high peak. 'But first I get married,' said Pasang. Though he already had a wife and seven children, his religion permitted him to marry more than one woman, and he had fallen in love with a girl in Lukla whose name was Yang Tshin. Pasang had made a pact with her parents that if he got to the top of Cho Oyu, they would give him their daughter for nothing; if he didn't, Pasang would pay them a thousand rupees and they would keep her. The wager was an immensely powerful reason for him to strive for the summit. It also made him a popular fellow, much in the news with stories such as 'Scaling Cho Oyu for love'.[11]

The Austrians were guests of honour at the 'little wedding' revelry in Namche, and then at the 'great wedding' ceremony in Lukla. A fortnight of festivities began with an enormous barrel of chang, the consequences of which appeared more alarming than Cho Oyu itself, Tichy wrote:

> We celebrated day and night: there was dancing, singing, drinking and eating. I can say without serious exaggeration that we were more or less drunk for two weeks. Pasang was much esteemed as a dancer, perhaps on account of his bandy legs, and was not sorry to be admired at all hours.[12]

During the more solemn ceremonies Pasang's son Kami, a Darjeeling chauffeur, described the conquest of Cho Oyu in metaphorical language: 'The Swiss were as strong as buffaloes, the Austrians as swift as ibex, and Pasang, the victorious eagle, had decided the contest.'[13]

NOTES

Chapter 1: Magnificent Obsession

1. An isolated 10,338ft peak south of New Zealand's highest mountain, Aoraki/Mt Cook (12,218ft). All heights will be given in feet, as used in the 1950s.
2. In organising this expedition Riddiford referred to it as the first New Zealand expedition to the Himalaya. However, there had been an earlier New Zealand-based overseas climbing expedition in 1938 to the Yunnan province in southwestern China. The all-women party led by Australian explorer Marie Byles, who learned her mountaineering skills in New Zealand, included New Zealand climbers Marjorie Edgar Jones, Dora de Beer, Fraser Radcliffe (another young Australian climber) and New Zealand guides Mick Bowie and Kurt Suter.
3. Norman Hardie, *On My Own Two Feet*, Christchurch: Canterbury University Press, 2006, 35.
4. Southwest of Mt Cook, the Landsborough is a remote, rugged tributary of the Haast River. It runs 50km parallel to the Southern Alps before meeting the Haast and flowing out to sea.
5. Wild deer were so abundant that Riddiford recalled Bill Beaven on one trip shooting a deer from his sleeping bag as it passed by the tent.
6. *Uncommon Law* (A.P. Herbert, Methuen, 1935) is an anthology of fictitious law reports first published in *Punch*.
7. Eric Shipton (1907–1977) and Frank Smythe (1900–1949) were two distinguished British Himalayan mountaineers who in 1931 shared the summit of Kamet, the highest peak climbed at that time.
8. Philip Temple, *The World at Their Feet*, Christchurch: Whitcombe & Tombs, 1969, 43.
9. Dan Bryant, *New Zealanders and Everest*, Wellington: A.H & A.W. Reed, 1953, 8.
10. H.E. Riddiford, 'Sefton from the south', *New Zealand Alpine Journal* (*NZAJ*), June 1948, vol XII, no 35, 217.
11. Ruth Adams, a keen amateur mountaineer, was a daughter of Ernest Adams, the owner of New Zealand's largest cake bakery. Relieved to learn his daughter was safe, Adams arranged for two giant fruitcakes to be air-dropped to the rescue party.
12. Philip Temple, *Castles in the Air*, Dunedin: John McIndoe, 1973, 143.
13. www.teara.govt.nz/en/mountaineering/page-8
14. Hardie, *On My Own Two Feet*, 62.
15. Temple, *Castles in the Air*, 143.
16. H.E. Riddiford, 'Tasman from the Balfour', *NZAJ*, 1949, vol XIII, no 36, 54–62.
17. Ibid., 56.
18. Ibid.
19. It was reached only once more that year, with Bill Beaven in the party (Hardie, *On My Own Two Feet*, 72).
20. H.E. Riddiford, 'A visit to the Burton', *The Canterbury Mountaineer*, 1949–50, vol 5, no 19, 58.
21. This is the official spelling adopted by the Royal Geographical Society. There are a number of variants.
22. Riddiford's address to the Wellington section of the NZAC, 1987.
23. Ibid.

Chapter 2: Master Planner

1. Archie Scott made the first ascent of Fettes Peak, 8051ft, in January 1935 with Christopher Johnson, an old boy of Fettes College, Edinburgh, and New Zealand climber Scott Russell, who

was later to play an important role in advocating the inclusion of New Zealanders in the 1951 Everest Reconnaissance party.
2. From a memorandum handed to Mr Doidge's private secretary a few days before the minister met Riddiford in Christchurch on 19 April 1950.
3. Riddiford to Doidge, 19 May 1950, Riddiford Correspondence.
4. Hardie to Riddiford, 30 May 1950, Riddiford Correspondence.
5. Hardie to Riddiford, 21 May 1950, Riddiford Correspondence.
6. Lowe to Riddiford, 31 May 1950, Riddiford Correspondence.
7. Riddiford to F.W. Doidge, minister of external affairs, 19 May 1950, Riddiford Correspondence.
8. Doidge to Riddiford, 11 September 1950, Riddiford Correspondence.
9. Hardie to Riddiford, 11 September 1950, Riddiford Correspondence.
10. Riddiford to Hardie, 20 October 1950, Riddiford Correspondence.
11. Hillary to Riddiford, 16 October 1950, Riddiford Correspondence.
12. Lowe to Riddiford, 6 November 1950, Riddiford Correspondence.
13. Riddiford to Braham, 18 November 1950, Riddiford Correspondence.
14. Ludwig Krenek was an Austrian schoolteacher who with Dr Fritz Kolb made the first ascent of Mulkila (21,380ft) in the Indian Himalaya on 7 September 1939. Shortly afterwards, on the outbreak of war, they were interned in India where they remained for many years. On their release they took up teaching appointments in India and made several more Himalayan expeditions, described in *Himalayan Venture* (Fritz Kolb, London: Lutterworth Press, 1959). At the time of the 1951 New Zealand expedition Krenek was teaching at Mt Hermon School in Darjeeling, and he later worked in New Zealand. In 1955 he joined the group of celebrated New Zealander Himalayan climbers pictured in Chapter 12.
15. Riddiford to Wade, 5 December 1950, Riddiford Correspondence.
16. Bill Beaven, interview with author, 17 June 2013.
17. Hillary to Riddiford, 6 February 1951, Riddiford Correspondence.
18. NZPA, 19 February 1951.
19. Also spelled Nilkantha.
20. Riddiford to Krenek, 26 April 1951, Riddiford Correspondence.
21. Lowe to Cotter, 11 April 1951, Riddiford Correspondence.
22. Hillary to Riddiford, 11 April 1951, Riddiford Correspondence. If Hillary had had his way it would have meant no 1951 Reconnaissance for him or Riddiford, and very little chance that the British would have opened their ranks in 1952 and 1953.
23. Riddiford to Hillary, 13 April 1951, Riddiford Correspondence.
24. Sri B.P. Joshi, deputy secretary to government Uttar Pradesh, to deputy commissioner Garhwal, Pauri, with enclosures, 16 May 1951, Riddiford Correspondence.
25. Lecture notes, 1953, Riddiford Archives.

Chapter 3: Awesome Elie

1. G. Lowe, *Because It Is There*, London: Cassell and Company, 1959, 12.
2. L.V. Bryant, *New Zealanders and Everest*, Wellington: A.H. & A.W. Reed, 1953, 8, 31.
3. Jack Ede, 'Elusive Elie', *Canterbury Mountaineer*, no 12, August 1943, 18.
4. L. Thompson, 'Oral Histories: The golden era of New Zealand climbing 1948–1955', NZAC archives, Hocken Collections, Bill Beaven, Folder 2.
5. H.E. Riddiford, 'Elie de Beaumont from the Burton', *NZAJ*, 1951, vol XIV, no 38, 28.
6. E.M. Cotter, 'Elie de Beaumont from the west', *The Canterbury Mountaineer*, vol 5, no 20, August 1951, 25–30.
7. Ibid., 26.

8   Ibid., 27.
9   Ibid., 28.
10 Ibid.
11 Riddiford, 'Elie de Beaumont from the Burton', 31.
12 Thompson, 'Oral Histories'.
13 With an incubation period of up to 21 days, chickenpox did not develop until Hillary was back in Auckland. While Riddiford and Cotter faced the 'displeasing prospect' of carrying five men's gear out to the coast, Hillary and Lowe were playing tennis at the Hermitage.
14 Mike Nelson, interview with author, 8 May 2015.
15 Lowe, *Because It Is There*, 13.
16 E.P. Hillary, *Nothing Venture, Nothing Win*, London: Hodder and Stoughton, 1975, 113.
17 E.P. Hillary, *View from the Summit*, London: Doubleday, 1999, 69.
18 Ed Cotter, interview with author, 15 January 2013.
19 Ibid.
20 Cotter's 1951 expedition diary.
21 P. Temple, *Castles in the Air*, Dunedin: John McIndoe, 1973, 116.

Chapter 4: En Route to Nilkanta

1   Riddiford's stockbroker friend and mountaineering mentor Archie Scott, who recommended the expedition to senior politicians in Wellington, wrote to Riddiford on 29 May that Hillary's remarks to New Zealand newspapers had made a bad impression in high circles. 'He was quoted saying that the expedition members didn't intend to do any serious exploration but all members were determined to enjoy themselves and have a good time. This is a very different story from that you told the Government when you asked for a grant of £3000.'
2   Riddiford to Helen Nicholl, 6 May 1951, Riddiford Correspondence.
3   From the undated text of an address given by Cotter on his personal memories of Ed Hillary, Cotter Archives.
4   Cotter to sister Cecily, 25 May 1951, Cotter Archives.
5   Riddiford to Helen Nicholl, 12 June 1951, Riddiford Correspondence.
6   Riddiford's address to the Wellington branch of the NZAC, 1987.
7   Now Kolkata.
8   Riddiford to Helen Nicholl, 6 May 1951. Riddiford Correspondence.
9   Now Chennai.
10 H.W. (Bill) Tilman, renowned Himalayan explorer and author. The New Zealanders were largely guided on their route by Tilman's 1937 book *The Ascent of Nanda Devi*.
11 Cotter's expedition diary, 30 May 1951.
12 Famed British mountaineer Frank Smythe called Nilkanta the 'undisputed queen of the Badrinath peaks', 'the most majestic and awe-inspiring peak of its height in the world' but also the most difficult in the Garhwal Himalaya (F.S. Smythe, *The Valley of Flowers*, London: Hodder and Stoughton, 1938, 62, 241).
13 A member of an Indian religious minority concentrated in the city of Bombay (Mumbai).
14 These two names were variously spelled in different accounts of the expedition. The author has chosen to use the spellings given by Ludwig Krenek when on 26 May 1951 he sent Riddiford a list of the three Sherpas who would accompany Pasang to Ranikhet. Riddiford Archives.
15 Riddiford to Helen Nicholl, 27 June 1951, Riddiford Correspondence.
16 Many Sherpas had the same name, often a source of confusion. The days of the week were popular: Dawa (Monday), Mingma (Tuesday), Lhakpa (Wednesday), Phurba (Thursday), Pasang (Friday), Pemba (Saturday) and Nima (Sunday) (B.G. Verghese (ed.), *Himalayan Endeavour*, Bombay: Times of India, 1962, 65).

17 A concise but informative account of this tragedy can be found in Irvine Lawrence's article 'Book chat' (*Canterbury Mountaineer*, August 1941, no 10, 102–03). More recently, in his 2015 book *The Ghosts of K2*, mountain writer Mick Conefrey provides a detailed account of the major role played by Pasang on this expedition.
18 Riddiford's address to the Wellington branch of the NZAC, 1987.
19 Ironically, since Hillary was a member of the failed 1952 British Cho Oyu expedition, it was to be Pasang Dawa Lama who, with the Austrian party of Herbert Tichy and Sepp Jochler, made the first ascent of 26,906ft Cho Oyu in 1954. An article on the Sherpas by Kohli and Verghese (Verghese, *Himalayan Endeavour*, 64) throws more light on the special qualities of endurance and determination Pasang Dawa Lama displayed. In 1958 in exceptionally severe gale-force conditions, Pasang made a second ascent of Cho Oyu, this time with an Indian expedition led by the same Keki Bunshah who, as a 21-year-old law student, accompanied the First New Zealand Himalayan Expedition on the hill walk to Badrinath. Keki Bunshah was also the deputy leader of the 1960 Indian Everest Expedition.
20 E.P. Hillary, *Nothing Venture, Nothing Win*, London: Hodder and Stoughton, 1975, 146.
21 E.P. Hillary, *High Adventure*, London: Hodder and Stoughton, 1955.
22 Riddiford to Helen Nicholl, 27 June 1951, Riddiford Correspondence.
23 Cotter's expedition diary, 6 June.
24 P. Temple, *The World at Their Feet*, Christchurch: Whitcombe and Tombs, 1969, 56.
25 F.S. Smythe, *Kamet Conquered*, London: Hodder and Stoughton, Uniform Edition, 1947, 278.
26 Cotter's expedition diary, 11 June.
27 Cotter's expedition diary, 16 June.
28 Eric Shipton, 'Mr Everest', famed British explorer-mountaineer who summited Kamet in 1931 (with Smythe) and played a major role in the reconnaissance of Mt Everest.
29 Cotter's expedition diary, 21 June.
30 According to Frank Smythe, who made the first ascent of Kamet in 1931, 'The Bhyundar Valley was the most beautiful valley that any of us had seen. We camped in it for two days and we remembered it afterwards as The Valley of Flowers … A valley of peace and perfect beauty where the human spirit may find repose' (Smythe, *The Valley of Flowers*, London: Hodder and Stoughton, 1938, 2, 5).
31 Chlorodyne is an opiate-based treatment for diarrhoea; thalazole is a synthetic opioid used to treat the same complaint.
32 L. Cleveland, 'Himalayan Journey', *Canterbury Mountaineer*, 1950–51, vol 5, no 20, 30.

Chapter 5: 'We Long Way Come'

1 Riddiford to Helen Nicholl, 27 July 1951, Riddiford Correspondence.
2 G. Lowe, 'Mukut Parbat: The reconnaissance', *NZAJ*, 1952, vol XIV, no 39, 176.
3 The note survives in the Riddiford Archives: 'Thurs 28th June: We reached this bridge yesterday at 3.15 pm, and found it down … Perc and Tenzing went downstream this morning and crossed snow bridge and we pulled these stringers across with rope at 10.15am. Both leaving for Pachmi Kamet to camp and return down tomorrow after a look towards the head. Wait for us at mouth of Pachmi Kamet tomorrow 29th June. Love and kisses, Geo and Perc.' Hillary added his bit: 'How's the diahrrorea [sic] – lucky fellow.'
4 Cotter's expedition diary, 30 June.
5 In his diary entry for 30 June, Cotter quotes extensively from Tilman's *Ascent of Nanda Devi*, which the party carried with them. This extract, Cotter notes, was on page 42.
6 H.E. Riddiford, 'Mukut Parbat: The ascent', *NZAJ*, 1952, vol XIV, no 39, 179.
7 Lowe, 'Mukut Parbat', 178.
8 Riddiford, 'Mukut Parbat', 181.

9   Cotter's expedition diary, 11 July.
10 Ibid.
11 E. Cotter, 'The Garhwal Himalayas', *Canterbury Mountaineer*, 1951–52, vol 5, no 21, 161.
12 Cotter's expedition diary, 11 July.
13 Riddiford, 'Mukut Parbat', 182.
14 Letter to Helen Nicholl, 27 July 1951.
15 Cotter, 'The Garhwal Himalayas', 161.

Chapter 6: Monsoon Woes

1   E.P. Hillary, *Nothing Venture, Nothing Win*, London: Hodder and Stoughton, 1975, 126.
2   E.P. Hillary, *View from the Summit*, London: Doubleday, 1999, 74.
3   Ibid., 125.
4   Ibid., 126.
5   Riddiford to Helen Nicholl, 27 July 1951.
6   E. Cotter, 'The Garhwal Himalayas', *Canterbury Mountaineer*, 1951–52, vol 5, no 21, 162.
7   Riddiford to Helen Nicholl, 27 July 1951.
8   Hillary, *View from the Summit*, 76.
9   Hocken Collections, MS 1164 1/6/14.
10 Riddiford to Helen Nicholl, 27 July 1951.
11 Note sent by Lowe to Riddiford, 27 July, Riddiford Archives.
12 Riddiford to Helen Nicholl, 31 July 1951.
13 G. Lowe, 'Three more summits', *NZAJ*, June 1952, vol XIV, no 39, 188.
14 Riddiford to Helen Nicholl, 5 August 1951.
15 Riddiford to Helen Nicholl, 17 August 1951.
16 E. Cotter, 'Peak 20,750ft and the return to Ranikhet', *NZAJ*, June 1952, vol XIV, no 39, 190.
17 Riddiford to Helen Nicholl, 17 August 1951.
18 Ibid.
19 Nima and Tenzing. Pasang had accompanied Riddiford to Nilkanta.
20 Riddiford to Helen Nicholl, 17 August 1951.
21 Ibid.
22 Ibid.
23 E. Cotter, 'The return to Ranikhet', *NZAJ*, June 1952, vol XIV, no 39, 192.
24 Riddiford to Helen Nicholl, 17 August 1951.
25 At no stage did Hillary and Lowe organise this expedition, though in 1997 Hillary claimed they did. 'We had tons of organising ability ourselves. We had just organised Mukut Parbat' (Peter Steele, *Everest and Beyond*, London: Constable, 1998, 199).
26 From a report dated 17 July 1952, Riddiford to the NZAC Overseas Expedition Committee, Riddiford Archives.

Chapter 7: Into the Crucible

1   Hocken Collections, MS 1164 1/11/18.
2   In his obituary for his father-in-law Jim Rose, (*NZAJ* 1990), Hillary said it was Rose who was the instigator of the invitation. Hocken Collections, MS 1164 2/87/1.
3   Letter from Roland Rodda, a member of the 1951 NZAC committee, to Murray Ellis, Roland Ellis's son, 3 October 1993. Hocken Collections, MS 1164 2/87/1.
4   Russell to Stevenson, 31 August 1951. Hocken Collections, MS 1164 1/6/14.
5   E. Shipton, *Upon That Mountain*, London: Hodder and Stoughton, 1943, 182.
6   As a major sponsor of the expedition, *The Times* was not impressed when they suddenly found out the party was up to six. Hardie to Riddiford, 8 October 1951, Riddiford Correspondence.

7 Hocken Collections, MS 1164 1/11/18.
8 P. Temple, *The World at Their Feet*, Christchurch: Whitcombe & Tombs, 1969, 60.
9 H.E. Riddiford, 'Because It Is There', *NZAJ*, 1960, vol XVIII, no 47, 414–15. In a letter to Norman Hardie, who reviewed Lowe's autobiography, Riddiford was adamant that the cable was from the NZAC, not from Shipton, and that the words 'any two of you to join the party' did not appear, though that was the gist of the message. Riddiford to Hardie, 17 December 1959, Riddiford Correspondence.
10 G. Lowe, *Because It Is There*, London: Cassell and Company, 1959, 18.
11 A. Johnston, *Sir Edmund Hillary: An extraordinary life*, Auckland: Penguin, 2007, 38. The citation given for this wording is Steele, *Eric Shipton: Everest and beyond*, London: Constable, 1998, 147. Steele himself provides no source. It seems Lowe and Hillary's version is wrong. The NZAC telegram quoted by Riddiford was in the Riddiford family's possession for some time before they lent it and it was lost: Anna Riddiford says the wording given by Riddiford himself is exactly as she and her husband Duncan Graham remember it. It is also unlikely that Shipton would have had Riddiford's contact details.
12 Riddiford to Helen Nicholl, 17 August 1951.
13 Lowe, *Because It Is There*, 19.
14 Ibid., 18.
15 Ibid.
16 Ibid.
17 Dan Riddiford wrote to Riddiford in Ranikhet on 16 August 1951, telling him he should not allow himself to be troubled by lack of money – the extended family would see he had enough for his requirements. Riddiford Correspondence.
18 E.P. Hillary, *Nothing Venture, Nothing Win*, London: Hodder and Stoughton, 1975, 130.
19 Hocken Collections, MS 1164 1/11/18.
20 'My momentary caprice was to have far-reaching results' (E. Shipton, *That Untravelled World*, London: Hodder and Stoughton, 1969, 187).
21 Steele, *Eric Shipton*, 149.
22 Lowe, *Because It Is There*, 19.
23 J. Grant, 'Peaks and troughs: The story of Ed Cotter', University of Canterbury, Christchurch, 1998, 7.
24 H.E. Riddiford, W. Lowe and E. Cotter, 'Expedition to the Garhwal Himalaya, 1951', *NZAJ*, 1952, vol X1V, no 39, 190.
25 Stevenson to Riddiford, 13 August 1951, Riddiford Correspondence.
26 Undated page of Cotter's letter home from Ceylon, probably September 1951. Cotter Correspondence.
27 Geoff Harrow, interview with author, 4 October 2013.
28 From the undated text of an address given by Cotter on his personal memories of Ed Hillary, Cotter Archives.
29 New Zealand Archive of Film, Television and Sound: ID 30262, 'NZ Himalayan Expedition, 1952', Track 4. [D417/4].
30 E.P. Hillary, *View from the Summit*, London: Doubleday, 1999, 77.
31 Riddiford to Helen Nicholl, 17 August 1951.

Part 2

1 Riddiford's great love of and interest in the mountains remained to the end: in his last few days he was re-reading Tilman's books on mountain travel with great delight. The lines quoted by Tilman are the final two lines of Rudyard Kipling's 1915 poem 'A Song in Storm'.

Chapter 8: Pioneer Spirit

1. A.H. McLintock (ed.), 'Riddiford, Daniel', Te Ara – the Encyclopedia of New Zealand: www.teara.govt.nz/en/1966/riddiford-daniel
2. Ibid.
3. Obituary, *Press*, 3 May 1911.
4. In *Committed to Escape* (2004), Daniel Johnston Riddiford wrote about his wartime experiences as a prisoner-of-war after his capture in North Africa in 1941, internment in six prison camps across three countries, and a successful third escape attempt in 1943, when he rejoined Allied forces in Italy. He was awarded the MC for his part in helping to lead a group of escaped POWs across Yugoslavia to freedom.
5. Anna Riddiford, interview with author, 10 June 2014.
6. John Arkwright, interview with author, 18 September 2014.
7. Helen Riddiford to Dan Riddiford, 24 January 1935, Riddiford Correspondence.
8. Belinda Cranswick, interview with author, 16 June 2014.
9. Earle Riddiford to Helen Nicholl, 23 November 1938, Riddiford Correspondence.
10. Head prefect at Wanganui Collegiate, John Arkwright later served with the NZRAF, going on to become the country's youngest wing commander. While stationed at the Wigram air base in Christchurch he frequently visited Earle.
11. John Arkwright, interview with author, 18 September 2014.
12. Eric Riddiford to Helen Riddiford, 15 July 1935. Supplied by Belinda Cranswick.
13. Obituary, *New Zealand Trotting Calendar*, 13 April 1955, 2.
14. Helen Riddiford to Dan Riddiford, 14 February 1937, Riddiford Correspondence.
15. In August 1942 Fred Tozer and Albert Jackson lost their lives in a wind-slab avalanche in the Cass Valley.
16. N. Hardie, 'Mt Sefton: The first 28 ascents', *The Canterbury Mountaineer*, vol 5, no 19, 123.
17. Address to Wellington branch of the NZAC, 1987. Taped recording supplied by the Riddiford family.
18. Letter to Helen Nicholl, June 1944, Riddiford Correspondence.
19. P.S. Powell, 'Volta Therma traverse', *NZAJ*, 1946, vol XI, no 33, 117.
20. H.E. Riddiford, 'A visit to the Douglas', *NZAJ*, June 1947, vol XII, no 34, 43.
21. Ibid., 44.
22. Ibid., 45.
23. Ibid., 46.
24. Ibid., 52.
25. Ibid.
26. H.E. Riddiford, 'Jagged and Tent Peaks', *NZAJ*, June 1947, vol XII, no 34, 90.

Chapter 9: The 1951 Everest Reconnaissance

1. E.H. Peck, the UK High Commissioner in New Delhi, warned Riddiford to be very cautious as the contract with *The Times* was an 'extremely exclusive form of world copyright' under which, if there was any breach of contract at all, *The Times* might refuse to fulfil its side of the agreement. Peck to Riddiford, 27 August 1951, Riddiford Correspondence.
2. Letter to Helen Nicholl, 24 September 1951.
3. Stevenson to Riddiford, 23 November 1951, Riddiford Correspondence.
4. Ibid.
5. Hillary to Riddiford, 24 November 1951, Riddiford Correspondence.
6. During a BBC interview after the 1951 Reconnaissance, Bourdillon was asked about food. His reply: 'Well, I do think it's important that there should be some.' Riddiford lecture notes, Riddiford Archives.
7. E. Shipton, *The Mount Everest Reconnaissance Expedition 1951*, London: Hodder and Stoughton, 1952, 16.

8 W.H. Murray, 'The reconnaissance of Mt Everest', *Alpine Journal*, November 1952, vol LVIII, no 285, 436.
9 Shipton, *The Mount Everest Reconnaissance Expedition 1951*, 44.
10 Ibid., 41.
11 Ibid., 50.
12 W.H. Murray, 'Himalayan adventure', *Weekly Overseas Mail*, Supplement, 17 May 1953, Riddiford Archives.
13 Shipton, *The Mount Everest Reconnaissance Expedition 1951*, 51.
14 Ibid., 55.
15 Ibid., 47–49.
16 Ibid., 40.
17 M. Ward, 'The exploration of the Nepalese side of Everest', *Alpine Journal*, 1992–93, vol 97, no 341, 219.
18 P. Steele, *Eric Shipton: Everest and beyond*, London: Constable, 1998, 156.
19 Address to Wellington branch of the NZAC, 1987. Taped recording supplied by the Riddiford family.
20 E.P. Hillary, *View from the Summit*, London: Doubleday, 1999, 82.
21 In hindsight Hillary gave Pasang much more credit. In sending his recommendations for sirdar for the 1953 Everest expedition, he wrote: 'Tenzing Bhotia first choice. Pasang Dawa Lama second choice – a terror after the money but is an excellent organiser, a first class mountaineer and has great determination to get to the top. Angtarkay is lacking in interest and drive nowadays.' Hocken Collections, MS 1164 1/11/18.
22 Hillary, *View from the Summit*, 82.
23 E.P. Hillary, *Nothing Venture, Nothing Win*, London: Hodder and Stoughton, 1975, 138.
24 Sirdar Pasang Dawa Lama to Riddiford, 11 December 1951, Riddiford Correspondence.

Chapter 10: Cho Oyu

1 P. Temple, *The World at Their Feet*, Christchurch: Whitcombe & Tombs, 1969, 69.
2 M. Conefrey, *Everest 1953: The epic story of the first ascent*, Oxford: One World, 2012, 29.
3 Ibid., 31.
4 Ibid., 40.
5 Eric Shipton, 'The expedition to Cho Oyu', *Geographical Journal*, Royal Geographical Society London, 119, 1953, 130.
6 Ibid.
7 E.P. Hillary, 'Attempt on Cho Oyu', *NZAJ*, 1953, vol XV, no 40, 4.
8 Hocken Collections, MS 1164 1/6/14.
9 H. Tuckey, *Everest: The First Ascent: The untold story of Griffith Pugh, the man who made it possible*, London: Rider, 2013, 29.
10 Shipton always found the impedimenta of a large party tedious (Astill, T., *Mount Everest: The reconnaissance 1935*, Southampton: T. Astill, 2005).
11 Tuckey, *Everest*, 55.
12 Ibid., 64.
13 Ibid.
14 R.C. Evans, 'The Cho Oyu expedition', *Alpine Journal*, vol LIX, no 286, May 1953, 12.
15 Shipton, 'The expedition to Cho Oyu', 133.
16 M. Ward, *Everest: A thousand years of exploration*, Glasgow: Ernest Press, 2003, 223.
17 E.P. Hillary, *View from the Summit*, London: Doubleday, 1999, 88.
18 Ibid.
19 Campbell Secord reportedly said, 'This is no good, Eric. You can't fly an aeroplane by having a debate' (Steele, *Eric Shipton: Everest and beyond*, London: Constable, 1998, 172.)

20 Conefrey, *Everest 1953*, 48.
21 M. Ward, *In This Short Span*, London: Victor Gollancz, 1972, 131.
22 Tuckey, *Everest*, 66.
23 Hillary, *View from the Summit*, 89.
24 Ibid., 90.
25 Evans, 'The Cho Oyu expedition', 13.
26 Norman Hardie, Obituary for H.E. Riddiford, *Press*, 8 July 1989, 4.
27 P. Steele, *Eric Shipton: Everest and beyond*, London: Constable, 1998, 173.
28 Roger Peren, interview with Anna Riddiford, June 2014.
29 Hillary to Hardie, 19 July 1952, Riddiford Correspondence.
30 Tuckey, *Everest*, 70.
31 Hillary described Pugh as 'an entertaining type but the perfect example of the impractical scientist'. Hillary to Hardie, 19 July 1952, Riddiford Correspondence.
32 A letter to Earle Riddiford (1 December 1952) from Nancy Summerhayes at the British embassy in Nepal relates how Jennifer Bourdillon suffered from a fever in Namche and on her trek over the mountains to Kathmandu. When diagnosed on her return to London, it turned out to be typhus. Riddiford Correspondence.
33 Hillary, *View from the Summit*, 88.
34 *The Times*, 8 April 1952.

Chapter 11: Fallout

1 As Harriet Tuckey put it, 'Criticism of Shipton was only acceptable to Hillary if he himself was doing the criticising' (Tuckey, *Everest: The first ascent*, London: Rider, 2013, 65).
2 Tuckey, *Everest*, 57.
3 Hocken Collections, MS 1164 1/6/14.
4 Hillary to Hardie, 19 July 1952, Riddiford Correspondence.
5 E. Shipton, 'The expedition to Cho Oyu', *Geographical Journal*, 119, 1953, 129–39.
6 P. Steele, *Eric Shipton: Everest and beyond*, London: Constable, 1998, 172.
7 On 3 November 1955 Marcel Kurz, editor of *Berg Der Welt* in Neuchatel, Switzerland, wrote to Riddiford telling him that Herbert Tichy, the Austrian climber who with Pasang had summited Cho Oyu, had praised Pasang Dawa Lama as one of the very best Sherpas. Riddiford was delighted to read of the ascent. On 29 November 1954 he wrote to Pasang in Darjeeling: 'I send you my warmest congratulations. Knowing your organising ability, and skill and determination, I realise that most of the credit for the success of the expedition probably belongs to you. Now you will get the recognition and fame you deserve as one of the best Sherpa mountaineers of all, and will be recognised in the same class as Tenzing, which is only what you deserve.' On the same day he wrote to Kurz: 'I was thrilled to read that Pasang Dawa Lama had got to the summit of Cho Oyu with one of the members of the Austrian expedition. It was he who went to the summit of Mukut Parbat with Cotter and myself and he also reached the summit of Chomolhari with Spencer Chapman. Knowing his exceptional organising ability and determination I expect much of the credit for the Austrian party on Cho Oyu belongs to him, and I am glad that this climb will bring him the recognition he deserves' (Riddiford to Kurz, 29 November 51, Riddiford Correspondence).
8 Steele, *Eric Shipton*, 178.
9 Ibid., 176.
10 Packard to Riddiford, 16 November 1952, Riddiford Correspondence.
11 Ellis to Riddiford, 10 July 1952, Riddiford Correspondence.
12 NZAC, 'Annual report', *NZAJ*, vol XV, no 40, 1953, 328.
13 Hocken Collections, MS 1164 1/11/18.
14 Ellis to Riddiford, 15 July 1952, Riddiford Correspondence.

15 Report from Riddiford to NZAC Overseas Expedition Committee, 17 July 1952, Riddiford Correspondence.
16 Hocken Collections, MS 1164 1/6/14.
17 Ibid.
18 Hocken Collections, MS 1164 1/11/18.
19 Hocken Collections, MS 1164 1/6/14.
20 Ibid.
21 Report from Riddiford to NZAC Overseas Expedition Committee, 17 July 1952, Riddiford Correspondence.
22 Hocken Collections, MS 1164 1/6/14.
23 Hillary, who had Shipton's ear, had suggested Harry Ayres rather than Riddiford.
24 Hocken Collections, MS 1164 1/6/14.
25 Ibid.
26 Hocken Collections, MS 1164 1/11/19.
27 Hocken Collections, MS 1164 2/66/3.
28 Hocken Collections, MS 1164 1/6/14.
29 Ibid.
30 Ibid.
31 Ibid.
32 Ibid.
33 Hillary consistently portrayed himself as a gung-ho adventurer always eager to forge on: 'nothing venture, nothing win'. It is safe to assume that he would not put this spin on events had he been the one to summit Mukut Parbat.
34 Hocken Collections, MS 1164 1/6/14.
35 Stevenson to Riddiford, 5 July 1953, Riddiford Correspondence.
36 Hocken Collections, MS 1164 1/11/19.

Chapter 12: New Directions

1 As it happened, Ayres would not have been able to join the 1953 expedition as the Public Service Commission would not allow him leave with pay, in spite of Riddiford's strenuous efforts on Ayres' behalf. 'The axe has fallen right on my neck – they could not have kicked me harder if they had tried' (Ayres to Riddiford, 10 September 1952, Riddiford Correspondence).
2 Basil Goodfellow, honorary secretary Himalayan Committee, to Riddiford, 13 November 1952, Riddiford Correspondence.
3 Riddiford to Helen Nicholl, 5 October 1952, Riddiford Correspondence.
4 Ibid.
5 Riddiford to Helen Nicholl, 31 October 1952, Riddiford Correspondence.
6 Riddiford to Hardie, 10 September 1952, Riddiford Correspondence.
7 Grandson of Canon Cecil Tyndale-Biscoe, founder of the Tyndale-Biscoe School in Srinigar, in the Kashmir Valley. Born in Srinigar, Hugh studied zoology at Canterbury University.
8 H.E. Riddiford, 'The east ridge of Malte Brun', *NZAJ*, vol XV, no 40, 1953, 139–44.
9 Ibid.
10 Pasang Dawa Lama to Riddiford, 23 November 1952, Riddiford Correspondence.
11 News of Riddiford's interest in Kangchenjunga had caused some panic in England, as Norman Hardie wrote home in 1953, Riddiford Correspondence.
12 'Pasang Lama (Pasang Dawa Sherpa) who was our Sirdar in 1950 has again served in that capacity during the last four months. A man of character and intelligence, scrupulously honest and completely reliable. He makes an excellent organiser. He purchases local produce economically, and is good at arranging transport. In addition he is a first-rate cook. As a mountaineer he is unquestionably in the very first rank. He was almost entirely responsible for

our success on Deo Tibba, a mountain difficult enough to have defeated six previous parties. Without him our expedition would have been something very different from what it was.' J. de Graaff, 4 November 1952, Riddiford Correspondence.
13 Riddiford to Helen Nicholl, 23 February 1953, Riddiford Correspondence.
14 Ibid.
15 *Evening Post*, 13 May 1953, 5, Riddiford Archives.
16 Riddiford Correspondence.
17 Harry Stevenson wrote complimenting Riddiford: 'I listened to the 8.45pm broadcast tonight and I must say you came over very well and what you said was excellent … I know how you must feel about it all, because if luck hadn't been against you, you would probably have been there too, and it was your effort on Mukut Parbat that gave New Zealanders the first opening' (May 1953, Riddiford Correspondence).
18 Lecture notes, 1953, Riddiford Archives.
19 Beaven was correct: on the evening of the 1953 Everest ascent, Hillary told Michael Ward that increasing the oxygen rate was like changing gear – everything went more easily (Ward, *Everest: A thousand years of exploration*, Glasgow: Ernest Press, 2003).
20 Beaven to Riddiford, June 1953, Riddiford Correspondence.
21 Ibid.
22 Riddiford to Helen Nicholl, 6 July 1953, Riddiford Correspondence.
23 Ibid.
24 Riddiford to Helen Nicholl, 14 September 1953, Riddiford Correspondence.
25 Undated note, Riddiford Correspondence.
26 Riddiford to Helen Nicholl, October 1953, Riddiford Correspondence.
27 Mountaineer, writer and explorer Colin Monteath rates this a significant climb by an under-rated expedition. Monteath, interview with author, 2 December 2014.
28 Riddiford to Helen Nicholl, 20 November 1953, Riddiford Correspondence.
29 Riddiford to Helen Nicholl, undated, Riddiford Correspondence.
30 Peren to Riddiford, January 1954, Riddiford Correspondence.
31 Back in New Zealand, a 'dinkum Kiwi' accent only strengthened the perception that Hillary was a genuine 'good keen bloke'.
32 Louis Armstrong.
33 Peren to Riddiford, March 1954, Riddiford Correspondence.
34 Riddiford to Helen Nicholl, 12 April 1954, Riddiford Correspondence.
35 Beaven to Riddiford, 15 November 1953, Riddiford Correspondence.
36 Riddiford to Helen Nicholl, 12 April 1954, Riddiford Correspondence.
37 Eulogy for Earle Riddiford, 29 June 1989, Riddiford Archives.
38 Hardie to Riddiford, 11 October 1954, Riddiford Correspondence.
39 See Appendix 1: Jim McFarlane.
40 Beaven to Riddiford, 8 May 1954, Riddiford Correspondence.
41 Beaven to Riddiford, 4 July 1954, Riddiford Correspondence.
42 McFarlane to Riddiford, 6 December 1954, Riddiford Correspondence.
43 Peren to Riddiford, August 1954, Riddiford Correspondence.
44 Riddiford to Helen Nicholl, 9 May 1955, Riddiford Correspondence.
45 Peren to Riddiford, 31 March 1955, Riddiford Correspondence.
46 Beaven to Riddiford, 30 July 1955, Riddiford Correspondence.
47 Riddiford to Ayres, 10 June 1955, Riddiford Correspondence.
48 Riddiford to Hardie, 10 June 1955, Riddiford Correspondence.
49 Bunshah to Riddiford, 19 February 1956, Riddiford Correspondence.
50 Belinda Cranswick, interview with author, 16 June 2014.

Chapter 13: Orongorongo Station

1. Belinda Cranswick, shared with author, 16 June 2014.
2. Sarah Riddiford, shared with author, 30 October 2014.
3. Anna Riddiford, interview with author, 10 June 2014.
4. It is fortunate he never knew the fate of his beloved Orongorongo homestead. After his death and shortly after the lodge was sold on to another syndicate, it was destroyed by fire on 29 June 1990. Earle had always been nervous about fire danger – he had bought his own fire engine from the Patea Fire Brigade – but on that day two chimneys were the only things left standing after a blaze that swiftly flared out of control.
5. 'Five footloose fathers in the Waipara', *NZAJ*, 1962, no 49, 63.
6. Riddiford to the treasurer, NZAC, 10 July 1976, Riddiford Correspondence. Many decades later, with the benefit of hindsight, the NZAC would make Ed Cotter a life member for his services to New Zealand mountaineering in the 1950s. Over three Himalayan expeditions, Riddiford's contribution was unquestionably greater than Cotter's.
7. Hocken Collections, MS 1164 2985/240.
8. Eulogy by Roger Peren, Wellington Cathedral, 29 June 1989, Riddiford Archives.
9. Ibid.
10. Tom Bourdillon wrote in his diary: 'Earle is a good man – old New Zealand family, sheep farmer, soldier and now lawyer, 30, and he is a gentleman, which Ed is not' (Tuckey, *Everest: The First Ascent: The untold story of Griffith Pugh, the man who made it possible,* London: Rider, 2013, 20).
11. E.P. Hillary, *View from the Summit*, London: Doubleday, 1999, 104. In this 1999 publication Hillary appears not to connect with his much earlier assessment of Riddiford's capabilities: when a radio interviewer asked him who was the best mountaineer he ever climbed with, he replied: 'Earle Riddiford, he had real courage coupled with an acutely analytical mind and I learned more from him than anyone else.' This anecdote is cited in *Everybody Hurts: A New Zealand story* by Rick Stevenson (Auckland: Hodder Beckett, 1995, 7–8). Stevenson explains that he met Riddiford on a number of occasions never suspecting he was ever a mountaineer. 'It was hard to get him to talk about himself – but I looked at him with a new respect after that.'
12. Bourdillon to Riddiford, 27 October 1953, Riddiford Correspondence.
13. E. Shipton, *The Mount Everest Reconnaissance Expedition, 1951*, London: Hodder and Stoughton, 1952, 40.
14. Bill Beaven, interview with author, 17 June 2013.
15. This is not the only occasion when Hillary turned his back on former friendships, as Harriet Tuckey found out while writing the biography of her father, Griffith Pugh. See Tuckey, *Everest*, 186.
16. Cotter to Rosemary Riddiford, undated, Riddiford Correspondence.
17. Editorial, *Press*, 4 June 1953, 8, Riddiford Archives.

Part 3

1. This extract from J.E. Flecker's verse drama *Hassan ... The Golden Journey to Samarkand* was a Cotter favourite often quoted in mountaineering publications.

Chapter 14: Born for Adventure

1. Cenotaph database: www.aucklandmuseum.com/war-memorial/online-cenotaph
2. Ed Cotter, interview with author, 15 January 2013.
3. Edmund Glover Cotter took a prominent part in local affairs in Greymouth: he even presided over an enthusiastic gathering at the Greymouth Opera House 'on the occasion of the Irish

Race Demonstration in favour of self-determination for Ireland' (*Grey River Argus*, 31 October 1919, 3).
4   Jude Cotter married Jim Horn; they now farm near Oxford, North Canterbury; interview with author, 22 March 2013.
5   J. Grant, 'Peaks and troughs: The story of Ed Cotter', University of Canterbury, Christchurch, 1998, 3.
6   Jude Cotter, interview with author, 22 March 2013.
7   M.J. Conway, 'Mt Stoddart', *The Canterbury Mountaineer*, August 1941, no 10, 14.
8   Cecily married Newton Brown, a stock and station agent, living for many years on the West Coast and in the North Island before succumbing to cancer in 1983.
9   Ralph and Margaret Cotter, interview with author, January 2015.
10 Ed's school reports show consistent first placings in class for English, a talent that was later reflected in all the articles he wrote for climbing journals.
11 That protection was removed in 1947.
12 Stuart Meares, 'The formation of the Christchurch Tramping Club', *The Canterbury Mountaineer*, Jubilee Edition, 1974–75, no 44, 10.
13 T.T. Robins, 'A hut at the Anti-Crow', *The Canterbury Mountaineer*, August 1941, no 10, 39.
14 T.T. Robins, 'Improvements to the Anti-Crow Hut, Xmas 1943', *The Canterbury Mountaineer*, August 1944, no 13, 24.
15 T.T. Robins, 'The Nevile Barker Memorial Hut on the White Col', *The Canterbury Mountaineer*, August 1945, no 14, 3–8.
16 T.T. Robins, 'The CMC huts', *The Canterbury Mountaineer*, August 1945, no 14, 9.
17 Tom Newth, 'Experimental bivvies', *The Canterbury Mountaineer*, August 1945, no 14, 51–53.

Chapter 15: Reaching for the Sky
1   Frank Haden to Wilf Layburn, email, 28 June 2005, Cotter Archives.
2   Robin Johnson, 'The Armoury Range', *The Canterbury Mountaineer*, 1946–47, no 16, 32.
3   Alan Evans, 'The Rakaia and Strachan Pass', *The Canterbury Mountaineer*, 1946–47, no 16, 26–31.
4   Robin Johnson, 'Mt Franklin between trains', *The Canterbury Mountaineer*, 1946–47, no 16, 75.
5   Stan Conway, 'The battle for Greenlaw', *The Canterbury Mountaineer*, 1946–47, no 16, 76.
6   Ed Cotter, 'Mount Rolleston: The Otira face,' *The Canterbury Mountaineer*, 1947–48, vol 4, no 17, 205.
7   David Hall, 'A Godley–Wataroa crossing', [sic] *The Canterbury Mountaineer*, 1947–48, vol 4, no 17, 129.
8   Ed Cotter, 'Harper and Speight', *The Canterbury Mountaineer*, 1948–49, vol 4, no 18, 302.
9   John Sampson, 'Mt Murchison evening climb', *The Canterbury Mountaineer*, 1948–49, vol 4, no 18, 303.
10 Anon, 'Aspiring traverse', *The Canterbury Mountaineer*, 1949–50, vol 5, no 19, 30–32. Other climbers on the mountain commented that Ed's parka was as dirty as the weather.
11 Geoff Harrow, interview with author, 4 October 2013.
12 'Burn to shine: The Craigieburn story', *NZ Skier Magazine*, undated interview with Ed Cotter, Cotter Archives.
13 T.T. Robins, 'Some reflections', *The Canterbury Mountaineer*, 1949–50, vol 5, no 19, 73.
14 'Burn to shine', Cotter Archives.
15 Geoff Harrow, 'Skiing notes', *The Canterbury Mountaineer*, 1949–50, vol 5, no 19, 103–04.

Chapter 16: Southward Bound

1. G. Lowe, *Because It Is There*, London: Cassell and Company, 1959, 19.
2. Ed Cotter, 'Three parties on Tasman: From Pioneer', *NZAJ*, June 1953, vol XV, no 40, 53.
3. Peter Bain, interview with author, 9 November 2014.
4. Ed Cotter, 'Rakaia climbs', *The Canterbury Mountaineer*, 1953–54, vol 6, no 23, 144.
5. Peter Bain, interview with author, 9 November 2014.
6. Cotter, 'Rakaia climbs', 146.
7. Cotter to Riddiford, 8 March 1954, Riddiford Correspondence.
8. J. Grant, 'Peaks and troughs: The story of Ed Cotter', University of Canterbury, Christchurch, 1998, 10.
9. Cotter to Riddiford, 16 January 1955, Riddiford Correspondence.
10. Alwyn Owen, 'Gunn, David John', from the Dictionary of New Zealand Biography: www.teara.govt.nz/en/biographies/4g25/gunn-david-john 257
11. Ibid.
12. J. Bradshaw, *The Land of Doing Without*, Christchurch: Canterbury University Press, 2007, 46.
13. Cotter to Riddiford, 16 January 1955, Riddiford Correspondence.
14. Bradshaw, *The Land of Doing Without*, 68.
15. Ibid., 74
16. Ibid., 82
17. Ibid., 86.
18. Jack Ede, *I've Lived Another Year*, Christchurch: Jack Ede, 2004, 259.
19. Bradshaw, *The Land of Doing Without*, 105.
20. Cotter to Riddiford, 16 January 1955, Riddiford Correspondence.
21. Ibid.
22. Bradshaw, *The Land of Doing Without*, 137.
23. Cotter to Riddiford, 10 August 1955, Riddiford Correspondence.
24. Ibid.
25. Bradshaw, *The Land of Doing Without*, 138.
26. Grant, 'Peaks and troughs', 11.
27. Ibid.
28. Ede, *I've Lived Another Year*, 259–63.

Chapter 17: The 1964 New Zealand Andean Expedition

1. In cuttings collected by Ted Cotter for a scrapbook he would later give his grandson, Guy.
2. Cordillera Real – 'royal' mountain range. About 125km long, southeast of Lake Titicaca.
3. Ed Cotter, 'Once upon a Cordillera', *NZAJ*, 1965, vol XXI, no 1, 18.
4. In July 1966 Alpamayo won this title after an international poll of climbers and photographers: https://en.wikipedia.org/wiki/Alpamayo
5. G. Hauser, *White Mountain and Tawny Plain*, London: Allen and Unwin, 1961, 198.
6. 'Let's do it tomorrow.'
7. J. Grant, 'Peaks and troughs: The story of Ed Cotter', University of Canterbury, Christchurch, 1998, 15.
8. A government-sponsored alpine club that turned out to have mainly skiers as members and only one mountain climber.
9. Mike Nelson, 'Astray in the Andes', *The Canterbury Mountaineer*, 1963–64, vol 10, no 33, 8.
10. Ibid., 9: 'There was still no sign of our errant guards. This exhibition of irresponsibility brought home to us the hard fact that in countries such as Bolivia one should not depend on gratuitous assistance.'
11. Ibid.

12 Ibid., 10.
13 Cotter describes Huaraz as a 'charming mountain town': six years later it was virtually destroyed by a magnitude 7.8 earthquake, with great loss of life.
14 Cotter, 'Once upon a Cordillera', 30.
15 Nelson, 'Astray in the Andes', 7.
16 The distinctive pyramid shape of this mountain has been suggested as the model for the Paramount Pictures logo.
17 Quitoraju, the name used in the Cotter and Nelson accounts of this trip, is the Hispanic spelling of Kitarahu.
18 H. Jacobs, 'A day in the Andes', *The Canterbury Mountaineer*, 1964–65, vol 10, no 34, 15.
19 Grant, 'Peaks and troughs', 15.
20 Nelson, 'Astray in the Andes', 12.
21 Cotter, 'Once upon a Cordillera', 37.
22 Ibid.
23 Ibid., 37–38.
24 *Press*, 26 August 1964.
25 *Expreso*, Lima, 12 July 1964, 3, Cotter Archives.
26 *Press*, 25 August 1964.
27 P. Temple, *The World at Their Feet*, Christchurch: Whitcombe and Tombs, 1969, 186.
28 *Press*, 6 August 1964.
29 Jen Cotter to Jude Horn, 2 July 1964.
30 J. Ede, *I've Lived Another Year*, Christchurch: Jack Ede, 2004, 328.

Chapter 18: Trailblazing the Hollyford

1 J. Bradshaw, *The Land of Doing Without*, Christchurch: Canterbury University Press, 2007, 152.
2 Ibid.
3 Ibid., 153.
4 State Forest Service file, Archives New Zealand, Dunedin. (Correspondence, Bradshaw to Cotter, 4 August 2006.)
5 'Hollyford Track': www.doc.govt.nz
6 No relation to Davey Gunn: www.milfordlodge.com/milford-sound-activities/milfordtrack-walking/holyford-track [sic]
7 Key Summit takes its name from providing the principal key to the water catchments of Otago and Southland. Some streams that drain the Divide join the Eglinton, emptying into Lake Te Anau; some find their way to Lake Wakatipu and the Clutha River; the rest, including the major Pyke tributary, descend into the Hollyford River to flow through Lake McKerrow to the sea (McClenagan, *Fiordland*, Wellington: A.H. & A.W. Reed, 1966).
8 Caples named the Hollyford Valley after his birthplace in Ireland (*Otago Daily Times*, 27 March 2012).
9 *Southland Times*, 22 March 1965.
10 Adventours brochure, Cotter Archives.
11 J. Grant, 'Peaks and troughs: The story of Ed Cotter', Christchurch, University of Canterbury, 1998, 18.
12 Ibid., 19.
13 Bradshaw, *The Land of Doing Without*.
14 www.hollyfordtrack.com
15 Grant, 'Peaks and troughs', 20.
16 In her back garden at New Brighton, Lis has another enormous tree: at the very top is a settee from which she can watch the Christchurch sunsets.

Chapter 19: Vailima and Beyond

1. Email to author, 5 September 2014.
2. Email to author, 17 December 2014.
3. Email to author, 7 March 2014.
4. See his 'Wayfarer' blog: http://bobmckerrow.blogspot.co.nz/
5. R. McKerrow, 'Forty years on: A climb with veteran mountaineer Ed Cotter', *NZAJ*, Centennial edition 1991, vol 44, 173.
6. Email to author, 28 January 2014.

Chapter 20: Everest at Last

1. *Press*, 2 February 1998.
2. Guy Cotter, interview with author, 5 September 2013.
3. Other experiments undertaken by Jim Cotter's team in 2008 looked at how breathing and brain flow are controlled awake and asleep and how these adapt with increasing time at altitude. More work in the same region in 2012 included experiments on blood vessel function, and fluid control and its relation to mountain sickness.
4. *Press*, 2 February 1998.
5. Bill Beaven, interview with author, 17 June 2013.
6. Colin Monteath, *Under a Sheltering Sky: Journeys to mountain heartlands*, Christchurch: Hedgehog House, 2005.
7. D. Morse, 'The Progress League's visit to the Waimakariri', *Canterbury Mountaineer*, Jubilee Edition, 1974–75, no 44, 13.
8. Interview recorded by David Harrowfield, 26 July 2000, CMC archives.
9. Ibid.
10. Cotter to Ted Moore, 14 August 2007.
11. Scott Russell, *Mountain Prospect*, London: Chatto and Windus, 1946, 156.

Conclusion

1. From Thomas Hardy's explanatory note to the first edition of *Tess of the D'Urbervilles*, November 1891. A prolific writer, St Jerome (347–420) is best known for his translation of the Bible into Latin.
2. Hocken Collections, MS 1164 1/11/27. Harriet Tuckey described Hillary's habit of 'deploying a calculatedly disarming modesty for which he was widely admired' (Tuckey, *Everest: The first ascent: The untold story of Griffith Pugh, the man who made it possible*, London: Rider, 2013, 254).
3. Guy Cotter, interview with author, 5 September 2013.
4. Hillary's accounts often focused on himself at the forefront of hair-raising adventures, as if he could not resist his own tale of derring-do. This was sometimes reinforced by a 'Famous Five' tone of writing, noted by Philip Temple in his review of *High Adventure* (Canvas magazine, *NZ Herald*, 24–25 May 2001, 28). Among numerous examples, after Everest Hillary conveyed the impression that he had pulled Tenzing up the Hillary Step, though Tenzing climbed it much as Hillary had done, protected by a rope. Tenzing, a vastly more experienced mountaineer, regarded Hillary's account of the final section of the climb as unfair (E. Douglas, *Tenzing: Hero of Everest*, Washington: National Geographic Society, 2003). Hillary also took credit for much of Griffith Pugh's work on the Silver Hut expedition (see Tuckey, *Everest*, 256–57).
5. www.theguardian.com/world/2013/mar/22/george-lowe
6. G. Lowe, *Because It Is There*, London: Cassell, 1959, 12.
7. Stephen Venables, 'The man who climbed Everest', *Geographical*, May 2008, vol 80, no 5. Article extract at www.questia.com
8. *Nine to Noon*, Radio New Zealand, 1 May 2014; 3ZB, 29 April 2014.

9   P. Steele, *Eric Shipton: Everest and beyond*, London: Constable, 1998, 148.
10 Hocken Collections, MS 1164 2/87/1.
11 Ibid.
12 Ibid., Stevenson to Ellis, 27 September 1991.
13 N. Hardie, 'Because it is there', *NZAJ*, 1960, vol XVIII, no 47, 417–18. Review reprinted with acknowledgement to the *Christchurch Star*.
14 Hardie to Riddiford, 9 December 1959, Riddiford Correspondence.
15 Riddiford to Hardie, 17 December 1959, Riddiford Correspondence.
16 H.E. Riddiford, Letter to the Editor, *NZAJ*, 1960, vol XVIII, no 47, 414–15.
17 M. Conefrey, *Everest 1953: The epic story of the first ascent*, Oxford: One World, 2012, xiv.
18 Perhaps Hillary was the ultimate victim, rather than the beneficiary, of all the publicity. As Harriet Tuckey sees it in *Everest* (188–89), Hillary was always under pressure to affirm his reputation as a high-altitude climber. 'In the bright afterglow of the Everest spotlight, he came to be viewed as a high-altitude climber of unparalleled skill and courage, though in reality his experience of climbing at extreme altitude was still limited.'
19 L.V. Bryant, *New Zealanders and Everest*, Wellington: A.H. & A.W. Reed, 1953, 35.
20 S. Barnett, *FMC Bulletin*, August 2013, no 193, 57.
21 Ibid., 57.
22 S. Barnett, *FMC Bulletin*, November 2015, no 202, 58.
23 G. Lowe and E.P. Hillary, *East of Everest*, London: Hodder & Stoughton, 1956, 33.
24 Geoff Harrow, interview with author, October 2013.
25 Norman Hardie, interview with author, 26 April 2013.
26 In what was designated as a scientific expedition, Hillary concentrated on the South Pole. Medical officer and dog expert George Marsh could not restrain his feelings in a letter to Riddiford from Depot 700 on 18 December 1957. With expedition deputy leader J.H. (Bob) Miller (later Sir J. Holmes Miller), Marsh was to make one of the longest Antarctic sledging traverses on record – 2500km from McMurdo Sound, exploring the mountains east of Beardmore Glacier. But he was incensed by Hillary's lack of interest in the scientific work of the expedition. 'As a leader he is too selfish to be a good one; and anything this expedition may achieve will be in spite of, rather than because of him. A man more concerned with what he can get out of it I have rarely seen. His obvious desire to reach the Pole, and some of the things he has stooped to in order to help this project, is little short of disgusting. This journey would bring back not one scientific fact, and stinks of personal publicity and gain' (Riddiford Correspondence).
27 J. Grant, 'Peaks and troughs: The story of Ed Cotter', University of Canterbury, Christchurch, 1998, 6.
28 Roger Peren, interview with author, 19 September 2014.
29 Mavis Davidson to Rosemary Riddiford, 15 January 1998, Riddiford Correspondence.
30 Rosemary Riddiford to Mavis Davidson, 6 February 1998, Hocken Collections, MS2985/240.
31 *New Zealand Books/Pukapuka Aotearoa, A Quarterly Review*, Wellington, October 1999, 14, Riddiford Files.
32 Philip Temple, interview with author, 3 June 2014.
33 'Canvas', *NZ Herald*, 24–25 May 2003, 28.
34 Michael Ward, *In This Short Span*, London: Victor Gollancz, 1972, 79.
35 Ibid., 131.
36 Murray Ellis was a member of what Hillary called 'The Old Firm', who drove to the South Pole: Hillary, Ellis, Jim Bates, Peter Mulgrew and Derek Wright. His son David Ellis makes the point that his father's disappointment relates more to Murray's experiences in Antarctica, where the unsung natural leader was Bob Miller, to whom everyone went for advice and decisions. Though Murray never wanted recognition for himself, he felt the talents of outstanding people should have been given due recognition by Hillary.

37 D. Ellis to Rosemary Riddiford, 17 April 2003, Riddiford Correspondence.
38 S. Russell, 'The centenary of the New Zealand Alpine Club', *Alpine Journal*, 1992–23, vol 97, no 341, 163.
39 Hocken Collections, MS 1164 2/71/1.

Appendix 2: What Happened to the Dream Team?

1 Hillary to Hardie, 19 July 1952, Riddiford Correspondence.
2 Jones to Hardie, 23 April 1953, Riddiford Correspondence.
3 British mountaineer Frank Smythe also wrote that Kangchenjunga 'is in everything but actual height an infinitely more difficult mountain than Everest, which technically speaking is an easy mountain' (Smythe, *The Kangchenjunga Adventure*, London: Hodder and Stoughton, 1946, 148). After the first ascent the mountain was not climbed again for 22 years – it was simply too long, too high, too cold, too hard. See also Band, *Summit: 150 years of the Alpine Club*, London: Collins, 2006.
4 N.D. Hardie, 'Five feet from the gods', *NZAJ*, June 1956, vol XVI, no 43, 280.
5 M. Ward, *Everest: A thousand years of exploration*, Glasgow: Ernest Press, 2003, 278.
6 B. Wilkins, *Among Secret Beauties*, Dunedin: Otago University Press, 2013, 15.
7 Hardie, email to author, 30 March 2016.
8 E.P. Hillary, *Nothing Venture, Nothing Win*, London: Hodder and Stoughton, 1975, 177.
9 'The expedition leader with five Sherpas failed to extract him. Next morning he was lifted out, but by then he was badly frostbitten' (Hardie, 'Obituary: Jim McFarlane, 1926–1997', *NZAJ*, 1997, vol 49, 121).
10 L. Thompson, 'Oral Histories: The golden era of New Zealand climbing: 1948–1955', NZAC archives, Hocken Collections, Bill Beaven, Folder 2.
11 Himalayan Trust UK release, ex Mary Lowe, undated, Cotter Archives.
12 L. Thompson, 'Oral Histories', Interview 4.

Appendix 3: British and New Zealand Expeditions to the Himalaya 1950–55

1 Bill Packard, 'The Annapurna Himal, Nepal, 1950', *NZAJ*, 1952, vol XIV, no 39, 216.
2 A.R. Roberts, 'The New Zealand Himalayan expedition, 1953', *NZAJ*, June 1954, vol XV, no 41, 393.
3 C.M. Todd, 'North-east of Api, West Nepal', *NZAJ*, June 1955, vol XVI, no 42, 54–60.
4 L.R. Hewitt, 'Masherbrum, 1955', *NZAJ*, 1956, vol XVI, no 43, 339–40.

Appendix 4: Pasang the Indestructible

1 Chapman described Pasang as going magnificently, his cheerfulness, determination and speed never flagging (Chapman, *Helvellyn to Himalaya, Including an Account of the First Ascent of Chomolhari*, London: Travel Book Club, 1941, 254).
2 H. Tichy, (1955) trans. B. Creighton, *Cho Oyu: By favour of the gods*, London: Methuen, 1957.
3 Ibid., foreword by John Hunt, 6.
4 Ibid., 29.
5 Ibid., 88.
6 Ibid., 94.
7 Ibid., 16.
8 Ibid., 125.
9 Ibid., 130.
10 Ibid., 156.
11 Ibid., 168.
12 Ibid., 180.
13 Ibid., 181.

BIBLIOGRAPHY

ARCHIVES

Archives New Zealand, The Department of Internal Affairs Te Tari Taiwhenua

Riddiford Correspondence: The Riddiford family's private collection includes personal letters from Earle Riddiford to his mother, and a large number of letters Riddiford received from other regular correspondents.

Riddiford Archives: includes all his files, letters and documentation relating to the First New Zealand Himalayan Expedition, plus correspondence and other material relating to the 1951 Everest Reconnaissance, Cho Oyu 1952, and planning for the NZAC Barun expedition in 1954. These archives also contain an extensive collection of cuttings, reviews and articles relating to mountaineering.

CMC Archives

Cotter Correspondence: includes diaries and letters from the First New Zealand Himalayan Expedition

Cotter Archives: includes miscellaneous correspondence, articles and speech notes

Hocken Collections – Uare Taoka o Hākena

BOOKS

Astill, T., *Mount Everest: The reconnaissance 1935*, Southampton: T. Astill, 2005.
Band, G., *Summit: 150 Years of the Alpine Club*, London: Collins, 2006.
Booth, P. *Edmund Hillary: The life of a legend*, Auckland: Moa Beckett, 1993.
Barnett, S., Brown, R. and Spearpoint, G., *Shelter from the Storm: The story of New Zealand's back country huts,* Nelson: Craig Potton, 2012.
Bradshaw, J., *The Land of Doing Without*, Christchurch: Canterbury University Press, 2007.
Bryant, L.V., *New Zealanders and Everest*, Wellington: A.H. & A.W. Reed, 1953.
Conefrey, M., *Everest 1953: The epic story of the first ascent*, Oxford: Oneworld Publications, 2012.
____, *The Ghosts of K2: The epic saga of the first ascent,* London: Oneworld Publications, 2015.
Douglas, E., *Tenzing: Hero of Everest*, Washington: National Geographic Society, 2003.
Ede, J., *I've Lived Another Year*, Christchurch: Jack Ede, 2004.
Evans, C., *Kangchenjunga: The untrodden peak*, London: Hodder & Stoughton, 1965.
Hardie, N., *On My Own Two Feet*, Christchurch: Canterbury University Press, 2006.
____, *In Highest Nepal*, Sydney: Allen & Unwin, 1957.
Hauser, G., *White Mountain and Tawny Plain*, London: Allen & Unwin, 1961.
Hillary, E.P., *High Adventure*, London: Hodder & Stoughton, 1955.
____, *Nothing Venture, Nothing Win*, London: Hodder & Stoughton, 1975.
____, *View from the Summit*, London: Doubleday, 1999.
Hillary, E.P. & P., *Two Generations*, London: Hodder & Stoughton, 1984.
Hunt, J., *The Ascent of Everest*, London: Hodder & Stoughton, 1953.
Izzard, R., *The Innocent on Everest*, London: Hodder & Stoughton, 1954.
Johnston, A., *Sir Edmund Hillary: An extraordinary life*, Auckland: Penguin, 2007.
Kolb, F., *Himalaya Venture*, London: Lutterworth Press, 1959.
Langton, G., *Armchair Mountaineering: A bibliography of New Zealand mountain climbing*, [Christchurch]: NZAC, 2006.

Little, P., *After Everest: Inside the private world of Edmund Hillary*, Sydney: Allen & Unwin, 2012.
Lowe, G., *Because It Is There*, London: Cassell, 1959.
Lowe, G. & Hillary, E.P., *East of Everest*, London: Hodder & Stoughton, 1956.
McClenagan, J., *Fiordland*, Wellington: A.H. & A.W. Reed, 1966.
Monteath, C., *Under a Sheltering Sky: Journeys to mountain heartlands*, Christchurch: Hedgehog House, 2005.
Noyce, W., *South Col: A personal story of the ascent of Everest*, London: Heinemann, 1954.
Russell, S., *Mountain Prospect*, London: Chatto & Windus, 1946.
Salisbury, R. & Hawley, E., *The Himalaya by the Numbers: A statistical analysis of mountaineering in the Nepal Himalaya*, Kathmandu: Vajra Publications (E-book), 2007.
Sharpe, R., *Fiordland Muster*, London: Hodder & Stoughton, 1966.
Shipton, E., *Upon That Mountain*, London: Hodder & Stoughton, 1943.
____, *The Mount Everest Reconnaissance Expedition, 1951*, London: Hodder & Stoughton, 1952.
____, *That Untravelled World*, London: Hodder & Stoughton, 1969.
Smythe, F.S., *The Valley of Flowers*, London: Hodder & Stoughton, 1938.
____, *The Kangchenjunga Adventure*, London: Hodder & Stoughton, 1946.
____, *Kamet Conquered*, London: Hodder & Stoughton, Uniform Edition, 1947.
Spencer Chapman, F., *Helvellyn to Himalaya, Including an Account of the First Ascent of Chomolhari*, London: The Travel Book Club, 1941.
Steele, P., *Eric Shipton: Everest and beyond*, London: Constable, 1998.
Stobart, T., *Adventurer's Eye: The autobiography of Everest film man Tom Stobart*, London: Odhams, 1958.
Temple, P., *The World at Their Feet*, Christchurch: Whitcombe & Tombs, 1969.
____, *Castles in the Air*, Dunedin: John McIndoe, 1973.
Tichy, H., (1955) trans. B. Creighton, *Cho Oyu: By favour of the gods*, London: Methuen, 1957.
Tuckey, H., *Everest: The first ascent: The untold story of Griffith Pugh, the man who made it possible*, London: Rider, 2013.
Ullman, J.R., *Man of Everest: The autobiography of Tenzing*, London: The Reprint Society, 1956.
Verghese, B.G. (ed.), *Himalayan Endeavour*, Bombay: Times of India, 1962.
Ward, M., *In This Short Span*, London: Victor Gollancz, 1972.
____, *Everest: A thousand years of exploration*, Glasgow: Ernest Press, 2003.
Wilkins, B., *Among Secret Beauties*, Dunedin: Otago University Press, 2013.
Wilson, J., *Joy of the Mountains: A climber's life*, Christchurch: Te Waihora Press, 2013.

JOURNAL ARTICLES

Anon, 'Aspiring traverse', *The Canterbury Mountaineer*, 1949–50, vol 5, no 19, 30–32.
Barnett, S., 'Beyond Everest: Inside the private world of Edmund Hillary', *FMC Bulletin*, August 2013, no 193, 56–58.
Barnett, S., 'First to the top: Sir Edmund Hillary's amazing Everest adventure', *FMC Bulletin*, November 2015, no 202, 58.
Cotter, E.M., 'Mount Rolleston: The Otira face', *The Canterbury Mountaineer*, 1947–48, vol 4, no 17, 205.
____, 'Harper and Speight', *The Canterbury Mountaineer*, 1948–49, vol 4, no 18, 302.
____, 'Elie de Beaumont from the west', *The Canterbury Mountaineer*, August 1951, vol 5, no 20, 25–30.
____, 'The Garhwal Himalayas', *The Canterbury Mountaineer*, 1951–52, vol 5, no 21, 154–63.
____, 'Three parties on Tasman: From Pioneer', *NZAJ*, 1953, vol XV, no 40, 53–54.
____, 'Rakaia climbs', *The Canterbury Mountaineer*, 1953–54, vol 6, no 23, 141–46.
____, 'Once upon a Cordillera', *NZAJ*, 1965, vol XXI, no 1, 18–38.

Cleveland, L., 'Himalayan journey', *The Canterbury Mountaineer*, 1950–51, vol 5, no 20, 30.
Conway, M.J., 'Mt Stoddart', *The Canterbury Mountaineer*, August 1941, no 10, 14–17.
____, 'The battle for Greenlaw', *The Canterbury Mountaineer*, 1946–47, no 16, 75–76.
Ede, J., 'Elusive Elie', *The Canterbury Mountaineer*, August 1943, no 12, 18–22.
Ellis, D., 'Higher ground: New Zealand's Himalayan achievements in the 1950's', *NZAJ*, 2005, vol 57, 108–24.
Evans, A., 'The Rakaia and Strachan Pass', *The Canterbury Mountaineer*, 1946–47, no 16, 26–31.
____, 'The Cho Oyu expedition', *Alpine Journal*, May 1953, vol LIX, no 286, 9–18.
____, 'New Zealand Himalayan expedition', *Geographical Journal*, 1955, 121, 129–35.
Hall, D., 'A Godley–Wataroa crossing', [sic] *The Canterbury Mountaineer*, 1947–48, vol 4, no 17, 125–31.
Hardie, N.D., 'Five feet from the gods', *NZAJ*, 1956, vol XVI, no 43, 280–87.
____, 'Mt Sefton: The first 28 ascents', *The Canterbury Mountaineer*, 1949–50, vol 5, no 19, 114–25.
____, 'Because it is there', *NZAJ*, 1960, vol XVIII, no 47, 417–18.
Harrow, G., 'Skiing notes', *The Canterbury Mountaineer*, 1949–50, vol 5, no 19, 103–04.
Hewitt, L.R., 'Masherbrum, 1955', *NZAJ*, 1956, vol XVI, no 43, 333–40.
Hillary, E.P., 'Attempt on Cho Oyu', *NZAJ*, 1953, vol XV, no 40, 4–13.
Jacobs, H., 'A day in the Andes', *The Canterbury Mountaineer*, 1964–65, vol 10, no 34, 13–16.
Johnson, R., 'The Armoury Range', *The Canterbury Mountaineer*, 1946–47, no 16, 32–33.
____, 'Mt Franklin between trains', *The Canterbury Mountaineer*, 1946–47, no 16, 75.
McKerrow, R., 'Forty years on: A climb with veteran mountaineer Ed Cotter', *NZAJ*, Centennial Edition 1991, vol 44, 171–74.
Meares, Stuart, 'The formation of the Christchurch Tramping Club', *The Canterbury Mountaineer*, Jubilee Edition 1974–75, no 44, 10.
Morse, D., 'The Progress League's visit to the Waimakariri', *The Canterbury Mountaineer*, Jubilee Edition 1974–75, no 44, 12–13.
Murray, W.H., 'The reconnaissance of Mt Everest', *Alpine Journal*, November 1952, vol LVIII, no 285, 433–52.
Nelson, M., 'Astray in the Andes', *The Canterbury Mountaineer*, 1963–64, vol 10, no 33, 7–13.
Newth, T., 'Experimental bivvies', *The Canterbury Mountaineer*, August 1945, no 14, 50–53.
Packard, W., 'The Annapurna Himal, Nepal, 1950', *NZAJ*, 1952, vol XIV, no 39, 206–20.
Powell, P.S., 'Volta Therma traverse', *NZAJ*, 1946, vol XI, no 33, 111–18.
Riddiford, H.E., 'A visit to the Douglas', *NZAJ*, 1947, vol XII, no 34, 43–52.
____, 'Jagged and Tent Peaks', *NZAJ*, 1947, vol XII, no 34, 89–91.
____, 'Sefton from the south', *NZAJ*, 1948, vol XII, no 35, 209–17.
____, 'Tasman from the Balfour', *NZAJ*, 1949, vol XIII, no 36, 54–62.
____, 'A visit to the Burton', *The Canterbury Mountaineer*, 1949–50, vol 5, no 19, 58–61.
____, 'Elie de Beaumont from the Burton', *NZAJ*, 1951, vol XIV, no 38, 26–33.
____, 'The east ridge of Malte Brun', *NZAJ*, 1953, vol XV, no 40, 139–44.
____, 'Because it is there', *NZAJ*, 1960, vol XVIII, no 47, 414–15.
____, 'Five footloose fathers in the Waipara', *NZAJ*, 1962, no 49, 58–65.
Riddiford, H.E., Lowe, W.G., & Cotter, E.M., 'Expedition to the Garhwal Himalaya, 1951', *NZAJ*, 1952, vol XIV, no 39, 170–93 (includes Riddiford, 'The approach to Garhwal and two attempts on Nilkanta'; Lowe, 'Mukut Parbat: The reconnaissance'; Riddiford, 'Mukut Parbat, the ascent'; Lowe, 'Three more summits'; Cotter, 'Peak 20,760 feet and the return to Ranikhet'.)
Roberts, A.R., 'The New Zealand Himalayan expedition, 1953', *NZAJ*, 1954, vol XV, no 41, 393–99.

Robins, T.T., 'A hut at the Anti-Crow', *The Canterbury Mountaineer*, August 1941, no 10, 38–40).
____, 'Improvements to the Anti-Crow Hut, Xmas 1943', *The Canterbury Mountaineer*, August 1944, no 13, 23–25.
____, 'The Nevile Barker Memorial Hut on the White Col', *The Canterbury Mountaineer*, August 1945, no 14, 3–8.
____, 'The CMC huts', *The Canterbury Mountaineer*, August 1945, no 14, 8–10.
____, 'Some reflections', *The Canterbury Mountaineer*, 1949–50, vol 5, no 19, 71–73.
Russell, S., 'The centenary of the New Zealand Alpine Club', *Alpine Journal*, 1992–23, vol 97, no 341, 161–63.
Sampson, J., 'Mt Murchison evening climb', *The Canterbury Mountaineer*, 1948–49, vol 4, no 18, 302–03.
Shipton, E., 'Everest: The 1951 reconnaissance of the southern route', *Geographical Journal*, 118, June 1952, 117–41.
____, 'The expedition to Cho Oyu', *Geographical Journal*, 1953, 119, 129–39.
Todd, C.M., 'North-east of Api, West Nepal', *NZAJ*, 1955, vol XVI, no 42, 54–60.
Ward, M., 'The exploration of the Nepalese side of Everest', *Alpine Journal*, 1992–93, vol 97, no 341, 21–221.

OTHER

Grant, J., 'Peaks and troughs: The story of Ed Cotter', Life History Project, Sociology 340, University of Canterbury, Christchurch, 1998.
Harrowfield, D., Taped interview with Ed Cotter, 26 July 2000, CMC archives.
'Hollyford track guide', Department of Conservation: www.doc.govt.nz
Langton, G., 'A history of mountain climbing in New Zealand to 1953', PhD thesis, University of Canterbury, Christchurch, 1996.
New Zealand Archive of Film, Television and Sound: ID 30262, *NZ Himalayan Expedition 1952*, Track 4 [D417/4].
New Zealand On Screen, *Aspiring*, The Gibson Group, 2006.
Taped address by Earle Riddiford to the Wellington division of the NZAC, 1987 (supplied by Anna Riddiford).
Thompson, L., 'Oral histories: The golden era of New Zealand climbing: 1948–1955', NZAC archives, Hocken Collections, Bill Beaven, Folder 2.

INTERVIEWS

Anna Riddiford
Belinda Cranswick
Bill Beaven
Bob McKerrow
Colin Monteath
David Ellis
Geoff Harrow
Guy Cotter
Jacqui Cotter
Jen Cotter
Jim and Ann Wilson
John Arkwright
Jude Horn

Lis Cotter
Mike Nelson
Norman Hardie
Peter Bain
Philip Temple
Ralph and Margaret Cotter
Rhondda Pope
Richard Riddiford
Roger Peren
Sarah Riddiford

ACKNOWLEDGEMENTS

Thanks to Rhondda Pope, the initiator of this project, and to Ed Cotter for the years of fun and friendship we have enjoyed. To Bob McKerrow, whose enthusiasm from the very start was so encouraging, and to Ed's climbing contemporaries Norman Hardie, Bill Beaven, Geoff Harrow and Peter Bain for their wise advice and unfailing support. Experts in the field Colin Monteath, David Ellis and Philip Temple helped me considerably by reading drafts and providing useful perspectives.

I am enormously grateful to Earle Riddiford's family – Belinda Cranswick, Anna Riddiford, Richard Riddiford and Sarah Riddiford – for access to Earle's photographs, letters and expedition documents, and their combined memory pool. Similarly, my sincere thanks to the Cotter family – Ed himself, Jen, Guy, Lis and Jacqui, who contributed the magnificent watercolour of Mukut Parbat for the cover. I also acknowledge my own family: John, Barb and Guy McKinnon, John Madgwick and Flora Pamment, Mike and Jennifer Blyleven, and David and Frances West, who have each supported me in their own way, from sharing mountaineering knowledge to helping with technical hassles.

Ed Cotter collected many photographic images over the years. Unfortunately a number were lost as a result of earthquake damage to his home, and for some of the items retrieved the provenance is obscure. As far as possible, the sources of photographs used in this work have been identified: should the origin be incorrectly ascribed, I apologise. Acknowledgement is also due to those who have kindly consented to the use of valuable personal correspondence: in a few cases the passage of time has made tracing descendants an insuperable task.

Those who allowed me the privilege of face-to-face interviews are acknowledged in the bibliography, but there were many others who also contributed stories, shared experiences, commentary and miscellaneous photos. They include Evangeline Riddiford Graham, Grant Southey, Maggie Stafsnes, Mary Lowe, Anne Harrison McGregor, Julia Bradshaw, Anna Cook, Steve Aiken, Jim Cotter, King Allen, Amanda Power, Gus Roxburgh, Limbo Thompson, Snow Ross and Grant Hunter. Thanks also to Maureen McCloy (CMC) for access to CMC archival tapes; the very helpful staff at Otago University's Hocken Collections; John Grant, for his invaluable Life History project; Gary Scott, Gibson Group; historian Graham Langton; helpful staff at Archives NZ; and Sam Newton, Margaret McMahon and Nerina Sutherland at the NZAC for their help with NZAC resources. It will also be hard for me to forget the efforts of Fly Fiordland in Franz Josef and The Helicopter Line based at Glentanner, whose pilots made the most of perfect conditions so that we could view close-up the Riddiford-inspired routes described in these pages.

To Rachel Scott, publisher at Otago University Press, my editor Imogen Coxhead and all the OUP staff, a huge thank you for your guidance as I edged slowly towards publication. I am grateful to Roger Smith, Geographx, for excellent maps that would not have been possible without the assistance of the NZAC DOW Hall Publications Fund, whose generous grant covered the cost. (By a curious quirk of fate, writer, historian and mountaineer David Oswald William Hall is the same David Hall who features in Chapter 15 of this book.)

Finally, I applaud my husband Herb Madgwick for his forbearance.

INDEX

Page numbers in **bold** refer to illustrations.

A

A.R. Harris and Co. 257, 258, 260
Abi Gamin 86, 89
Acland family 266
Adams, Ruth 18, 20, 228, 306
Adventure Consultants 269, 272–78
Aiken, Steve 261–62, 274
Alabaster, Lake **213**, 249
Alaknanda Gorge **94**, 95, 96
Alaknanda River 59, **65**, **66**, **94**
Aldridge, Lois **205**
Algie, R.M. 27, 30
Allen, King 223, 252, 254
Allen, Sydney and Doris 223, 226
Allot, Viv 255
Alpamayo 226, 235–39, **236**, **237**, 242–43
Ama Dablam 168, **278**
Amazon, Mt 199
Amazons Breasts 209
Ancohuma **227**, 228, 229, **229**, 230, **231**, **232**, 243
Anderson, Andy **194**
Andrews and Beaven Ltd 307
Ang Dorje 277
Angtarkay 126, 127, 131
Annapurna IV 25, 138, 302, 308
Antarctica 167, 168, 220, **244**, 244–45, 273, 292, 303; Anglo–American physiological expedition 168
Anti-Crow Hut 191–92, **192**, 200
Aoraki/Mt Cook 21, **24**, 25, 44, 220–22, 272, 292, 303–04, 306
Aoraki/Mt Cook region **22–23**
Arichiri **227**, 229, 232, 243
Arichiri Este **227**, 243
Arkwright, Alys (Awa) 111, 113, 157–58
Arkwright, Henry 111
Arkwright, John 111, 113, **164**, 173
Arkwright, Rosalind 111, 113
Armoury Range 199
Arnold, Jan 273
Arrowsmith Range 119, 207
Artesonraju 234

Arthur Ellis and Co. 29
Arthurs Pass Association 307
Arthurs Pass National Park 200, 202, 206, 271, 303, 306; *see also* names of individual peaks
Aspiring Hut **205**
Aspiring, Mt 116–17, 202, **203**, **204**
Avalanche Peak 177, 178, **179**, **203**, **204**, 306
Aylmer, Mt 36, **37**
Aymara Indians 228
Ayres, Harry 20, 44, 133, 154, 155, 157, 167, 291, 293, 306; First New Zealand Himalayan Expedition 28, 30

B

Badri 297, 298
Badrinath 53, 54, **55**, 56, 59, 60, **61**, 62, 63, **65**, 66, **66**, 67, 69, 70, 71, 298
Badrinath-Mana Pass 32
Bain, Peter **169**, 207, 209, **283**, 284
Balbala Glacier **65**, 92
Balfour Glacier 20–21, **22**, **24**
Balfour Range 21
Balfour Valley 21
Ball, Gary 272–73
Banks Peninsula 191, 259, 267, 271
Bannie, Mt 118
Bardolph, Mt 199
Barker Hut 192, 201
Barnett, Shaun 290–91
Barun area *see* New Zealand Alpine Club Barun Valley Expedition 1954
Barun Glacier **125**, 131, 147, 149, 150, 151, 304
Baruntse **125**, 166, 306, 307, 309
Baxter, James K., 'In the Matukituki Valley' 202
Beaven, Bill: Bealey Spur bach **174**, 307; British Expedition to Mount Everest 1953 158, 161; climbing career 306–07; climbing with Riddiford and praise of abilities 292, 306; Dog Tuckers group

283; Elie de Beaumont Maximilian Ridge climb 36, **38**, **39**, 39–41, **43**, 43–44, 45, 274, 292; English Lake District climbing 161, 306; and Hillary's comments about Riddiford 180; Himalayan Dinner, Christchurch 1955 **169**; marriage and children 167, 307; New Zealand Alpine Club Barun Valley Expedition 1954 165–66, 306–07; rescue of Ruth Adams 20, 306; Riddiford's 'Dream Team', First NZ Himalayan Expedition **14**, 25, 30, 306–07; Riddiford's wedding 165; sailing 305; skiing 307; Southern Alps climbing 15, 16, 17–18, **18**, **19**, 20–21, **21**, 24, **24**, 31, 117–19, 158, **159**, 176, 177, 178, 306, 307; *Stepping Stones to Everest* (film) 181; tribute to Ed Cotter 278–79

Beaven, Don 32, 117, 303, 306

Beaven, Gay (née Hall) 167, 307

Beere, Rawdon 157, 165

Bhote Kosi River **124**, 141

Big Bay 211; plane crash 212, 214

Blakeney, Tom 153

Bodkin, W.A. 31

Bohny, Hans 207

Bonar Glacier 202

Bonington, Chris **263**

Bourdillon, Jennifer 138, 147

Bourdillon, Tom 123, **123**, 128–29, 132, 133, 138, 143–44, **146**, 147, 150, 161, 180

Bowie, Mick 20, **169**

Braham, T.H. 30, 32

Brake, Brian, film of Mt Aspiring climbing expedition 201–02, **203**, **204**

British Alpine Club 97, 152, 153, 165, 302, 306; 40th Everest Anniversary 288

British Everest Reconnaissance Expedition 1935 25, 35

British Expedition to Cho Oyu 1952 134, **146**, 312; attempt on Cho Oyu 144–45; coolies 141; discord among climbers 142–43, 144; exploratory climbs after abandonment of Cho Oyu attempt 138, 141, 144, 147, 150, 151; finances 138, 152–53; food, gear and equipment 138, 141, 144; friction between New Zealanders 133, 137–38, 143, 149, 152, 155, 156, 179–80, 181–82, 294; illness of climbers 141, 143, 144, 145, 149; leader and members 309; objectives 137; organisation 138; reconnaissance 141–43; Sherpas 144; Shipton's report 149–50; testing ground for 1953 Everest expedition 150–51; trek in to Namche Bazar and Lunak 139, **139**, **140**, 141

British Expedition to Mount Everest 1953: conquest of Everest 160–61, 162–63, 285, 290, 306, 309; *Conquest of Everest* (film) 162; Hillary and Lowe's lectures and appearances 162–63; leader, members and sirdar 209; radio broadcast 162; Riddiford's exclusion 143, 150, 151; Riddiford's lectures 161; Shipton's removal from leadership 142, 150–51, 154

British Reconnaissance Expedition to Kangchenjunga 1955 310

British Reconnaissance to Mount Everest 1951: British members 123, **123**, 132–33, 134; coolies 122, 127; decision on which two New Zealanders to go 100–04, 278, 288, 289–90, 291, 294; Dudh Kosi Valley and Nup La 133, 294; finances 99, 101, 102, 122, 152; food 104, 122, 123, 126, 128; gear and equipment 126; Hillary's and NZAC requests to include two New Zealanders 89, 97–100, 287, 288; Khumbu Icefall route 121, 126, 128–29, **130**, 131–33, 134, 182, 308; leader, members and sirdar 308; planning and organisation 87, 126–27; Riddiford's lecture 160; Sherpas 126, 127, 128, 129, 131; Tesi Lapcha Pass and journey to Kathmandu 134–36

British West Nepal Expedition 1950 25, 54, 119, 308

Browne, Carrol 266

Browne, Mike 264, 265, 266

Brunner, Mt 16, **22**, 117, 118

Bryant, L.V. (Dan) 25, 35, 47, 98, 99, 168, **169**, 290, 295

Bunshah, Keki 53, 56, 60, **61**, 62, 168

Burns, Mt 17

Burton bivvy 39–40, **40**, 43, 45

Burton Glacier 24, 36, 40

C

Callery Glacier 36, 39

Callery Saddle 36, 39

Callery Valley 39, 43, 274

Cameron Glacier 119
Cameron River 207
Cameron Valley **208**
Canterbury Mountaineering Club (CMC) 29, 48, 67, 102, 188, 191–96, 205, 226; Dew Drop Inn bar **189**; Ed Cotter as president 259–60; hut building 191–93, 202, 205, 207; New Zealand Masherbrum Expedition 1955 310; skiing section 202, 205–06; training camps 195–96, 199; women members 191, 205–06
Canterbury University College 115
Canterbury University Tramping Club 15, 16, 115, 303, 306
Caples, Patrick 248
Carrington, Gerald (Charlie) 281
Carrington Hut 191, 195–96, 199
Carty, D.A. 24, 45
Cashmere Sanatorium 189–90; Fresh Air Home for Children 190
Cass 194
Cawley, Bob 177
Cawley, Nancy 278
Chamar 162, 309
Chamrao Glacier 69, 74, **75**, **77**, 297, 298, 299; Dakkhni Chamrao Glacier **65**, 74, 76, 77, 78, 80; Uttari Chamrao Glacier **65**, 76, 89, 92
Chancellor Dome 265
Chancellor Hut **263**
Chapman, F. Spencer 311
Chapman, Ray **169**, **208**, 209
Chartres, Johnny 215
Chartres, Ruth 218
Chearucu Valley, Cordillera Real **227**, 228, 229, 232
Chispani 141
Cho Oyu **124**, 131, 134, 150, 168; *see also* British Expedition to Cho Oyu 1952
Chomolhari 311
Chopicalqui 228
Christchurch Boys' High School 190–91, 196, 202
Christchurch earthquake damage 282–83
Christchurch Tramping Club 281; *see also* Canterbury Mountaineering Club (CMC)
Christmas, Roger **208**
Christopher Col 16, 117–18
Chule **124**, 141, 143
Climber, The 294–95

Climbers Col 31, 36
Club Andino Boliviano 228
Coast-to-Coast race 206
Cockburn, Daryl 173, 180
Colledge, Ray 138, 143, 144, **146**, 147
Commonwealth Trans-Continental Crossing 167
Conquest of Everest (film) 162
Conway, Stan **169**, 197, 200, **200**, 201, 207, **208**, 209, 211
Cook, Anna **174**, 274, 297, 298
Cook, Derek **174**, 176, 177, 244, 307
Cook, Edward **174**
Cook, Mt *see* Aoraki/Mt Cook
Cook, Phil 153, 155
Cook River 20, **22**, 24
Copland Pass **22**, 115, 119, 261, 265
Copland Valley 116, 117, 118
Cordillera Blanca 226, 232, **235**, 243
Cordillera Real 226, **227**, 228, 243
Cotter, Ann (née Hindmarsh) 189
Cotter, Anton 225, **225**, 252, **257**, 269–71, **270**
Cotter, Cecily 50, 185, **187**, 190, **221**
Cotter, Dulcibel (Dulcie) Minnie (née McCarthny) 185, 186, **187**, 189–90
Cotter, Edmund Glover 185, 186, 189
Cotter, Edmund (Ed) McCarthny
    climbing and outdoors life **183**; Antarctica **244**, 244–45; Aoraki/Mt Cook climbs 44, 220–22; British Reconnaissance to Mount Everest 1951, exclusion 100–03; California **264**, 265–66; Canterbury Mountaineering Club, and friends 188, 191–96, **192–96**, 198–202, **200**, **201**, **205**, 206–11, **208**, **210**, 259–60, **263**, 264, 281; New Zealand Alpine Club life membership 269; climbing with son Guy, including to Everest Base Camp 269–72, **270**, 274, **275**, 276, **276**, **277**, **278**, **279**, **280**; Dog Tuckers group **283**, 284; Elie de Beaumont Maximilian Ridge climb 31, 35–41, **37**, **39**, **40**, **42**, **43**, 43–45, 274, 281; guiding 218, 220, 264, 265; Himalayan Dinner, Christchurch 1955 **169**; Hollyford tourism venture 'Adventours' 214, 217–20, **246**, 247–52, **251**, **253**, **254**, 254–55; Hollyford Valley mustering 211–12,

212, **213**, 214–20, **216**, **217**, **218**, **219**; introduction to climbing 188; Lowe, renewed contact in later years 267, **267**, 282; New Zealand Andean Expedition 1964 224–244, **227**, **231**, **232**, **235**, **236**, **237**, **240**, **241**, **244**; rafting **266**, 266–67; relationship with Hillary 180, 181, 287, 292; sailing 259, 260–61, **261**, **262**, 263, 266, 267; skiing 202, 205, 274, 298; *Stepping Stones to Everest* (film) 181, 182; at unveiling of Hillary's statue **181**

First New Zealand Himalayan Expedition 1951 **13**; in Badrinath 60, 62, 69, 70, **70**, 89, 93–94; diaries 47, 51–52, 56, 58, 62, 64, 66, 69, 70, 71, 73, 75, 78–80, 84, 103; general climbing in the area **90**, **91**, 92, 93; handwalking across makeshift bridge **286**; Mukut Parbat climb 69–80, **75**, **77**, **81**, **82**, 82–86, **84**, 87–88, 89–90, 96, 100, 274, 278, 288, 290–91, 298; with Natar Singh **92**; Nilkanta attempt 62–67; plans and preparation 28, 29, 31, 32, 33; Riddiford's invitation 206, 273–74; travel 47, **48**, 48–53, **51**; trek in to Badrinath 53–54, 56, 58–60, **59**, **61**, 62

personal life: childhood and family background 185–90, **187**, **188**; children 225, **225**, 255–57, **256**, **257**, 258, 269–78. **270**, 283; Edith Cavell rest home, Christchurch 283; education 187, 190–91, 196, 198; employment 197–98, 207, 211–20, 222, 247–57, 258; in Fiordland with Riddifords and friends **166**; grandchildren and great-grandchildren 283; Invercargill life 255–57; marriage to Jen **223**, 223–24, **224**, 256–57; mother's tuberculosis and effect on family life 189–90; personal attributes 278–79, 281, 284, 291; photo with sisters and brother **221**; photographic business, Gore 220, 222, 225, 244, 255; relationship with Rhondda Pope 259, 260, **260**, 261, 262–63, 264, 283; Riddiford's wedding **164**, 165; separation from Jen 258; Vailima, Christchurch 257, 259, 260, 261, 262, **267**, **282**, 283

Cotter, Edmund Rogerson 185
Cotter, Edmund (Ted) Wallace 185, 186, 187, **189**, 190, 192, **192**, 198, 271
Cotter, Elisabeth (Lis) 224, 225, 225, 248–49, **256**, 256–57, **257**, 271
Cotter, Guy 185, 224, 225, **225**, 243, 255, **256**, **257**, 264–65, 285; Adventure Consultants 269, 273–78; Everest 272–73, 274, 276, **276**, **277**, **278**, **279**; guiding 272–73; New Zealand Alpine Club life membership 269; Rolleston ascent, as a child 269–71, **270**; Seven Summits quest 273; Southern Alps climbing 271–72; United States climbing 272, **273**
Cotter, Harry 189
Cotter, Jacqueline (Jacqui) 224, 225, **225**, 248–49, 252, **256**, **257**, 265
Cotter, Jennifer (née Allen) 185, **223**, 223–24, **224**, **225**, 250, 252, 256, **256**, 257, 257, 258; New Zealand Andean Expedition 1964 224–25, 228, 229, 230, 232, **233**, 240, 243–244
Cotter, Jim 276, 278, **279**
Cotter, Judith (Judy or Jude) 185, 187, **187**, 188, 190, 198, 202, **221**, 243–44
Cotter, Martha (Marolin) Shaw (née Glover) 185
Cotter, Ralph 186, **187**, **188**, 189, 198, **221**
Cotter, Victoria Violet (née Wallace) 185, 189
Cradock, Nick 271, 274
Craigieburn Valley 202
Craigieburn Valley Ski Club 206
Croatia 267
Croll, Wynne 222
Cuthbert, John and Bob 306

D

Da Tenzing 141
Daku (Tenzing Norgay's wife) **175**, 180
Dampier, Mt 20, 24
Daniell, E. 107
Darjeeling 29, 30, 32, 142
Darran Mountains 248
Davidson, Mavis 155–56, 178, 292–93
Davie, Mt 116
Dawa Thondup 307
Dawson, Russell **208**
Deadmans Hut 214
Dechen, Mt 303

INDEX 343

Deerstalkers' Association 168
Delhi 97, 102, 104, 312
Demon Trail 255
Dhakwani 58
Dhanushkodi 50
Dhaulagiri 272, 312, 313
Dhuali River 59
Dick, Doug 155, 289
Dingla 121, 122–23, 127
Dog Tuckers group **283**, 284
Doidge, F.W. 27, 29
Douglas Glacier 16, 117, 118
Douglas Pass 118
Douglas Valley 115
Drawbridge, John 202
'Dream Team', First New Zealand Himalayan Expedition, May–August 1951 **14**, 15–17, 25, 30, 302–07
Dudh Kosi **124**, 131, 133
Duplat, Roger 89
Dutt, G.N. 134
Dyson, Brian 274

E

Earnslaw, Mt 116
Ede, Jack 35, 220–22, 244, 245
Elie de Beaumont **23**, 35, 36, **37**; Maximilian Ridge **10**, **23**, 24–25, 31, 35–41, 37, **42**, 43–45, 274, 281, 287, 292
Elliot, Mt 16
Ellis, David 294–95
Ellis, Murray 288, 294, 295
Ellis, Roland 29, 97, 152, 153–54, 156, 285, 288, 294
Ennis, John 200–01
Erewhon Col and Peak 209
Evans, Alan **196**, 199, 202
Evans, Charles 138, 139, **142**, 144, 145, **145**, 146, **146**, 147, 161, 163, 165, 302
Evans, G.S. 107
Evans, Mt 209
Everest Foundation 226
Everest, Mt: Adventure Consultants 272, 273; Ed Cotter's trip to Base Camp 274, **275**, 276, **276**, **277**, **278**; first ascent by Hillary and Tenzing 160–61, 162, 285, 290, 306, 309; Mallory and Irvine 16; Mt Everest region **124**–25; national park investigation 303; see also British Everest Reconnaissance Expedition 1935; British Expedition to Mount Everest 1953; British Reconnaissance to Mount Everest 1951

F

Fastness Peak 116
Feasey, Eric 44
Federated Mountain Clubs of New Zealand (FMC) 28, 167, 168
Fettes Peak 16, 115
First New Zealand Himalayan Expedition, May–August 1951: climbing of unnamed peaks 90, **90**, 91, **91**, 92; contribution to New Zealand Himalayan successes 90–91, 92–93, 279, 281, 285–95; 'Dream Team' **14**, 15–17, 25, 30, 302–07; finances 30, 31, 32, 33, 51, 53, 90, 91, 101; food 29, 32, 47–48, 56, 60, 64, 66, 75, 76, **76**, 80, 82, 88, 90, 92, 93; gear and equipment 29–30, 32–33; members and sirdar 308; misconceptions 285, 287–88; monsoon 90–91, 92–93; Mukut Parbat climb 69–80, **75**, **76**, **77**, **78**, **79**, **81**, **82**, 82–86, **84**, **85**, 87–88, 90–91, 156, 182, 274, 278, 287, 288, 290–91, 295; Nilkanta attempt 62–67, 156; plans and preparation in New Zealand 27–34; porters 30, 33, 54, 56, **57**, 58–59, 60, 62, 66–67, 71, **71**, 73, 74–75, 90, 93, **96**; preparation in Ranikhet and trek in to Badrinath 53–54, 56, **56**, **57**, 58–60; return to Ranikhet 94–96, 97, 99, 100, 102, 104; Riddiford family expedition 2015, to retrace steps 297–301, **299**, **300**, **301**; sahibs 13, **13**, **63**; Sherpas 12, **12**, 30, 32, 53–54, 58, 59, **63**, 66, 71, 74, 75, **76**, 80, 82, 83, 88, **90**, 90–91, 93
Foot, Allan 220–22
Footloose Fathers 307
Foster, Mt 17
Fox Glacier 20, **22**, 44, 45, 284
Franklin, Mt 199
Franz Josef 25, 44, 264, 265
Franz Josef Hotel 43
Fraser, Patrick 248
French, Mt **204**
French Ridge **203**, **204**
French Ridge Bivouac 117, **201**
Fresh Air Home for Children, Cashmere Sanatorium 190
Fyfe Pass 118
Fyffe, Mt 271

G

Garhwal Himalaya 27, 30, 31, 32, 33, **65**, 298; *see also* First New Zealand Himalayan Expedition, May–August 1951
Gelgun 135
Gerard, David 33
Ghastoli **65**, 69–70, 71, **71**, 73–74, 75
Gibbs, Ian Ogilvie 158, 159, **159**, **164**, 165, 176
Gibson Group, *Aspiring* (film) 202, **203**, **204**
Gillett, Frank 200
Gizeh, Mt 200
Glacier Dome 44, 221
Gladiator (peak) 118
Glenburn Station 110, 111
Goat Pass 206
Godley Valley **23**, 206
Godley–Whataroa crossing of Main Divide 197, 201
Goodfellow, Basil 153
Gore 220, 222, 224, 225, 244, 250, 251, 255
Graaf, Jan de 160
Greenlaw, Mt 116, 200
Greenstone Valley 248
Gregory, Alfred 138, 141–42, 144, 145, **145**, 146, **146**, 150
Grey, Mt 191
Gummer, John 117
Gunn, Davey 211–12, **212**, **213**, 214–20, **216**, 247, 248, 255
Gunn, George 248
Gunn, Lake 250
Gunn, Murray 214, 215, 218–19, 247, 255
Guyachung Kang **124**, 131, 142

H

Haast Range 117
Haast Ridge 158
Haden, Frank 197
Hadleigh, near Masterton 110
Hadlow School **110**, 111
Haidinger, Mt **22**, 207
Hall, David 201, 341
Hall, Rob 271–73
Hamilton, Neil 306
Hamiltons' jetboats 211

Hannah, W.E. (Bill) **169**, **208**
Hardie, Enid (née Hurst) 31, 138, **174**, 302, 306
Hardie, Jane **174**
Hardie, Norman: at Beavens' Bealey Spur bach **174**; British Expedition to Mount Everest 1953 157, 158, 302; career, climbing and retirement activities 302–03, 306; Cora Lynn bach 175; Dog Tuckers group **283**; English Lake District climbing 161; and Hillary 149, **181**, 302, 303, 305; Kangchenjunga ascent 167–68, 310; New Zealand Alpine Club Barun Valley Expedition 1954 165, 302, 307; opinion of Riddiford's leadership qualities 291; rescue of Ruth Adams 20, 306; Riddiford's 'Dream Team', First NZ Himalayan Expedition **14**, 25, 28–31, 302–03; and Riddiford's participation in Cho Oyu expedition 138, 145, 152; sailing 305; Southern Alps climbing 15–16, 17–18, 20–21, 24–25, 118, 119, 176, 177, **177**, 178, 303; *Stepping Stones to Everest* (film) 181
Hardie, Ruth **174**
Harper, Mt 116, 201
Harpers Rock 17, **22**, 117, 118
Harrington, H.J. **169**
Harris, Andy 273
Harris, Murray **208**
Harris Saddle 218, 248
Harris, Wyn 257
Harrison, J. (John) **169**, 222, 303
Harrison, J.B. (Jock) **169**
Harrow, Geoff 67, 102–03, **169**, 191, 198, 202, 205, 209, **283**, 306, 307
Hauser, Günther 226
Hearfield, Brian 177, 220–22
Hector, James 248
Heuberger, Helmut 312, 313
Hewitt, L.R. **169**
Hewitt, Nellie and Francis 111
Hicks, Mt **22**, 272
Hidden Falls 212, 214–15, 248, 249, 250, 252
Hill, David and Phoebe Morris, *First to the Top* 291
Hillary, Edmund Percival: Antarctic expeditions 167, 303; Booth, Pat, *Life of a Legend* 287; British Expedition

to Mount Everest 1953 and ascent of Everest 157, 158, 160–61, 162, 163, 285, 290, 306, 309; canoeing on Esk River, England 20, 28; climbing achievements 285; Elie de Beaumont Maximilian Ridge climb 36, 39–41, **40**, **42**, 44–45, 292; guided climbing 20, 28, 291, 293; *High Adventure* (1955) 150, 294; Hill, David and Phoebe Morris, *First to the Top* 291; Himalayan Dinner, Christchurch 1955 **169**; knighthood 161; Little, Paul, *After Everest* 290–91; *Nothing Venture, Nothing Win* (1975) 44, 87–88, 101, 150; opinions about achievements 285, 286, 287–88, 289, 290–91, 292–95; post-Everest lectures and appearances 162–63; relationship with Cotter 180, 181, 287, 292; relationship with Riddiford 133, 136, 143, 155, 156, 179–81, 287, 291, 292, 293, 294; search for meaning in life 292; Southern Alps climbing 18, 20, 199–200; unveiling of statue, Hermitage, Mount Cook 180–81, **181**; *View from the Summit* (1999) 44, 87, 88, 150, 179–81, 287, 293; visit to Orongorongo Station **175**, 180

British Expedition to Cho Oyu 1952 **146**, 150, **151**, 153; attempt on Cho Oyu 144; climbing of peaks in the area 144, 145; crossing of Nup La pass 146–47; exploration of Barun Valley 147; friction between New Zealanders 133, 137–38, 143, 150, 179–80; lecture 157; reconnaissance 141, **142**, 143; Shipton's invitation 138

British Reconnaissance to Mount Everest 1951: inclusion in expedition 100–04, **127**, 288, 289, 291; Kangshung Glacier route 131; Khumbu Icefall route 129, 182; New Zealand Alpine Club support 101, 102, 122; request to Shipton for inclusion of two New Zealanders 89, 98; Tesi Lapcha Pass and journey to Kathmandu 134–36

First New Zealand Himalayan Expedition 1951 **13**; in Badrinath 60, 62, 69, 89, 93–94; climbing of unnamed peaks 90, 91, 92, 93; lead climbing 44–45, 87–88, 104; Mukut Parbat climb 69–80, **75**, **82**, 82–86, 87, 89–91, 103, 274, 287, 288, 291; with Natar Singh **92**; Nilkanta attempt 62–67; plans and preparation 28, 29, 31–32, 33, 292; travel 47–53, **48**, **49**, **51**; trek in to Badrinath 53–54, 56, 58–60, 62

New Zealand Alpine Club Barun Valley Expedition 1954: leadership 154, 155–56, 161, 165; recommendation 152; rescue of McFarlane from crevasse 165, 166, 291, 304–05

Hillary, Peter 271
Himalayan Club 30, 33, 47, 53, 69
Himalayan Committee, Royal Geographical Society 97, 122, 137, 139, 150–51, 152, 153, 154, 288
Himalayan expeditions 308–10; *see also* British Everest Reconnaissance Expedition 1935; British Expedition to Cho Oyu 1952; British Expedition to Mount Everest 1953; British Reconnaissance to Mount Everest 1951; British West Nepal Expedition 1950; First New Zealand Himalayan Expedition 1951; New Zealand Alpine Club Barun Valley Expedition 1954
Himalayan Trust 303
Hinchey, Joe 198
Hochstetter Dome 36
Holland, Sidney 104
Hollyford (Gunn's) Camp 214, 215, **216**, 216–17, 252, 255
Hollyford Conservation Trust 247
Hollyford River **218**, 220, **246**, 247, 248
Hollyford tourism venture, 'Adventours' 214, 217–20, **246**, 247–52, **251**, **253**, **254**, 254–55
Hollyford Tourist and Travel Company 255
Hollyford Track 247, 248, 255
Hollyford Valley 211–12, **212**, **213**, 214–20, **216**, **217**, **218**, **219**, 248, 249, **253**, **256**, 269
Hopkins, Mt 17
Huachana **227**, 232, 243
Huascarán 226, 228
Hughes, David 118
Humbolt Falls 249
Hunt, John 151, 154, 157, 158, 161, 162, 302, 311

I

Invercargill 255–57
Ireland, John 235, **235**, 239, 240, 242
Irvine, Andrew 16
Isobel, Mt 15

J

Jacobs, Harold 228, 229, **229**, 230, **231**, **232**, 235–40, **236**, **240**, 242–43
Jagged Peak 119
Jamestown 248, 249
Jasamba **124**, 143, 144, 145
Jaynagar railhead 139
Jellicoe, Mt 20
Jenkins, Jack 214, **218**, 219
Jillet, Chris 264
Jöchler, Josef (Sepp) 312, 313
Jogbani 104, 121, 122, 127
Johnson, Robin 191, 193, **193**, **194**, **196**, 199, 201
Jones, J.H. Emlyn 302
Jones, Sutton 212
Jones, Warren 44
Joshimath 59, 94, 297, 298

K

K2 expedition 1939 54, 311, 313
Kaipo Valley 212
Kalinghat 58
Kamet 53, **65**, **68**, **81**, 90, 298
Kangchenjunga 150, 152, 160, 162, 165, 167–68, 302, 310
Kangshung Glacier **125**, 131
Kasiri 229, 230
Kasiri Aguja **227**, 229, 230, 243
Kasiri Oeste **227**, 229, 243
Katie's Col 20, 21
Kelly, Allen **208**
Kelly, Suze **276**
Kennedy, W.A. 206
Key Summit 248
Khathmandu 134, 136, 137, 147, 166
Khati 74
Khumbu Icefall 121, 126, 128–29, **130**, 131–33, 134, 182, 308
Kraayvanger, Caroline 172
Krenek, Ludwig 30, 32, 54, **169**
Kuari Pass 58, **59**, 297–98, 299
Kyetrak (Gyabrag) Glacier 144

L

La Perouse Glacier 20, 21
La Perouse, Mt 18, 20, **21**, **22**, 24, **24**, 306
Lake … *see* name of lake, e.g. McKerrow, Lake
Lake District Outward Bound school 306
Lands and Survey Department 168
Landsborough River 16, 17, 18, 118
Landsborough Station 18, 169
Landsborough Valley 18, **19**, 115, 116, 177, 306
Lauper Peak 209
Law, Mr and Mrs T.G. 104
Leary, Mt 116
Lendenfeld Peak 207
Lewis-Jones, Huw 287
Lhotse II 165
Lilburn, Douglas 202
Linda Glacier 221
Little Homer Saddle 249
Livingston, Mt 201
Lombard, A.E. **151**
Longwood, near Featherston 108, 111, 113
Lowe, Mary 267, **267**
Lowe, Wallace George: *Because It Is There* (1959) 99, 150, 207, 287, 288–90; British Expedition to Mount Everest 1953 160, 162, 163, 307; British Reconnaissance to Mount Everest 1951, exclusion 100, 101, 102, 104, 294; canoeing on Esk River, England 20, 28; Elie de Beaumont Maximilian Ridge climb 36, 37, 39–41, **42**, 44–45, 292; *Letters from Everest* 287; New Zealand Alpine Club Barun Valley Expedition 1954 155–56, 166, 306–07; post-Everest lectures and appearances 162–63; relationship with Riddiford 143, 152, 155, 179, 180, 181–82, 289–90, 291, 294; renewed contact with Cotter in later years 267, **267**, 282; Southern Alps climbing 28, 35, 199–200, 201, **201**, **205** British Expedition to Cho Oyu 1952 **146**, 150, **151**, 153; attempt on Cho Oyu 144; climbing of peaks in the area 144, 145; crossing of Nup La pass 146–47; exploration of Barun Valley 147; friction between New Zealanders 133, 137–38, 143, 145, 150, 152, 155, 179–80, 181–82, 294; reconnaissance 141, **142**, 143; Shipton's invitation 138

First New Zealand Himalayan Expedition 1951 **13**; in Badrinath 60, 62, 69, **70**, 89, 93–94; climbing of unnamed peaks 90, 91, 92; lead climbing 44–45, 87–88, 104; Mukut Parbat climb 69–80, **75**, **82**, 82–86, 87–88, 89–91, 103, 274, 287, 288, 291; Nilkanta attempt 62–67; plans and preparation 28, 29, 31, 32, 33; travel 47–53, **48**; trek in to Badrinath 53–54, 56, 58–60, **59**, 62
Loyacjirca 242, 243
Lucknow 53, 101, 102, 104
Lukla 313
Lunak **124**, 141, 142, 146

M

Macaulay, M.E. 44
Mackay, Don: climbing with Cotter, 1979 272; friendship with Wilsons 256, **262**, 263; New Zealand Andean Expedition 1964 228, 229, 230, **231**, 232, **233**, **235**, 235–36, 237–40, 242, 243
Madeline, Mt **213**, 217, 249
Madras Express 51–53
Mahitahi Valley 16
Makalu **125**, 131, 141, 273, 285, 306
Makalu II **125**, 165
Makarora 18
Malapur 136
Mallory, George 16
Malte Brun **23**, 158, 160
Mana (peak) **65**, 90
Mana (village) 60, 62, **65**, 66, 71, 73, 74; villagers **72**, **93**
Mana Pass 71, 73, 79
Manapouri 219, 220
Manapouri and Te Anau campaign 305
Mannering, Guy 211
Marian Corner 212, 214
Marlborough Sounds 259, **261**, 263
Marshall, Colin 116
Martins Bay 211, 212, 214, 215, **217**, 247, 248, 249, 250, 251, 254, 255; Māori settlement 248
Masherbrum 209, 211, 310
Masterton 111–12
Maud Francis Glacier **203**
Mavora Lakes 219, 220, 248
Mayank 297

McCallum, Graham **169**, **175**
McClure Peak 206
McFall, Dave 297, 298, 299
McFarlane, Jim: climbing career 303–05; and Cotter 194; Himalayan Dinner, Christchurch 1955 **169**; New Zealand Alpine Club Barun Valley Expedition 1954 165, 166, 291; Riddiford's 'Dream Team', First NZ Himalayan Expedition **14**, 25, 30, 303–05; sailing 305; Southern Alps climbing 15–16, 17–18, **18**, **19**, **21**, **24**, 24–25, 118, 303–04
McFarlane, Nola 304
McFetrick Peak 264
McKellar, David 248
McKenzie family 248
McKenzies Lagoon 249
McKerrow, Bob 264, 291
McKerrow Glacier 118
McKerrow, Lake 212, 214, 248, 249, 250, **254**
McPherson, Donald **264**, 265, 266
Menlung area 146
Menzies, Bruce 115, 199
Milford Track 247, 255
Milne, Geoff 201, **205**; First New Zealand Himalayan Expedition 28, 31
Milner, H.T. **169**
Mingha Bivvy **194**
Mingha River 206
Mingha Track 193
Mitchell, Jeremy 259, **260**
Mitchell, Jethro **260**
Mitchell, Julian 259, 260, **260**
Mitchell, Katie 259, **260**
Moffat, Mt 201
Monteath, Colin, *Under a Sheltering Sky* 279, 281
Montgomery, Jock 176
Morris, John 44, 306
Mount … *see* name of mountain, e.g. Elie de Beaumont
Mueller Glacier **22**, 117, 118
Mueller Pass 16, 177
Mukut Parbat: ascent by Riddiford, Cotter and Pasang 69–86, **79**, **81**, **82**, **84**, **85**, 87–88, 96, 100, 102, 156, 182, 274, 278, 288, 290–91, 295; Hillary and Lowe's failure to summit 87–88, 90–91, 100, 103–04, 287, 288, 291; objective of First

New Zealand Himalayan Expedition 32, 53, 96; Riddiford family expedition 2015 297–301
Murchison, Mt 116, 201
Murray, Bill 123, **123**, 127, 129, 131, 133, 138
Musapani 73

N

Namche Bazar 104, 121, **124**, 128, 133, 134, **135**, 141, 147, **151**, 313
Nanda Devi 25, 53, 54, 75, 89, 274, 298
Nangpa Glacier 141
Nangpa La Pass **124**, 134, 141, 142, 143, 144, 145
National Film Unit 202
National Geographic Society 163
Nau Lekh 307
Nelson, Jean (née Adams) 224, 228–29, 230, 232, 235, 267
Nelson, Mike 224, 226, 228, 229, 230, 232, **233**, 234, **235**, 235–36, 237–40, 242, 243, 267
Nepal 28
Nevado Loyacjirca 242, 243
New Zealand Alpine Club (NZAC) 29, 32, 97–98, 99, 102, 122, 162, 206, 226, 288, 294; Auckland section 47; Canterbury–Westland section 15, 116, 117, 304; Otago section 116; Overseas Expedition Committee 149, 152, 153; Riddiford's membership terminated 177–78; Southland section 223, 304, 305; Wellington section 160
New Zealand Alpine Club Barun Valley Expedition 1954 302, 306–07; fundraising 160; Hardie and Beaven 165–66, 302, 306–07; members and sirdar 309; planning, and selection of leader 138, 149, 152–56, 161, 306, 309; rescue of McFarlane from crevasse 165, 166, 291, 304–05; Riddiford's recommendations 152
New Zealand Andean Expedition 1964 224–244, **227**, **229**, **231**, **232**, **233**, **234**, **235**, **236**, **237**, **240**, **241**, **244**
New Zealand Antarctic Expedition 167
New Zealand Chamar Expedition 1953 162, 309
New Zealand Karakoram Expedition 1955 209, 211

New Zealand Masherbrum Expedition 1955 310
Newmarch, Frank 154
Newth, Tom 192–93, **193**, **194**, 200, 306
Ngāi Tahu Tourism 255
Ngojumba Glacier 141
Nicholl, Harry 114
Nilkanta 32, 53, 58, 60, **61**, 62–64, **65**, 66–67, 69, 91–93, 156, 298
Nima: British Reconnaissance to Mount Everest 1951 121, 122, 126, 132, 134–35, 136; First New Zealand Himalayan Expedition, May–August 1951 **12**, 54, **55**, 66, 67, 75, **76**, 92
Nup La **124**, 133, 146–47, 294

O

O. & R. Beere & Riddiford 165
Odell, Noel 16, 25, 29, 168, **169**, 287
Okhaldunga 141
Orion 31, 33, 48–50
Orongorongo Lodge 176
Orongorongo Station 107–08, 114, 169–70, **171**, 171–72, **172**, 173, **173**, **174**, **175**, 175–76, **176**
Orongorongo Valley 167
Overton, near Marton 111, 113, 114, 158
Owen, Barry 206
Oxford University Exploration Club Expedition to West Nepal 1954 309–10
oxygen use 139, 147, 150, 161

P

Pachmi (west) Kamet Glacier 69, 71, 73, 74, 80, 85, 88
Packard, Bill 16, 18, 25, 29, 32, 54, 119, 151, 168, **169**, 181, 182, 302, 306, 308
Packard, Geraldine 302
Pangboche **124**, 128
Pangbuk Valley 147
Pasang Dawa Lama: British Reconnaissance to Mount Everest 1951 121, 122, 126, 128, 129, 131, 132, 133, 134–35, 136; Cho Oyu 150, 168, 311–13; correspondence with Riddiford 159–60; First New Zealand Himalayan Expedition, May–August 1951 **12**, 32, 54, **55**, 59, 66, 71, 73, 74, **75**, **76**, 83–84, **84**, 85, 86, 88, **90**, 92; Jan de Graaf's Himalayan expedition 160; Mukut Parbat climb 96, 103, 298; Nilkanta

attempts 92–93; second wife 313; Tichy's high opinion 311–13
Pattle, Jack 207, **208**
Penney, Phil 265
Peren, Gillian **164**
Peren, Roger 146, 158–59, 163, 166, 167, 178, 292
Perry, H.E. 220
Perry, Mike 260
Pethangtse 309
Pilgrim, Bob 116
Pilgrim, Eric 196, 199
pilgrim route to Badrinath shrine 59–60, **60**, 94, 95
Pioneer Hut 207
Pioneer Pass 44, 45
Pistol, Mt 199
Pollux, Mt 177
Pope, Rhondda 259, 260, **260**, 261, 262–63, 264, 283
Powell, Paul 116
Power, Amanda 262
Public Trust Office, Christchurch 197–98
Pugh, Griffith 139, 141, **142**, 143, 144, 145, **145**, **146**, 147, 150, 168, 303
Pumori **124**, 131, 273
Pyke Hut 250, 252
Pyke River 249, 255
Pyke Valley 212, 215, **219**, 248

Q

Quarterdeck Pass 117, **204**
Queenstown 248, 265
Quitoraju 234, **241**, 242, 243

R

Rakaia River 209
Rakaia Valley 193
Ramni 56
Rangitata Rafts 266
Ranikhet 32, 33, 51, 53, 95, 97, 99, 100, 102, 104, 143, 301
Red Lion Peak 209
Rees Valley 116
Revillagigedo Island, Alaska 266
Riddiford, Alice (née McGregor) 109
Riddiford, Anna 109, 168, **170**, 172, **173**, 179, 180, 181, 297, 299, **299**, **300**, 300–01
Riddiford, Belinda 113, 166–67, **167**, 168–69, **170**, 172, **173**, **174**, 220

Riddiford, Dan (Earle's uncle) 108, 110, 111, 113, 114
Riddiford, Daniel (1814–1875, Earle's great-grandfather) 107–08
Riddiford, Daniel Johnston (Earle's cousin) 100, 101, 108, 157, 164
Riddiford, Edward Joshua ('King') 108, 111
Riddiford, Eric 109, 114
Riddiford, Freddy (Earle's grandson) 297, 299, **299**, **301**
Riddiford, Frederick (Earle's grandfather) 108–09
Riddiford, Frederick Earle (Earle's father) **108**, **109**, 109–10
Riddiford Graham, Evangeline 297–301, **299**, **301**
Riddiford Graham, Oonagh 297, **299**
Riddiford, Harold Earle
 climbing: Aoraki/Mt Cook climb 44, 45; British Expedition to Mount Everest 1953 143, 150, 151, 157, 158, 160, 162, 179; contribution to New Zealand Himalayan successes 90–91, 92–93, 279, 281, 285–95, 307; Elie de Beaumont Maximilian Ridge climb 36–37, **39**, 39–41, **40**, 43–45, 274; Himalayan Dinner, Christchurch 1955 168, **169**; introduction to mountains 113; leadership abilities 291–92; lectures on Himalaya 158, 160, 161; New Zealand Alpine Club Barun Valley Expedition 1954 152, 153, 155–56; Orongorongo Valley 167; relationship with Hillary 133, 136, 143, 155, 156, 179–81, 287, 291, 292, 293, 294; relationship with Lowe 143, 152, 155, 179, 180, 181–82, 289–90, 291, 294; rescue of Ruth Adams 20; Southern Alps climbing 15, 16, 17–18, **18**, **19**, 20–21, **24**, 24–25, 27, 115–19, 158, 167, 176–77, **177**, **178**
 climbing: British Expedition to Cho Oyu 1952 134, **146**, 150, 153; disagreement with Shipton 143, 144, 145–46; friction between New Zealanders 133, 137–38, 143, 145, 150, 152, 155, 294; hospitalised on return to New Zealand 146, 152, 158, 160; organisation 138; sciatica 144, 145

climbing: British Reconnaissance to Mount Everest 1951: Dudh Kosi Valley and Nup La 133, 294; inclusion in expedition 100–04, **127**; Khumbu Icefall route 128–29, **130**, 131–32, 133, 134, 182, 288; New Zealand Alpine Club support 101, 102, 122, 152; search for pass leading to West Rongbuk Glacier 129, 131; Tesi Lapcha Pass and journey to Kathmandu 134–36

climbing: First New Zealand Himalayan Expedition 1951 **13**, **14**; in Badrinath 60, 62, 69, 70, 89, 90, 92, 93–94; lunch break with Sherpas **90**; Mukut Parbat climb 69–80, **82**, 82–86, **84**, 87–88, 90, 96, 100, 102, 156, 182, 274, 288, 290, 295; Nilkanta attempts 62–67, 91–93, 156; plans, preparation and organisation 15, 25, 27–34, 47–48, 96, **96**, 100, 101, 103–04, 156, 287, 288, 289–90, 292; Riddiford family expedition 2015, to retrace steps 297–301, **299**, **300**, **301**; travel 47–53, **48**; trek in to Badrinath 53–54, 56, 58–60, 62

health: angina attacks 178; back injury, Cho Oyu expedition 146, 152, 158, 160; dysentery 62, 67, 71, 87, 89, 100, 134, 143, 301; heart attack 176

personal life: childhood and family background **105**, 107–13, **112**; children 166–67, **167**, 168–69, **170**, 171–73, 175, 180, 297; death, funeral and tribute 107, 178; education **110**, 111, 113, **113**, 115; grandchildren 178, 297; Karori home 163, 167; legal studies and career 13, 108, 115, 116, 157, 165, **168**, 171, 176; marriage to Rosemary 160, 161, 162, 163–65, **164**, 173, **174**, 175, 297; Orongorongo Station 169–70, **171**, 171–72, **172**, 173, **173**, **174**, **175**, 175–76, **176**; war service in the Pacific 116, **117**; wide circle of friends 159, 165, **166**, 175

Riddiford, Harriett (née Stone) 107, 108
Riddiford, Helen (née Easton, later Nicholl) **108**, **109**, 109–11, 113, 114, 162, 164

Riddiford, Richard 168, **170**, **174**, 181, 297, **299**, **300**
Riddiford, Rosemary (née Johnston): at Beavens' bach, Bealey Spur **174**; children 166–67, 168; David Ellis's letter 294–95; and Hillary's hostility to Earle 180, 181; marriage to Earle 160, 161, 162, 163–65, **164**, 173, 176, 178, 180, 220, 297; Mavis Davidson's letter 292–93; Orongorongo Station 169–70, 171–72, **172**, 173, **174**, 175; visit to Ed Cotter **166**
Riddiford, Sam 297, **299**, 301
Riddiford, Sarah 168, **172**, 172–73, **173**, **174**
Riddiford, Trish **109**, 110, 111, 114, 157
Riddiford, Val **109**, 110, 111, 114
Riddiford, Vivian 110
Roberts, Adrian 256
Roberts, Athol 160, 162
Roberts, Bob 193
Robins, T.T. (Nui) 192, **192**, 193, 205
Rodda, Roland 288
Rolleston, Mt 15, 177, **178**, 199, 269–71, **270**, 303, 306; Otira face 200–01
Rose, Jim 149, 154, 155, 156, 288
Ross Dependency Research Committee 168
Ross, 'Snow' and Joyce 260–61
Routeburn Valley 218, 248
Roxburgh, Guy 262
Royal Geographical Society (RGS) 150, 302; 40th Everest Anniversary 288; Himalayan Committee 97, 122, 137, 139, 150–51, 152, 153, 154, 288
Russell, Scott 97–98, 99, 138, 152, 284, 295

S

Sage, John 116
Sampson, John **195**, **196**, 199, **200**, 201, 202, 205
Santa Cruz valley, Peru 234, **234**, 240, **240**
Sanyal, B. 33
Saraswati Gorge 71, 73
Saraswati River **65**, 69, 70–71, **71**, 73–74, 79
Satopanth Glacier 53, 62, **65**
Satopanth Valley 93
Scott, Archie 27, 219–20
Scott Creek 115, 119
Scott Peak 118–19
Secord, Campbell 138, 139, 143, 144, **146**, 150

Sefton, Mt 15, 17, 18, 20, **22**, 115, 118
Seymour Peak **200**, 201
Sharks Tooth peak, Southern Alps 115
Shaw, George 211
Shaw, Warren 220
Sherpas: Athol Roberts' expedition 160; British Reconnaissance to Mount Everest 1951 126, 127; Everest region 127–28, 134, 276; First New Zealand Himalayan Expedition, May–August 1951 12, **12**, 30, 32, 53–54, 58, 59, **63**, 66, 71, 74, 75, **76**, 80, 82, 83, 88, **90**, 90–91, 93; Tichy's Cho Oyu expedition 1954 312; *see also* names of individual Sherpas
Shipman, Jim **196**, 199
Shipton, Eric 16, 64; British Everest Reconnaissance Expedition 1935 25, 300; British Expedition to Cho Oyu 1952 133, 137–47, **142**, 149, 150–51, 182; British Expedition to Mount Everest 1953, exclusion from leadership 142, 150–51, 154, 158; British Reconnaissance to Mount Everest 1951 87, 89, 97–99, 100–01, 104, 122, 123, **123**, 126–27, 128, 129, 131, 132–33, 182; Hillary's opinion 149, 153–54; Outward Bound school, Lake District 161, 306; praise for Riddiford 180; Riddiford's disagreements 143, 144, 145–46
Sierra Range 116, 117, 118–19
Sikkim 29, 30, 54, 162, 302
Silberhorn, Mt 21
Singh, Gopah 69, 70, 92
Singh, Natar **92**
Skellerup Rubber 198, 207
skiing 202, 205–06
Smith, Ian **208**
Smith, Nick 247
Smyth Johnson & Stevens 165
Smythe, Frank 16, 59
Snelson, Kenneth 54
Snow Dome 209
South, Grant 266, **266**
Southern Alps 17, 35
Spearpoint, Mt 199
Speight, Mt 201
Spence, Mt 17
Spencer Glacier **23**, 24, 36, 41, 45
Spencer, M. 117

Spencer Valley 41, 43
St Matthews College kindergarten 111
Stafsnes, Maggie **264**, 265–66
Steele, Peter 287
Stepping Stones to Everest (film) 181–82
Stevenson, Harry 97–98, 99, 101, 102, 122, 152, 153, 154, 288, 295
Stewart, Malcolm 193
Stoddart, Mt 188
Strachan, Mt 16, 177
Strachan Pass 199
Sullivan, Mick 20, 175
Summerhayes family 136
Suter, K. **169**
Swiss expedition to Everest 1952 137, 141, 150

T

Taparacu **227**, 230, 243
Tapper, Jules 255
Tartare Saddle 43, **43**, 45
Tasman, Mt 20, 21, **22**, 44, 207
Tasman Saddle **23**, 36, 272
Tasman Ski Club 304
Taupo 159
Te Awaiti Block 107, 108
Te Wāhipounamu World Heritage Area 18, 248, 255
Tekano Glacier 119
Temple, Mt 117
Temple, Philip 20, 45, 243, 293–94
Tengboche 128
Tennant, Judy **164**
Tent Peak 119, 207
Tenzing Norgay **175**, 180, 294, 309
Tenzing, Yila **12**, 54, **55**, 69, 74, **76**, 79, 83, 92, 311
Tesi Lapcha Pass 134–36, 149
Thame **124**, **140**, 141, 144
Therma Glacier 116, 117
Thomas, C.S. 115
Thompson, Limbo **283**
Thomson, Mt 17, **22**, 115
Thundu **12**, 54, **55**, 66, 67, 70, 71, 73, **76**, 92, 93
Tibet 27, 28–29, 30, 74, 80, 133, 142, 143, 144
Tichy, Herbert, *Cho Oyu* 311–13
Tilman, H.W. (Bill) 25, 58, 74–75, 138, 260, 300

Todd, Chris 271–72
Todd, Colin 306, 307, 309, 310
Tora, Wairarapa 109, 114
Tothill, John 228
tourism, Fiordland 214, 217–20, **246**, 247–52, **251**, **253**, **254**, 254–55
Townsend, Mt 16, 118
Tozer, Fred 115
training expedition 28, 29, 30, 35–45, 287
travel 30, 31, 32–33, 47–53
Treadwell, Mandy **173**
Trisul Peak 168
Tutoko Lodge 249
Tutoko, Mt 217, 248, 249
Tyndale-Biscoe, Hugh 158, **159**

U

Uli Biaho spire 274
Union Steamship Company 30
Uttar Pradesh 31, 33

V

Vailima, Christchurch 257, 259, 260, 261, 262, **267**, **282**, 283
Valley of the Flowers World Heritage Site 67
Vampire, Mt 17, 117
Venables, Stephen 287
Vignes, Gilbert 89
Volta Glacier 116, 117

W

Wade, R.H. 27–28, 29, 30, 33
Waiau River 266
Waimakariri River 188, 199
Waimakariri Valley 15, 191
Waitaha River **266**
Walker, Harry **189**, 193, 202, **219**
Walter, Mt 41
Wanaka 264–65
Wanganui Collegiate 113
Ward, Mike 123, **123**, 128–29, 132, 133, 138, 143; *In This Short Span* 294
Warizata, Bolivia 228, 232
Warrior, Mt 199
waterfront dispute 1951 32–33, 47
Watson, R.H. (Bob) **169**, **208**, 209
Welcome Flat 119, 261–62
Welcome Pass 115, 119
Wellington Club 171
West Matukituki Valley 117
West Rongbuk Glacier 129
Western Cwm **125**, 128, 129, 131, 132, 288, 308
Whataroa Valley 36, 197, 201
Whitcombe, Mt 209
Whitcombe Valley 209, **210**
Whymper Glacier 36, 37, **37**, 39
Whymper Saddle **23**, 36, **38**, 45
Wicks Glacier 115
Wiessner, Fritz 54
Wilkins, B. **169**, 304, 305
Will, Jennifer **164**
Wilson, Ann 258, **261**, 263
Wilson, Jim 258, **261**, **262**, 263, 289, 303
Wolfe, Dudley 54
Woods, Mike 271–72
Woollens, Bruce 30
World Expeditions India 297
World War I 185
World War II 116, **117**, 185, 214

Y

Yeoman, Martin 286
Young, Hugo 271

Z

Zemu Glacier 29
Zora Creek **18**